India & Pakistan
Pathways Ahead

India & Pakistan
Pathways Ahead

Editors

Amitabh Mattoo
Kapil Kak
Happymon Jacob

UNIVERSITY OF JAMMU

Centre for Strategic and Regional Studies
University of Jammu, Jammu

in association with

KNOWLEDGE WORLD

KW Publishers Pvt Ltd
New Delhi

KNOWLEDGE WORLD

A KW Publishers Book
www.kwpublishers.com

Published in India by

Kalpana Shukla
KW Publishers Pvt Ltd
5A/4A, Ansari Road, Daryaganj, New Delhi 110002
email: knowledgeworld@vsnl.net / online.kw@gmail.com

ISBN: 978-81-87966-66-1

Typeset by Black Innovation, New Delhi
Printed at Chaman Offset Printer, New Delhi

Contents

Peace Building in Jammu Kashmir

India-Pakistan Relations: The Way Forward

Conclusion

Preface

The publication of this book was delayed for over one year. Barring some of the usual editorial tweaking that had to be done, the book was deliberately delayed so that the full steam of the rapidly improving India-Pakistan relationship could be captured. The contours of India-Pakistan relations kept changing on a regular basis since the conceptualisation of this ambitious project, persuading us to recast its metanarratives in the last two years of India-Pakistan relations, a period that arguably coincided with the most vibrant epoch in India-Pakistan détente. While the peace process started with the usual note of caution, it went through phases of turbulence and the test of time, leaving India-Pakistan watchers befuddled, and has now reached a level of self-sustainability. We have now gone forward from thinking as to what needs to be done to avoid a failure of the peace process to thinking what can be the best results of this process, with a view that the process has to lead to some outstanding mutual gains.

This book has been conceptualised, thematised and written to assess the ongoing peace process between India and Pakistan. At least two features seem to distinguish the current state of India-Pakistan relations with reference to Kashmir from the past: one, the Pakistani leadership and most serious Kashmiri leaders have now gone back on their demand for altering the borders between the two countries; two, most of the leaders have now enunciated what they would like to achieve in terms of a settlement of the Kashmir issue. In other words, cold peace no longer characterises Indo-Pak relations: there is a constructive engagement towards fulfilling common regional goals and aspirations. Sixty years of neighbourly existence have always been far from good neighbourly. Thus, to chart a new course all at once is not easy. Breakthroughs are difficult to achieve in India-Pakistan relations. Thus, every small measure goes a long way in constructing the larger picture. Movement of people and goods between the two countries has increased manifold, in an unprecedented manner; myths about the other are gradually vanishing; the leadership in both countries is identifying common grounds to engage themselves in; and, the unstoppable forces of a rapidly changing world are forcing the countries to think out of the box. This may indeed be the opportune time for creating a common vision for a common destiny.

Generations of Indians and Pakistanis have grown up on a staple diet of hatred of 'the other'. The other was posited in a variety of shapes and forms, from being the enemy country to the country of enemies. Each believed that the other's sole reason for existence was to obliterate the country in question. From textbooks to newspapers to movies, the identity of the 'other' was that of an enemy. Multi-track diplomacy comprising politicians, public personalities, performers, academics, students, traders and the general public achieved the impossible, of demystifying the enemy images.

Sixty years of fighting have only convinced India and Pakistan of its futility and that the struggle today is against common problems. Terrorism, poverty, ecological and environmental problems, religious extremism are the new enemies: just to cite an example, both countries now have a joint anti-terror mechanism to chart out ways and means to fight terrorism in the subcontinent.

One of the important reasons for such enlightenment can be ascribed to the entry of global forces such as economic globalisation and consequent economic opportunities, the South Asian Association for Regional Cooperation (SAARC) vision of creating the South Asian Free Trade Area (SAFTA), South Asian Economic Union, etc. Both countries realise that unrealistic zero-sum games are of no benefit to either.

This book is a rare compilation of articles by leading luminaries on India-Pakistan relations, some of the most ardent India-Pakistan watchers of the subcontinent. Articles vary from the changing nature of geo-politics in the subcontinent, cross-border terrorism, Track two diplomacy, Indus Waters Treaty, and views from Jammu, Kashmir and Leh. Questions regarding the irreversibility of the peace process and the possibility of its failure are also addressed in the book.

We hope that this volume will further enrich the existing literature and discourse on India-Pakistani relations.

April, 2007

Amitabh Mattoo
Kapil Kak
Happymon Jacob

Notes on Contributors

Amitabh Mattoo is the Vice Chancellor of the University of Jammu. He is also Professor of International Relations at Jawaharlal Nehru University, New Delhi. He has served as a member of India's National Security Advisory Board, and the Task Force constituted by the Indian Prime Minister on Global Strategic Developments. He has been visiting Professor at Stanford University, University of Notre Dame and University of Illinois, Urbana Champaign, and has authored many books and articles on international relations and foreign policy.

Air Vice Marshal **Kapil Kak** AVSM VSM (Retd.), formerly of the flying branch of the Air Force, is a well-known defence and security affairs analyst who earlier served as Deputy Director of the Institute for Defence Studies and Analyses, New Delhi. He also did a stint as Advisor (Strategic Studies), University of Jammu (2002-2006), and continues to be the Additional Director, Centre for Air Power Studies, New Delhi, since its inception in 2002.

Happymon Jacob teaches Strategic Studies at the Department of Strategic and Regional Studies, University of Jammu. He is also a Visiting Fellow at the Nelson Mandela Centre for Peace and Conflict Resolution, Jamia Millia Islamia University, New Delhi. Jacob is the Coordinator of the Pugwash Kashmir Initiative, and has been associated with the Observer Research Foundation, Centre for Air Power Studies and the Delhi Policy Group. Jacob's publications include *HIV/AIDS as a Security Threat to India* (Manohar, 2005) and *The Rise, Fall and Resurgence of the Taliban* (Observer Research Foundation, 2005).

Air Commodore **Jasjit Singh**, AVSM, VrC, VM (Retd.), is Director, Centre for Air Power Studies, New Delhi, and a former Director of the Institute for Defence Studies and Analyses, New Delhi (1987-2001). He was Convenor of the Task Force to set up the National Security Council and Member of the National Security Advisory Board and is also a Fellow of the World Academy of Arts and Sciences. He has authoured/edited more than three dozen books and lectured extensively at defence and war colleges in India and abroad.

Devika Sharma is a Research Consultant with the Confederation of Indian Industries. Ms. Sharma was previously with the Observer Research Foundation, New Delhi. She is also a Doctoral Candidate at the Centre for

International Politics, Organisation and Disarmament, School of International Studies, Jawaharlal Nehru University, New Delhi.

Kalim Bahadur retired as Professor of South Asian Studies at the School of International Studies, Jawaharlal Nehru University, New Delhi. He is one of India's leading commentators on Pakistan. His publications include *The Jamaat-i-Islami of Pakistan* (New Delhi, 1977), *Democracy in Pakistan: Crises and Conflicts* (New Delhi, 1988) and *South Asia in Transition: Conflicts and Tensions* (New Delhi, 1986).

Alumni of Columbia University, Graduate School of Journalism (1982), **Malini Parthasarthy** has written extensively on a range of key socio-political issues that have a bearing on India's peace and security. A feisty and deeply secular advocate of Press freedom, she has often picked up cudgels against state and central governments in the public interest. She is currently Joint Editor, *The Hindu.*

Sushant Sareen is Executive Editor, Public Opinion Trends (POT), New Delhi. After serving for a year in the Railways, he resigned to join POT, a news agency that monitors news in South Asia. He was associated with the Observer Research Foundation as the Honorary Director of the Pakistan Centre and is the author of *The Jihad Factory: Pakistan's Islamic Revolution in the Making* (2005).

Rajesh Rajagopalan is Associate Professor, School of International Studies, Jawaharlal Nehru University, New Delhi, and was earlier Senior Fellow at the Institute for Defence Studies and Analyses and Observer Research Foundation, New Delhi. He also served as Deputy Secretary in the National Security Council Secretariat, Government of India (2000-2001), and is the author of *Second Strike: Arguments About Nuclear War in South Asia* (New Delhi, Penguin, 2005).

Pervez Hoodbhoy is Professor of physics at Quaid-e-Azam University, Islamabad, Pakistan, and is the recipient of the Baker Award for electronics (1968) and Abdus Salam Prize for mathematics (1984). He is the chairman of *Mashal,* a non-profit organisation which publishes books in Urdu on women's rights, education, environmental issues, philosophy, and modern thought. He is one of the most respected peace activists in Pakistan.

Wilson John is a Senior Fellow at the Observer Research Foundation. His areas of research include Pakistan and terrorism, not necessarily together. He has four books to his credit: *An Admiral's Fall* (1999), *Karachi: An International Terrorist Capital in the Making* (2004), *Pakistan's Nuclear Underworld (2005), and Terrorism in South Asia* (co-edited 2005) and is regularly published in both India and abroad.

A.K. Pandey is an officer of the Indian Foreign Service. He is presently High Commissioner of India to Maldives. Prior to his present appointment, he was a Joint Secretary at the Ministry of External Affairs, in New Delhi. Shri Pandey earlier served as Senior Fellow at the Institute for Defence Studies and Analyses, and was also a Joint Secretary in the Prime Minister's Office.

Major General **Afsir Karim** AVSM (Retd.), has commanded an Infantry Division of the Indian Army and is a well-known military scholar who has authored several books on strategic and military affairs. He was a member of India's National Security Advisory Board (1999-2001) and is the editor of the security affairs journal *Aakrosh*. He was formerly the editor of the *Indian Defence Review*.

Rekha Chowdhary is Professor and Head of the Department of Political Science, University of Jammu. She is also currently the Coordinator for the UGC's Special Assistance Programme on research and analysis of the politics of Jammu and Kashmir.

P. Stobdan heads the Department of Strategic and Regional Studies, University of Jammu, and was earlier Senior Fellow at the Institute for Defence Studies and Analyses, New Delhi. He is an expert on issues concerning Asian security affairs covering Central Asia, Inner Asia, including Xinjiang, Tibet, Myanmar and the Himalayan region. He has served as Director, Indian Cultural Centre, Embassy of India, Almaty, Kazakhstan, and as Joint Director, National Security Council Secretariat, New Delhi.

Prof. **Noor Ahmad Baba** is a Professor and Head of the Department of Political Science, Kashmir University, Srinagar, and has written extensively on issues relating to Jammu and Kashmir.

Prem Shankar Jha is the former editor of the *Hindustan Times, The Economic Times* and *The Financial Express* who has also served as information advisor to the Prime Minister of India. He is the author of several books, including *The Perilous Road to the Market: The Political Economy of Reform in Russia, India* *and China,* and *Kashmir 1947: The Origins of a Dispute,* and is a regular columnist with several leading publications.

Pran Chopra is a well-known political analyst and was chief editor, *The Statesman.* His publications include *India's Second Liberation; Scene Changes in Kashmir, India and Pakistan* and *The Supreme Court Versus the Constitution: A Challenge To Federalism* (Edited).

Radhavinod Raju is a senior Indian Police Service (IPS) Officer of the J&K cadre and co-author of the book, *Triumph of Truth: Rajiv Gandhi Assassination -- The Investigation* (New Delhi, New Dawn Press Inc.). He currently serves as Joint Director of the Central Bureau of Investigation, New Delhi.

Satish Kumar is a former Professor of diplomacy in the School of International Studies, Jawaharlal Nehru University, New Delhi. His publications include *CIA and the Third World: A Study in Crypto-Diplomacy,* and *Rana Polity in Nepal: Origin and Growth.* He is the editor-in-chief of *India's National Security Annual Review.*

Frédéric Grare is a visiting scholar with the Carnegie Endowment for International Peace, Washington. He served at the French Embassy in Pakistan and was Director of the Centre for Social Sciences and Humanities in New Delhi from 1999 to 2003. His publications include *India, China, Russia: Intricacies of an Asian Triangle,* with Gilles Boquérat, eds., (New Delhi, India Research Press, 2003); *Pakistan and the Afghan Conflict, 1979-1985: At the Turn of the Cold War* (Karachi, Oxford University Press, 2003); *Political Islam in the Indian Subcontinent: The Jamaat-i-Islami* (New Delhi, Manohar, 2001).

India-Pakistan Relations: Towards a Grand Reconciliation?

Amitabh Mattoo

At a certain point I lost track of you.
You needed me. You needed to perfect me.
In your absence you polished me into the Enemy.
Your history gets in the way of my memory.
I am everything you lost. You can't forgive me.
I am everything you lost. Your perfect enemy.
Your memory gets in the way of my memory.
I'm everything you lost. You won't forgive me.
I hid my pain even from myself; I revealed my pain only to myself.
There is everything to forgive. You can't forgive me.
If only somehow you could have been mine,
what would not have been possible for the world?

– Agha Shahid Ali, *The Country Without a Post Office* (1997).

The conflict between India and Pakistan is easy to describe, but painfully difficult to understand. "Enduring rivalry," "sustained conflict," "ugly stability": these terms, often used by scholars of international relations to capsule the relationship, are, sadly, more often than not, "Occidental" attempts at forcing an Eastern intellectual puzzle into a preconceived Western mould. Unfortunately, the India-Pakistan relationship is, and has been, about almost everything that matters: history, memory, prejudice, territory, identity, religion, sovereignty, ideology, insecurity, trust, betrayal and much, much more, in a very *desi* way. Agha Shahid Ali's poem (quoted above), written in a different context about Kashmir, works as one powerful metaphor for the relationship:

I am everything you lost. You can't forgive me.
I am everything you lost. Your perfect enemy.

At what level does one, therefore, analyse the relationship: at the level of the international system or in inter-state terms, or does one address the inter-society dimension or focus at the human level? And where does one look for remedies? This essay argues that the only way that this relationship can move forward is by systematically beginning a process of reconciliation at *every* level. Only through such a 'grand' reconciliation will it be possible for India and Pakistan to live comfortably next to each other and for communal relations in the subcontinent to heal, well and truly. Given the nature of South Asian polities, this process of reconciliation can only be state driven initially, but once there is enough backing, push and momentum, the process can accelerate and move on, into an auto mode. Fortunately, there is space, at least for now, with the top leadership in the two countries seeking a shift in the policies of the past. The reconciliation, were it to happen, would, of course, be grand in its design and vision, but incremental in its process and execution: several flakes that would come together and snowball into an unstoppable avalanche of peace. Will it be possible to make use of this opening to make a real change? Will important stakeholders – civil society, big business and academia – make full use of this opportunity? And will those institutions of the state – driven as much by past orthodoxies as by present "vested" interests – let this incipient peace process bloom? As one Indian diplomat put it: "The people have made peace, the leaders want to make peace, but the establishments are still unwilling to adjust."

The Traditional Debate on Pakistan

Pakistan evokes passion like few other countries, especially in northern India. Anger and nostalgia, hatred and sympathy, contempt and fear combine to produce an intensity of emotions that are difficult to reduce to a well defined analytical category. Traditionally, the security community in India has been overwhelmingly in support of a policy of aggressively countering Pakistan. We term them the *subedars*. Only a minority has wanted to ignore and benignly neglect Islamabad: the *saudagars*. And a microscopic few wanted New Delhi to be proactive in promoting peace – even to the extent making unilateral concessions. These are the *sufis*. These opinions need to be fleshed out.

Most of the *subedars* argue – and often with considerable evidence – that New Delhi, despite persistent efforts, has been unable to inject a modicum of civility and stability in bilateral relations. For them, the Pakistan conundrum presents perhaps the most intriguing example in the history of state-to-state relations since the Treaty of Westphalia. They believe that neither military defeat, nor constructive engagement, nor unilateral gestures, nor passive disregard and not even international pressure seem to be able to reduce the pathological hostility that the Pakistani state bears towards India, and which – in this view – goes much beyond the problems in Kashmir. They view the Pakistani state, and its most important institution – the army – as having an anti-India posture as its *raison d'etre*, and consequently argue that only a dramatic reconstruction of the Pakistani state would create the possibility of peace in South Asia.

Evidence is provided by the *subedars* from the pre-2004 history of India-Pakistan relations, and the manner in which the whole spectrum of policies adopted by New Delhi towards Islamabad has floundered. Twice, in the 1998-2004 period, it is pointed out, New Delhi has publicly engaged Pakistan. The Lahore Summit of February 1999 raised expectations that a new détente in the subcontinent was in the offing, and indeed the summit documents included an imaginative set of cooperative measures, particularly on the nuclear issue. So much so, that several do-gooders prematurely nominated Prime Ministers Vajpayee and Sharif for the Nobel peace prize. But even more prudent analysts seemed to have been convinced that the overt nuclearisation of the subcontinent would help Pakistan to acquire the confidence and maturity to normalise its relations with India without being burdened by the existentialist fears that had plagued it since 1947, but particularly since 1971.

In the event, according to subscribers of this view, Pakistan – instead of seeking to project itself as a responsible nuclear power – sought to use the cover of nuclear weapons to escalate the conflict in Kashmir, burying the Lahore process under the heights of Kargil. Similarly, the Agra Summit failed primarily – in this view – because Pakistan was unwilling to concede that no normalisation of relations is possible as long as Islamabad continues with its policy of sponsoring violence and terror across the border. It is believed that India had been willing to concede at Agra much more than it had done during the last decade, including setting up of a high level bilateral group to discuss Kashmir and only Kashmir. But whatever was left of the spirit of Agra evaporated after the September 11 terrorist attacks and particularly after the terrorist attack on the Jammu and Kashmir (J&K) Legislative Assembly complex in Srinagar on October 1, 2001.

According to the *subedars*, Lahore and Agra were only the public face of a policy of engagement that New Delhi has been attempting to construct at various levels. More important, India had not been shying away from discussing what Pakistan has termed as the core issue of Kashmir. It is now well known that a special envoy of Prime Minister Vajpayee had been discreetly meeting a Pakistani counterpart, in the weeks after the Lahore Summit, to discuss a possible resolution of the Kashmir issue. It is even believed that the two interlocutors had been mandated by their respective prime ministers to find a solution for Kashmir before the dawn of the 21st century, and met several times in Islamabad and New Delhi before Kargil and the military coup by General Musharraf derailed the process.

Similarly, it is argued by the *subedars* that New Delhi had persisted in its efforts to initiate a peace process with the Kashmiri separatists, even with that section which it knows is deeply beholden to Pakistan and is in constant communication with elements within the Pakistani establishment. A quiet dialogue with the Kashmiri separatists and militants had been continuing for at least couple of years before 2004. But it became clear that any time that there was a real chance of translating discreet drawing room parleys into a more public political process, Pakistan would use all means at its disposal, including direct physical threats, to subvert the process. In other words, Islamabad was unwilling to even let Kashmiri leaders, who it had sponsored, sustain a meaningful dialogue with New Delhi's representatives.

Neither, according to the *subedars*, have unilateral gestures of goodwill and cooperation made a difference. India's continued treatment of Pakistan as a most favoured nation has not been reciprocated by Islamabad and, it is believed, that the report of the South Asian Association for Regional Cooperation (SAARC) Eminent Persons Group, which recommends imaginative time-bound steps to promote regional economic integration, has been given short shrift by Pakistan, despite the presence of one of its former foreign secretaries as part of the group. New Delhi's decision, before the Agra Summit, to unilaterally relax visa rules or its decision to open further crossing points on the border have failed or had little effect in the absence of Pakistani reciprocity. Pakistan's unwillingness to give visas to Indian artistes, its attempts at blocking Indian television channels, have meant that the hope that there could be a détente from below, a genuine breakthrough because of greater people-to people contact, too, has been dashed.

Most of the *saudagars* believe that any cost benefit analysis would suggest that ignoring the military regime in Pakistan is the most prudent option. The *saudagars* say that India can and should bypass Pakistan and indeed South Asia, as it emerges as a major economic player in the international system. Indeed, for more than one year after the Kargil War and before the Agra Summit, India passively disregarded Islamabad. The *saudagars* were convinced that Pakistan was in such a deep internal crisis that it was best left alone. Economically, it was on the verge of collapse, politically, it had descended into yet another praetorian phase and socially, it was one of the most divided societies in the world.

But there has always been a small section of Indian opinion that believes that New Delhi – more than ever before – has a stake in the future of Pakistan. A few years ago, Prime Minister Vajpayee unambiguously stated that Pakistan's stability was also in India's national interest and this is echoed by the *sufis*. They argue that Vajpayee's statement is not a political slogan, but a harsh reality. True, Pakistan's demise may finally bury whatever is left of the two-nation theory, but that would be too heavy a price merely to prove that a mistake – huge as it may have been – was made 60 years ago. Pakistan needs to survive, not just for the sake of its own citizens, but also for the health of the whole of South Asia.

They argue that on paper, the option of ignoring Pakistan may seem desirable, but in reality it is an unsustainable option. It is extremely difficult to ignore Pakistan if Islamabad does not want to be left alone. As long as Pakistan continues its support for militancy and violence in Kashmir and other places, and seeks to portray South Asia as a region on the brink of a nuclear war, it will be almost impossible to look the other way.

It was Pervez Hoodbhoy, a nuclear physicist at Islamabad and an anti-nuclear activist, who put it most graphically: "Pakistan's state is already fractured by multiple violent ethnic and religious conflicts. Disintegration into molecular civil war with fiefdoms and warlords is a terrible possibility. India will find, too late, that it has created a South Asian nuclear Somalia for a neighbour."[1] Hoodbhoy's sentiments have been echoed by a variety of respondents. They argue that a nuclear Pakistan, on the verge of economic and political disintegration, will be a danger to the whole region. Even the *subedars* would agree that deterrence stability requires a modicum of political stability and control. In other words, political turmoil and economic chaos in Pakistan can create conditions in which nuclear stability in South Asia could be seriously threatened.

But the political and economic health of Pakistan is of concern to the *sufis* for other reasons as well. Ethnic turmoil in Pakistan could easily spill over to India and the country's balkanisation could even lead to a huge refugee problem in India. Similarly, self-styled warlords could well expand their narcotics and gun-running businesses into India. In larger terms, the crumbling of the Pakistan economy could have a ripple effect on the Indian economy as well. South Asia will begin to be viewed as a zone of turmoil and lead to erosion in investor confidence as well as possible flight of capital even from India. But, perhaps most crucially, the collapse of Pakistan will inevitably lead to a larger cultural demoralisation. It will suggest that even after years of independence, South Asians are still not able to acquire firm control over their nations. It will suggest a failure at developing coherent systems of governance. South Asia, not just Pakistan, will become an international object of ridicule and the whole project of nationhood in the region may become deeply suspect.

The *sufis* also argue that a policy of confrontation has not worked and is unlikely to do so in the future. Two nuclear states, in today's international system, cannot afford repeated acts of brinkmanship and recent experience has suggested that there are clear limits to which a military confrontation can be escalated. They suggest that even the idea of limited war floated by some strategists is rife with dangers: military, diplomatic and political.

The Changes in Pakistan

In the course of a television interview in 2006 with an Indian journalist, President Pervez Musharraf abandoned decades of the most sacredly held *mantras* of Pakistan's Kashmir policy: plebiscite and the United Nations (UN) Security Council resolutions. During the course of the conversation, the general even ruled out supporting an independent Kashmir. In the past too, he has signalled a shift, and this has been in evidence for the last two years. The first major policy shift in Pakistan's Kashmir policy came when in December 2003, during an interview with Reuters, Musharraf offered to set aside Islamabad's 50-year-old demand to implement UN resolutions on Kashmir.

It is also clear that there is greater convergence today between the positions of Prime Minister Manmohan Singh and President Musharraf on Kashmir than there has been between any two leaders of India and Pakistan in the last forty years. This change has been visible since their first summit meeting in New Delhi in 2005. Both have ruled out a change of borders or an exchange of territories. Instead, they want the borders to be made irrelevant in order to ensure a free flow of people, goods, services and ideas across the Line of Control (LoC). It is also clear to both that there cannot be any visible dilution of political sovereignty. And both are committed to some form of devolution of powers on both sides of the LoC. There are, of course, real differences over joint supervision and demilitarisation, but President Musharraf seems to have today conceded much more than any Pakistani leader in the past.

Is this for real? Does Mr. Musharraf really want a final reconciliation with India based on a grand compromise? Or is this, as most of the Indian establishment thinks, merely *chaalbazi* to get a foothold in Kashmir? The reality, however, is that even by the most diabolic understanding of President Musharraf, India needs to engage with Pakistan and its leader's views on Kashmir in its own national interest.

Clearly, President Musharraf is not an easy man to understand, precisely because he appears to be exactly what you expect him not to be: transparent, straight and flexible.

Indeed, for an army commando, it is strange the way that he can almost disarm his audience with his words. During a lengthy interaction a group of us had with him in Islamabad earlier last year, he was ready to answer any question – even those targeting him personally – without showing the slightest rancour. And throughout the two hours, he came across as someone who genuinely wanted to make peace with India. For a few minutes, at least, even his otherwise most fierce opponents (and this included *subedars* of the Indian establishment) were ready to concede that the general was a most reasonable man. Only later did it seem that this was a case of the speediest "Stockholm syndrome." After all, how could a former *Mohajir*, an India-hating army commando who authored Kargil and ditched us in Agra, be a sincere man to be trusted?

The fact is that for Indians, the trust deficit in Pakistan begins, as was illustrated in the last few pages, right at the top. Sections of public opinion, aided, of course, by a cynical establishment, cannot bring themselves to believe that President Musharraf could really want an accommodation with India. Why should someone who witnessed the horrors of partition want to be friends with us? Why should someone who spent his career in the Pakistan Army, presumably fed on a daily diet of anti-India propaganda, suddenly want to cozy up to the eastern neighbour? And why should someone who plotted the great betrayal at Kargil and let down the venerable Vajpayee at Agra suddenly become a messiah of peace? The tragedy, of course, is that the Indian establishment has rarely, if ever, accurately gauged the mind of leaders from Pakistan. Understanding the mind of Pervez Musharraf, probably the most agile and complex of recent Pakistani leaders, requires an ability that goes beyond backgrounders and pre-conceived notions of Muslims, Pakistanis and generals.

The reality, however, is that people do change; all the time, as a matter of fact. We tend to often judge military leaders by the absolute standards of robots, not as mere human mortals who can think and act differently if circumstances change. President Musharraf has, as we all know, done many U-turns in the past, especially after 9/11. The Musharraf of Agra, who chided Indian editors at breakfast, is not the Musharraf of the television interview. But is Musharraf now willing to do the mother of all U-turns, change forever Pakistan's policy on Kashmir?

The proof, as they say, is in the eating or perhaps just in tasting the recipe. Engage Musharraf, play with his ideas, suggest alternatives, but do not reject his proposals because of his past obnoxiousness. In any case, it is in India's interest to be seen as dialoguing with the Musharraf proposals for a variety of reasons. Let us be clear, only the most straitjacketed can argue that

President Musharraf's recent proposals do not demonstrate flexibility. Whether or not this new shift demonstrates a fresh willingness to compromise and make peace with India, or is merely a ploy to gain entry in Kashmir needs to be carefully studied.

Consider, however, the response from the Kashmir Valley. Almost every major political force, from mainstream to separatist, from the National Conference of Farooq Abdullah to Mufti Sayeed's People's Democratic Party, to the All Parties Hurriyat Conference, has welcomed the proposals. Indeed, the only group in the Valley to outrightly reject the Pakistan leader's ideas is, ironically, the pro-Pakistan hardline Jamaat-i-Islami leader, Ali Shah Geelani. If at least in part, New Delhi's Kashmir policy is to win the hearts and minds of the Kashmiri people, then it is important not to reject outright the flexibility inherent in the Musharraf ideas.

Similarly, because the Pakistan president's proposals seem reasonable, they are being taken seriously internationally. And precisely for this reason, it is vital to constructively engage with them. But beyond these tactical domestic and international considerations, is the possibility that Mr. Musharraf may have actually changed. The only way to find out if this indeed is the case is by dealing with him.

Engagement should in no case mean lowering the strategic guard or the vigil that is essential in Jammu and Kashmir. Indeed, the only real test of Pakistan's intentions will be a permanent end to violence in Jammu and Kashmir, an end to infiltration and an end to a policy that was created to bleed India through a thousand cuts. But if Pakistan does want to take steps in that direction in abandoning that misguided policy, it would be a tragedy if we did not help it do so, merely because of a history of bitterness and bureaucratic inertia and only because India could never bring itself to trust a man called Musharraf.

There are several other reasons why Pakistan may well be changing fundamentally. And this change can generate maximum acceleration if it can be met with an Indian policy of reconciliation.

The traditional, narrow, militaristic, framework of national security continues to operate in Pakistan. But the truly momentous developments of the 1990s have finally provoked a rethinking and there are signs, albeit still weak, that Pakistan may adopt a fresh holistic paradigm of national security by the first years of the new millennium. Or at least, expand its existing framework to take greater cognisance of the larger dimensions of security. Perhaps the most significant development of the 1990s has been the steady democratisation of the debate on national security. Within the media, and in policy institutes and non-governmental organisations (NGOs), there are new voices that are beginning to challenge conventional wisdom and orthodox prescriptions. Prime Minister Nawaz Sharif's emphasis on economic stability, and his unwillingness to play the India card during the 1997 election campaign, arguably, reflect this new emerging trend.

A detailed nationwide poll by the news magazine *Herald* in 1997, after 50 years of Pakistan's independence, was particularly revealing. Forty-two per cent of the respondents thought that Muslims of the Indian subcontinent were better off before partition and the creation of Pakistan. In Karachi, the city with a large *Mohajir* population, the majority (52.8 per cent) believed that Muslims are worse off after partition. Forty-seven per cent believed that Jinnah intended Pakistan to be a modern democracy rather than a religious state. More than 60 per cent in Islamabad/ Rawalpindi and nearly 58 per cent in Quetta supported this proposition.

A majority of the respondents thought that Pakistan has been harmed by periods of martial law and 47 per cent thought that West Pakistan's politicians and army were responsible for the creation of Bangladesh. Only 41 per cent held India or Sheikh Mujib responsible. Forty-nine per cent wanted military spending to be cut. Respondents in Karachi, Lahore, Multan and Sukkar were less supportive of the idea, while the majority in Peshawar, Quetta and Islamabad/Rawalpindi were in favour of cuts. Seventy-two per cent held that since the creation of Pakistan, religious parties have done more harm than good and 67 per cent believed that the economic crisis in Pakistan is the country's own fault rather than the International Monetary Fund's. Indeed, 59 per cent wanted friendlier relations with India, and only 29 per cent believed that Pakistan would fight a war with India in the next five years. Sixty-seven per cent do not want the kinds of restrictions imposed on women as were imposed by the Taliban in Afghanistan. Seventy-five per cent were opposed to the government having the right to intercept mail and tap telephones. An overwhelming 80 per cent believed that health and education are responsibilities of the state. Seventy-one per cent were supportive of family planning and 90 per cent of the respondents were of the opinion that AIDS posed a serious threat to Pakistan.

A 1996 comprehensive opinion poll of the elite on the nuclear issue, which the author of this paper helped design, was also revealing: even while 56 per cent of the respondents identified Kashmir as the first or second most important issue facing the country, 53 per cent of the respondents accorded this status to economic stability. The issues of ethnic conflict and religious sectarianism, the Afghan refugee presence and poverty were all considered more important than the nuclear weapons issue or the question of external military assistance and weapons supply.

There are at least six inter-related factors that have led to this new thinking and especially to the questioning of Pakistan's traditional security paradigm. First, was the disintegration of the Soviet Union and the weakening of the alliance with the United States. The beginning of the withdrawal of Soviet forces from Afghanistan in 1990 signalled the end of the Cold War, and ended Pakistan's status as a frontline state as the United States lost interest in the region. This was starkly reflected in the Bush Administration's reversal of course and refusal to certify Pakistan's non-nuclear status in 1990, leading to an abrupt cut-off of aid under the Pressler Amendment. No other action could have demonstrated so clearly to the Pakistanis the strategic "opportunism" of the United States and its unreliability as an ally. While, on the one hand, the aid cut-off created a widespread sense of victimisation and outrage at this dual-standards treatment, it also revealed, on the other, the declining strategic importance of Pakistan in the post-Cold War era. Subsequent measures by the Clinton Administration did seek to limit the damage to US-Pakistan relations, but it was clear to most Pakistanis that Islamabad's relations with Washington are unlikely to return to the "heady" days of the 1980s in the foreseeable future.

Second, was Islamabad's failure to achieve a decisive push over the Kashmir issue. Kashmir was, and continues to be, a key political concern in Pakistan. Even now it is clear that no government in Islamabad can afford to be seen to compromise on the Kashmir issue. Kashmir still looms very large in its popular consciousness. But what also seems to have become clear gradually, even at the popular level, is that a "victory" on Kashmir cannot be simply engineered through a combination of strategies that were employed until the mid-1990s: diplomatic, political and military support to the Kashmiri militants, on the one hand, with attempts to secure international support for Pakistan's position and a commitment from the international community to intervene in the dispute, on the other. The refusal of both China and the United States to adopt a more active posture of support on the issue has brought this realisation home. This refusal of open support for Pakistan's Kashmir policy became evident when both China and the United Stated did not support Pakistan during the latter's Kargil misadventure in 1999.

Third, was the culture of drugs and guns that was bred during the Afghan crisis and continues to flourish even today. It was this "Kalashinikov and heroin culture," together with the presence of hundreds of thousands of Afghan refugees, that has played havoc with Pakistan's civil society; made it a central pivot of the international drugs traffic network; made Peshawar a breeding ground for international terrorists; and was responsible for putting Pakistan on the US watch list for terrorist states. In short, the after-effects of the Afghan crisis have made Pakistanis acutely conscious of the internal threats to their state and society. Indeed, today Pakistan suffers more from terrorist activities than India even as the terror infrastructure in Pakistan is sustained for 'bleeding' India.

Fourth, was the growing consciousness about Pakistan's underdevelopment – the poor quality of life even as compared to other countries in the region. Pakistan ranks 144 out of 170 nations in the Physical Quality of Life Index, below nations such as Bangladesh and Haiti. In almost all Human Development Indicators, Pakistan is well below India, Bangladesh, Sri Lanka, Bhutan and the Maldives. What is most startling is the lack of progress after fifty years, whether it is in terms of access to health, drinking water, sanitation, or the literacy rate. In addition, Pakistan's external debt and liabilities stood at $35 billion in 2005.

It is becoming clear that the increasing defence burden is taking a huge economic toll. The Islamabad-based Human Development Centre's *Human Development Report*, 1997, is a good source of evidence. In 1994, Pakistan spent 7 per cent of its Gross Domestic Product (GDP) on defence or nearly 27 per cent of the total central government expenditure. This is higher than in any other South Asian country. In the decades of the 1980s and 1990s, Pakistan spent between 5.7 to 7.22 per cent of its GDP on defence while India spent between 2.83 and 4.00 per cent. The per capita defence expenditure amounts to about $26, and with the eighth largest army in the world, Pakistan spends about four times on defence what it does on education and health. There has been an annual real increase of 5.2 per cent in military expenditure from 1947 to 1996. There is a growing elite consciousness about the deleterious consequences of seemingly abstract statistics, and this awareness has started slowly permeating to the grassroots.

Fifth, was the creation of a nuclear option that has given Pakistan the confidence to pursue more creative thinking on defence and national security. Although it was some time in the mid-1980s that Pakistan acquired its nuclear capability, the full implications of the nuclear option became clear in the 1990s. The "nuclear crisis" in 1990 itself must have revealed the deterrent potential of nuclear capability to the Pakistanis. More important, the ability of Pakistan's nuclear weapons to offset India's conventional advantage and Pakistan's lack of strategic depth have not gone unnoticed in its media or in academia. In other words, conventional warfare is not an easy option for a country that has too little or no strategic depth, but such a situation can be salvaged with the introduction of nuclear weapons into the country's strategic calculations. This confidence has been instrumental in its more rational and temperate posture towards India.

Sixth, was the collapse of law and order in Sindh and the virtual outbreak of a civil war between supporters of the Mohajir Quami Movement (MQM) and the government. The breakdown of law and order in Karachi, the huge number of casualties, and the collapse of the entire imagery of all assumed notions of Islamic solidarity and brotherhood, have starkly revealed the limits – in the post Bangladesh period – to which a nation-state can be sustained on the basis of a common religion in the absence of the growth of economic potential or other common values. The situation in Balochistan and the Northwest Frontier Province (NWFP) has only added more credibility to this realisation.

Conclusion

This essay has suggested that Pakistan is changing, and changing fast. Parts of the polity are in deep crisis. The recent groundswell of public opinion against the president's decision to suspend the chief justice, the continuing debate over President Musharraf's future, the deep tensions within Balochistan, the anarchy in Balochistan and the Federally Administered Tribal Areas (FATA), are good evidence of a country on the boil. This should not, however, be any cause of celebration in India, but should invite deep introspection. Fortunately, there are tendencies within Pakistan that recognise the deep flaws within the polity and the mistakes of past policies, and the need to make a strategic shift, particularly in terms of Pakistan's relations with India. These currents need to be strengthened by New Delhi, by unilateral gestures, if necessary. India also needs to pay attention to the new flexibility demonstrated by President Musharraf and the growing constituency in support of a second-best settlement on Kashmir. The *subedars*, the *saudagars* and the *sufis* need to come together and shape a Pakistan policy that has three elements: maintain a security vigil and sustain a deterrent capability at all levels; engage Pakistan at all levels to further cooperation in areas where business is possible; and prepare for a fundamental change in Pakistan's policy in core areas, including on Kashmir, and grab the opportunity wherever and whenever it presents itself. A grand reconciliation may seem like a utopian idea, but it is only by sticking to such a mega-blueprint on the easel can one begin – through small strokes of the brush of cooperation – to visualise the vast promise that a new phase in India-Pakistan relations holds for the region.

Notes

1. Pervez Hoodbhoy, "Surviving South Asia's Nuclear Whirlpool," Paper presented at the RCSS conference on "Future of Security Studies in South Asia," at Ahungalla, Sri Lanka, July 14-16, 1998, p.2.

Regional Dimension

Geo-Politics in Southern Asia and its Impact on India-Pakistan Relations

Happymon Jacob

Introduction: The New Geo-Politics in the Southern Asian Region (SAR)[1]

The onward march of history has always been unstoppable, be it in human civilisation, technological development or even in the case of the rise and fall of great powers. The turn of the Southern Asian Region (SAR) has come to have its date with history. Once ignored and neglected by those who matter in the conduct of international relations, the region today is experiencing an unprecedented degree of change in its internal and external environments which have the potential to radically alter the political destiny of the region.

In retrospect, while the arrival of the post-Cold War world did impact upon the SAR, the transformation was still fraught with geo-strategic uncertainty, after-effects of the Cold War in the region, insurgencies, and acute economic problems. Even though cessation of the Cold War did provide the countries of the region with an opportunity to be masters of their own destiny, most countries in the region lacked the wherewithal to do so. While the West freed itself of the ill effects of the Cold War in the 1990s, the Third World countries continue to bear its brunt. In other words, the end of the Cold War did not particularly change the fate of the Third World in a positive manner. In contrast, the current transformation in the SAR is far more revolutionary in nature and has the inherent capacity to positively alter the decades-long geo-political configuration in the region.

This chapter argues that there are tectonic geo-political transformations taking place in the Southern Asian region. These transformations are likely to have a positive impact on the current balance of power in the region in general and Indo-Pak relations in particular.

The following factors are the four pillars, this chapter reasons, of the great transformation that today's Southern Asia is witnessing: (a) The global war on terrorism; (b) Indo-US relations; (c) Sino-Indian entente; and (d) India's emergence as a major power.

The key aim of this chapter is to argue that the transformations underway in the SAR will undeniably have an impact on Indo-Pak relations. The correlations of global and regional forces today seem to be in favour of a positive momentum towards resolving the deeply-entrenched Indo-Pak enmity. This chapter will analyse the transformations underway in the region in general and will describe how these will have an impact on Indo-Pak relations in particular.

From Struggle for Power to Struggle for Well-Being

The Neo-Liberal Peace Thesis

Economic incentives may not deter states from engaging in geo-political games that they are structurally in sync with. In other words, power struggles, arms races and geo-politics are not likely to come to a grinding halt in this region in the foreseeable future. However, globalisation, the prospects of economic gains, shared aversion to terrorism, and the post-Cold War global power configuration are more likely to determine these than the intention to gain power and friends merely for the sake of being militarily powerful. From an International Relations theory perspective, therefore, it may be said that the classical realist explanation as to why states engage in power struggles is of less relevance for this argument. For the classical realists, power is for the sake of power: states aspire and struggle for power because national interest is defined in terms of power. Structural realists, on the other hand, argue that power is not for the sake of power: power helps to achieve security which is necessary for a state in an anarchic states-system. While this perspective more usefully explains what is happening in the SAR today, even this would not be able to completely capture what has been happening in the region in the last couple of years. It is the neo-liberal peace thesis that, in fact, better explains the Southern Asian geo-politics. While not resting merely on the strength of neo-liberal institutional prescriptions, this understanding argues that even in the absence of peace-making or cooperative institutions, peace can be a feature of relations among states if they believe peace is profitable. To consider an example, today it would not be out of place to say that China is forced by economic pragmatism to reconsider its decades-long rivalry with India since, for China, which is emerging as a global power of economic and military consequences, what is more important today is sustaining its growing economy and getting the advantages of globalisation which it entered only at an advanced stage, than perhaps entering into a military confrontation with India.

Indian Ocean Geo-Politics

Would the Indian Ocean geo-politics lead the region to more chaos or increased cooperation? Analysts have argued that even as the Indian Ocean region becomes a busy hub of international trade, with the littoral states indulging in what Donald Berlin calls "great base race"[2] and the US increasing its present engagement with it, it is likely that the Indian Ocean would soon become a theatre of conflict rather than cooperation.

The Indian Ocean region is of immense strategic significance. Alfred Thayer Mahan had predicted: "Whoever controls the Indian Ocean, dominates Asia. This ocean is the key to the seven seas in the twenty-first century, the destiny of the world will be decided in these waters." Its importance comes from two factors: volume of trade and problems of piracy. Around 360 ships pass through the Indian Ocean on a daily basis. Ships carrying almost $200 billion worth of oil pass through the Strait of Hormuz every day out of which $70 billion worth of oil goes through the Strait of Malacca. Berlin writes:

> Currently, about 25 per cent of all oil used by America passes through Indian Ocean sea lanes and the Persian Gulf region, and the United States also depends on the Indian Ocean for the shipment of about 50 different strategic materials, including tin, nickel, iron, lead, and copper. Burma and Bangladesh, which are rich in minerals, are also seen by other key states as important future energy sources. The same is true of Central Asia and the Caspian Basin. Many of the military infrastructure initiatives described in this essay thus are explainable in part in terms of their proximity to the Persian Gulf, Central Asia or the energy-rich Bay of Bengal and the Malacca Strait, gateway into the Indian Ocean.[3]

Indeed, for all the major powers, including the US, China and Japan, the Indian Ocean is of great economic and strategic importance. A quarter of America's imported energy passes through the Indian Ocean region. In the case of India, "[O]ver 97 per cent of India's trade by volume and 75 per cent by value is sea-borne."[4]

The second reason for the importance of the Indian Ocean is the increasing security threats to the ships cruising these waters. The International Maritime Organisation reports that the Malacca Strait, South China Sea and Indian Ocean are the most affected by piracy.[5] Narco-terrorism and gun-running in the Indian Ocean are also issues of concern today.

There are also military security reasons for the importance of the Indian Ocean. The attempts by the Chinese to increase their presence in the ocean are looked upon suspiciously by both Japan and the US. India's increasing presence in the ocean is troubling for both China and Pakistan. Under such circumstances, it would be rational to argue that the Indian Ocean is quickly becoming a theatre of conflict rather than of cooperation. However, going by what has been happening so far, it would be out of place to say so. Consider the following.

First of all, countries are unlikely to turn the Indian Ocean region into a theatre of conflict because many countries depend heavily on the ocean for trade in energy and other items. Thus, turning the region into a theatre of conflict would be disadvantageous for the countries and their economies. Secondly, countries are increasingly realising that they need to put in place cooperative mechanisms to safeguard the security of the ocean. Indeed, this is precisely what is happening in the region today. To cite a few examples, sixteen countries (ASEAN—Association of Southeast Asian Nations members and China, South Korea, Japan, Bangladesh, India, and Sri Lanka) concluded the Regional Cooperation Agreement on Combating Piracy and Armed Robbery Against Ships in Asia (ReCAAP) in November 2004.[6] The first ever Indo-US naval exercise "Malabar" was held from September 26 to October 3, 2002, in which over 1,500 Indian and American naval personnel had taken part. Singapore and India signed an agreement in 2003 to improve maritime and counter-terrorism cooperation. Later, in September 2004, India and the Indonesian Navy conducted joint patrols close to the Strait of Malacca. In fact, India has been visiting almost all the Indian Ocean littoral states to improve maritime cooperation in the region.

If the suggested measures mentioned under the US-supported Proliferation Security Initiative (PSI) are extended to the Indian Ocean, it will lead to further cooperation in the region, provided certain objections raised against PSI are adequately addressed. PSI aims to implement effective interdiction of shipments of weapons of mass destruction (WMD) or missiles and related items.[7] The new US-led Container Security Initiative (CSI) is another step in the direction of enhancing cooperation in the Indian Ocean region. India has already joined the initiative after some initial hesitation. The Indian Ocean Rim Association for Regional Cooperation (IORARC) which was launched in Mauritius in 1997 is another organisation for increasing cooperation. The association, which has countries such as India and China on board, comprises 18 member states and facilitates trade and investment in the region. The above analysis suggests that even as there exist possibilities of an arms race in the Indian Ocean region, it is more likely that the economic stakes involved here are powerful enough to deter any such eventuality and would, eventually, on the other hand, lead the region towards cooperative security.

Terrorism: The Great Unifier?

Terrorism or support to terrorism as a state policy does not sell in the conduct of international relations any more. On the one hand, the international community, especially post-9/11, has grown intolerant to terrorism in any form, be it in the name of "moral and diplomatic support" or "freedom struggle." On the other hand, countries which have traditionally supported terrorism have been facing the blowback effects of it in ways manifold.

The post-September 11 international environment has forced Pakistan to abandon terrorism as a policy of statecraft. First came the abandoning of the Taliban regime under acute US pressure followed by the softening of posture on Kashmir. The Pakistan government was forced to ban a large number of militant groups and curb cross-border infiltration after the 2002 military stand-off with India. The Inter-Services Intelligence (ISI) also was under the scanner for some time. This radical *volte-face* was a result of US pressure, intolerance of any forms of terrorism by the international community and the realisation by the Pakistani establishment that talking to India was a more judicious way of getting a better deal on all outstanding issues than waging a proxy war against it. As a respected Pakistani journalist Zahid Hussain wrote in the Pakistani news magazine *Newsline* "[T]he use of militancy as an instrument of policy was no longer acceptable under any pretext."[8]

Apart from Pakistan, other countries were also taking steps to rein in terrorist groups. The Liberation Tigers of Tamil Eelam (LTTE) was internationally banned and China started focussing more on the situation in Xinjiang, claiming "that these separatists are no different from other Islamic terrorists that are the focus of the global 'War against Terror'."[9] Bhutan took stern military steps to clear the camps of the terrorists, holed up in its territory, who were waging an insurgency in India's northeast. The US and Britain were also voicing their concerns about terrorism in Kashmir. As Malini Parthasarathy points out in her chapter in this book:

> India's campaign against Pakistan's perceived support to cross-border terrorism found a resonance internationally in the new context of the international campaign against terror. Thus, the United States and the United Kingdom became less ambiguous in their endorsement of India's position that complicating the attempt to address the dispute with Pakistan over Kashmir was the consistent support provided by forces in Islamabad to the terrorists

> operating in the Valley. The US and its allies, while appreciating the support extended by Musharraf to their coalition, made it clear to the Pakistani leader that he would have to stop supporting the *jihadi* groups in Kashmir.[10]

Secondly, apart from the realisation that the international community would not tolerate terrorism any more, it had also become costly for the countries that were supporting terrorism. For Pakistan, it was not just its Kashmir campaign that was backfiring—its Afghan campaign too had cost it very dearly.[11]

As Sushant Sareen notes in one of the later chapters of this book:

> The need to wind down or tightly control the *jihad* against India was equally the result of the blow-back of this policy inside Pakistan – the mushrooming militias, the social regression that the growing radicalism brought about in the society, the economic fallout of *jihad* on business and investor climate, the deteriorating law and order situation and the consequent loss of internal sovereignty.[12]

Terrorism, as discussed above, is likely to bond the international community together in the days to come as it has now become a more dangerous international menace than a weapon that states would use to achieve their geo-political gains. This global metanoia will indubitably have its regional impact.

The India Effect

India as an emerging power has the potential to realign the power configuration in the region. Economic strength, democratic ethos, projection of soft power, large skilled population in the working age group, technological advantages, military capabilities and a "strategy of tolerance" (for want of a better term) will make India a power to reckon with in the region and the world at large. The strategy of tolerance will singularly give India an advantage in its future foreign policy endeavours.

The emergence of India as a power of consequence has been predicted by many authors.[13] The significance of India's power will be predicated on the fact that it will not just be a hard power of global military consequences but, unlike many great powers of the day, its power will have two defining features. On the one hand, it will be what Joseph Nye calls a soft power of great and long-lasting impact. On the other, it will also be a strong military power. This soft power has many dimensions: vibrant economy, popular culture, vast Diaspora, technological edge, etc. The Indian economy, according to the Goldman Sachs Report no.99, "could be larger than Japan's by 2032" and "could be larger than all but the US and China in 30 years."[14] The report further claims that "India has the potential to show the fastest growth over the next 30 and 50 years. Growth could be higher than 5 per cent over the next 30 years and close to 5 per cent as late as 2050 if development proceeds successfully." India, being the largest English-speaking country in the whole world and with trained manpower in health care, information technology among others, will increase its power base with such a powerful Diaspora to back it up. Indian presence in the Silicon Valley, and US scientific, technical and educational institutions is unmatched by any other country. The image of the country is getting radically altered by the expatriate Indians who are doing much better than anybody else in their host countries. To quote from the *Indian Express*:

> As per the last official census in the UK, the average income of Indians living in Britain was about 15 per cent higher than the national average, while in Canada, it was 20 per cent higher. In the US, where this has been meticulously documented by a report, We the People: Asians in the United States, that was issued by the US government some time ago and was based on the 2000 census, émigré Indians have the highest per capita income of any ethnic group, including the Chinese.[15]

It is also important to note that for a country to emerge in the world scenario, one, it needs to be noted by others, and, second, the policy elite in the country in question realises the potential of the country to emerge as a big power; in other words, it should have the will power to be a big power. In India's case, the international community is noting India's ability to come forth on the world stage and the Indian elite is growing more and more confident in dealing with the rest of the world.

India has also become a major source of global research and development (R&D) with a large number of multinationals having established their R&D labs in the country. India's cultural influence will not be ignorable. Its films, music, food and popular culture have takers all around the world. If predictions about India's 7-8 per cent per annum economic growth are anything to go by, its economy will turn out to be exceptionally large and diversified.

Southern Asia is the new global epicentre of conflict and prosperity. In one sense, the region holds the key to the future of the world: ignore the region and one will find that economic deprivation and extremism thrive in the region which will go on to upset the global order. The region also has a lot of potential for wealth-creation, be it in terms of energy, trained manpower or others. The international community sees India as a major actor in the region, a country that shares the enlightened values of the Western world, to help the international community, given its own advantages, to transform the region. For one, the US thinks that "[I]t should pay closer attention to India's role in the regional balance."[16] In many ways, therefore, the West seems to realise that India can be its strong ally in the onward march to global peace and prosperity.

Another important India factor that supposedly attracts the regional powers, despite their shared suspicion of a huge country in their neighborhood, is its declared and demonstrated lack of territorial ambitions which can be termed as a strategy of tolerance. India behaves like a passive elephant; it is dominant perforce, not by force. In other words, India is a reluctant hegemon. This was amply demonstrated when in 2000 the Sri Lankan government asked India to intervene in their country to save the lives of 120,000 Sri Lankan soldiers when they were surrounded by 4,000 Tamil rebels after the fall of Elephant Pass which is considered to be the gateway to Jaffna. Moreover, India is widely considered to be a defensive power which has never initiated a war in the history of its existence.

The US Factor

The US support for India's vision for global power status was already evident during the regime of Bill Clinton. The Bush Administration has followed it up without the strings that the Clinton Administration attached to its support for India. The February 2006 visit of President Bush to India and the nuclear treaty signed between the two countries is evidence enough to suggest that US would have no problems in having India become a global power, even though it may not actively aid India to be one. The nuclear deal provided India with an entry into the nuclear club which so far has been the privilege of the five recognised nuclear powers. By signing the treaty, US has made exceptions to its own laws, or has promised to do so. The pro-India tilt has also translated into a sterner posture towards Pakistan. India is likely to benefit from a relationship with the US if the latter does not use a "carrot and stick" policy while dealing with India. It will also not be in India's interests to be a US henchman guarding the Southern Asian outpost vis-à-vis China. Increased closeness with the US, while ensuring its strategic autonomy, will help India realign the forces of the region in its favour.

The Sino-Indian Entente

China will be forced to rethink the anti-India tenor of its relations with Pakistan and come closer to India by way of mending fences for its own smooth sailing to great power status and to have relative stability in the region.

Growing Beyond Self-Indulgence: Sino-Indian Entente

There are two contending schools of thought regarding Sino-Indian relations. One school believes that China is a threat.[17] The other believes that China is an opportunity.[18] Yet another strand of thinking would posit China as both a threat and an opportunity: engage but be cautious.

The first school makes its arguments in the light of the historical experiences and military prowess of the country. They prescribe, in the words of Mohan Malik: "...hyperrealists…draw attention to the vast gap between Beijing's declaratory and operational policies vis-à-vis India and argue that China will never be territorially satiated."[19] Malik shows how the military capability of China threatens India: "..the traditional India-China rivalry is augmented by China's groundwork for a naval presence along maritime chokepoints in the South China Sea, the Malacca Strait, the Indian Ocean and the Strait of Hormuz in the Persian Gulf to protect its long-term economic security interests."[20]

He also counters the argument that the Sino-Indian economic relationship is complementary, arguing that it is competitive: "Both look to the West and Japan for advanced technology, machinery, capital and investment. China has long regarded India as a large potential market and has shown interest in India's information technology (IT) prowess. But Indians see China as a trade predator and fear being left behind China's robust growth rates."[21]

C. Raja Mohan belongs to the "woo China" school. He writes,

> ...for the first time in decades, both China and India are confident about their own political future and their ability to play a larger role in world affairs. As economic reforms of the last couple of decades have begun to increase the relative economic weight of both China and India, they now have a sense of regaining their national destiny. The new generation of Indians and Chinese are less furtive in their attitudes to the world and see the future with optimism rather than pessimism.[22]

But how much trade is conducted between the world's second largest and fourth largest economies? Not much. However, it is rapidly increasing. As Amita Batra and Arvind Virmani point out, "[I]n 2003-04, Sino-Indian bilateral trade touched a high of US$ 7 billion, up to 47 per cent over 2002-03, the year in which bilateral trade also rose by 60 per cent. In 2004-05, two-way trade touched $ 9 billion, almost 10 times that of the figure a decade ago."[23] They point out that there are economic complementarities between the two countries. Raja Mohan points out one of those areas of cooperation wherein India can propose to benefit China by providing its expertise in services such as management, consultancy, accounting and legal services. Alka Acharya relates this cooling off of Sino-Indian relations to the "fundamental change in the political thinking in both countries, especially since the late 1980s."[24]

Even as there are competing views regarding the state of Sino-Indian relations, it would not be wrong to conclude, for reasons laid out in the following sections, that China and India are on a historic journey towards resolving their problems.

India and the US vs China?

A related question is whether the US wants to use India to balance out China's rise as a power of global consequences. The answer is "yes" and "no." Yes, because the US, the lone superpower that it is, would very much like to maintain the basic feature of the realist world, balance of power. No, because the Chinese economy, as is well known, is more integrated to the US economy than is the Indian economy. The Sino-US trade relationship benefits both of them and so a flare-up would hurt both of them. Politically, therefore, it is unwise to say that the US wants to destroy China or outsource its war against China to India.

A Path Sauntered ad Maximum: Sino-Pakistan Relations

Pragmatism based on new perceptions of power politics in the world and the region is also impacting upon the "all weather friendship" between China and Pakistan. This is not to deny that Pakistan is of great strategic significance to China. China has many important uses of Pakistan: Pakistan is close to the sea routes of oil, it buys Chinese weapons, and it gives Pakistan a strong presence in the intersection of three regions – South Asia, Central Asia and West Asia. However, there has been a perceptive change in China's Pakistan policy. China has changed its stance on Kashmir – it no longer says that there should be a plebiscite on Kashmir as it did from 1960 to 1980. Today, China is of the opinion that it is a matter that needs to be solved between the two countries – a stand taken by Deng in 1980. China has also refused to support Pakistan's attempts to internationalise the Kashmir problem. Moreover, post-9/11, China has consistently asked Pakistan to stop supporting terrorism, something which China itself is concerned about. In one sense, it could be said that even if China wants to weaken India, it would not want it to be done through terrorism as it would be disastrous for China also. China would prefer to, if at all it would, weaken India through military means. John Garver points out two reasons why a war in China's neighbourhood would not be in Chinese interests:

> War in China's neighborhood, especially one between two significant powers like India and Pakistan, could easily spoil the international environment for China's

> development drive. An India-Pakistan war would cause the flight of foreign investment, businessmen, and tourists spending foreign currency, from adjacent regions of China. An India-Pakistan war would also make difficult profit-driven economic cooperation between China and the belligerent countries. It would disrupt the flow of Chinese goods via nearby belligerent countries to global markets. It would necessitate tighter internal security controls that would be antithetical to market-driven economic activity. And it would force increased military spending and preparedness at the expense of increased attention to China's economic and social development needs. In short, an India–Pakistan war would retard China's drive to raise itself to a modest level of prosperity by the middle of the twenty-first century. The second reason for Beijing's desire to avoid an India–Pakistan war over Kashmir is that such a war would endanger two fundamental elements of China's South Asia strategy: (1) maintaining Pakistan as a balance to India; and (2) improving relations with *all* the states of South Asia.[25]

China also refused to support Pakistan in times of conflict with India. There was no Chinese support to Pakistan during all the wars that Pakistan fought with India, including the one in Kargil.

This shows that what China is interested in is to keep India under check, not to destroy India. If China does not support Pakistan to wage a war against India nor support Pakistan to reclaim its "jugular vain" i.e. Kashmir, there is even less possibility that China would support Pakistan to continue with its proxy war against India.

Can India Enact the *Mandala* Theory in Southeast Asia?

Can India do a Pakistan to China in Southeast Asia? Does it want to do so? Kautilya's *Mandala* theory would prescribe that India make strategic allies in the Southeast Asian countries as the country between India and Southeast Asia, i.e., China, is not India's friend, and also because the Southeast Asian countries are not very comfortable with China. How uncomfortable the Southeast Asian countries are with China is measurable by how far they would be willing to go along with India in ganging up against China. I would argue that while there are obvious elements of discontent in Southeast Asia vis-à-vis Chinese strategic domination in the region, they are not yet enough to be used against China.

India has been engaging the ASEAN countries in a variety of ways, ranging from trade to maritime cooperation. The ASEAN countries also have been making investments in India. The ASEAN countries and India share land borders and maritime boundaries. ASEAN has also accepted India into its fold. While this cooperation can be seen as merely economic in nature with no defence-strategic underpinnings, arguments have also been made into the contrary.[26]

Moreover, it is also unlikely that the ASEAN countries will play into the hands of Indian strategies amongst them vis-à-vis China, as the ASEAN countries, economically prosperous and the leading lights among them being the role models of globalisation, would not like to have an enemy in China. Moreover, as Kripa Sridharan argues, "[T]here is a feeling that India will play into the hands of those who are desirous of checkmating China or may fall prey to the embryonic designs of Russia to create a Moscow-Delhi-Beijing bloc in order to balance the US."[27] This also contributes to the lessening of a possibility of an enactment of *the Mandala* theory in Southeast Asia.

...and Indo-Pak Relations

What does the above analysis hold for Indo-Pak relations? The first proposition that can be gleaned from the above analysis is that the region is moving towards greater stability, lasting peace and increased prosperity. Secondly, the forces of economic development and globalisation are more likely to determine the contours of geo-politics in the region in the days to come than ethnic violence, inter-state rivalries and moribund geo-political games. It is evident that for once the geo-strategic context of Indo-Pak relations has changed in favour of an amicable solution to their long-pending problems. In other words, the present milieu is not one that would tolerate promotion of terrorism in the SAR; as a result, states are likely to abstain from supporting terrorists. The above analysis also throws up the following futuristic conclusions. Under the present circumstances where China is attempting to settle its territorial dispute with India and wants to become a global economic power, it is unlikely to support Pakistan fight a war against India which will invariably have its impact on China too. China is also likely to impress upon Pakistan to give up on supporting terrorism in Kashmir as it does have spillover effects on the Xinjiang region of China.

The United States, having signed the historic nuclear treaty with India to grant the latter the much sought after entry into the nuclear club, has finally decided to takes sides with India in the geo-politics of Southern Asia. One of the major reasons seems to be that the US wants to have a trouble-free Southern Asia. But why India over Pakistan, its own trusted ally for the last so many decades? Primarily because the US wants to have a trouble-free Southern Asia, it wants to have a trouble-free country which believes in the strategy of tolerance. Secondly, India, in many ways, stands for the values that the US wants the world to have; it is another way of telling the Southern Asian countries to emulate India's example in democracy and economic liberalisation. This US tilt towards India can either be rejected by Pakistan or it can be resigned to it. If Pakistan decides to object, it is unlikely to achieve much, given the kind of problems it faces today. The better option, one could reason, is to accept it and move forward. This will invariably mean that Pakistan goes back on its rhetoric against India and on Kashmir. Let us look at this argument in all possible dimensions.

Considering that Pakistan's internal problems and politics have always had their impact on Kashmir and India, let us assume that if Pakistan has to struggle to confront a twin problem, it will invariably have an impact on India. What will Pakistan do vis-à-vis India and Kashmir as and when the twin problem it faces becomes too difficult to contain? There are two possibilities. First, it will up the ante in Kashmir. In other words, we will see an increase in Pak-sponsored militancy in Kashmir in order to divert the attention of the media, the international community and the domestic audience so that it can crush the rebellion in Waziristan and Balochistan and bring the situation back under control. The second possibility is that Pakistan will look for an honourable exit route from Kashmir so that it can save itself from disintegration resulting from civil war, faction fighting, military overstretch, spillover effects of terrorism, etc.

Which of these options is Pakistan likely to adopt? It is rational to suggest that Pakistan will adopt the latter option as it would be far less difficult than the former one. The former option would involve defying the international community, ignoring the spillover effects of terrorism internally, bearing the costs of confrontation with India which is growing militarily and economically stronger and having to put up with all the risks and pressures associated with this.

India, in all probability, will be the natural big power of the region in the decades to come. This, when combined with India's strategy of tolerance, will stop Pakistan from making adventurous decisions. India's emerging preeminence and traditionally appreciated defensive-posturing, along with a host of other internal and external factors laid down in this chapter, will make Pakistan look foolish if it tries to turn the emerging balance of forces in the region by way of a continuation of proxy wars and promotion of terrorism and fundamentalism. The post-tsunami relief efforts by India in the neighbouring countries, and the increasing demands by Sri Lanka requesting India to involve itself in the peace process in that country, along with the role that the international community thinks India should play in the affairs of the region, show the increasing preeminence of the country.

As reasoned out above, peace is likely to prevail in the Indian Ocean region as it suits all the stakeholders. The great number of vital stakes involved in the region will make the interested parties in the Indian Ocean region, which include most global powers apart from the regional ones, keep it a zone of no-conflict. This will preempt the concerns that are being raised today of a possible "base-race" or armed confrontation in the Indian Ocean region in the days to come.

Traditionally, India has been faced with a two-front problem: a border dispute with China, and Pakistan sponsored terrorism in Kashmir, combined with elements of home-grown insurgency. While years of sustained diplomatic initiatives and a strategy of tolerance by India are now bearing fruit, it is now Pakistan that is faced with a twin problem: Waziristan and Balochistan. While Waziristan has always resisted Pakistan's rule, the events post-9/11 have worsened the situation there. The Pakistani state machinery is losing control over Waziristan. The Taliban leaders and local militias have declared the creation of a parallel Islamic state in this land of warring tribes. Close to a hundred thousand Pakistani soldiers are unwilling to get out of their barracks to fight the insurgents. Balochi nationalists have become bolder over the years to resist and confront the discrimination they have traditionally faced from the government in Islamabad. While what we have in Waziristan is an Islamic fundamentalist movement, it is a nationalist movement that we are witnessing in Balochistan. The increasing amount of resistance, armed clashes and undesirable international attention in those two fronts will keep Pakistan preoccupied, which will mean a decline in its capability to go on engaging India on Kashmir as it has done for many decades now.

However, Afghanistan is likely to be a wild card in this scenario of peace and tranquillity for the region. The US-Pakistan designs in Afghanistan have the potential to disrupt the ongoing process of peace and reconciliation in that country. While Pakistan wants to maintain its lost strategic leverage in Afghanistan, the US is apparently willing to let Pakistan play its games in Afghanistan: the US today is only concerned about an exit route from the Afghan challenge. However, the emerging situation in Afghanistan does not have the potential to disrupt the region as a whole, let alone disrupt the ongoing Indo-Pak peace process.

Notes

1. The term Southern Asian region may be defined as the following: "A geographic region of the Asian continent bordered in the north by the countries of Central Asia and in the south by the Arabian Sea and the Bay of Bengal, extending westward into Iran and eastward into China, including Afghanistan, Pakistan, India, Nepal,

Bangladesh, Burma, Bhutan and Sri Lanka." Available on the website of the European Environment Information and Observation Network (EIONET). http://www.eionet.eu.int/gemet/concept?cp=7951&langcode=en. This article uses the term "Southern Asia" primarily because it is assumed here that South Asian geo-politics in the days to come will impact upon Southern Asia and vice versa. Moreover, the geo-political games in the region can be better understood through the larger prism of Southern Asia than other traditional and narrower ones.

2. Donald L. Berlin, "The "Great Base Race" in the Indian Ocean Littoral: Conflict Prevention or Stimulation?" *Contemporary South Asia* 13 (3), September 2004.
3. Berlin, Ibid., p. 250.
4. Vijay Sakhuja, "Cooperative Security in the Straits of Malacca: Policy Options for India," ORF Issue Brief. Available at http://orfonline.org/analysis/issuebiref.pdf
5. International Maritime Organisation, "Report on Acts of Piracy and Armed Robbery Against Ships - Annual Report 2002," April 17, 2003. Available at www.imi.org
6. John F. Bradford, "The Growing Prospects for Maritime Security Cooperation in Southeast Asia." Available on the net at http://community.middlebury.edu/~scs/docs/Maritime%20security%20cooperation%20in%20Southeast%20Asia.pdf
7. The participating countries will commit themselves to the following things: 1. undertake effective measures, either alone or in concert with other states, for interdicting the transfer or transport of WMD; 2. share information and intelligence regarding the movement of suspected cargos, and; 3. strengthen the existing framework of national laws and export controls, multilateral treaties, and other tools that help prevent the spread of WMD and missiles. See Happymon Jacob, "Proliferation Security Initiative and Global Policing," *ORF Strategic Trends,* Vol. I, Issue. 4, October 20, 2003. Available at http://www.observerindia.com/strategic/st031020.htm
8. Zahid Hussain, "Kashmir: The Long Road to Peace," November 2004. Available at http://www.newsline.com.pk/NewsNov2004/cover1nov2004.htm
9. Marika Vicziany, "State Responses to Islamic Terrorism in Western China and Their Impact on South Asia," *Contemporary South Asia,* 12 (2), June 2003, p. 243.
10. Malini Parthasarathy, "Engaging Pakistan: From the NDA to the UPA," one of the chapters in this book.
11. For more on how the Afghan campaign cost Pakistan dearly, see Noor Muhammad Jadmani, "Afghanistan: Its Impact On Pakistan's Economy," National Institute of Public Administration (Karachi, Pakistan) journal, Vol.8, No.1. Available at http://www.nipa-khi.edu.pk/Noor%20Muhammad%20Jadmani-MAR.pdf; Happymon Jacob, *The Rise, Fall and Resurgence of the Taliban,* (Observer Research Foundation in association with Samskriti Publishers, 2005).
12. Sushant Sareen "Another Shot at Bilateralism? Compulsions, Constraints and Calculations Behind the Peace Process." One of the chapters in this book.
13. Stephen P. Cohen, *India: Emerging Power* (Washington, DC: Brookings Institution Press, 2001); Baldev Raj Nayar and T.V. Paul, *India in the World Order: Searching for Major Power Status* (Cambridge: Cambridge University Press, 2003); Ashley J. Tellis, *India as a New Global Power: An Action Agenda for the United States* (Washington: Carnegie Endowment, 2005); Sumit Ganguly, *India as an Emerging Power* (Portland: Frank Cass, 2003).
14. Dominic Wilson and Roopa Purushothaman, "Dreaming With BRICs: The Path to 2050," *Global Economics Paper,* No. 99, Goldman Sachs.

15. Subhash Agarwal, "India's Changing Image Abroad," *Indian Express*, December 24, 2005.
16. Condoleezza Rice, "Promoting the National Interest," *Foreign Affairs*, 00157120, Vol.79, Issue 1, January / February 2000.
17. For more on this, see writings by Amitabh Mattoo, "India-US Relations: Sanctions and Beyond," *AGNI: Studies in International Strategic Issues*, Vol. 3, No. 3, January-May 1998, pp.596; and Mohan Malik, "India-China Relations: Giants Stir, Cooperate and Compete," *Asia's Bilateral Relations* (Honolulu: Asia-Pacific Centre for Security Studies, 2004)
18. For more on this, see Raja Mohan, "Sino-Indian Relations: From Security Dilemma to Strategic Cooperation," *Security and Society*, Vol.2, No.1, 2005; and Kanti Bajpai, "State, Society, Strategy," in Kanti P. Bajpai & Amitabh Mattoo, eds., *Securing India: Strategic Thought and Practice* (New Delhi: Manohar Publishers and Distributors, 1996).
19. Mohan Malik, "Eyeing the Dragon: India's China Debate," in Satu P. Limaye, ed., *Asia's China Debate*, (Asia Pacific Centre for Security Studies, December 2003), p.5.
20. Malik, Ibid., p.3.
21. Mlaik, Ibid.
22. Raja Mohan, n.18, p.51.
23. Amita Batra and Arvind Virmani, "India-China Economic Relations," *Security and Society*, Vol.2, No.1, 2005, p.106.
24. She further claims that "[A] conscious decision was taken in 1998 to set aside contentious issues, downplay differences and allow the economic forces to play their part in reinforcing the links and imparting the necessary dynamism." Alka Acharya, "Transcending the Territorial Imperative: A Political Approach to Changing the India-China Dynamics," *Security and Society*, Vol.2, No.1, 2005, pp. 76-77.
25. John W. Garver, "China's Kashmir Policies", *India Review*, Vol. 3, No. 1, January 2004, p.5.
26. Swaran Singh claims, "Although ASEAN countries would not admit it publicly, one of the considerations ASEAN took into account for according such bigger status to India was definitely the issue of China's rising power profile and especially its naval incursions into the South China Sea as also China's expanding acceptance worldwide." He goes on to argue that "Indo-Vietnam nuclear cooperation has often been analysed as India's response to the Chinese involvement in Pakistani nuclear research activities." Swaran Singh, in Frederic Grare and Amitabh Mattoo, eds., *India and ASEAN: The Politics of India's Look East Policy* (New Delhi: Manohar Publishers & Distributors 2001) p.199.
27. Kripa Sridharan, "Regional Perceptions of India," in Grare and Mattoo,eds., Ibid., p.79.

Nuclear Stability in South Asia: Issues and Challenges

Jasjit Singh

The issues of nuclear stability between Pakistan and India have obviously attracted a great deal of attention. But considering that Pakistan had acquired what the then army chief and the person who controlled the nuclear programme, General Aslam Beg had claimed, a "credible" nuclear deterrent by early 1987, and most estimates agree that India had transited from an open option to weapons capability by that time, it is surprising indeed that no concerns or debate about nuclear stability took place till after the May 1998 tests. There was certainly great focus on nuclear non-proliferation in the 1990s, especially on India, as expressed in the *mantra* of "cap, reduce and eliminate" nuclear weapons in South Asia. There was an expressed concern in Western countries about the risk of war and possible escalation to nuclear dangers during the crises of the 1987 Brasstacks and the 1990 and 1994 tensions, while daily live shooting and artillery barrages between the military forces of the two countries went on across the Line of Control (LoC) in the Jammu and Kashmir (J&K) state. But there is little in the strategic literature about the issues and challenges of nuclear stability during that period. This aspect is much more a post-test phenomenon although still viewed in terms of the Cold War experiences.

It also needs to be noted that there are at least two dyads of nuclear weapon states in the region: India-China and India-Pakistan. But we don't hear anything about nuclear stability issues and challenges about the first case. Are we to assume that the India-China situation is substantively stable, or more stable than the India-Pakistan situation, and, hence, of less concern? Or are we to assume that both players in the India-China equation are rational, stable actors? And if that is so, does it imply that Pakistan is the only actor among the three which is intrinsically irrational, or at least more of a risk taker than the other two? In fact, any objective examination would lead to that conclusion. If that is so, should we not be looking at the factors that make it conducive to greater nuclear stability than the India-Pakistan case?

The fundamental difference between the East-West nuclear deterrence and strategic stability issues during the Cold War and that in South Asia is the distinct and almost overwhelming asymmetry in strategic terms between Pakistan and India, while there is much more equivalence between China and India. And this has an impact in making the Pakistan-India paradigm far more complex than those of the Cold War or for that matter the one between China and India. This also means that we need to be cautious about either judging the deterrence-stability issues or applying the lessons and experiences from the East-West nuclear confrontation to the regional situation without closely looking at the specifities of the region.

If there is one dominant factor that affects nuclear deterrence and strategic stability in South Asia, it is the existence of strategic asymmetries that have influenced political relations, driven domestic perceptions, shaped military policies and the prospects of peace and stability in the region. And yet these asymmetries are a reality that cannot be wished away, or means and methods of developing strategic stability, leave alone friendly relations between Pakistan and India instituted with any degree of success. It is not intended to go over the nature and extent of these asymmetries here, except in so far as they impact nuclear deterrence. At the same time, it is obvious, though almost inevitably ignored, that issues of peace and security in South Asia cannot be addressed in any meaningful way unless China is included in the discussions. In fact, there is an obvious lesson in undertaking a comparative assessment of the nature, degree and future of strategic stability between China and India to help develop greater strategic stability between Pakistan and India.

Nature of Nuclear Deterrence

While there is extensive strategic literature and historical record of nuclear deterrence since 1945, it seems we have not really looked at some critical aspects that perhaps have far more relevance in the post-Cold War world and for the second-tier nuclear weapon states which are not treaty-bound with the first-tier nuclear states like the United States and the Russian Federation. One important issue concerning deterrence and strategic stability is about *what is sought to be deterred* by a country with its nuclear weapons. This seems such a simple question that we all tend to ignore it. But this has a profound impact on the strategic posture, the generation of capability and its likely employment, with obvious implications for deterrence and strategic/crisis stability. The second aspect concerns the *type of deterrence* that a country opts for. This also has rarely been explored essentially beyond the strategies formulated between the United States and the Soviet Union. For example, there has been little serious examination of the type of deterrence paradigm that China has adopted since the past forty years ago which has seen little change since its early days and is perceived as credible. As regards the first aspect, a country could choose from any one (or all) of the three broad deterrence goals where nuclear weapons are expected to deter:

1. Nuclear weapons of another state;
2. Conventional military forces of another state; and/or,
3. Sub-conventional war waged by a state (normally through terrorism and/or irregular covert war) and/or non-state actors with or without assistance/ sponsorship of a state or its sub-state entities like intelligence agencies.

The challenge for nuclear deterrence (and strategic stability) is significantly different in each case, being the least complex in the first and most complex and difficult in the third. Confining nuclear deterrence to the threat of nuclear weapons inherently has greater scope for stability than in the other two cases. There is no doubt that serious problems emerge in the case of deterrence failure due to any reason. But such problems would aggravate seriously where a doctrine/strategy for war-fighting with nuclear weapons is adopted since this would rapidly escalate to maximum use of such weapon by both sides. Obviously, this would be mutually suicidal since both sides would end up with cataclysmic destruction. That is the reason for the Reagan-Gorbachev declaration in 1986 that nuclear war cannot be won, and, hence, must never be fought. Thus, nuclear strategy for nuclear war-fighting would naturally lead to deep instability since first-use, preemption, decapitation, etc. would also enter the strategic calculus, leading to hair-trigger alerts even in peace-time. This is why tactical nuclear weapons enhance instability.

In fact, the first option allows for a strategy where nuclear weapons need not be used first, and, credibility of deterrence can be built on second strike/retaliation (to first strike) capabilities. Even a cursory examination would indicate that this strategy allows for a significantly simpler, smaller and less costly deterrence posture.

The second option actually creates serious complications for the nuclear deterrence strategy. The actions of the adversary in employing its conventional military power are likely to be influenced, if not governed, by a multiplicity of factors, many of them ambiguous. One may simply be an assumption that a nuclear response to use of conventional forces would actually not take place. Further refinement of this logic would take us to an assessment of the levels of "thresholds" being critical factors in the success or failure of the deterrence strategy. There are obviously innumerable variables and ambiguities in this process. Such assessments about the adversary, at best, would remain subjective and prone to error. While it can be argued that these factors would inhibit — or at least limit — any use of conventional military forces, it is clear that potential for strategic and crisis instability would remain high. This is even more problematic where the weaker power initiates a war on the assumption that mere existence of nuclear weapons would limit the adversary's choices even in the conventional military arena.

But what happens if the country with the larger and more potent conventional military capability also possesses nuclear weapons? Logically, these would deter the country with the smaller/weaker conventional military power from holding out a nuclear threat or use them without the risk of nuclear retaliation. At what point in the use of asymmetric conventional forces would the smaller/weaker power hold out a nuclear threat that is credible? One less ambiguous situation would be one where the use of conventional forces actually threatens the very survival of the adversary's nation-state, leaving it with no alternative to the proverbial "Samson Option" that is believed to have shaped Israel's nuclear strategy for decades and goaded it to hold out the threat of nuclear weapons use in the early stages of the 1973 Yom Kippur War. The real issue affecting nuclear stability, therefore, is not the size and capability of conventional military power between two states, but the degree and extent to which it is actually employed and the effect it is able to achieve. If the state with the more powerful conventional military power to deny the adversary any potential for success at the conventional level itself does not push for political and military goals that threaten the existence of the smaller/weaker state, stability may be expected to prevail. Such (politically and militarily) limited use of superior conventional military power, in fact, makes the nuclear weapons capability of the smaller/weaker adversary redundant.

The challenge of deterring non-state actors and terrorist groups with nuclear weapons approaches the levels of impossibility as there are no real and satisfactory answers to the question about how to successfully do so. This becomes even more problematic when the terrorists are operating from sanctuaries across established frontiers. And the situation becomes unmanageable if the terrorists get hold of nuclear weapons. The most logical solution to this challenge would be the universal abolition of nuclear weapons and iron-clad inspections-verification regimes and control mechanisms to ensure that no diversion of fissile material or technology takes place. But the dominant powers are not interested in moving toward this direction. This is one reason why the use of proxy war employing guerrilla fighters has been seen as a strategic foreign policy tool to achieve political goals.

The United States used guerrilla fighters as "Mujahideen" to fight its nuclear adversary, the Soviet Union and the government in Kabul. Pakistan, which acquired enormous expertise and weaponry as the "frontline" state for the US, in turn, initiated its own proxy war using *jihadis* against India. It is significant that it waited to do so till it acquired, in the words of its former army chief, a "credible (nuclear) deterrent" and announced the new doctrine of offensive-defence where the "war" would be fought on Indian territory.

As regards the second aspect, there are a number of levels of deterrence strategies that can be pursued, depending on what a country expects to deter, at what costs, and in what ways? The different levels at which nuclear deterrence strategies can function are listed below:

- Maximal
- Minimum
- Recessed
- Extended
- Existential
- No deterrence

There is no standard template for nuclear deterrence and it has taken different forms with different countries and on different occasions. The United States and the USSR adopted a maximalist approach to nuclear deterrence, relying on massive retaliation with tens of thousands of nuclear weapons deployed across the world on hair-trigger alert. The UK and France adopted a more modest approach, but still adopted the doctrine of massive retaliation along with their North Atlantic Treaty Organisation (NATO) commitments.

China adopted a fundamentally different approach with a minimum deterrence strategy, relying in addition to a no-first-use doctrine. As a consequence, its arsenal did not rise above a few hundred even when it was fully developed. Cost was obviously not the reason for this policy since continuation of modernisation of the arsenal that it possessed was more expensive than building more warheads and delivery system of existing types as the costs of research and development would already have been absorbed.

The central point that this author wishes to note is that the *lower the level at which nuclear deterrence doctrine and strategy are planned for, the greater the potential for strategic and crisis stability*.

Indian Nuclear Doctrine and Strategy

India has, in effect, adopted a nuclear strategy which is best described by "recessed deterrence" based on the doctrine of "no-first-use" (NFU) of nuclear weapons. China has also pursued a similar doctrine and strategy. To that extent, there is a high degree of consonance between the doctrine and strategy of the two countries. No known nuclear threat has been held out between the two countries. The last known armed conflict between them was in 1967 though major disputes continue to plague their relations. It, therefore, must be recognised that the Chinese nuclear posture, while perhaps the most dominant factor in Indian thinking about the need for nuclear weapons, in actual terms did not pose an urgent and aggressive threat to India and New Delhi remained far more relaxed in relation to Chinese nuclear capabilities without ignoring the existential threat. And, hence, India sought to work for universal nuclear disarmament as a means of dealing with the challenge posed by nuclear weapons. In the meanwhile, it kept its options open even though this policy carried its own costs.

A key error made by most people in the country and outside is that if Pakistan was the concern and cause of India's nuclearisation, then the simpler, less costly and more effective policy choice for New Delhi would have been to sign the nuclear Non-Proliferation Treaty (NPT) and force Pakistan to follow suit. Under those circumstances, Pakistan would have been placed permanently in an inferior position in terms of conventional military capability. Its risks of waging a *jihadi* proxy war would have far outweighed any perceived benefits that it might have tried to achieve. The experience of 1965 is instructive. Both India and Pakistan did not possess nuclear weapons capability. Pakistan's launching of its 5,000-strong Force Gibraltar guerrillas quickly led to India's robust military response to dislodge the Pakistan Army from strategic locations on the ceasefire line to plug the infiltration routes like those through Haji Pir Pass and other points. But that option was obviously risky after 1987 by which time Pakistan had acquired a nuclear deterrent. Unfortunately, the Pakistani elites assumed that this automatically would deter India from any robust conventional retaliation also. And, hence, the escalation to launch a regular invasion across the Line of Control (LoC) in 1999.

Many Pakistani experts make a fundamental error of assuming (and arguing on that basis) that India's NFU strategy is not "acceptable" to Pakistan, that it is a propagandist articulation, or that it does not provide any reassurance that India would not carry out a preemptive nuclear launch. Even those in Pakistan's strategic planning division have argued from a similar point of view that India's NFU is a "flawed argument."[1] Such assessments indicate the unwillingness or inability to understand the true dimensions of the NFU doctrine and deterrence.

India's doctrine is meant to convey the principles on which its nuclear weapons may be employed to deter, and how it would use nuclear weapons if deterrence fails. In turn, this also implies that the development of capabilities would also be in accordance with those principles. The purpose of a nuclear doctrine is less to "reassure" a potential adversary and more to make it amply clear what is expected to be deterred (nuclear weapons threat or use, conventional military attack , etc) and how nuclear deterrence is to be achieved. Above all, it has to clearly convey what actions the attacker should expect in case he uses nuclear weapons first. It is *the consequences of that first strike that determine the foundation of the target country's successful deterrence strategy* since the prospect of retaliation must be factored into the decision to strike.

While the Chinese establishment and strategic community are well-versed in the "no-first-use" based nuclear doctrine and strategy, we are not certain whether the Pakistani elites have grasped the true import of the Indian nuclear doctrine. The Pakistani strategic community, whether in or outside the government, of course, are at full liberty to interpret the Indian doctrine as they wish. But they could make a grievous error in rejecting the core of the doctrine which would guide development and employment of nuclear weapons by India. Even a nominal commitment to strategic stability demands that potential adversaries analyse each and every element of each other's nuclear doctrine and strategy objectively. This becomes even more important for ensuring the credibility of one's own nuclear deterrent since it has to deter the posture of the adversary. After all, the deterrent must be credible in the eyes of the adversary and not just one's own perceptions based on assumptions that may be far removed from what the adversary plans to do under situations that require deterrence as well as those when nuclear deterrence fails.

It is in this context that we need to understand the Indian *nuclear doctrine and strategy of retaliation only*. Fundamentally, this doctrine is far more conducive to enhancing strategic stability than a first use doctrine and strategy since it permits a posture of "recessed deterrence." Questions, of course, have been raised about the credibility of such a strategy. Would India wait for, say, New Delhi to be hit with nuclear weapons before it retaliates? But two factors need consideration. First, for more than half a century, second strike capability has been considered the litmus test of credible nuclear deterrence for a variety of reasons. A strategy of retaliation only assumes that the adversary's first strike would get through. But that assumption has to be made even in the case of a first strike strategy. Second, a first strike doctrine and strategy would inevitably lead to an extremely high state of alert, the capability to launch on warning/attack, and so on. This is a recipe for an arms race, very high costs and complex command and control systems, including the need for airborne command systems. It is this paradigm of nuclear strategy that creates greater risks and dangers of accidents, miscalculation and preemption, thus, increasing the prospects of nuclear instability.

Pakistan would perhaps not want to take any chances and depend upon the declared doctrine and assume that India may even launch a preemptive nuclear strike. But this also must rationally address the question: what would be the political and military scenarios when India would stand to gain in striking first, or need to undertake such a strike? One, of course, is that India starts to lose a conventional war to a degree that it is left with no option but to rely on nuclear weapons use. This is exactly the posture of Pakistan, regardless of the semantics in which it gets wrapped.

But that is also the reason why India is unlikely to allow its conventional military capability to draw down to an extent where its reliance on nuclear weapons increases. On the other hand, rational defence planning clearly points to maintaining a conventional military capability at a higher level after the entry of nuclear weapons into the deterrence paradigm. It can be argued that this would put additional pressure on Pakistan, leading to generating a (conventional) arms race at one level, and increasing Pakistan's dependence on nuclear weapons at another. Pakistani military and strategic thinkers have been highly critical of India's conventional superiority and justify their nuclear weapons and the first-use doctrine to counter that superiority. But this is exactly the central issue because of the strategic asymmetry which would continue into the future since, besides India's need for maintaining a credible superiority in conventional capability (to reduce its own dependence on nuclear weapons), India's security and defence concerns are not limited to Pakistan, regardless of what Pakistanis and their friends may keep stressing.

One can always question whether India would actually pursue its NFU strategy or decide to use nuclear weapons first. Statements about the right of preemption have been cited in support of conclusions that India might do so without examining why it would resort to such a situation. The primary reason why India would not, in its own interest, resort to first use is that it is unlikely to provide *assured decapitation* of the Pakistani nuclear arsenal. In such a case, India would risk a counter-strike. And even if that happens with one nuclear bomb, a first strike on Pakistan (which no doubt causes far greater damage to Pakistan) could hardly justify the risk and consequences of retaliatory damage to India itself. This was the classical lesson of the Cuban missile crisis where the United States could have wiped the USSR and Cuba off the face of earth, but no one could guarantee that a single nuclear warhead would not get through. Given India's capabilities, geography, etc, its current doctrine provides it with the optimum choices to achieve its aim of nuclear deterrence being confined to deterring the use and threat of nuclear weapons.

Pakistan's Nuclear Doctrine

On the other hand, Pakistan has to take into account the situation where its first use of nuclear weapons (whether under the rubric of "all options" or for a pre-emptive decapitation strike, etc) would lead to an "assured retaliation" by India leading to, as the doctrine says, "unacceptable punishment" to Pakistan for launching the strike. There can be a theoretical formulation that assumes that a Pakistani strike would decapitate India's nuclear arsenal. Pakistan's acquisition of longer-range ballistic missiles would suggest some such thinking, at least in targeting the command and control system of India. But what everyone must seriously and objectively assess is whether even a full-scale Pakistani nuclear strike would eliminate India's nuclear arsenal to the degree where sufficient nuclear retaliation with the surviving arsenal would not be possible.

This is why the Indian doctrine and strategy clearly lays great emphasis on survivability of the arsenal (which includes redundant capabilities, including command and control system). The basic NFU strategy does not require hair-trigger alerts and responses. As for the command and control system, its operational chain to implement the NFU strategy in a situation where a first strike has taken place, would naturally have to ensure that this is kept highly classified for obvious reasons. It is also clear that decision-making for retaliatory strike would be far simpler than if first use (or its variations like launch on warning, or launch under attack) was to be contemplated.

Since Pakistan's *raison d'etre* for acquiring nuclear weapons was the perceptions of Indian *conventional* military superiority, which, in the words of former Foreign Minister Mr. Agha Shahi, "hangs like a Sword of Damocles" over Pakistan, it would be unwilling to commit to an NFU doctrine.[2] But the problem is that responsible people in Pakistan who have spoken and written on their nuclear doctrine indicate a serious problem. For example, the Director General, Strategic Planning Division, Lieutenant General Khalid Kidwai in 2001 had defined four thresholds which would trigger Pakistan's launch of a nuclear strike.[3] At least two of these can hardly claim any credibility as a rational basis for launching a nuclear strike against India.

This, in turn, conveys an impression that the Pakistani elites have either not given sufficient thought to their nuclear strategy or they are relying heavily on fantasies. In the process, Pakistan seems to be devaluing its own nuclear deterrence by threatening a preemptive nuclear strike. On the other hand, more responsible articulation (for example, from President Pervez Musharraf himself) focusses on use only in case Pakistan's survival is threatened, presumably by Indian military actions and not by domestic causes of state failure.

Pakistan has pursued a proxy war in J&K on the assumption that the nuclear umbrella makes it a "low cost" option for deterring India from using its conventional military superiority for a punitive response as it had started to do in August 1965 through "hot pursuit" of infiltrators which then led to Pakistan escalating by launching a full-fledged conventional offensive named "Operation Grand Slam" to take Kashmir. Since India has not actually launched similar military action like the one in 1965, Pakistan was probably emboldened to launch a military offensive across the Line of Control in the Kargil sector in the summer of 1999, a good decade after its proxy war through cross-border infiltration and *jihadi* terrorism started. The assumption is that a covert war for 16 years, superimposed with an overt war lasting 42 days, deterred India from resorting to an assertive conventional military response all due to the success of the Pakistani nuclear deterrent!

Some Stability-Instability Issues

Strategic stability in the subcontinent is much more likely to be affected by the nature of asymmetry as a consequence of sub-conventional war rather than mere existence of nuclear weapons. The Pakistani elites have been deeply disturbed by the Indian nuclear doctrine which is seen by some as "aggressive, and a provocative strategy" which could only enhance strategic instability. This leads to the inevitable question of whether Pakistan has fully grasped the nature and impact of the Indian nuclear doctrine and strategy? Or of their own?

The Pakistani elites seem to have been rattled by the concept of limited war under the nuclear overhang (articulated officially by the Indian defence minister in January 2000) and the possibility of a conventional war/use of military force (in 2001-02) launched by India below the nuclear threshold and above the sub-conventional war that Pakistan believes to have perfected as its own strategy. The limited war concept has been interpreted as "exceedingly dangerous" if pursued by India (presumably being not dangerous if carried out by Pakistan, as it indeed did in 1999!). Concepts like Pakistan would "unleash a storm" if India crossed an inch of the Line of Control hardly contribute to stability. Few stop to consider that if Pakistan can exploit the strategic space below the nuclear threshold, what would stop India from doing the same thing? Only the tactics might be different.

India may not pursue a retaliatory covert war, but it would always have the option to launch a limited conventional war which would have limited political and military aims (for example, of punitive operations to force an end to the covert war through terrorism rather than a decisive military victory to destroy the major military forces of Pakistan). This could take a long time and may not lead to unambiguous success since such use of force would have to be carefully calibrated in smaller doses than a sledgehammer approach which could be destabilising in political-psychological terms. This strategy would place the onus of escalation on Islamabad. Up to a certain level, such escalation would remain in the conventional arena. But, rationally, its extension to the nuclear level would require circumstances which either threaten the other country's survival itself or circumstances like annihilation of its military forces and/or loss of highly valuable territory. Surgical air strikes spaced out in time or a localised border conflict is hardly the type of situation that could lead to such annihilation or create dangers to the survival of Pakistan as a state.[4]

In other words, the greatest likelihood for escalation toward strategic instability is likely to originate in sub-conventional war and acts of terrorism which may require offensive punitive retaliation. This is what happened on December 13, 2001, when India mobilised with a clear intention to launch a conventional war if terrorism was not to be rolled back. It is to the credit of the Pakistani leadership that it altered the long-held belief in pursuit of the covert war and committed itself to ensuring that Pakistani territory would not be allowed to be used to pursue any form of terrorism. If that was not forthcoming, or further escalation took place, like it did in the terrorist attacks in mid-May 2002 in Jammu, the movement toward war was inevitable till further commitments were made to end infiltration across the borders.

Developing Strategic Stability

The fear of retaliation with nuclear weapons (and understanding of the effects of the use of nuclear weapons) remains the central rationale of successful deterrence. This is why *second strike capability had become so critical for nuclear deterrence credibility against nuclear weapons threat* during the Cold War. India's NFU is simply the generation of a second strike retaliatory strike capability without maintaining a first strike strategy (with all its complications). Pakistan, on the other hand, seeks to deter both a conventional war as well as a nuclear weapons threat. With both countries possessing nuclear weapons, the probability of the first contingency will remain extremely low beyond a border local and/or limited war. But its goal of successfully deterring the Indian nuclear weapons threat holds credibility only against an Indian first strike. Its own first strike against India that does not completely decapitate the Indian nuclear arsenal would only invite an assured retaliatory strike "leading to unacceptable punishment," making it suicidal for Pakistan. It is difficult to believe that such elementary but unambiguous logic has not been discovered by their elites.

The Pakistani leadership may be expected to take such a risk — as the proverbial "Samson Option" — only if the very survival of the country as a sovereign state is threatened by an Indian military action. This would imply destruction of its military machine and/or occupation of large/valuable territory by India. This, in turn, broadly defines the nuclear threshold for Pakistan. And as long as India operates short of such situations, nuclear stability would remain operative, the rhetoric of politicians and strategic experts notwithstanding. In other words, the Indian strategy clearly makes Pakistan's nuclear arsenal redundant or simply irrelevant in a limited war.

What political goals India would seek to achieve through seeking a Clausewitzian military victory is itself subject to question. The only possible ambiguous situation may be in case India tries to reoccupy Pakistan Occupied Kashmir. But India had shown no inclination to do so for four decades when no nuclear weapons threat could complicate its choices. In fact, signing the Shimla Agreement in July 1972 clearly sent a signal that New Delhi had settled down to the Line of Control as the de-facto international border between India and Pakistan. It can also be argued that assuming that the Kashmir dispute was essentially settled into a new status quo, India then decided to proceed with the decision a few months later to carry out the peaceful nuclear explosion that it had been working on for years. On the other hand, it is Pakistan that has sought to alter this status quo.

The Indian nuclear doctrine and strategy forces Pakistan into a situation wherein it either also adopts a similar doctrine, or something very close to it for use in extremis. Therefore, what is needed, and is absent, is an ongoing serious objective analysis of the doctrine and strategy for employment of nuclear weapons by both sides, undertaken individually as well as jointly. The generation of strategic literature about nuclear weapons strategies and their implications had gone a long way in helping to create strategic stability during the Cold War once both sides accepted the reality of their own vulnerabilities. We need to initiate the process of objective strategic literature which also addresses the issues of scenarios, options and their implications, even where there are disagreements.

Conventional Conflict: The Key to Nuclear Stability

At the same time, we need to recognise that the secret of successful nuclear deterrence and strategic stability actually lies more in the domain of conventional and sub-conventional conflict rather than in the mechanics of nuclear capabilities and strategies. As long as sub-conventional armed conflict (through support of terrorism, however defined) continues, it would always have the potential to trigger a larger conventional war, which, in turn, could slip out toward the nuclear thresholds which may remain ambiguously understood and poorly defined. Defining a threshold may not be an easy process although India has defined it clearly in its doctrine by pinning it to a first strike by an adversary on its territory or its forces. Pakistan, at some stage, would have to define its threshold in a more credible manner, even if initially it moves toward an articulated doctrine and strategy of use of nuclear weapons "in the last resort." This would be a useful move toward greater stability while enhancing the credibility of its nuclear deterrence which stands undermined by postures like the use of nuclear weapons if India even crosses the borders.

At the same time, deeper and sincere discussions and exchange of views between the strategic communities of Pakistan and India (from both government and non-government sectors) is needed on issues of conventional military power, doctrines and strategies. This requires much greater transparency in military postures than is currently available, especially in respect of Pakistan.

It would, of course, be ideal if political relations between the two countries are improved to the level where nuclear weapons (which also implies conventional forces and covert wars) actually become redundant. However, this is likely to remain in the domain of wishful thinking for a very long time. But what would be needed most for future stability would be a serious consideration of conventional arms control, including force reduction agreements. This may seem unrealistic at this stage. Both India and Pakistan have been the target of global and country-specific arms control and denial regimes under the rubric of non-proliferation. But closer scrutiny would show that conventional arms control would be an essential ingredient of building strategic stability.

Conventional arms control strategies would need to consider the expected nature of war and the strategic-military doctrine to conduct such wars in future. Here the Chinese strategic thinking is useful to note since all the potential adversaries that it may have to deal with militarily are nuclear weapon states (or, like Japan and South Korea, protected by them). China has the largest military force in the world today. Its military doctrine has moved from the notion of "People's War" of the 1950s, 1960s and 1970s, to "People's War Under High-Tech Conditions" in the 1980s, to the current approach termed "Limited, Local War Under High-Tech Conditions." China views the primary threat as a local-regional war which would be a "limited war, fought in a restricted geographic area for limited objectives, with limited means and a conscious effort to curtail destruction."[5] But it is clear that the shift of doctrine to "high-technology warfare" implies that China's "defence strategy is largely an offensive-oriented strategy reflecting the People's Liberation Army's (PLA's) shifting emphasis towards the 'active' versus the 'defensive' side of war preparations."[6] Inevitably, the evolving high-technology hardware would be heavily biased towards a "swift offensive strike because technological innovations have increasingly blurred the boundaries between offensive and defensive weaponry. Indeed, the revolution in military affairs (RMA) is all about how to maximise the offensive."[7] China expects such a war to have the following general characteristics:

- War would be fought with comparatively small, highly trained joint forces using mostly long-range, precision-strike weapons made available by the ongoing revolution in military technology.
- The objective in such warfare is to defeat the enemy rapidly by inflicting strategic and operational paralysis through attacks on his weaknesses. This kind of war will not require annihilation of the enemy or physical occupation of his territory. This multi-dimensional war will unfold in all dimensions (air, sea, ground, space, and the electromagnetic spectrum) simultaneously.
- Air power and precision strikes are now the primary means of conducting warfare, with ground operations secondary.[8]

This type of war, of course, represents a revolutionary change from the traditional PLA concept of People's War, which assumed a strategically defensive total war fought primarily by ground forces and a comprehensively mobilised population against an invading enemy seeking to destroy and occupy the People's Republic of China (PRC). It appears that China's doctrine for war is tailor-made for air and space power, which can have a major impact by waging an independent air campaign against vital targets and supporting other arms of the military.

Indian defence planning would need to pay close attention to building the requisite capabilities for the type of war which may get imposed on us, not only to win such a war, but to ensure that the requisite level of deterrence and strategic stability is built into that planning. But the case of combat air power is probably symptomatic of the nature of challenges ahead. We may be focussing maximum attention to the less critical areas since it is the Indian Army that needs to watch the build up of air power capabilities across the frontiers far more critically than what appears to be the case since the ground forces are likely to face the consequences of an adverse air power balance the most. The head of the Chinese Air Force has publicly sought a greater role for the PLA Air Force declaring that the Chinese Air Force will strive for a transformation from the air defence type to an offensive and defensive type as soon as possible. He announced, "At the turn of the century and in the early part of the new century, the air force will have a batch of new-types of early warning aircraft, electronic-equipped fighter planes, and ground-to-air missiles" and that the air force *"must give more prominence to air offensive,* gradually integrate offensive and defensive, and build up a crack, first-rate air strike force"[9] (emphasis added). The principal area where China appears to be making advances in coercive military capabilities involves air power, to include missiles and information operations."[10] In keeping with the shift in priorities, the heads of the air force and navy have been brought into the Central Military Commission (CMC) for the first time in China's history.

If our wars, like those that China officially plans for, would be local, border wars, then the logical conclusion would be that major land battles, especially those that might lead to deep strikes and/or destruction of major military formations/"decisive" military victory would be risky from the point of view of escalation to the nuclear threshold, then it is logical to conclude that large size of forces would not be usable to the degree they were traditionally employed in the past. Advances in modern technology have in any case shifted the importance of mass to precision firepower. The worst situation that could trigger unintended consequences would be the likelihood of strategic surprise which leaves the defending country with few options but to rapidly escalate to offset the advantage that surprise might provide the adversary. Hence, arms control needs to be pursued as a military strategy to assist in enhancing stability.

It is in this context that the CFE (Conventional Forces in Europe) Treaty holds out key lessons. The core of the treaty was the reduction of offensive forces by mutually negotiated agreements based on a mutually accepted definition of such categories of weapons. The definition of what are considered destabilising conventional weapons, in fact, has been universally accepted in the UN Register for Conventional Arms. In other words, what we need to evolve are mutually accepted force reductions involving armoured forces, etc that leave the ratio of forces essentially unaltered, but allow for strategic defensive strategies. Such an approach would create a firebreak between escalation to nuclear weapons by limiting the potential for a surprise conventional attack.

Notes

1. See Air Commodore Khalid Banuri, "Strategic Plans Division of Pakistan" in Peter Lavoy and Christopher Clary, eds., *Strategic Stability in South Asia,* Conference, June 29-July 1, 2004, Centre for Contemporary Conflict, Bradford.
2. Agha Shahi, in Fasahat H. Syed, ed., *Nuclear Disarmament and Conventional Arms Control Including Light Weapons,* Rawalpindi Cantt., 1997, p.421.
3. Paolo Cotta-Ramusino and Maurizio Martellini, "Nuclear Safety, Nuclear Stability and Nuclear Strategy in Pakistan: A Concise Report of a Visit by Landau Network-Centro Volta." Available at http://www.mi.infn.it/~landnet
4. The worst outcome could be a regime change in Pakistan as happened in 1999.
5. Thomas R. McCabe, "The Chinese Air Force and Air and Space Power," *Air & Space Power Journal,* Fall 2003.
6. You Ji, "The Revolution in Military Affairs and the Evolution of China's Strategic Thinking" *Contemporary Southeast Asia,* Vol. 21, No. 3, December 1999, p. 355.
7. Ji, Ibid., p.355.
8. The PRC's Central Military Commission concluded in December 1995 that the ground battle was now secondary to the air battle. See Mark Stokes, "China's Missile, Space, and Conventional Theatre Missile Development: Implications for Security in the Taiwan Strait," in Susan M. Puska, ed., *People's Liberation Army after Next* (Carlisle Barracks, Pa: Strategic Studies Institute, US Army War College, 2000), p. 109. This, however, may not necessarily apply to other theatres. See also China's Defence White Paper 2004.
9. "Air Force Commander Liu Shunyao on Air Force Transformation," FBIS-CHI-1999-1107, dated November 7, 1999.
10. *Annual Report on the Military Power of the People's Republic of China,* Report to Congress by Secretary of Defence (Washington: US Government, 2002), p. 11.

Theorising Territory and Borders in the India-Pakistan Conflict

Devika Sharma

Introduction

The conflict between India and Pakistan has been an enduring one;[1] one that has resisted better relations since the two states gained independence in 1947. Mutual suspicion and animosity arising from the wellspring of the two-nation theory and the violence that attended partition in 1947 have proved difficult to uproot from the minds and hearts of the people of India and Pakistan. Differences borne of religion have since found expression in a long lasting, intractable and complex conflict over territory. The India-Pakistan conflict has been explained by and large by citing the following three prominent arguments. Firstly, ambivalent colonial policies of the British before 1947 exacerbated the already simmering Hindu-Muslim rivalry.[2] Secondly, Cold War politics and American grand strategy pitted India and Pakistan against each other as both found themselves on opposing sides.[3] Thirdly, the geo-political reality of the region set the stage for the 'inherent' clash between the insecurities of a comparatively smaller and weaker country such as Pakistan vis-à-vis the hegemony of a regional big power such as India.

However, the nature of the conflict between these two historical enemies has seldom been studied from the border-territory-identity perspective. Since 1947, India and Pakistan have fought four wars (1948, 1965, 1971 and 1999) and their relations continue to be marred by frequent border skirmishes and an ongoing proxy war over Kashmir. National chauvinism and religious bigotry have helped create a perplexing conflict that is territorial. This essay examines the India-Pakistan conflict in the context of the insights offered by an inter-disciplinary prism of critical geo-politics, cultural geography, anthropology and constructivism. The aim of the article is to suggest that the growing literature on territorial disputes and border theory offers interesting ways of looking at the India-Pakistan conundrum by understanding the nature of the dispute and identifying ways in which the conflict can be transformed and perhaps even resolved. The objective of the article is threefold: one, to present the theoretical formulations which frame the study of territorial conflicts; two, to contextualise the India-Pakistan conflict within this framework and mention the bordering processes that have helped spawn the conflict; third, to identify potential areas that can help engineer a more flexible and dynamic border regime, highlight processes already underway towards that end and cite the obstacles on the path.

Theory of Borders and Territorial Conflicts

Until recently, borders and territorial conflict were only partially explained by international relations theory (neorealism as well as liberal institutionalism) and political geography. Chris Brown asserts, "Neither modern political theory nor international relations theory has an impressive record when it comes to theorising the problems posed by borders, frontiers and identity."[4] Given the primacy both approaches afford to the anarchical international system, being unit-level features of sovereign states, borders are completely overlooked. Both approaches to international relations envisage different outcomes from the same starting point, even where borders are concerned. Forced to self-help for the sake of their survival in conditions of international anarchy, states, according to the neorealists, have no choice but to shore up their military and economic capabilities vis-à-vis each other. Eternally caught in a zero-sum game, security concerns compel states to militarily defend and barricade their borders. This static understanding of borders is juxtaposed with the liberal institutionalist approach, which asserts that states can learn to trust each other by joining international regimes and organisations; through economic cooperation, states can break out of the billiard-ball allegory proffered by the neorealists.[5] Inter-state cooperation allows borders to become porous and lose their barrier-effect. Contiguous countries, in conflict over territory, can avoid war by becoming mutually relevant to one another through processes of integration, interdependence and "a high rate of transactional exchange."[6]

The political geography approach to territorial conflicts conforms to the basic tenets of neorealism. Accordingly, conflicts over territory are perceived as being enduring in nature and most likely to lead to militarised disputes and war. The impact of geography on conflict has been studied in great depth by scholars such as John A. Vasquez, Paul R. Hensel, Gary Goertz, Paul F. Diehl, Harvey Starr, and so on.[7] What lies at the heart of this debate is that territory has a high salience value both in terms of tangibles like economic resources, strategic advantage, population centres such as cities and capitals, as well as in terms of intangibles such as prestige, honour, national identity, and so on. As a result, stakes in a territorial dispute are high on both sides of the border, making it difficult for states to back down or settle for what might be construed as a compromise by the people. Analysts have identified territory, proximity, opportunity and willingness in explaining the propensity for conflict between contiguous dyads.[8] Being post-colonial developing states, contiguity and proximity has been a facilitating factor (although not a determinant itself) of the territorial conflict between India and Pakistan. Despite their forced entry into the nuclear club, both India and Pakistan lack the military might to project force further than their immediate neighbourhood.[9]

Territories and the political-juridical boundaries that frame them are neither static nor inert concepts. Territory is not intrinsically given to conflictual behaviour. The tangible and intangible values attached to territory are not everlasting in terms of their meaning or influence on states and their people. The reification of the territorial sovereign state, with its emphasis on the exclusive, single-point perspective[10] fails to grasp the role of identities and constructions of inter-subjective understandings that mould borders in a conflictual or coexistent manner. Both neorealists and neoliberals fail to explain the discursive construction of borders; the former focus on politico-military borders disproportionately whereas even though the liberal institutionalist approach recognises the possibility of porous, non-competitive borders, they completely disregard the role of identity and culture in aiding or curbing the process.

Borders have both a symbolic or metaphorical meaning as well as a material reality. Borders are essentially discursive products that segregate people into "us" and "them" "categories." Anssi Paasi suggests that it is the "iconography of boundaries" that constructs the history and meaning of a particular territory.[11] Boundary narratives provide the people with common experiences, a history and memories that bind them together. This suggests that borders can be cultural constructs while being political or physical entities. The nation-state project and processes of nation-building demand the "invention" of artificial political borders that encompass a culturally homogeneous space in which the political culture extends to the sovereign edges of this space.[12] According to Jason Askleson, "The construction of reality, quite simply, depends on borders…meaning, content, form and discourse…are formulated by, through, over and under different kinds of borders and boundings".[13]

Since borders are primarily constructions of identity, the constructivist paradigm offers the best approach to the study of borders. According to the constructivist approach, cooperation between states can be better explained by the distribution of knowledge and inter-subjective beliefs rooted and reproduced through social practices than the distribution of power.[14] With its emphasis on identity and culture, constructivism can account for the "construction" of identity and interest that borders entail.[15] "The internality and externality of the 'other' are not matters of fact and history but of construction and cognition."[16] Constructivism and the identity-based understanding of territorial conflicts enable us to see borders as dynamic and ever-changing products of peoples' sense of self and the other. Who we are is determined by who we are not. Borders are constituted by state-driven nationalist discourses and are de-constructed by those border communities that are silenced by the "territorialisation of identities," often only once the state allows them the space to express their identities.[17] This approach can help explain relations between contiguous dyads and why some disputes get resolved while others remain highly emotive issues. For example, despite being at war, the dispute over the accession and the exact location of the border between the state of Kutch in India and the province of Sindh in Pakistan was settled by the International Court of Justice. In 1954, the issue was raised, and in 1968, an international three-man tribunal awarded about 350 square miles of the northern part of the disputed Rann to Pakistan and allotted the rest to India. Furthermore, the agency of states and communities in changing the status quoist understanding of borders brings to the mainstream the importance of identity and interest formation in understanding world politics. "The understanding of borders as social and dynamic institutions offers the possibility for the transformation of border identities through bottom-up processes of change emanating from social processes on both sides of the border divide."[18]

The Territorialisation of Identity in South Asia

Although the conflict over Kashmir has set the stage for and the direction in which India-Pakistan relations have moved over the years, other comparatively minor and seemingly less intractable disputes over the Tulbul Navigation Project/Wullar Barrage[19] and Sir Creek[20] and now over the Baglihar Dam, have become entangled with the quarrel over Kashmir. National chauvinism and religious bigotry have helped create a conflict that is primarily territorial in nature. A brief overview of the territorial dispute between India and Pakistan shows how the international and the domestic aspects of the conflict have become so profoundly intertwined. In Pakistan's view, Jammu and Kashmir's (J&K's) Hindu king, Maharaja Hari Singh's accession to India did not reflect the commonly held aspirations of the Kashmiri people, as he was not an elected representative.[21] However, before the legality of the Instrument of Accession could be ascertained, a war broke out in October 1947, aided and abetted by Pakistani-sponsored tribals. A UN-imposed ceasefire in 1949 artificially divided the state of J&K, a line that represented both militaries' ground positions after the war. After the Shimla Agreement between India and

Pakistan in 1972, the Ceasefire Line (CFL) was converted into the militarily held Line of Control (LoC). However, the LoC north of coordinate NJ 9842 until Indira Col in the Karakoram was never accurately delineated and was the "missing piece," in Robert Wirsing's words.[22] Since the occupation of the Siachen Glacier by Indian forces in 1984, both India and Pakistan continued to exchange fire across these uninhabitable heights until the mutually agreed ceasefire on the LoC, Line of Actual Control (LAC) and the border in November 2003. By 1999, years of bad governance and growing grievances among the people of J&K coalesced into a full-fledged armed insurgency. Internal unrest in the state was manipulated by Pakistan, which morally, financially and militarily aided militant activity in India. Today, the people of the Vale of Kashmir feel alienated from a political centre that has not addressed their needs. The demand for greater autonomy in Kashmir is based on the "territorial" aspirations of a people who find themselves marginalised from the mainstream. This "peripheral" nation finds itself at the edge of the state's borders – geographically as well as socio-economically.[23]

The salience of the territory under dispute between India and Pakistan is high in terms of tangible as well as intangible values. This underlines why both India and Pakistan find it difficult to backpedal on issues connected to territory, why sabre-rattling accompanies dips in bilateral relations and why both sides ostensibly seem willing to suffer the costs of an enduring conflict. It is also one of the fundamental reasons why the conflict is a zero-sum game. The fact that the demand for autonomy and secession in Kashmir is inextricably linked to the dispute between Pakistan and India and the clandestine support the Kashmiri insurgency receives from across the border has only complicated matters further. States riddled by more than one movement of territorial separatism cannot afford to appear soft on secessionists. Appearing tough and inflexible has the benefit of deterring similar challenges from emerging elsewhere.[24]

Why are India and Pakistan unwilling to yield on Kashmir and other less intractable boundary disputes?[25] Years of "cultural othering"[26] has assisted in the construction of the border as the epitome of all differences by erasing similarities among the people and by making the border a palpable entity even for people living far from the border. British policies and arbitrary lines denoting the control the Indian and Pakistani militaries exercised have helped spawn artificial borders with no resonance on the ground, particularly in the frontier where cultures merge rather than abruptly abut each other.

The India-Pakistan border as a whole represents a region of "peripheries, of infiltration, transition or separation"... the defence of which is necessary for the supposed "purity" of the "centre."[27] The Radcliffe Line that bifurcated the India-

Pakistan border in the culturally homogeneous region of Punjab followed no consistent criteria. The border bisected homes, villages, canals and communication lines. It also failed to divide the communities fairly, leaving large populations of Hindus, Muslims and Sikhs on the "wrong" side of the border.[28] The border was reflected in a precise form only in the mental images of politicians, lawyers and intellectuals and failed to become part of the socio-cultural imagination or identities of the people.[29] While the border was projected as a natural cultural divide, stories that might have highlighted the cultural oneness of the border region became "footnotes in the triumphant progress of the independence movement."[30] The Unionist Party of Punjab before 1947, for example, worked towards strengthening the forces of Punjabiyat and was a cross-communal mix of Hindus, Sikhs as well as Muslim agriculturalists.[31] History has been used by both India and Pakistan to territorialise the nation. Historical narratives and myths such as the idol-breaking episode by the Sultan of Ghazni at the Somnath Temple in 1025 AD are used as themes for the portrayal of an unreal cultural divide between Hindus and Muslims. Mubarak Ali points out how Pakistan has always occupied a distinct cultural zone in the Indus region, which de-links the cultural identity of Pakistan from South Asia and pushes it towards a Middle Eastern one.[32] Similarly, the socialisation of young children in India and Pakistan in subjects such as geography and history has further entrenched the "naturalness" of the border dividing India and Pakistan. Krishna Kumar's comparative study of Indian and Pakistani school textbooks reveals that "what happened in the past is intertwined with the current and evolving perception of the other," thereby prompting people to accept partition as a result of the realities of a "primordial divide" that existed between India and Pakistan long before partition.[33] At the time of independence, for example, only 3 to 5 per cent of the population of Pakistan spoke Urdu, a figure turned on its head by subsequent policy that encouraged the learning of Urdu as a language of Pakistan.[34]

The LoC in Kashmir is even more arbitrary in nature than the Radcliffe Line as it was supposed to be a temporary line until a resolution was to be implemented. Travel and people-to-people interaction is difficult along the length and breadth of the India-Pakistan border, and until recently, it was next to impossible across the LoC in Kashmir. It was only with the peace talks between India and Pakistan in 2004-2005 that people from both sides could travel across the LoC.[35] Although the LoC (740 km) indiscriminately separates villages, families and even houses, even this section of the border between India and Pakistan has been subjected to a processs of "cultural othering." According to the Kargil Committee Report, the CFL/LoC represents a broad ethnographic and cultural divide. The report emphasises that the people of Azad Kashmir (under Pakistan) are mainly of Hazara-Pathan and Punjabi stock, the Northern Areas are mainly Central Asian in character, whereas the Sufi-Rishi tradition that created Kashmiriyat is peculiar to the Valley of Kashmir.[36] The reality is more complex; cultural similarities cut across the LoC and differences exist within both Pakistan Occupied Kashmir (PoK) and India Occupied Kashmir. On the Indian side, a Hindu Dogri-speaking Jammu jostles for space with predominantly a Buddhist Ladakh and a Mulsim Kashmir Valley. On the other hand, Baltistan, which forms part of present-day Pakistan's Northern Areas, is ethno-linguistically closer to the Ladakhi-Balti (Tibetan) speaking region across the LoC.[37]

The India-Pakistan border is infused with an inter-subjective meaning and understanding that is adversarial. The border exists everywhere, in the hearts of the people and in the way Hindus and Muslims see each other, both across the border as well as within them. By viewing territories as constructed and borders as multi-dimensional in nature, the possibility of conflict transformation on the Indian subcontinent is possible to imagine. If territory is constructed, it can just as easily be deconstructed. To this end, a start has been made, both along the border in J&K as well as across Punjab, which will be discussed in detail below. Before that, however, it is important to mention examples of other territorial conflicts between contiguous dyads that were transformed from being conflict-ridden to peaceful and are, hence, instructive for the analysis of the India-Pakistan territorial dispute.

The Finnish-Russian border was a heavily militarised one during and after World War II. It was also fed with ideological differences: the capitalist world vis-à-vis the Communist and Western versus Eastern Christianity. The war between Finland and Russia during World War II over the contiguous territory of Karelia, led to Finland's loss of large areas of the Karelian Isthmus. Today, the Finnish-Russian border marks the European Union's boundary with the outside world; yet, special border projects and regimes deal with cross-border cooperation and similar concerns of the borderland, developments which were met with reluctance by some sections of the military and security elite who perceived increasing cross-border activity as a strategic threat, even though no real threat existed.[38] In another instance, until the adjoining border region of Alsace and Lorraine was restored to French sovereignty in 1945, both France and Germany carried out assimilationist policies during the territory's occupation by both countries over the centuries; education helped to demonise the "other." Yet, today, the region stands at the heart of European integration and cross-border cooperation between the two countries. In the apt words of Reverend Joseph Musser in the border city of Strasbourg at the French-German border, "Here in Alsace, Franco-German reconciliation is not just an abstract concept – it is a daily reality."[39] On the Asian continent, October 2004 saw the end of a 300-year old dispute between Russia and China when the two sides signed a historic supplementary agreement on the joint development of the islands in the Amur, Ussuri and Argun Rivers.[40]

Just like the India-Pakistan border, politico-military borders that were culturally constituted through processes of othering and were barriers to economic cooperation separated the contiguous dyads mentioned above. As the examples suggest, borders that were once militarised did undergo a peaceful transformation. The reasons why this transformation occurred are myriad – ranging from change in the international environment like the dissolution of the Cold War, the growing vitality of the European Union, the trumping of military concerns by benefits accruing from economic exchange and joint development, external pressure by third parties, public lethargy and a corresponding change in the political climate, and so on. It is difficult to pinpoint one pivotal factor in the transformation of territorial/border conflicts. However, what emerges from a brief overview of the transformation of territorial conflicts elsewhere is that at the base of it, the conflicting collective identities of the people underwent a process of gradual transformation. It also brings to light the preeminent role the state plays in orchestrating this change – by providing the right atmospherics and lifting barriers to economic interaction, by creating institutional linkages and by allowing space for the expression of flexible and possibly translocal identities.[41]

Deconstructing the Border

The illusory nature of the India-Pakistan border is most striking for those border communities whose voices have been marginalised or completely silenced by xenophobic voices and statist concerns; communities who are in a position to challenge the state's official discourse on the 'nation'. Firm control on travel and exchange between the two sides of the borderland has made it difficult for younger generations to counter the state-directed territorialisation of memories of a shared past, particularly in the Punjab region. The study of border regions and the communities who live there is important to give the communities living near the border a sense of 'agency' in deciding their fate. Communities such as the Punjabis, Sindhis, Mohajirs, Mirpuris, Kashmiris, the Chib community,[42] the Gujjars and Bakkarwals need to find a voice in determining their own future and the direction that India-Pakistan relations can take. There is need for greater interaction between these communities on either side of the border in order to enrich and possibly challenge state-centric notions of identity, belonging and conflict resolution.

It is clear that the political-military nature of the border has facilitated the construction of the border as culturally, read religiously, opposed and this has in turn prevented a vibrant economic trade and exchange regime from developing. The outbreak of war soon after independence closed off any possibility of the integrated development of the region. Instead, both countries gave up their "utilitarian complementarities in a remorseless hunt for economic independence which would serve political demands for sovereignty."[43] Even though the economies of India and Pakistan have shed the complementarities they possessed at the time of partition, there are definite benefits that can accrue to the people on both sides through trade and exchange. This can even have a positive "spill-over effect" on the security concerns of the two countries, as explored in detail by E. Sridharan.[44] Some movement and the right noises have been made in this direction. The Chief Minister of Pakistan's Punjab Province Chaudhary Parvez Elahi invited Indian businessmen and traders to take part in joint exhibitions and discussions, although nothing emerged from this. The year 2005 also witnessed the "great and historic" and as yet, riven with uncertainty, gas pipeline deal among India, Pakistan and Iran that proposes to pipe gas to India from Iran's South Pars field via Pakistan.

Therefore, the state is in a particularly pivotal position to, according to David Newman, not really to open up common space but identify border regimes that enable "differences to be valued rather than feared."[45] 2004-2005 saw some successes in the advancement towards taking the sting out of the border that separates India and Pakistan. At the forefront is the intra-Kashmir dialogue and interaction. In April 2005, the Muzaffarabad-Srinagar road carried families across the LoC for the first time, and there are proposals to finalise the opening of other road routes as well, such as the Poonch-Rawalakote network.[46] In June 2005, the All Parties Hurriyat Conference's moderate faction travelled across the LoC and met with leaders and mediapersons in PoK, and emphasised that any future resolution of the Kashmir problem must take the Kashmiri people into account. In July 2005, the Delhi Policy Group and the Centre for Dialogue and Reconciliation brought together 13 delegates from Muzaffarabad, Mirpur, Skardu, Gilgit, and 50 representatives from J&K and New Delhi to discuss Kashmir's problems and deepen understanding.[47] The recent spate in goodwill has translated into increased interaction across other sections of the border as well, like the recent agreement to open bus services between Amritsar and Nankana Sahib in Pakistan and Amritsar and Lahore, bringing Wagah into the news for reasons other than the by now infamous war-like ceremony enacted by the border security forces of both countries. Work is also on to operationalise the Munabao railway station that will connect Rajasthan to Karachi, a part of the border that was forgotten for 40 years. Interaction between civil society groups, the media, prominent people from the cultural, sports and political worlds are together helping create a multi-track diplomacy – diplomacy that helps not only change governmental policy but also the way people think.[48]

A lot still needs to be done and numerous impediments stand in the way of making the India-Pakistan border more permeable and creating space for 'translocal' identity formations to emerge. As the third round of composite dialogue starts in January 2006, there are innumerable obstacles that can jeopardise the peace process. The continuing cycle of violence in Kashmir perpetrated by insurgents, mercenary fighters and security forces, the infiltration and support of terrorists from across the border,[49] the unpredictability of Pakistan's internal polity,[50] the absence of democracy in Pakistan,[51] the lack of greater autonomy in Kashmir, the role of the US in changing the strategic concerns of both India and Pakistan, both countries' quest for greater military prowess in the background of a nuclearised South Asia, visa limitations, the appalling human security situation[52] and the low level of economic development in Kashmir, are just a few concerns that can arrest progress towards lasting peace. There will always be constituencies on both sides that will try to hold back the peaceful resolution of the conflict. Notwithstanding the above-mentioned problems, the very deconstruction of the bordering process itself is fraught with difficulties, in particular two. Firstly, years of diligent and consistent efforts by states may not succeed in weakening the "us" and "them" dichotomy. For example, after the fall of the Berlin Wall in 1989 and the unification of East and West Germany, Germans continued to speak of a "wall in the mind" that separated societies divided by separate histories, disparate levels of economic development and by mentalities shaped through distinct social systems.[53] Secondly, giving communities (including communities living in the border region) a voice in determining their future does not always mean that it will be a voice in favour of weakening cultural and economic barriers and making borders more porous. For example, since the European Union's (EU's) open frontiers policy, Alsace Lorraine's industry has faced stiff competition from a far stronger German economy. Political analysts suggested that the support for Le Pen, candidate for the 2002 presidential elections, and his far right xenophobic National Front was a reaction to Alsace Lorraine's sense of abandonment from Paris.[54]

Growing scepticism in the countries of Western Europe represents a growing fear that further integration and market liberalisation will disrupt the social fabric of Western Europe as a result of the free flow of people across porous borders with Eastern Europe. Similarly, even though Russia and China have resolved their border dispute, the threat of a Chinese "invasion" in the form of Chinese goods and cheap labour has increased anti-China feelings in the scarcely populated border stretches of eastern Siberia.[55] The Minuteman Project along a 23-mile section of the US-Mexico border echoes similar fears of increased illegal immigration into the United States from Mexico. In April 2005, volunteers of the armed civilian vigilante group mounted a round-the-clock search for illegal migrants, an example of the animosity towards outsiders who are perceived as criminals and threats to the livelihood and security of the citizens of the US states bordering Mexico.[56]

Religion has often been cited as a particularly divisive force in India-Pakistan or Hindu-Muslim relations. However, religion is just one of various attributes of culture, such as language, ethnicity, kinship, tradition, and so on. We know from events in South Asia itself that religion can be as divisive a factor as ethnicity and language, and on the Indian subcontinent, differences between religions are more apparent and constructed than real. In his book, Amitava Kumar, for example, quotes the findings of the Anthropological Survey of India according to which, "popular cultural expression cuts across religion" identifying social traits such as settlement, food, marriage, economy, social organisation as common between regions rather than religions and caste. According to the report, Hindus share 96.77 per cent traits with Muslims and 88.99 per cent with Sikhs and Muslims share 91.18 per cent with Buddhists and 89.95 per cent with Sikhs.[57]

Conclusion

The resolution of the territorial dispute with Pakistan is undoubtedly entangled with the question of India maintaining its territorial integrity over Kashmir and Pakistan believing it rightfully belongs to it. India's and Pakistan's approach to the status quo is markedly different; while India seeks to reaffirm the status quo through negotiations and possibly turn the LoC into an international border, Pakistan seeks its alteration. Perceiving borders as discursive constructs explicitly coiled around the idea of the "nation-state" underlines the growing interest in identity and culture in the study of international relations theory.[58] An interesting shift in emphasis on identity clashes in conflicts has been analysed in detail by Jay Rothman and Marie L. Olson. According to them, state and power-centric politics as modes of managing conflict do not address the deep underlying identities of the people and fail to "redefine processes and relationships in the process."[59] Although the efficacy of the authors' prescription for resolving identity-based conflict cannot be conclusively confirmed, they suggest that interactive conflict resolution and a four-tiered model can help in breaking the barrier of identity.[60] In conclusion, two important indicators are worth highlighting and perhaps reiterating.

Far from a borderless world, the world's states are still caught up in boundary-determining exercises and territorial disputes. According to Beth Simmons, the world's most permeable borders exist between countries that have "well-established political jurisdictions."[61] However, this does not explain why India and Pakistan accepted the Kutch Award (mentioned above) or signed the Indus Waters Treaty and why the US and Canada continue to have ownership disputes over areas such as the Machias Seal Island, Strait of Juan de Fuca, Dixon Entrance, Beaufort Sea, etc despite have the longest permeable and non-militarised border in the world. Clearly, the answer lies in the way the conflict is constructed by the state by its official discourse that binds it with the constructed collective identities of the 'nation' on either side. Building fences, however 'good', is not enough. Conflict over territory has to address the identity and inter-subjective values of the communities and introduce developmental programmes and social projects that help in transforming the identities of the people. The first step in lifting barriers to people-to-people interaction between groups like the Pakistan-India People's Forum for Peace and Democracy, is by opening road and rail routes and building bridges and through cooperation in more fields such as the pipeline deal, etc. However, it is just as important to obliterate school syllabi that make future generations in India and Pakistan what Amitava Kumar has called "textbook enemies."[62] It is, therefore, important that nationalist narratives and fundamentalist ideologies on both sides of the border are brought under the hammer. Border development projects in managing cross-border water resources, and support for the development and expression of the cultural oneness of the border region are some mechanisms that can carry on alongside "bigger" initiatives on conflict resolution, thereby transforming the borderland from an alienated to a coexistent one.[63] The future states of the world will have to also think of alternatives to the Westphalian territorial state. More creative and imaginative answers that are not imprisoned by ethnocentric motions of exclusive territoriality and mutually exclusive jurisdiction, notions implicit in the sovereign state system, need to be crafted. Although perhaps a solution appears impossible, the time has come to discuss joint mechanisms of development, authority and jurisdiction over the disputed territories and a special regime for Kashmir needs serious reflection.

The state in post-colonial countries such as India and Pakistan is in a particularly preeminent position to transform territorial conflicts and institute mechanisms that bring economic and cultural commonalities to the fore. Although differences will continue to exist, it is important to reach a point where "increased cooperation and interaction across borders can lead to greater trust, transparency and to a sense of security in the identity of the people on both sides of the border such that these differences cannot lead to war again."[64] What the strategic community on both sides has to realise is that territory is much more than border demarcations and the stubborn grasp on disputed land. Territory is about the symbolic meaning and inter-subjective understandings that extend far beyond the border region and deep into the psyche of the people. It is for this reason that territory is a constructed reality, a reality that nonetheless has a tangible physical existence. Agreement on border delineations and respect for territorial integrity will be bereft of meaning if cross-border cooperation does not instill a sense of purpose in the people who are affected by the border and the larger populace who deserve more than official historiographies that narrow their vision. Pipelines, roads, rails and bridges might not alter the territorial 'status quo' between India and Pakistan; they will, however, create stakes in maintaining peace in each other's territory.

Notes

1. According to the Correlates of War Project (COW) Militarised Dispute data sets, enduring rivalries are those that experience at least six disputes in a time period lasting 20 years. Those between this category and those that experience isolated rivalries (two or fewer disputes, 10 years apart) are termed as proto-rivalries. India and Pakistan fall in the proto-rivalry category as disputes that occur within 10-15 years of each other are considered to be part of the same rivalry. India and Pakistan have fought four wars in the past and a proxy war continues between armed militants and the security forces in J&K. For more on the COW data sets, see http://correlatesofwar.org/
2. According to Sucheta Mahajan, the vacillating nature of British policies and their conflicting interests allowed communalism to wreak havoc during and after partition. Mahajan claims that the British allowed communal tendencies to boil as they tried to appease both the Congress as well as the Muslim League for their own strategic interests even after power was handed over by the British. See Sucheta Mahajan, *Independence and Partition: The Erosion of Colonial Power in India* (New Delhi: Sage Publications, 2000), pp. 143-204.
3. After independence, Pakistan turned to America for military and economic assistance to shore up its strength vis-à-vis India. The United States declared its neutrality and refused to aid Pakistan under the terms of the Agreement of Cooperation, while refusing to militarily intervene in India's favour either during

the 1965 War. In the words of Husain Haqqani, it was Eisenhower's Cold War policy that clearly established Pakistan as the eastern anchor of America's Middle Eastern policy and marked the beginning of a client-patron relationship that was damaging to Pakistan. Lecture on "Pakistan: Between Mosque and Military," at the India International Centre, December 21, 2005, New Delhi.

4. Chris Brown, "Borders and Identity in International Political Theory," in Mathias Albert, David Jacobson and Yosef Lapid, eds., *Identities, Borders and Orders: Rethinking International Relations Theory* (London: University of Minnesota Press, 1999), p. 117.

5. Simple iterative interaction can lead to cooperative outcomes. International institutions, regimes, laws, treaties help provide the necessary transparency, predictability and institutionalisation that make cooperation under uncertain circumstances relatively easy.

6. Harvey Starr and G. Dale Thomas occupy a middle ground in the explanation of territorial conflict. Rather than endorsing a linear relationship between territorial contiguity and conflict, Starr and Thomas suggest that conflict is most likely to become militarised in the 'area' where both opportunity (levels of ease of interaction) and willingness to engage in combat (salience) are sufficiently high and not necessarily when they are either at the highest or lowest levels as hypothesised by Vasquez and Deutsch respectively. See Starr and Thomas, "The Nature of Borders and International Conflict: Revisiting Hypotheses on Territory," *International Studies Quarterly*, 49, 2005, pp. 123-139.

7. See John A. Vasquez, *The War Puzzle* (Cambridge: Cambridge University Press, 1993), Vasquez, "Why do Neighbours Fight? Proximity, Interaction or Territoriality?," *Journal of Peace Research*, 32, 1995, pp. 277-293; Paul K. Huth, "Enduring Rivalries and Territorial Disputes, 1950-1990," *Conflict Management and Peace Science*, 15, 1996, pp. 7-41; Paul Hensel, "Charting a Course to Conflict: Territorial Issues and Interstate Conflict, 1816-1992," *Conflict Management and Peace Science*, 15, 1996, pp. 43-73; Gary Goertz and Paul F. Diehl, "Taking Enduring out of Enduring Rivalries," *International Interactions*, 21, 1995, pp. 291-308. Also see, Arie M. Kacowicz, "The Problem of Peaceful Territorial Change," *International Studies Quarterly*, 38, 1994, pp. 219-254.

8. Although territorial issues are more likely to escalate into militarised disputes, contiguous territory is more prone to undergo processes of militarisation. Furthermore, proximity makes states "relevant" to each other, and, hence, "willing" to defend their heartland or homeland. Scholars such as Vasquez assert that a lack of contiguity and a coincidence between borders and natural frontiers lower the stakes and reduce the chance of war. See Paul F. Diehl, "Territorial Dimensions of International Conflict: An Introduction," *Conflict Management and Peace Science*, 15, 1996, pp. 1-6.

9. States other than great powers cannot engage in militarised conflicts of an enduring nature except with other states in their immediate neighbourhood or region. See Jaroslav Tir and Paul F. Diehl, "The Political Geography of Enduring Rivalries," Paper presented at the Conference on New Methodologies for the Social Sciences: The Development and Application of Spatial Analysis for Political Methodology, March 10-12, 2000, Boulder, Colorado. Available at http://www.colorado.edu/IBS/PEC/spatial/papers/tir_diehl.paper.pdf

10. According to John Ruggie, it was the Renaissance that imposed its single-point perspective on the system of rule. See "Territoriality and Beyond: Problematising

Modernity in International Relations," *International Organisation*, 47:1, 1993, pp. 139-174.

11. Anssi Paasi, "The Role of Identities and Boundaries in the Contemporary World", presented at 5th Nordic-Baltic Conference in Regional Science, October 1-4, 1998, Parnu, Estonia. Available at http://www.geo.ut.ee/nbc/paper/paasi.htm
12. Ernest Gellner, quoted in Carlo J. Bonura Jr., "The Occulted Geopolitics of Nation and Culture," in Gearoid O' Tuathail and Simon Dalby, eds., *Rethinking Geopolitics* (London: Routledge, 1998), pp. 86-105.
13. Jason M. Ackleson, "Discourses of Identity and Territoriality on the US-Mexico Border," in Nurit Kliot and David Newman, eds., *Geopolitics at the End of the Twentieth Century: The Changing World Political Map* (London: Frank Cass Publishers, 2000), p.159.
14. Theo Farrell, "Constructivist Security Studies: Portrait of a Research Program," *International Studies Review*, 4, no. 1 (2002): p.49-72.
15. Brown, n.4, pp.117-136.
16. Bonura Jr., n.12, pp. 91.
17. According to Agnew, identities are territorialised into an "us" pursuing universal values (politics) and "them" practising different and nominally inferior values. See John A. Agnew, *Mastering Space: Hegemony, Territory and International Political Economy* (London: Routledge, 1995), p. 87.
18. Michelle Pace and Stephan Stetter, "A Literature Review on the Study of Border Conflicts and Their Transformation in the Social Sciences." Available at http://www.euborderconf.bham.ac.uk/publications/files/stateoftheartreport.pdf
19. The dispute over the Wullar Barrage and the Baglihar Dam are not territorial disputes *per se*. However, both disputes emphasise the problem in harnessing energy from rivers that do not respect political borders and have the potential of being detrimental to communities living downstream. The Tulbul/Wullar and Baglihar disputes bring to light 'territorial' disputes over rivers that straddle or cross international borders, boundaries that demarcate adjacent coastlines and the Exclusive Economic Zones (EEZs).
20. The Sir Creek dispute is over a tidal channel in a small stretch of the 20,000 sq km badlands along a 38 km estuary that separates the state of Gujarat in India from the province of Sindh in Pakistan. There is an urgent need to "delimit the boundary along the creek as well as demarcate the maritime boundary from the mouth of the creek seawards in the Arabian Sea." See Bharat Bhushan, "Tulbul, Sir Creek and Siachen; Competitive Methodologies," *South Asian Journal*, 7, January-March 2005. Available at http://www.southasianmedia.net/Magazine/Journal/7_competitive_methodologies.htm
21. The accession of the state of Jammu and Kashmir to India denied a strategically pivotal region to Pakistan, denying it strategic depth as well as a firm foothold in Indian territory. In addition, the accession of J&K to India was a blow to the two-nation theory that was the basis of Pakistan's partition from India. There were suspicions within the Muslim League that Lord Mountbatten had influenced the final decision of the Radcliffe award in favour of India.
22. Robert Wirsing, *India, Pakistan and the Kashmir Dispute: On Regional Conflict and its Resolution* (New Delhi: Rupa, 1994), p. 75.
23. The term peripheral nation has been defined on the basis of economic and political power, and the minority community's identity, language and religion vis-

a-vis the majority community. See James Anderson and Liam O'Dowd, "Borders, Border Regions and Territoriality: Contradictory Meanings Changing Significance," *Regional Studies*, 33:7, 1999, pp. 593-604. Also, it is important to underline the fact that the 'peripheral nation' is mainly the Muslim community that constitutes the majority in the Valley and not the Buddhist community of Ladakh, or the Hindus of Jammu.

24. See Barbara F. Walter, "Explaining the Apparent Indivisibility of Territory," Graduate School of International Relations and Pacific Studies, University of California, San Diego, March 2001. Available at www.yale.edu/leitner/PEC-Walter.pdf
25. The unprecedented level of intra-Kashmir interaction undoubtedly was a result of some concessions being made by both India and Pakistan. India recognised the need to include the Hurriyat in the India-Pakistan talks on Kashmir and Musharraf agreed to let the process go ahead, despite India's categorical refusal to change any borders between the two.
26. A term used by Michael Crang; communities form cultural identities through a process by which people of a community recognise not only themselves but can also identify others. Cultures help make sense of space and develop meaning for people, thereby perpetuating culture within that space. See Michael Crang, *Cultural Geography* (London: Routledge, 1998), p. 60.
27. Anderson and O' Dowd, n.23, p. 596.
28. Gurdaspur with a considerable Muslim population was awarded to India whereas Lahore with a Hindu population went to Pakistan.
29. Mushirul Hasan, "Memories of a Fragmented Nation: Rewriting the Histories of India's Partition," in Amrik Singh, ed., *Partition in Retrospect* (New Delhi: Anamika Publishers, 2000), pp. 339-360.
30. Ian Talbot, *Inventing the Nation: India and Pakistan* (London: Oxford University Press, 2000), p. 163.
31. The Unionist Party was discredited by nationalists as well as the supporters of the two-nation theory for being either pro-British or anti-Pakistan and soon caste and religious forces destroyed the Punjabi flavour of the party.
32. Mubarak Ali, "Pakistan's Search for Identity," in Paul Brass and Achin Vinayak, eds., *Competing Nationalisms in South Asia* (New Delhi: Orient Longman, 2002), Chapter 10.
33. Krishna Kumar, *Prejudice and Pride: School Histories of the Freedom Struggle in India and Pakistan* (New Delhi: Penguin, 2002), p. 29.
34. Interestingly, Urdu was the mother tongue of people who migrated from present-day India during partition and not of the people in Pakistan.
35. It is important to note that the peace initiatives in Kashmir will always be precariously placed vis-a-vis a rise in militant infiltration and violence.
36. *The Kargil Committee Report*, February 23, 2000, p. 39.
37. For more on the state of Baltistan, read M. Hasnain Sengge Thsering, "Key Issue in Contemporary Balti Language and Script," paper presented at the Eighth Himalayan Languages Symposium, University of Bern – Institute of Linguistics, September 2002, available at: http://members.tripod.com/~INDIA_RESOURCE/baltiyul.html. According to Luv Puri, even though Muzaffarabad in POK was part of the Kashmir province before 1948, it was linguistically and culturally similar to the Jammu region and not the Vale of Kashmir. See Luv Puri, "Softening the Line of Control," *Himal*, November 2004. Available at

http://www.himalmag.com/2003/november/commentary_2.htm

38. Anssi Paasi, "Boundaries as Social Practices and Discourse: The Finnish-Russian Border," *Regional Studies*, 33:7, 1999, p. 675.

39. See Katrin Bennhold, "Old Europe, New Ideas: A Look at What Works," *International Herald Tribune*, August 10, 2005.

40. In the past, the islands in the middle of the Argun, Amur and Ussuri Rivers had been a serious bone of contention between Russia and China. In 1969, these islands, for example, the Damansky Island (Chinese – *Zhenbao*) on the Ussuri was the site of a serious gunbattle. Another curious example is the little known island in the middle of the river Bidasoa which flows along a section of the Franco-Spanish border. This uninhabited island had been under conflict between the people living on either side of the border and its ownership switched from France and Spain. Today, under the impact of an open frontier policy within the EU, both France and Spain rotate their jurisdiction of the island every six months. See Zoe Bray, "Boundaries and Identities on the Franco-Spanish Frontier," CIBR Working Papers in Border Studies, CIBR/WP02-2. Available at www.qub.ac.uk/cibr/WPpdffiles/CIBRwp2002_2_rev.pdf

41. For more on a perspective on the state from the frontier, see Alex Maroya, "Rethinking the Nation-State from the Frontier," *Millennium*, 32:2, 2003, pp. 267-292.

42. The Chib community traces its origin to a 12th century saint; however, after partition most of the community migrated to Punjab in Pakistan while others stayed back in Akhnoor, Jammu in India. See Luv Puri, "Sentinels of Peace," *The Hindu*, September 5, 2004.

43. Graham Chapman, "Religious vs. Regional Determinism: India, Pakistan and Bangladesh as Inheritors of Empire," in *The Geopolitics of South Asia: From Early Empires to India, Pakistan and Bangladesh* (Aldershot: Ashgate Publishing, 2000), p.125

44. E. Sridharan, "Economic Cooperation and Security Spill-Overs: The Case of India and Pakistan," in Michael Krepon and Chris Gagne, eds., *Economic Cooperation and Regional Security* (Report 36, The Henry L. Stimson Centre, October 2000). Available at http://www.stimson.org/southasia/pdf/sridharanpdf.pdf

45. See David Newman, "On Borders and Power: A Theoretical Framework," *Journal of Borderland Studies*, 18: 1, 2003, pp. 13-26.

46. See Amit Baruah, "Peace Process Irreversible, say India, Pak," *The Hindu*, April 18, 2005. Also, according to Luv Puri, other routes such as the Suchetgarh-Sialkot road, the Mirpur-Bimber-Rajouri or Mughal road and the intra-Poonch route could go a long way in bringing separated families closer to each other.

47. Read the Joint Statement from the three-day Intra-Kashmir dialogue by the Centre for Dialogue and Reconciliation, Delhi Policy Group and the Forum for Regional Voices. Available at http://www.fnst.de/webcom/show_article.php/_c-705/_nr-48/printmode-true/i.html

48. See Manjrika Sewak, *Multi-Track Diplomacy Between India and Pakistan: A Conceptual Framework for Sustainable Security*, Policy Studies 30 (Colombo: Regional Centre for Strategic Studies, 2005).

49. This is true despite the completion of the fencing of the border by India and President Musharraf's commitment to rein in extremist Islamic forces.

50. Since 1947, Pakistan's governmental structure has been personality oriented. Decades of military rule and weak democratic moments have disallowed any

vibrant institutions from emerging, institutions which could give a voice to the people of Pakistan beyond the freedom of the Press to the airing of grievances and differences in identity.

51. According to Sarah McLaughlin Mitchell and Brandon C. Prins, mature democracies are capable of settling contentious territorial disputes by accepting the status quo, unlike democratising or non-democratic states. See "Beyond Territorial Contiguity: Issues at Stake in Democratic Militarised Interstate Disputes", *International Studies Quarterly,* 43:1, 1999, pp. 169-183. Another growing body of literature looks at the role leaders and their time in office in resolving specific territorial disputes. See Giacomo Chiozza and Ajin Choi, "Guess Who Did What. Political Leaders and the Management of Territorial Disputes, 1950-1990," *Journal of Conflict Resolution,* 47:3, 2003, pp. 251-278.
52. Not only are the social indicators poor for the state, even civic amenities are in short supply, not the least for refugees who have had to migrate from the Valley. Many innocent people have suffered the consequences of living in a state of constant militarisation, which further fills common people with hatred, whether it is over disappearances, fencing and mining activities of the military.
53. For more, see Wilfred Skor, "East Germans Between Euphoria and 'Ostalgia,'" and Pramod Talgeri, "The Identity Formation of the Reunited German Nation", in Rajendra K. Jain, ed., *Germany in the Nineties* (New Delhi: Radiant Publishers, 1998).
54. Rory Carroll, "The Alsace Vote for Le Pen was just a Protest, Wasn't it?", *The Guardian Weekly,* Saturday April 27, 2002, available at: www.guardian.co.uk/france/story/0, 11882,706168,00.html.
55. See Yulia Latynina, "Selling Russia Down the River," *The Moscow Times,* February 9, 2005.
56. See Jerry Seper, "Border Vigil Ends on Wary Note," *The Washington Post,* May 1, 2005.
57. Amitava Kumar, *Husband of a Fanatic* (New Delhi: Penguin, 2004), p. 87.
58. Read Michael C. Desch, "Culture Clash: Assessing the Importance of Ideas in Security Studies," *International Security,* 23:1, 1998, p. 151 and 58 Marysia Zalewski and Cynthia Enloe, "Questions about Identity in International Relations," in Ken Booth and Steve Smith, eds., *International Relations Theory Today* (Cambridge: Polity Press, 1995).
59. Jay Rothman and Marie L. Olson, "From Interests to Identities: Towards a New Emphasis in Interactive Conflict Resolution," *Journal of Conflict Resolution,* 38: 3, 2001, p. 294.
60. Rothman and Olson, Ibid., pp. 289-305.
61. Beth A. Simmons, "Rules Over Real Estate. Trade, Territorial Conflict and International Borders as Institutions," *Journal of Conflict Resolution,* 49:6, 2005, p. 843.
62. Kumar, n.57, pp. 80-125.
63. For more, see Oscar Martinez, *Border People: Life and Society in the US-Mexico Borderlands* (Tuscon: University of Arizona Press, 1994).
64. Henry McDonald, "Across the Great Divide," *The Guardian,* October 27, 2002.

India–Pakistan Relations: From the Past to the Present

Reconstructing the Evolutionary Narrative

Kalim Bahadur

Origins of Muslim Separatism

Partition of India in 1947 was the result of the developments of the last one hundred years of the complex Indian history. Muslim separatism or Muslim nationalism grew out of the political, social, and economic developments of that period. Broadly speaking, four factors could be considered for the growth of Muslim separatism which later took the form of the "two nation theory." First, the British policy of divide and rule. Second, the emergence of the Muslim middle class. Third, growth of communal sentiments. Fourth, the mistakes committed by the Indian National Congress.

The British were in India as the colonial rulers and had no intention or interest in the integration of the Hindu and Muslim communities. One of the many political steps taken by the British which could be considered as a step for divide and rule was the partition of Bengal in 1905 which was aimed at creating a Muslim Province, "where Islam would be predominant and its followers in the ascendancy" and further "that would invest the Mohammedans of Eastern Bengal with a unity which they had not enjoyed since the days of Old Mussalman Viceroys and Kings."[1] Another step was the 1909 Act which introduced separate electorates under which a separate representation was granted to Muslims who also retained the right to vote in the general electorate.[2] The separate electorate and the other policies of the government encouraged Muslims to think that their interests as a religious community were different from, and in some ways even contradictory to, those of other communities.

Muslim trading communities like the Memons, Khojas, Bohras and Chiniotis believed that a separate homeland for the Muslims would be free from non-Muslim competition, presenting greater opportunities for them. Educated Muslims, particularly from the Aligarh Muslim University, were active in the Muslim League which was the reflection of the strong middle class nationalism. Many Muslim business magnates contributed liberally to the coffers of the Muslim League.[3]

The pan-Islamic movement in the early decades of the century followed by the Khilafat movement had promoted Muslim nationalism when "latent appreciations of religious attitudes were resuscitated, and Islamic emotions, long dormant, once more became powerful."[4] Though the *Ulema* had opposed the two nation theory and condemned the concept of Pakistan, religion nevertheless played a very important part in popularising the Muslim League's agenda. The Deoband *Ulema* had opposed Pakistan because of their traditional conception of Islam, and also because the leadership of the Pakistan movement was led by the Western educated elite.[5] Pakistan was presented by the Muslim League as a Muslim Utopia that would banish the harsh drudgeries of life. *Maulanas* and *pirs* were used frequently to spread the word.

The Muslim League was greatly helped in widening the gulf between the two communities by the mistakes committed by the Congress in the provinces where they had formed the governments in 1937. To mobilise Muslims in favour of its agenda, the Muslim League had to demonise the Congress as anti-Muslim and to argue that the Hindus sought to deprive the Muslims of their cultural identity.[6] The Congress leadership failed to understand the cross currents within the Muslim community. The alienation of the Muslims from the Hindus had been increasing ever since the failure of the Khilafat movement. The Hindu idiom of the Congress greatly helped the Muslim League propagandists. The cow protection movement, the introduction of Hindi textbooks which glorified Hindu heroes and several other real or imaginary grievances spread by the Muslim League activists provided grist to the mill of the Pakistan movement.[7]

Some Pakistani and Indian historians believe that the first seeds of Pakistan were sown by Sir Syed Ahmed Khan and many others consider the famous Urdu poet and philosopher Sir Muhammad Iqbal as the father of Pakistan. However, there would be no controversy about Jinnah being the progenitor of the country. Sir Syed Ahmed Khan wanted the Muslims to adopt English education and closely cooperate with the British rulers but he had not thought of separate nationhood though he frequently used the word nation for community. There is the contrary view that Sir Syed was the real father of Pakistan because all the arguments that Jinnah later advanced for partitioning the subcontinent were the same which Sir Syed used while opposing the Congress.[8] Iqbal believed that for Muslims, Islam alone provided the ideal worth living and dying for. He demanded the creation of a Muslim India within India by the merger of the Muslim majority areas of north and northwest India into a single state.[9] Some Pakistani scholars have claimed that what Iqbal meant was a separate Muslim state within the British Empire, not necessarily within the Indian federation. However, others have quoted Iqbal's letter to E. J. Thompson in which he said that it was a mistake to call him a protagonist of the scheme called Pakistan. He went on to say that Pakistan was not his scheme. Further, he clearly stated, "[I] propose to create a Muslim province within the Indian Federation."[10]

The name Pakistan is taken from a pamphlet issued by one Chaudhari Rahmat Ali, in 1932, who was a student at the Cambridge University, along with three other students, including one Mohammad Aslam Khan Khattak. The title of the pamphlet was "Now or Never." Later, Aslam Khan Khattak went to London to call on Mohammad Ali Jinnah who was practising law there in the early Thirties. Jinnah told Aslam Khan that he had read the pamphlet and was very unhappy about it. He said to Khan, "[W]hy destroy the one great and good thing the British had done in India by unifying the heterogeneous elements into a united whole? Muslims and Hindus had to learn to live as friends and brothers."[11]

The so-called Pakistan Resolution was passed on March 23, 1940, by the Lahore session of the All India Muslim League. Jinnah was in full form at this session, championing the cause of Pakistan which for him was not negotiable. The British had initiated talks with the Indian leaders as World War II drew to a close. However, it appears from the developments during Jinnah's hectic talks with the Congress and the British in 1946, that by accepting the Cabinet Mission Plan he did not rule out the possibility of a compromise short of partition of the country. Jinnah's tactic was to state his maximum demand – the outright acceptance of a sovereign Pakistan comprising the undivided provinces of northwestern and eastern India – and leaving the Congress and the British to produce an alternative formula which would give him the substance of what he was after.[12] The acceptance of the Cabinet Plan had left Bengal and the Punjab undivided, to the relief of the League leaders from these provinces. There were certain advantages for the Muslim provinces in the plan and Jinnah could have reconciled them to it.[13] Some critics of Jinnah had hinted that his acceptance of the Cabinet Mission plan showed he was ready to compromise on something less than the demand made at the Lahore session of the All India Muslim League.[14] This view is stoutly opposed by some other Pakistani scholars who counter that the acceptance of the Cabinet Mission plan by Jinnah was the first step towards acquiring a sovereign and separate state of Pakistan.[15]

Lord Mountbatten, who became the viceroy of India in March 1947, had come with the mandate to partition India, irrespective of what the Congress was demanding or what Jinnah was arguing for. Churchill had wanted Lord Wavell, the predecessor of Mountbatten, to divide India, as noted by Wavell in his diary, "between Hindustan, Pakistan, Princestan." Churchill's brief for

Mountbatten, when he gave his approval to his appointment was clear: if the British could not hold India, then it was best to divide her.[16] Various explanations have been given for the speed with which Lord Mountbatten had gone to impose partition on the Indian subcontinent. The Pakistanis have accused him of all kinds of conspiracies. They have alleged that he manipulated the Radcliffe Boundary Commission which was to draw the boundaries of the two countries, in favour of India against Pakistan.[17] There were no carefully thought out plans to tackle the difficult task of dividing the country. In fact, the date for the transfer of power in the countries was fixed on the spur of the moment by the viceroy.[18] There were dire warnings from all sides, particularly from the British provinces in Punjab, the Northwest Frontier Province (NWFP), and Bengal that the situation was explosive. There were communal riots in Bihar and East Bengal. Simultaneously, with the intense negotiations with Viceroy Mountbatten, bitter controversies about the two nation theory and the demand for Pakistan between the Congress and the Muslim League were aggravating the hatred and enmity among the two communities. The first major communal violence had broken out in Calcutta in August 1946 when the Muslim League had given the call for Direct Action. Communal violence had also started in Punjab after the Muslim League had started the agitation to bring down the Khizer Hayat government in the province. After the Mountbatten award was announced on June 3, 1947, widespread communal violence began in the Punjab, the NWFP, and Bengal and many other parts of India. Large scale migration of minorities from the two countries began.

The Problems of Partition

Partitioning the country which had grown as one politically, socially, and economically integrated country over the last one century, was no easy task. Most of the conflicts and disputes between India and Pakistan originated during the process of dividing the subcontinent. As mentioned earlier, the partition resulted in large scale migration of minorities from both countries. Pakistan had a large number of Hindus in both wings of the country and a significant number of Sikhs in West Pakistan. India had a large Muslim population which had chosen not to migrate and at present their number is more than the total population of Pakistan. It had been decided to partition the Punjab and Bengal; a referendum was to be held in the NWFP and in the Sylhet district in East Bengal. Bitter controversies erupted between the two countries after independence about the division of assets and also regarding the demarcation of the boundaries.

One of the problems regarding the assets was the division of the cash balances, in which the Pakistani side believed their due share had not been given to them. Pakistan alleged that this was done with the sinister intention of financially crippling the new state. Ultimately, Mahatma Gandhi had to intervene and he went on a fast demanding that India give Pakistan its due share. Pakistan protested on the question of the division of military equipment, most of which was lying in India, and most of the ordnance factories were located in the Indian territory. Pakistan was to get one-third of all military equipment as its share. These controversies were reflective of the bitterness that had been generated by the atmosphere at the time of independence. The problem of the properties left behind by the Hindus and Sikhs in Pakistan and those that were left by Muslims in India was a sore point in both the countries. There were two other major issues which continue to poison the atmosphere and comprise the roots of the running conflicts between the two countries.

The distribution of water has been one of the two major issues of contention between the two countries. All the five rivers of Punjab originate in the Indian territory before entering Pakistan. There was a provisional agreement at the time of independence that the amount of water which Pakistan was getting would not be changed. The dispute was settled with the help of the World Bank when the Indus Waters Treaty was signed in 1960 between the Prime Minister of India Jawaharlal Nehru and General Ayub Khan, the then president of Pakistan. The treaty provided that the waters of three rivers i.e., the Indus, Jhelum and Chenab, would go to Pakistan, while the waters of three rivers, that is, Ravi, Beas and Sutlej would go to India.[19] The World Bank had also provided a grant of Rs.1,000 crore for the construction of canals, dams and reservoirs to store the waters of the Indus and Jhelum. There have been disputes about the various projects started by India on the rivers flowing into Pakistan which Pakistan believes violate the Indus Waters Treaty.

The most complex problem of the partition was the question of the five hundred odd princely states. Some of them like Hyderabad and Jammu and Kashmir were larger than some of the provinces, whereas some were tiny principalities. The rulers of the larger states had ambitions of becoming independent once the British withdrew from India. The majority of the population of some of the states was Hindu whereas the ruler was Muslim, like in Hyderabad and Junagarh, while in some of the states, the majority of the population was Muslim while the ruler was Hindu, like the state of Jammu and Kashmir. Although the partition plan had made no definite arrangements about the future of the princely states, however, it was provided that the rulers would accede to one of the two new dominions, India and Pakistan. There were some suggestions that the will of the people might be ascertained for the purpose of opting for India or Pakistan. However, Jinnah had rejected the suggestion, saying that the decision of the ruler was enough. According to the Mountbatten Plan, the ruler had only to take into consideration the contiguity which meant that a state located in the territory of one dominion could not accede to the other. However, three states became the cause of conflict between India and Pakistan. The states of Hyderabad and Junagarh were located within the territory of India. The situation of Jammu and Kashmir was different in the sense that it was located contiguous to the territory of both India and Pakistan.

The anti-feudal movement in Jammu and Kashmir had been led by Sheikh Mohammad Abdullah of the Muslim Conference since the early Thirties. The Muslim Conference was close to the ideology of the Indian National Congress. Sheikh Abdullah, addressing the Muslim Conference on March 26, 1938, had said, "[F]irstly we must end communalism by ceasing to think in terms of Muslims and non-Muslims when discussing our political problems."[20] In 1939, the Muslim Conference named itself National Conference which helped it to unite all the people of the state in the struggle against the autocratic rule of the maharaja. Jinnah had visited Kashmir in the summer of 1944 to persuade Sheikh Abdullah to support the Pakistan movement but did not succeed. In 1944, the National Conference gave an outline of a socialist form of responsible government in Jammu and Kashmir, with the Maharaja, as the constitutional head of the state. It reflected a liberal and secular approach to politics which was entirely different from that of the Muslim League. The Constitution envisaged by the New Kashmir programme was based on equality of all citizens, irrespective of religion, race and nationality of birth in all spheres.[21]

On the eve of independence, the maharaja of Kashmir signed a Standstill Agreement with both India and Pakistan which meant that there would be no change in the situation till the Maharaja had made up his mind on the state to which he would accede to. In the meantime, communal riots had broken out in some of the borders districts of Jammu. Large scale infiltration had also started from Pakistan into Kashmir of criminal elements who were on a spree of looting and killing.[22] By the third week of October 1947, tribals from across the NWFP, obviously sponsored by Pakistani agencies, launched a massive aggression into the territory of Jammu and Kashmir.[23] The Maharaja's armed forces and his administration collapsed in the face of the attacks and he escaped to Jammu. It was in this situation that the Maharaja decided to accede to India and requested for help from New Delhi in the face of blatant aggression. It is well known that the Pathan attacks had been organised and led by Pakistan Army personnel. The Maharaja's accession to India has not been accepted by Pakistan, alleging that it was obtained through fraud and violence. Most legal authorities have accepted the legality of the accession.[24] The Maharaja also appointed an interim government headed by Sheikh Abdullah. After the accession, India attempted to persuade Pakistan to stop supporting the raiders, an appeal which was ignored by Pakistan. It was in this situation that India decided on December 27, 1947, to appeal to the United Nations.

The state of Junagarh, a comparatively small state located in what is now the state of Gujarat was another problem. The nawab of Junagarh acceded to Pakistan on August 15, 1947, against the wishes of the people. Later, however, the nawab fled to Pakistan while the then prime minister of the state requested the Government of India to take over the administration of the state. Pakistan accused India of committing naked aggression. Hyderabad was a different proposition.[25] India knew that the nizam of Hyderabad had ambitions to declare independence which was certainly not acceptable to India. New Delhi was patient and offered several options to the nizam for a satisfactory arrangement which would have safeguarded his position. However, under the Pakistani encouragement, no agreement could be possible except for New Delhi to take police action and integrate the state. Kashmir has become a perpetual symbol of Pakistan's feeling of injustice done to it by India. It has been called the "unfinished agenda of partition" and General Zia-ul-Haq called it the "core issue." If it is the unfinished agenda, which means that Pakistan has to complete this task, then unsurprisingly, India Pakistan relations through all the ups and downs of history since 1947 have revolved round this one issue. Pakistan has gone to war for Kashmir in 1947, 1965 and 1999. The controversies generated by the process of partition and the bitterness and rancour left by them, convinced the Pakistani elite that India had not accepted Pakistan and was out to undo it. Indians mourned partition while Pakistanis celebrated it; Indians were proud of the commonalties of culture in both countries while Pakistanis were embarrassed by such a proposition as it questioned the two nation theory. The question to ponder over is whether Kashmir is the cause of Pakistan's hostility to India or is Kashmir the product of Pakistan's enemy image of India?

Pakistan's Insecurity

Many of the issues which were the offshoots of the controversies described above like the Sir Creek, Siachin, Wullar Barrage, etc., were added to aggravate the hostility between the two countries. Pakistan being smaller in population and size, weaker in economic resources and military strength, developed a permanent feeling of insecurity and vulnerability in relation to India. This compelled it to join US sponsored military alliances. India and Pakistan had appeared on the scene when the world was divided into two camps. One was the camp of the Western countries led by the United States and the other was the socialist camp led by the Soviet Union. Whereas India chose to stay non-aligned with both the military camps, Pakistan decided to align itself with the Western bloc. There is evidence that Pakistan had contacted the United States as early as September 1, 1947, for military aid.[26] The respective choices reflected the world view of the leaders of the two countries, which has not changed in spite of the passage of so many decades. In the early Fifties, Pakistan joined the US sponsored military alliances SEATO (Southeast Asia Treaty Organisation) and the CENTO(Central Treaty Organisation) mainly to make up for its insecurity against India, while the United States claimed that the military alliances were aimed at the threat of Communist aggression. Obviously, there was no threat to Pakistan from Communism from any side. Pakistan perceived the threat from India. With its joining the US sponsored military alliances, Pakistan's military assumed greater importance in its power structure. American involvement in Pakistan became more visible and Pakistan's entanglement and commitment increased in this period.[27]

India had been able to frame its Constitution soon after independence which came into effect on January 26, 1950. The principles and the ideology of the Indian National Movement had made it clear that India would be a secular, democratic and parliamentary form of political system. Regular elections have been held since then which have demonstrated the strength and stability of India's democratic institutions. The leaders of the Muslim League had led the Pakistan movement on Islamic slogans, without doing any intellectual exercise as to what political system Pakistan would have. Jinnah had never used the term "Islamic state" though he repeatedly claimed that the Muslims demand Pakistan, where they could rule according to their own code of life and according to their cultural growth, traditions and Islamic laws. His address at the inaugural session of the Constituent Assembly of Pakistan in which he almost prescribed a secular system for Pakistan came as a bolt from the blue for the Islamic zealots. Attempts have been made to suppress it, interpolate it and to ignore it.[28] Jinnah had deliberately played down the Islamic content of Pakistan in order to present the Pakistan demand not only in terms of modern political parlance and phraseology but also in terms of universally acceptable principles of nationhood.[29] Even Iqbal had supported the secular system of Turkey because, according to him, Islam does not prescribe any specific system of polity which falls under the temporal affairs of life.[30] Pakistan was understood by the common mass of Muslims as an Islamic state where justice would prevail and by the rising middle classes where there would be no competition from the well entrenched Hindu businessmen, etc. At first, the Muslim League leaders paid lip-service to Islam. In 1949, the Pakistan Constituent Assembly adopted the Objective Resolution which provided that Muslims shall be enabled to order their lives, in the individual and collective spheres, in accordance with the teachings and requirements of Islam. This was not meant to make Pakistan a theocracy as stated by the then Prime Minister of Pakistan, Liaquat Ali Khan. It was, in fact, meant to steal the thunder of the *mullahs'* sails. The *Ulema*, who had opposed Pakistan, were claiming that since Pakistan had been promised to be an Islamic state, the same needed to be built now. By 1952, the Bengali language movement erupted in East Pakistan. The Pakistani elite, instead of meeting the demand, decided to meet it by the slogan "Islam in danger."[31] However, when the document of the Constitution was ready, the then the Governor General, Ghulam Mohammad dissolved the Constituent Assembly in 1953, an unprecedented and unconstitutional action that had the full support of the military and its Comander-in-Chief (C-in-C), General Ayub Khan. This may be considered as the beginning of the military's alliance with the bureaucracy. The Governor General, Ghulam Mohammad, forced the then Prime Minister, Mohammad Ali Bogra, on the threat of dismissal and arrest, to reconstitute his government in which General Ayub Khan was inducted as the minister of defence while retaining his position as the C-in-C of the army.[32] It took a while for the new Constituent Assembly to come into being and draft the 1956 Constitution. The elections under the new Constitution were slated for 1959 but in early October 1958, General Ayub Khan launched the military coup and President Iskander Mirza declared Martial Law and abrogated the Constitution. Within a few weeks, President Mirza was sent into exile to the UK and Ayub Khan appointed himself the president. Scholars have argued that in Pakistan, effective power within the state apparatus lay in the hands of the military-bureaucratic oligarchy from the very inception of the state, rather than with the political leadership. The coup of 1958 was merely a formalisation of the real situation.[33]

The Praetorian State

Pakistan has been ruled directly or indirectly by the military for most of the period since independence. In fact, the first Martial Law was imposed in Lahore on March 6, 1953, during the anti-Ahmediya agitation. The circumstances that led to the declaration of Martial Law were "the complete breakdown of the administrative machinery and total collapse of civil power."[34] The Martial Law administrator was General Azam Khan who controlled the mass violence against the Ahmediya community within a few hours but later he took over some of the functions of the civil authorities like the cleaning of the drains and managing the traffic. The 1953 Martial Law in Lahore has been considered the key-stone in the arch of military coups in Pakistan.[35]

General Ayub Khan ruled for four years as the Martial Law administrator. He believed that the Western type of democracy did not suit the psyche of the people of Pakistan and, therefore, he enforced the Basic Democracy. It was the period when some kinds of controlled democracy were in fashion viz., the Guided Democracy of Sukarno in Indonesia and the Panchayat Democracy of King Mahendra in Nepal. A new Constitution was prepared and enforced the 1962 Constitution. Ayub's system of Basic Democracy has come to be called "constitutional autocracy." The general during his rule enforced some progressive laws, notable among them being the Muslim Family Laws Ordinance, 1961.This measure marked the high-point of Islamic modernism in Pakistan and was arguably the greatest innovation of the Ayub era. Ayub had also introduced land reform; however, the land ceiling had been kept so high that it did not have any impact.[36] The Muslim Family Laws Ordinance was opposed by the *Ulema* at that time but Ayub stood up to the pressure. The ordinance also survived General Zia's Islamisation in the Eighties and it is still on the statute book of the country.

General Ayub Khan also launched the 1965 India-Pakistan War, the second Pakistani attempt to seize Kashmir by force. The short and sharp conflict with India in the Rann of Kutch had encouraged General Ayub Khan to believe that if the Kashmir problem had to be solved, then the Kutch strategy had to be followed because the international arbitration after Kutch had gone in Pakistan's favour. He was encouraged in this misadventure by Zulfikar Ali Bhutto.[37] The then C-in-C of the Pakistan Army General Mohammad Musa, had his reservations about the success of the plan.[38] The war ended in a stalemate. It did not bring Pakistan any closer to the solution of the problem of Kashmir. The 1965 War was the high water mark of General Ayub's regime; thereafter his decline began which ended in his downfall as the result of a country-wide mass movement against his rule and for the restoration of democracy in 1968-69. He was succeeded by General Yahya Khan who conducted the first free and fair election for the National Assembly which was also to frame the new Constitution of Pakistan. The election produced the mandate in favour of the Awami League, which had led the autonomy movement in East Pakistan, and rightfully should have been allowed to form the government. Any constitutional arrangement in which Bengalis enjoyed a majority, to which they were rightfully entitled, was not acceptable to the civil bureaucracy and the defence establishment from the early days of Constitution-making in the country.[39] The political crisis provoked the civil war after the army attacked the Bengali nationalists. The Indian Army had to go in support of the Bengalis. The war ended after the defeat of the Pakistani armed forces and the emergence of independent Bangladesh. The India-Pakistan Shimla Agreement in July 1972 not only provided for the release of about one hundred thousand prisoners of war but it also laid the ground for the future relationship between the two countries. Pakistan's military was discredited after the fall of Dhaka. Zulfikar Ali Bhutto, leader of the Pakistan People's Party, took over from the discredited General Yahya Khan when Pakistan was reeling under defeat and humiliation. He took steps to punish those military leaders who were responsible for the fiasco in East Pakistan. However, he did not do much lest the military step into politics again. On the contrary, he promised to make the Pakistan Army the strongest in Asia. It was the Pakistan Army that proved to be his nemesis. He was toppled in a military coup by General Zia-ul-Haq in 1977 and hanged on the charge of murder in April 1979.

General Zia-ul-Haq had no legitimacy whatsoever, and, therefore, he used Islamisation and the focus on the issue of Kashmir to gain the support of the religious lobby. It was during his regime that Pakistan became the frontline state in the American campaign against the Soviet intervention in Afghanistan. He promoted religious parties, sectarian groups and supported *madrassas* which became the factories for producing *jihadis* for fighting in Afghanistan and in the state of Jammu and Kashmir. His policy in Afghanistan had an Indian dimension also. He thought that a friendly regime in Kabul would give Pakistan strategic depth in case of a confrontation with India. Rigid interpretations of Islamic injunctions and jurisprudence were introduced during the eleven years of the Zia regime. The Deobandi *Ulema* and the Jamaat-i-Islami intelligentsia guided his brand of Islamisation.[40] Over the years, as a result of the *mullahs'* successful bargaining and the military's tacit and overt support, religious activism has become a function of the Pakistani state.[41]

The two terms each of the governments of Benazir Bhutto and Mian Nawaz Sharif respectively from 1988 to 1999 were democratic in name only as by that time, the military had become the final arbiter in all national decision-making. This situation was given the informal institutional sanction in the shape of the 'troika,' comprising the president, the prime minister and the army chief at the apex of the power structure. Mian Nawaz Sharif's second term also saw the third Kashmir War in Kargil launched by the Pakistan Army in the summer of 1999. Prime Minister Sharif had denied at the time that he had been briefed by the army about its plans to occupy the Kargil heights. In any case, there is no denying that it was General Musharraf's war for he took over power by toppling Nawaz Sharif a few months after the Kargil War of October 1999.The Kargil misadventure failed just as the two earlier wars for Kashmir had ended in a fiasco. No benefit came to Pakistan from what had initially been projected as an act of military brilliance. Losing both military and political battles, Pakistan's position had become unsustainable.[42] General Musharraf's coup showed that the civilian government which had been elected by a two-thirds majority could not withstand the power of the military. General Musharraf's regime is the fourth military regime in the history of Pakistan. All four military rulers had given almost the same reasons for their takeover. All the four went back to square one and set about creating a new constitutional and political system in the country. Ayub set up the Basic Democracy system, Yahya Khan conducted the election but ended in a civil war, Zia-ul-Haq set about Islamising the country, and now General Musharraf has also created a façade of democracy.

Military's Corporate Interests

The military during the decades of its rule in the country has developed a vested interest in remaining in power. It was during the Ayub regime in the late Fifties and Sixties that Ayub began the practice of inducting military officers in lucrative civilian jobs. This system was continued by General Zia on a much larger scale. Musharraf has sent about 500 uniformed officers in control of government agencies and state run corporations.[43] There has been a tradition of awarding agricultural land to military personnel which has been continuing since the British regime and which has now reached scandalous levels when the best possible land, particularly the newly reclaimed land, has been awarded to military personnel and foundations for a pittance.[44] The armed forces have expanded their role in business and industry. The army's own departments are involved in civilian road construction, engineering projects, power projects, etc. The military's logistics cell is not only used for military transport but also for civilian transport. The Pakistan Ordnance Factories (POF) produces goods for the military but also for civilian use which are also exported. Every military has a charitable trust which is normally set up for the welfare of the retired military personnel. But Pakistan has three: the army runs the Fauji Foundation, the air force the Shaheen Foundation and the navy has the Baharia Foundation. The Fauji Foundation has acquired many industrial concerns and become one of the largest industrial concerns in Pakistan. The total assets value of the Fauji Foundation and its various projects in 1996 was Rs. 8,005 million.[45] Naturally, all these assets which benefit the large military establishment would be at risk in case a civilian democratic regime comes to power. Any situation which reduces the military establishment would not be tolerated. The conclusion is that the Pakistan's entrepreneurial army, which is gripping and penetrating national institutions would not back off from the country's political scenario.[46]

There has been some improvement in the relations between India and Pakistan during the last two years. Two phases of the composite dialogue have been completed on a positive note. Many confidence-buildings measures (CBMs) have been taken which have brought relief to large sections of the divided families of Jammu and Kashmir on both sides of the Line of Control (LoC). Some other humanitarian CBMs like the agreements on the question of missing fishermen, prisoners, and new bus connections have also been welcomed on all sides. Yet there has been no progress on any of the components of the composite dialogue like the issues of Jammu and Kashmir, Siachen, Sir Creek, Wullar Barrage, and expansion of trade, etc.[47] It is clear that as long as the military in Pakistan remains in control of the levers of power, there is little hope of any breakthrough in the relations between India and Pakistan.

Notes

1. Madan Gopal, *Indian Muslims: A Political History (1858-1947)* (Bombay: Asia Publishing House, 1964), p.91.
2. Gopal, Ibid., p.109.
3. Yunas Samad, *A Nation in Turmoil: Nationalism and Ethnicity in Pakistan 1937-1958* (New Delhi: Sage Publications, 1995), p.97.
4. Wilfred Cantwell Smith, *Modern Islam in India* (London: Victor Gollancz, 1946), p.202.
5. Ziya-ul-Hasan Faruqi, *Deoband School and the Demand for Pakistan* (Bombay: Asia Publishing House, 1963), p.124.
6. Husain Haqqani, "Partition is History, Leave it in the Past," *Indian Express*, June 9, 2005. Reprinted in www.carnegieendowment.org/publications/
7. P. Hardy, *The Muslims of British India* (Cambridge: Cambridge University Press, 1972), p.228.
8. Rafiq Zakaria, *Rise of Muslims in Indian Politics* (Bombay: Somaiya Publications Pvt Ltd, 1970), p.12.

9. Bimal Prasad, *Pathways to India's Partition: Volume I: The Foundations of Muslim Nationalism* (New Delhi: Manohar, 1999), p.31.
10. www.thefridaytimes.com. September 3, 2003.
11. Mohammad Aslam Khan Khattak, *A Pathan Odyssey* (Oxford: Oxford University Press, 2004), p. 14.
12. Khalid Bin Sayeed, *Pakistan: The Formative Phase 1857-1948* (Karachi: Oxford University Press, 1992), p.145.
13. Ayesh Jalal, *The Sole Spokesman* (Cambridge: Cambridge University Press, 1985), pp.198-199.
14. Jalal, Ibid., p.189.
15. *The Friday Times*, September 3, 2003.
16. Cited in Rafiq Zakaria, *The Price of Partition* (Mumbai: Bharatiya Vidya Bhavan, 1998), p.143.
17. Ijaz Husain, *Kashmir Dispute: An International Law Perspective* (Lahore: Service Book Club, 2000), p.111.
18. Zakaria, n.16, p.169.
19. Sreedhar and John Kaniylil, *Indo-Pak Relations: A Documentary Study* (New Delhi: ABC Publishing House, 1993), pp. 206-210.
20. Lars Blinkenberg, *India-Pakistan: The History of Unsolved Conflicts* (Munkgaard: Dansk Udenrigspolitisk Instituts, 1972), p.65.
21. Sisir Gupta, *Kashmir: A Study of India Pakistan Relations* (New Delhi: Asia Publishing House, 1967), p.69.
22. Pakistan claimed that a revolt against the maharaja had already erupted in Poonch before he had signed the Instrument of Accession. See Husain, n.17, p.76.
23. Ayesha Jalal, *The State of Martial Rule* (Cambridge: Cambridge University Press, 1990), p.58.
24. Blinkenberg, n.20, p.91.
25. Blinkenberg, Ibid., p.98.
26. M.S. Venkataramani, *Pakistan mein Amerika ka kirdar* (Lahore: Avon Corporation, 1988), p.17. Translated by Qazi Javed.
27. Hamid H. Kizilbash and Khawar Mumtaz, *Changes in US Foreign Policy and Pakistan's Options* (Lahore: South Asia Institute, University of Punjab,1976), p.3.
28. Sharif al Mujahid, *Quaid-i-Azam Jinnah: Studies in Interpretation* (Karachi: Quaid-i-Azam Academy, 1981), pp.229-277.
29. Ibid., p.237.
30. www.dawn.com, January 1, 2002.
31. Hamza Alavi, "Social Forces and Ideology in the Making of Pakistan," *The Friday Times*, December 6-12, 2002.
32. *Dawn* (Karachi edition), August 11, 1957.
33. Hamza Alavi, "Class and State" in Hasan Gardezi and Jamil Rashid, eds., *Pakistan the Roots of Dictatorship: The Political Economy of a Praetorian State* (New Delhi: Oxford University Press, 1983), p.65.
34. Rajendra Sareen, *Pakistan-The India Factor* (New Delhi: Allied Publishers Private Ltd, 1984), p.147.

35. *Defence Journal* (Karachi), November 1957.
36. Ian Talbot, *Pakistan: A Modern History* (New Delhi: Oxford University Press, 1998), pp.165-166.
37. Hasan Abbas, *Pakistan's Drift into Extremism* (New Delhi: Pentagon Press, 2005), p.45.
38. General (Retd.) Muhammad Musa, *My Version* (Lahore: Wajidalis, 1983), p.23.
39. Jalal, n.23, p.175.
40. "Pakistan: The Mullahs And The Military," International Crisis Group Asia Report No.49.
41. Ibid., p. 22.
42. Ahmad Faruqui, *Rethinking the National Security of Pakistan* (Aldershot: Ashgate Publishing Company, 2003), p.16.
43. www.satribune.com/archives/oct 7_13_02
44. Hasan-Askari Kazmi, *Military, State and Society in Pakistan* (London: Macmillan Press Ltd, 2000), p.236.
45. Kazmi, Ibid., p.237.
46. Ali Waqar, "Army Will Not Leave Politics: Tariq Ali," *Daily Times*, October 14, 2005
47. www.dawn.com/2005/09/10/op

Engaging Pakistan: From the NDA to the UPA

Malini Parthasarathy

Daunting Historical Baggage

Deeply embedded as it is in the historical consciousness of the people of the subcontinent, replete with memories of shared living and the painful experience of an acrimonious divide, the subject of the relationship between the two countries, India and Pakistan, continues to be seen as a matter of contention. It remains an issue gingerly approached by governments on both sides of the border, and, unfortunately so, in the eyes of the public in both countries, most often its handling is regarded as one of the key tests of the particular regime's nationalist credentials or political worthiness. This point requires underlining and scrutiny—the peculiarity that 60 years after India and Pakistan became independent states, the historical overhang of mutual bitterness and suspicion continues to cast an undesirable shadow on the efforts to pursue creative and forward-looking political approaches on either side. Otherwise imaginative and sensitive individuals with outstanding leadership abilities are overtly transformed into cautious and defensive politicians, afraid to break new ground in this one arena of bilateral relations. What is it that makes our politicians and leaders so afraid to tread new ground? Why does a Vajpayee or Musharraf have to encase and enmesh his ideas or initiatives in a web of tired rhetoric and belligerent posturing even as these new creative and promising formulations are unveiled, merely to ensure that his own personal credibility in the eyes of the people remains undented by the suggestion that he might be "going soft" on the other side? Why do the tentative overtures made by one side to the other have to periodically alternate with strident posturing? If the April 2005 Summit meeting between India's Prime Minister Manmohan Singh and Pakistan's President Musharraf seemed to open up fresh political space, the tenor of the New York encounter between the two, later in September 2005, seemed to have relapsed into the old crusty testiness and contentiousness.

The most striking example of the timorousness that prevails in the political approach to the subject in recent times was the launch of the Gujral Doctrine in January 1997 which won much international acclaim for its undertaking that India would not insist on reciprocity in its dealings with its smaller neighbours, yet did not include Pakistan in the ambit of the new promised benevolence. The ironic part was that the then Prime Minister, I.K.Gujral was perhaps one of the few Indian politicians most empathetic to the cause of better relations with Pakistan and was deeply committed to the project of healing the bitterness with India's estranged twin, yet given the historically loaded political context of the bilateral relationship, refrained from making what could have been a potentially radical gesture. It was, of course, another matter that Gujral did go on to initiate a round of creative diplomacy with Pakistan's leadership, setting a more expansive framework for the reconciling of perceptions on the bilateral agenda. The point is that despite the latent desire of leaders on both sides of the border to move forward and offer "out-of-the-box" approaches to the various issues on the agenda, the inhibiting factor of the daunting historical baggage of mutual mistrust, kept alive too, in generous measure by cautious bureaucracies on either side, remains a barrier to creative political initiatives such as the Lahore Agreement gaining momentum as a catalyst for consolidation of the process of normalisation.

The same may be said for Pakistani leaders as well. Whether it be a Benazir Bhutto, a Nawaz Sharif or a Pervez Musharraf, each of whom was evidently eager to make a mark for herself or himself as someone committed to warmer relations with India, any attempt to break free of the traditional mould of the approach to the bilateral relationship, particularly the all-consuming focus on Kashmir, had to be carefully strategised. Most often that strategy would be to offer a new peace offering but ensure that it was encased in a tissue of angry and combative rhetoric. An example would be General Musharraf's significant address on January 12, 2002, which perhaps signalled the most important strategic shift in Pakistan's official policy in recent times—putting conspicuous distance between the Pakistani state, widely regarded as a sponsor of the *jihadi* terrorism that was the bane of India's attempt to heal the situation in Jammu and Kashmir, and the *jihadi* groups. While it was the first time that a Pakistani leader acknowledged publicly and thereby gave credibility to India's charge that terrorism in Kashmir had the support of certain agencies in Pakistan, Musharraf knew that he was walking on thin ice and took care to avow afresh emphatically that Pakistan would continue its moral and political support to the Kashmir movement.

Thus, in attempting to generate fresh political thinking on this important task of narrowing the gap between the two countries, it would have to be first acknowledged that whatever be the political or ideological orientation of the governing formation in New Delhi and Islamabad, the issue of building closer ties with each other remains hostage to the political apprehension that this is a matter involving national honour and sovereignty, affecting the national psyche. The net result is that India-Pakistan relations are often imprisoned in the unyielding embrace of the old adage, "The more things change, the more they remain the same." The same complaints are dredged out with dreary predictability. On the Indian side, cross-border terrorism; on the Pakistani side, the failure to make progress in the dialogue on the "core issue of Kashmir." This results in a situation where despite history often being seen to have been made as in the signing of the Lahore Agreement, the Musharraf-Manmohan Singh Summits in Delhi in April 2005 and earlier in New York in September 2004, and in such historic steps as allowing a bus service between Delhi and Lahore, and more significantly, between Srinagar and Muzaffarabad, the overall framework of the bilateral relationship does not seem to lend itself to a dramatic transformation into a new paradigm of sustained cooperation, that would be more in tune with a radically changed global context.

Another piquant paradox that stands out in the recent developments in the arena of India-Pakistan relations is that leaders such as Atal Behari Vajpayee, a representative of a Hindu nationalist party traditionally seen as having reservations about the interlocutory worthiness of the estranged neighbour have taken the most creative strides forward in this regard. Likewise, Pakistan's President Pervez Musharraf, seen as the architect of Kargil, has undertaken significant efforts to clear the political context for forward movement in bilateral negotiations, thus, defying the stereotype that Pakistan's military establishment had stakes in preserving the hostility with India. It may be true that Vajpayee's own desire to "go down in history" as making peace with Pakistan and Musharraf's own inclination to prove his internal critics wrong, that as the leader of a military-led regime, he would be a hardliner in respect to normalising ties with India, might have fuelled their willingness to invest in the peace-making process and thereby injected fresh momentum into the context of the bilateral relationship.

The Consequences of Bin Laden

Yet it must be noted that the real pressure injected into the context of the bilateral relationship and which resulted in greatly enlarging the political space for constructive engagement between India and Pakistan was the dramatic change in the international context after the terrorist attacks by a group owing allegiance to the ominous Saudi-born Osama Bin Laden, in the United States on September 11, 2001. There is little doubt that the National Democratic Alliance's (NDA's) own political arguments in relation to Pakistan's strategic approach to the dispute on Kashmir, were unexpectedly buttressed by the weight of world opinion ranging firmly and categorically on one side against what it had newly confronted—the monstrosity of terrorism. The discovery that the Al Qaeda had a worldwide network, including the *jihadi* groups active in terrorist activities in Kashmir was a fortuitous circumstance coming to the rescue of the NDA regime's policy approach to Pakistan, which helped India to build a moral support base in the international arena against cross-border terrorism. Musharraf's own strategic decision to support the international coalition against terrorism may have given him tremendous credibility on the world stage, giving legitimacy to his leadership of Pakistan, until then, a hotly contested issue within his country, but put him on the back foot as regards Pakistan's covert support to *jihadi* terrorism in the Kashmir Valley, thus, allowing Indian diplomacy to regain some momentum.

It is instructive to note how much strategic and political space was wrested by India in relation to Pakistan in the wider context, not so much as a result of the Vajpayee-led regime's own diplomatic initiatives which, in any case, after the Kargil episode, had been placed on the backburner, but because of the sudden revulsion worldwide against *jihadi* terrorism. If Vajpayee's initial eagerness to make history reflected in the visit to Lahore and the unveiling of the Lahore Declaration in February 1999, after the Musharraf coup and Kargil, those inclinations had long been buried. The first tentative step to break the ice with the new military leader of Pakistan, General Musharraf — the Agra Summit of July 2001—ended as is well known in failure as fundamental differences between the two sides over cross-border terrorism and Kashmir stalled the launching of a fresh declaration. The Ministry of External Affairs spokesperson expressed "disappointment" that although a new journey had begun with Pakistan, "the destination of a joint statement has not been reached."[1] What was intriguing was that although the Agra Summit was said to have ended inconclusively, it was decided that the two sides would keep talking and that the tentative dialogue that had begun at long last since the unpleasant developments of the past—the military coup and Kargil—would not be snapped.

But after September 11, and the global campaign against "Islamic terrorists" got underway, the leaders of the NDA regime appeared to suddenly change their minds as to the necessity of engaging Pakistan, apparently banking on a conjecture that Pakistan would be identified as a source of Islamic terrorists and Musharraf would soon face international isolation. They clearly did not anticipate that Musharraf would make his own pragmatic leap towards strategic cooperation with the United States, which would obviously strengthen his own hand in the regional context. He made the tactically bold decision to distance himself from the Islamist extremists and jumped with alacrity onto the bandwagon of the international coalition led by the United States. The NDA regime calculated instead that Musharraf would be isolated in the new scheme of things, the then Home Minister, L.K. Advani and the then Defence Minister, George Fernandes, stepped up their critical and sharp rhetoric against "Pakistan-sponsored terrorism" in Kashmir and accused Pakistan of being a sponsor of *jihadi* terrorism.

It was clear that the September 11 incident had left its mark on the India-Pakistan engagement, with the issue of cross-border terrorism now becoming the central focus of the Vajpayee Administration's approach to relations with Pakistan. As it happened, the relationship with Pakistan plunged to new and abysmal depths after the terrorist attacks on the Srinagar Legislative Assembly in October 2001, to be followed by the deadly suicide attack on Parliament House in New Delhi that December after which India snapped all ties with Pakistan, including air links. Thus, the Vajpayee era which had seen the high point of Lahore which unveiled a new vision of cooperation and confidence-building between the two countries also saw the relationship at its lowest ebb by January 2002.

Vajpayee in his New Year Reflections of 2002 was unflinchingly clear that he saw Pakistan as the principal sponsor of the deadly terrorism that was trying to unravel the Kashmir Valley. "It often happens that the road to the future is rendered difficult by roadblocks placed by the past. One such roadblock for us, indeed, the biggest, is Pakistan's consistent and continuing anti-India policy, beginning with its refusal to accept the constitutionally validated and democratically endorsed accession of Jammu and Kashmir to India...," he said, asserting that "what they could not achieve through open military aggression, they never will achieve through cross-border terrorism."[2] He went on to link Pakistan with the December 13 terrorist attack on Parliament House: "The terrorist attack on our Parliament on December 13 has shown beyond a shadow of a doubt that the anti-India forces in Pakistan are prepared to wreak any havoc on our soil. It was an attack on our sovereignty, on our national self-respect and it was a challenge to our democratic system...".[3] He further warned that "...India does not want war....but we have a sovereign right to defend ourselves against cross-border terrorism which is a proxy war that is already thrust on us. Pakistan will be solely responsible for the consequences of encouraging terrorism against India and when expedient, turning a blind eye to terrorist groups with trans-national linkages operating from its soil..."[4]

India's campaign against Pakistan's perceived support to cross-border terrorism found a resonance internationally in the new context of the international campaign against terror. Thus, the United States and the United Kingdom became less ambiguous in their endorsement of India's position that complicating the attempt to address the dispute with Pakistan over Kashmir was the consistent support provided by forces in Islamabad to the terrorists operating in the Valley. The US and its allies, while appreciating the support extended by Musharraf to their coalition, made it clear to the Pakistani leader that he would have to stop supporting the *jihadi* groups in Kashmir. With the then US Secretary of State, Colin Powell urging Musharraf, on the one side, to end support to the *jihad* in Kashmir and Vajpayee, on the other, to deescalate the military build-up in the Valley, the UK was adding its voice. British Prime Minister Tony Blair, in a stopover in New Delhi on January 6, 2002, virtually endorsed India's stand that acts such as December 13 had to be completely rejected or condemned by Pakistan if there was to be a dialogue. Blair told reporters categorically at a Press conference in Delhi that "there are two sides to this equation. On the one hand, there has to be complete rejection of terrorism and end to support to it in any form. And then meaningful dialogue can begin."[5] Interestingly, Blair did not, as is often wont with most international leaders visiting Delhi and Islamabad, change his stance after meeting Musharraf in Islamabad. In a joint Press conference with Musharraf, Blair said that the international community expected the Pakistani leader to take action against five militant groups. The British prime minister also specifically referred to the two terrorist attacks in India—the October 1 attack on the Jammu and Kashmir Legislative Assembly in Srinagar and the December 13 attack on Parliament House in New Delhi—and emphasised that Pakistan should denounce such incidents in categorical terms.[6]

Thus, the pressure was mounting on Musharraf to distance himself unambiguously from *jihadi* terrorist groups, which were now seen worldwide as operating not only in Kashmir but as supporting flanks of the Al Qaeda, which greatly bolstered India's campaign against cross-border terrorism. It was largely in response to the international pressure that Musharraf made his famous January 12, 2002, address to the Pakistani people in which he banned the Jaish-e-Mohammed and the Lashkar-e-Tayyeba, the two terrorist groups which India had identified as behind the deadly attacks in India. While maintaining his stand that Pakistan would continue its moral and political support to the "Kashmir movement," Musharraf had in effect begun to distance himself from the *jihad* in Kashmir. In June 2002, the then US Deputy Secretary of State, Richard Armitage delivered to the Vajpayee government a "substantive commitment" from Pakistan on "permanently" ending cross-border infiltration across the Line of Control (LoC).[7] Of course, it was also indicated that the United States which was applying this pressure on Musharraf, so helpful to India's argument, likewise expected some "early reciprocal actions" on India's part in terms of a "step-by-step" deescalation of the stand-off.

What all this indicates is that the political and strategic space that seemed to have opened up in India's favour and placed it at a slight advantage in the global scales vis-à-vis Pakistan was largely the result of the changed international context which now saw terrorism, particularly Islamist terror, as a deadly enemy. As Musharraf began an intensive cooperation with the US and its allies in the battle with the Al Qaeda, it became increasingly difficult for him to sustain the pressure on India that was being sustained by Pakistan's covert support to the *jihadi* groups operating in the Kashmir Valley. The Pakistani president found himself more and more at loggerheads with the extremist Islamist groups in Pakistan and his consequent emphatic espousal of an argument that Pakistan must stand for "moderate Islam" rendered it much easier for India to reappraise its relationship with Pakistan and General Musharraf and thereby move forward. It is important to note that without the strategic decision of Pakistan's President Musharraf to project himself as leading Pakistan in the direction of a more "moderate Islamic state" and setting his face against religious extremism, a decision that reflected his own political quandary, being forced to align with the Western powers in the context of the upsurge of Al Qaeda terrorism, India might not have been able to make the headway with him that it has done.

In his musings on his website which he launched on February 24, 2005, Musharraf explains the thought process behind his decision.

> Nine Eleven came as a thunderbolt. I confronted acute challenges on one side, but also saw great opportunities on the other. I decided on the route of opportunities.....it was a tough decision to side with the US and the coalition to fight terrorism. Domestic opinion was divided but I saw that the vast majority of moderates were behind me, while the religious extremists got violently against....the schism between the minority of extremists and the vast majority of moderates kept increasing. The nation was faced with the challenges of sectarian and religious terrorism....Today, we face the uphill task of bringing about a societal renaissance by ridding Pakistan of the dominance of an extremist minority and establishing the unequivocal authority of the silent dormant, vast moderate majority...[8]

In a candid explanation of his willingness to distance himself from support to the Kashmir terrorists, Musharraf goes on to point out that with the US and coalition forces battling the Al Qaeda and the Taliban, Pakistan was faced with four serious accusations. These were: "(a) All the terrorist activity in Afghanistan had its base in Pakistan; (b) All the freedom struggle in Indian Held Kashmir was Cross-Border Terrorism from Pakistan; (c) All nuclear proliferation in the world had its source in Pakistan; (d) Pakistan is an intolerant militant extremist society." Thus, reasons the Pakistani president, he had " to battle against these accusations singlehandedly to cool international temperatures against Pakistan." He concludes that he had "succeeded considerably, but not sufficiently to project the reality of Pakistan as a progressive, moderate Islamic State."[9]

There is little doubt that without the fact of the international community having made clear that terrorism was now Enemy No 1, and its elimination the highest priority as far as the international agenda was concerned, India's argument that cross-border terrorism sponsored by Pakistan was an impediment in the normalisation of ties would not have received the worldwide empathy it did. India now had the strategic advantage that international pressure was working in its favour and Musharraf was now forced to distance himself, at least in an official or formal sense, from the terrorist campaign in Kashmir. In a sense, the success of the Vajpayee regime's strategic approach to Pakistan was largely based on a fortuitous circumstance that the international mood had changed after September 11, 2001, and there was now zero tolerance for terrorism or any such attempts to change the ground situation in any troubled area using violence and force.

But it was also clear that the same international pressure was working on New Delhi to be more responsive in its dealings with Islamabad. As much as the Western powers warmed up to the Pakistani president, there were subtle hints to India that it would have to shed some of its diplomatic rigidity towards Pakistan. The Vajpayee Administration sensed an opportunity to do just that. Its successful conduct of elections to the State Assembly in Jammu and Kashmir, which had received international approbation for being "free and fair" had been a shot in the arm for its strategic calculations in Kashmir. Vajpayee, evidently happy to use at long last his famed political skills and rekindle his own inclinations to build a historic peace with Pakistan, took the subcontinent by surprise when at a public rally in Srinagar, on April 18, 2003, he seemed to use the forum to announce his government's desire to restart talks with Pakistan. In a significant gesture to Musharraf that India now saw him as an interlocutor that it could do business with, Vajpayee recounted how he had made efforts to build a harmonious relationship with Pakistan. "As prime minister of the country, I wanted to have friendly relations with our neighbours and I went to Lahore. But it was returned with Kargil. We still continued and invited General Pervez Musharraf to Agra but again failed....We are again extending a hand of friendship but hands should be extended from both sides. Both the sides should decide to live together. We have everything which makes us to have good relations."[10] He was also careful not to jettison India's negotiating premise that cross-border terrorism would have to end and the terrorist training camps in Pakistan-Occupied Kashmir dismantled if there were to be meaningful talks. At a Press conference the next day, at the end of his visit to Srinagar, Vajpayee reiterated his desire for peace but laced it with a cautionary note, "We want to tread the path of friendship but a lot depends on Pakistan's response. I reiterate that only talks can resolve all the issues."[11] What was remarkable was the turnaround in India's diplomatic stance. Until then, Delhi had maintained that talks would be of no use in the context of cross-border terrorism but now the insistence had been diluted and the emphasis was now on restarting the dialogue.

Resuming the Composite Dialogue

As is well known, India and Pakistan moved through the year to restart the confidence-building process which included restoration of rail, road and air links, the appointment of fresh high commissioners on either side, the revival of sporting links, including cricket, with both sides taking care to express periodically their reservations. On the one hand, India maintained that progress on the confidence-building measures (CBMs) would have to be in tandem with "firm and credible action" on Pakistan's part against cross-border terrorism and to "dismantle the infrastructure of support to terrorism."[12] Pakistan for its part was careful to remind the world that its participation in a process of confidence-building would not in any way dilute its insistence on a dialogue on the "core issue" of the status of Kashmir. But the welcome point was that the dialogue which had gone into a hiatus since December 2001 was now on and there seemed to be no turning back. Thus, after the high point of the Lahore Declaration which had committed India and Pakistan to "intensify their efforts to resolve all issues, including the issue of Jammu and Kashmir" and more specifically to "intensify their composite and integrated dialogue process for an early and positive outcome of the agreed bilateral agenda,"[13] New Delhi and Islamabad were now poised to pick up the threads of what was a promising track to normalisation. For Musharraf, who knew that the Vajpayee Administration had warmed to the former Prime Minister, Nawaz Sharif as an interlocutor they could trust, particularly being the co-architect of the path-breaking Lahore Declaration, it was a triumph of sorts. He was now being invited to a substantive engagement with India on a sustained basis.

It was clear that the Vajpayee Administration wanted to be perceived as being responsive to the positive signals from the other side. In late November 2003, India and Pakistan finally agreed to a formal ceasefire along the International Border (IB), the Line of Control (LoC) and the Actual Ground Position Line (AGPL) in Jammu and Kashmir, in what was described as the first such comprehensive agreement of its kind.[14] What was significant was that while the Vajpayee government took care to warn that the ceasefire that was being proposed would not include terrorists violating the sanctity of the LoC, it appeared keen to signal that it wanted to turn the page with Islamabad. Asked about Pakistan's "unreliability" in the past, the then Defence Minister, George Fernandes, traditionally regarded as a hardliner on relations with Pakistan observed that " in relations between nations there comes a time when one does find a need to come to terms and resolve whatever problems that exist. And therefore, for the two neighbours like India and Pakistan, when the Prime Minister (Vajpayee) made a third offer, despite whatever may have happened in the interregnum, the latest response by the Pakistan Prime Minister shows a lot of hope. Therefore, one should not take it lightly and dismiss it."[15]

The determination on both sides to take the bilateral relationship back to the high road of peace had Vajpayee making another historic trip to Pakistan, this time to Islamabad, where, on the sidelines of the South Asian Association for Regional Cooperation (SAARC) Summit in January 2004, Vajpayee and Musharraf formally launched another phase of the peace-building process between India and Pakistan by a joint statement on January 6, announcing the commencing of a process of "composite dialogue" in February 2004. In another significant indication of Musharraf's determination to take Pakistan out of the strategic trap of linkages with extremist forces, the language of the Joint Statement appeared to accommodate more than halfway India's concerns with regard to cross-border terrorism. "Prime Minister Vajpayee said that in order to take forward and sustain the dialogue process, violence, hostility and terrorism must be prevented. President Musharraf reassured Prime Minister Vajpayee that he will not permit any territory under Pakistan's control to be used to support terrorism in any manner."[16] Of course, Pakistan's traditional emphasis on the Kashmir issue was included. "President Musharraf emphasised that a sustained and productive dialogue addressing all issues would lead to positive results...... The two leaders are confident that the resumption of the composite dialogue will lead to peaceful settlement of all bilateral issues, including Jammu and Kashmir, to the satisfaction of both sides."[17] It was interesting that for Vajpayee, personally, who made no secret of his desire to be remembered in Indian history as the leader who brought peace with Pakistan, his tenure as prime minister had two high points as regards relations with Pakistan. If there was the crowning moment of the Lahore Declaration at the beginning of his innings, which saw India and Pakistan commit themselves after a long while to a grand vision of sustained cooperation towards the goal of a final peace between themselves, at the end of his term, the January 6 statement which restarted the composite dialogue, seemed to put India and Pakistan back on the high road to peace.

It was indeed a vivid illustration of the contradictions that underlie the context of India-Pakistan relations. The NDA, led by the Bharatiya Janata Party (BJP), a party that had high political stakes in maintaining pressure on Pakistan, feeding as it would have to, the traditional suspicions and misgivings of its Hindu nationalist constituency, had the opportunity of ushering in landmark agreements opening up fresh political and diplomatic space enabling India and Pakistan to reengage each other in a constructive manner and forward-looking direction. That this could happen was clearly a consequence of the strong international campaign against terrorism which compelled Pakistan's Musharraf to change political direction and steer his country towards becoming a "moderate Islamic state." Yet it was also a result of Vajpayee's personal inclinations to make history and end an unpleasant chapter in India's post-independence history. Those inclinations drove Vajpayee to transcend his own particular political circumstances and context in reaching out to Pakistan. So pleased was the former prime minister with the progress that had been made in this difficult arena, that addressing a public meeting in Jammu in April 2004, just before the national elections, he said: "Weapons cannot solve problems between the two nations. Cannon shells have now been replaced with cricket balls."[18]

Moving Ahead with the UPA

The Congress-led United Progressive Alliance (UPA), at the helm since May 2004, has fewer ideological or political compulsions that could come in the way of its formulating a comprehensive policy approach to relations with Pakistan. But it is clear that the Congress and its Prime Minister, Manmohan Singh who appears committed to accelerating the peace process with Pakistan, are still guarded and cautious in their policy formulations, preferring an incremental approach rather than a sweepingly strategic shift from the NDA's policies in this regard.

Given that the UPA led by the Congress is essentially a coalition of centrist and left-oriented political forces, the democratic and political space to chart a more forward-looking and expansive diplomatic course with Pakistan undeniably exists. It is also clear that the UPA intends to stay the course with respect to the pursuit of the composite dialogue. Prime Minister Manmohan Singh and his government were quick to indicate their commitment to the composite dialogue process by adhering to the schedule of the various secretary-level meetings that had been outlined as necessary steps of the dialogue process in February 2004, including the expert-level talks on nuclear CBMs. One heartening feature of the new phase was that during the foreign secretary talks in June 2004, soon after the UPA took over, apart from the foreign secretaries of both countries "expressing satisfaction over the ongoing process of dialogue and confidence-building between the two countries,"[19] New Delhi submitted to Islamabad a set of Kashmir-specific proposals on transport links, trade, cultural cooperation, the environment and people-to-people contacts. This gesture went some distance in acknowledging Islamabad's emphasis on keeping Kashmir in focus in the dialogue process, even as it was meant as a signal to the Kashmiri people that New Delhi was sincere in its intention of healing the ground situation in the Valley.

The second reaffirmation of the Manmohan Singh Administration's earnestness in sustaining the dialogue with Pakistan was, of course, the meeting that the prime minister had with the Pakistani President Musharraf in New York, in September 2004 where it was categorically asserted that both leaders "reiterated their commitment to continue the bilateral dialogue to restore normalcy and cooperation between India and Pakistan."[20] More importantly, the continuity of the composite dialogue process put in place in January 2004 when Vajpayee visited Islamabad was underlined with the two leaders stating that "in the spirit of the Islamabad joint Press statement of January 6, 2004, they agreed that CBMs will contribute to generating an atmosphere of trust and mutual understanding so necessary for the well-being of the peoples of both countries." It was evident that India and Pakistan saw the Manmohan-Musharraf meeting as being an important landmark in the process of confidence-building between India and Pakistan. In Musharraf's own words: "The New York joint statement between me and Prime Minister Manmohan Singh finally is a quantum leap forward towards resolution of all disputes, including the core issue of Jammu and Kashmir. There is light visible at the end of the tunnel."[21]

It was evident that the optimism and the forward-looking spirit that now prevailed in the relationship was enduring enough to manifest in a visit to

Delhi in April 2005 by Pakistan's President Musharraf to watch India-Pakistan cricket, an opportunity the Pakistani leader seized upon to suggest to the Indian government that a summit be held between the two leaders. While an exuberant Musharraf declared that his hand was "extended to clap," Manmohan Singh was similarly warm in emphasising that while "we cannot rewrite the past but we can build a more secure future."[22]

But it was also apparent that both leaders were reluctant to abandon the frameworks of their respective strategic discourses. For his part, Musharraf continued to highlight the centrality of Kashmir in all the efforts at conflict resolution by calling for a display of "courage and flexibility" on the part of the leadership to bring about "a permanent resolution of all disputes, including Kashmir." Manmohan Singh reiterated India's stance that "practical ways and means "must be found to resolve all issues between the two countries "in a reasonable, pragmatic manner, cognisant of ground realities."[23]

Yet while the two sides appeared to be cautious in their formulations, it was clear that a serious attempt was being made on the ground to bring fresh air into a stale context. India made it clear that it had no reservations about Musharraf meeting the Hurriyat leaders, reflecting a new confidence in its own handling of the situation in Jammu and Kashmir. Musharraf seemed to step back from his earlier insistence that progress on other issues was tied to progress on the Kashmir dispute, even as both sides agreed to step up bus and rail links, freer movement across the Line of Control in Kashmir, and significantly seemed to have a shared appreciation of the proposals for gas pipelines from Iran and Turkmenistan via Pakistan to India. What stood out in the summit meeting of April 2005 was that both countries chose to underline that they had "determined that the peace process was now irreversible."[24]

Yet indicating once again the inherent fragility of the engagement between India and Pakistan, given the underlying political fears on both sides, of being perceived by their domestic constituencies as "going soft" on each other, barely five months later, when Prime Minister Manmohan Singh met President Musharraf over dinner in New York on September 14, there was a new chill in the air. If the joint statement issued afterwards dutifully reaffirmed the two leaders' "commitment to the decisions taken at the meeting in New Delhi" and paid homage to the concerns of both sides, avowing that they would not "allow terrorism to impede the peace process," on the one hand, and also expressing a commitment to ensure a peaceful settlement of all issues, particularly Jammu and Kashmir,[25] it was also clear that the familiar ghosts had reared their heads again.

Underscoring as it did, the vulnerability of the entente, held hostage as it is to a number of factors, including both countries' increasing proximity to the United States, the fact that both Musharraf and Manmohan Singh in their New York sojourn seemed to revert to their own national stereotyped positions, Musharraf raising the Kashmir issue in the UN General Assembly and Manmohan Singh pointedly reminding America and the international community in his various encounters in the United States of the image of Pakistan as a breeding ground for terrorism, shows that even as new ground is undeniably being broken in the relationship, the old roadblocks remain.

It is clear that Prime Minister Manmohan Singh and his colleagues in the UPA Administration who are politically free of the historical and ideological reservations that dogged the NDA's policy approach to Pakistan have a unique opportunity to tread a new path in the relationship. What are the pitfalls that could trip up the Manmohan Singh regime's strategic and diplomatic engagement of Pakistan? There seem to be a few roadblocks that must be got out of the way if history is to be made in this regard. The first is the danger of adopting a hide-bound approach to the diplomatic tasks ahead.

The first warning signal came in the early days of the Manmohan Singh Administration when the External Affairs Minister, K. Natwar Singh seemed to suggest that the Shimla Agreement would be the principal touchstone for the dialogue process. Given that much water has flowed under the bridge since Shimla, and much better frameworks are in place that provide comprehensive scope for a creative engagement of each other, this suggestion appeared to dampen spirits on both sides of the border. Natwar Singh's statement caused a flutter in Pakistan with its Foreign Minister, Khurshid Mehmood Kasuri saying pointedly in a statement that a "rhetoric restraint regime" must be observed to avoid misunderstanding and that if Shimla was invoked to move forward and find solutions, Pakistan had no problem but if it was being suggested for the purpose of freezing the Kashmir issue, it would not work. ...If one agreement were a panacea, we would have resolved our problems long ago...Instruments cannot be selectively invoked to shelve pressing problems. We must use statesmanship to resolve issues. And I believe that we are in the process of doing that."[26] Another stratagem from past Congress Party approaches to Pakistan which has long outlived its political utility in a radically altered global context was to revive the issue of American arms sales to Pakistan and factor it in as a caveat in the dialogue process. In December 2004, when US Defence Secretary Donald Rumsfeld visited New Delhi, India's "concern" over US arms supplies to Pakistan and its view that this would "affect the peace process" between India and Pakistan was conveyed to him by Defence Minister Pranab

Mukherjee. Whether reviving such old and crusted arguments serves any strategic or diplomatic purpose is unclear, especially since there is much scope in the changed context in the subcontinent to put in place new priorities of emphasis and indeed break new ground in bilateral relations.

What the UPA needs to guard against is the allowing of the old elements of traditional bureaucratic reserve to creep back into its policy-making which could prevent a potentially forward-looking and constructive engagement of Pakistan. By being overly cautious and retreating into cliched and bureaucratic formulations just to highlight its different political orientation, the UPA would be doing itself a disservice. If it does not imaginatively draw its policy approaches from the democratic and culturally pluralist wellsprings that are at the base of the UPA coalition, this could narrow the scope for creative diplomacy in a crucial phase. If the UPA takes into account the best strands of the earlier policy approaches while discarding some of the more politically questionable elements, and more important, is unafraid to take the dialogue forward in new directions, it has the chance to begin a new chapter in the subcontinent's history, truly ending more than five decades of what is an unnecessary estrangement.

Notes

1. C. Raja Mohan, "Kashmir, Cross-Border Terrorism Derail Talks," *The Hindu*, July 17, 2001.
2. Atal Behari Vajpayee, "We Shall Triumph Against Terrorism," New Year message published in *The Hindu* and other newspapers, January 1, 2002.
3. Vajpayee, Ibid.
4. Vajpayee, Ibid.
5. Atul Aneja, "India Could Resume Talks if Terrorism Ends: Blair," *The Hindu*, January 7, 2002.
6. B. Muralidhar Reddy, "Musharraf Willing to Address India's Concerns," *The Hindu*, January 8, 2002.
7. Raja Mohan, "Musharraf Vows to Stop Infiltration: Armitage," *The Hindu*, June 8, 2002. Armitage told reporters in New Delhi after meeting Vajpayee that in his talks with Pakistani leaders the day before, General Musharraf had pledged to "stop cross-border terrorism permanently."
8. Pervez Musharraf, "From the President's Desk"—Section on his website launched on February 24, 2005, detailing events and major decisions in his life. Available at http://www. Presidentofpakistan.gov.pk/From the Presidents Desk.aspx
9. Musharraf, Ibid. This section contains to date the most candid account of the reasoning behind Musharraf's decision to publicly commit himself to containing the *jihadi* terrorist groups operating in Kashmir.
10. Shujaat Bukhari, "PM Extends 'Hand of Friendship' to Pakistan," *The Hindu*, April 19, 2003.

11. Shujaat Bukhari, " Waiting for Pak Response to Offer of Friendship: PM," *The Hindu,* April 20, 2003.
12. Amit Baruah, "Pak must Take Credible Steps," *The Hindu,* May 8, 2003. The report quoted the Ministry of External Affairs (MEA) spokesman, in an official reaction to the Jamali proposals of May 6, 2003.
13. The Lahore Declaration, February 21,1999.
14. Amit Baruah, Sandeep Dikshit, "Ceasefire in Place," *The Hindu,* November 26, 2003. The report quoted the MEA spokesman's characterisation of the ceasefire agreement between India and Pakistan, taking effect from the midnight of November 25.
15. Sandeep Dikshit, "Guns Fall Silent Along Border," *The Hindu,* November 27, 2003.
16. India-Pakistan Joint Press Statement, Islamabad, January 6, 2004. Available at http://www.satp.org/satporgtp/countries/india/document/papers/indo_pak-6jan04.htm
17. Ibid.
18. Luv Puri, "Vajpayee for Permanent Peace with Pakistan," *The Hindu,* April 15, 2004.
19. Joint Statement issued by India and Pakistan after the two-day foreign secretary-level talks, June 28, 2004. Available at http://www.iiss.org
20. India-Pakistan Joint Statement, September 24, 2004, after the meeting of Prime Minister Manmohan Singh and President Pervez Musharraf in New York. Available at http://pmindia.nic.in/speech
21. Musharraf, n.8.
22. Harish Khare, "I Have Come with a Message of Peace," *The Hindu,* April 17, 2005.
23. Khare, Ibid.
24. India-Pakistan Joint Statement, April 18, 2005.
25. India-Pakistan Joint Statement in New York, September 14,2005
26. B. Muralidhar Reddy, "Kasuri Calls for 'Rhetoric Restraint Regime'," *The Hindu,* June 1, 2004.

Another Shot at Bilateralism?

Compulsions, Constraints and Calculations Behind the Peace Process

Sushant Sareen

Has Anything Changed?

What does it take for nation-states to renounce irredentism? Normally, nothing short of a cataclysmic event like a destructive war or a natural calamity of fearful proportions – an earthquake or a tsunami! Sometimes a military stalemate exhausts nation states and forces one or both to decide in favour of the benefits of peace over the cost of continuing conflict. In other cases, a comprehensive defeat on the battleground changes the objective conditions in a way that irredentist claims are put on the backburner until such time that they either cease to matter or else are raised when one state gets in a position to once again press its claims. There are also a few cases in which with the passage of time (normally a few hundred years), nation-states peacefully settle their claims over a territory they covet.

But what happens if none of the above conditions hold? In other words, what are the chances of a peace process between two contending nation-states succeeding if there has neither been a devastating war nor a comprehensive defeat of one country by another, neither of the two states is exhausted by the conflict nor has enough time passed for either state to enter into peace negotiations in a spirit of compromise because the 'core issue' is no longer a 'core issue', and a natural calamity is not seen as an opportunity to affect a paradigm change in relations but as an opportunity to maximise political capital? Can nation-states still change a policy objective which they consider cardinal to their existence without ground realities having changed? Can nation-states be rational and wise and change the course of their irredentist and revanchist policy without having gone through the paces necessary for affecting such a change?

The answers to the above questions lie at the core of any analysis of the peace process currently underway between India and Pakistan. The big question is: what are the prospects for a peace deal between the two countries with nothing material having changed on the ground as far as the 'core issue' of Jammu and Kashmir is concerned? Pakistan has not stopped coveting the Indian state. India appears to have no intention of compromising on either sovereignty or territory in Jammu and Kashmir. The *jihad* factory based in Pakistan is doing business as usual inside India. Pakistan is no longer internationally isolated. And with international aid flowing into the country, Pakistan is no longer facing the economic crunch that could have forced a major rethink in policy in that country. Pakistan continues to stymie Indian initiatives to improve relations through a slew of confidence-building measures (CBMs) designed to develop stakeholders in the peace process. A large section of the public in Jammu and Kashmir continues to be alienated and disaffected and India has still not managed to change the political climate in the state. There are still no significant political stakeholders in the peace process on either side. In a sense, all the factors that have led the problem in Jammu and Kashmir to erupt continue to remain in play.

And yet, some things have changed. For instance, there appears to be a change in the mindset of a large section of the public in both India and Pakistan. Significantly, this change has been witnessed among people who would earlier revel in demonising the other side and who had close linkages with the establishments in either country. Perhaps the starkest example of the changing mindset was the attitude of the spectators during the cricket series between India and Pakistan in the spring of 2004. The scenes that were witnessed during that landmark series were unimaginable until they happened. The fact that everyone – from the most well-heeled youngsters (who would have most certainly have family and friends from within the ruling establishment, including the army, bureaucracy, political and business elite) to the most humble – cheered India to victory, signalled a huge change in the mindset of the people in Pakistan.

Equally important has been the changing notion of security among influential sections of the establishments in both countries. The realisation that economic and human security is as important as military security makes it imperative to strike a balance between the two, something which is not possible in a state of perpetual conflict, especially with a country that is economically much stronger and can spend you into ruin. So does this mean that the establishments' mindset too has changed? If it has, then it would imply that rationality and wisdom have crept into policy-making and perhaps this will manifest itself after a lag.

Another very important change has been the end of the "Punjabi civil war." Not long back, it was the two Punjabs that defined the state of hostility between the two countries. But today, the peoples of the two Punjabs seem to be keener than anyone else in a cooperative relationship between India and Pakistan.

There is far greater interaction between the peoples of the two countries than at any time in the past six decades. Delegations of politicians, retired civil and military officials, journalists, academicians, lawyers, judges, businessmen, farmers, engineers, doctors are crossing the border practically every day. This civil society interaction has played a big role in changing the perceptions and mindsets on both sides. At times, it appears as though this civil society initiative is leading the governments by the nose and forcing them into adopting more flexible attitudes.

To be fair, the two governments have taken some remarkable initiatives over the last few years. The bus service across the Line of Control (LoC) and the opening of additional points along the LoC for providing relief and rehabilitation to the earthquake affected families, the agreement to reopen consulates in Mumbai and Karachi, the agreement to start a rail service between Rajasthan and Sindh, the commitment of both sides to the composite dialogue process despite nothing substantial having emerged out of it in the last couple of rounds of negotiations, the ceasefire along the LoC have all contributed in a major way to lending a momentum to the peace process.

Indeed, both sides seem to be showing greater flexibility than they have ever done in the past. For instance, India has given up its insistence on cessation of all cross-border terrorism before it entered into any sort of a dialogue with Pakistan. Even on the cross-LoC movement, India gave up its stand on the travel documents required for crossing the LoC. Pakistan too has shown flexibility and is no longer harping on the UN resolutions as the only solution to the issue of Jammu and Kashmir. Pakistan has also tightened the leash over the *jihadi* groups which were earlier operating with impunity. Perhaps the most striking example of Pakistan's flexibility is the Kashmir formulation of its military ruler, General Pervez Musharraf, who no longer treats Jammu and Kashmir as one entity but as seven regional units and who has spoken of making "borders irrelevant" as a possible solution to the dispute over Kashmir.

But despite all the positives in the equation, the negatives could still play the spoiler. The fact that the ground situation remains more or less the same means that there is a disconnect between overt postures and covert practices. May be this is a function of the lag of changing mindsets translating into changing policy. May be this is a function of the inability of the state to bottle up the monsters it has created in its phase of strategic overreach through the use of asymmetric warfare. Or perhaps the policy of wresting Kashmir remains in place and only the tactics and the strategy to achieve this objective have changed because of the changed domestic and international situation.

The Road to Bilateralism

Many in India see Pakistan's acceptance of a bilateral dialogue with India as a victory of India's long standing policy of not allowing any interference by extra-regional powers to intervene in South Asian disputes. On the face of it, Pakistan's engagement on a bilateral track with India was a sign of its failure to internationalise the Kashmir issue and its acceptance of the Indian position. Pakistan always opposed bilateralism because normally this suits the stronger country which can keep any countervailing force at bay through direct negotiations with a weaker country. On the other hand, a weaker country always wants international mediation because this way it manages to balance the power differential with the powerful country. A related problem for Pakistan has been that if it gives up its insistence on the UN resolutions on Kashmir, then it is left with no case on Kashmir. A bilateral process necessarily puts the UN resolutions on the backburner. But in a situation where Pakistan found no powerful backers for its insistence on implementation of the UN resolutions, coupled with assurances that India would engage Pakistan in serious and meaningful talks aimed at resolving the dispute over Jammu and Kashmir left Pakistan with no option but to enter into a bilateral track. But it would be taking a very simplistic view to conclude from this that Pakistan has accepted to play the game on India's terms.

Because of Pakistan's discomfort with the traditional definition of bilateralism, Pakistan evolved its own definition, which runs counter to how India defines bilateralism. Nearly six decades after partition, despite speaking the same language and vocabulary, the nuances of the words being used by one side are not understood by the other. It is almost as though the idiom used by the people and establishments of the two countries has changed so much that neither side understands nor is able to comprehend what the other side is saying. This is exactly what has happened in the case of bilateralism.

In India, we take bilateralism to mean that two countries sort out their issues between themselves and without involving any third party. The sum and substance of the Indian understanding of the term is that it junks the UN resolutions on Kashmir and avoids any international interference in the issue. This, in turn, helps India to maintain the status quo in Kashmir.

For Pakistan, bilateralism was defined first by Zulfikar Ali Bhutto way back in 1976. According to Bhutto:

> ...bilateral foreign policy means that there must be a minimum of reciprocity in bilateralism. If there is not a minimum of reciprocity in bilateralism, it

> cannot be called a bilateral foreign policy. That means there must be an agreement on certain fundamental matters. Otherwise, what is bilateralism? In that case, bilateralism is sterile. You cannot take pride in a bilateral foreign policy with your adversaries, whose interests conflict with your interests... If a State has a conflict of a fundamental nature with you, as for instance, it does, not recognise your frontiers, or it does not accept certain basic interests of Pakistan, you cannot say you have a bilateral relationship with that country.[1]

Bhutto's formulation holds true even today. General Pervez Musharraf has hinted this on more than one occasion. In fact, he has even said that if the bilateral track doesn't work (which according to Pakistan means that India doesn't agree to abandon Kashmir), then Pakistan will be forced to take the issue once again to the international community. But to be able to junk the bilateral track, Pakistan will have to show to the world that it is just not working, something which they cannot do at present simply because in the eyes of the world the bilateral track is proceeding smoothly.

If anything, the bilateral track suits Pakistan much more than India. For one, Pakistan has an exit route if the bilateral track doesn't deliver an agreement on Kashmir. Pakistan can always say that it tried bilateral talks with India with utmost sincerity but Indian insincerity left it with no choice but to go back to demanding international intervention in the Kashmir dispute. In international forums, Pakistan believes it enjoys greater sympathy than India, provided it can repair its image as an epicentre of Islamic terrorism and give the insurgency in Kashmir the colour of an independence struggle rather than an Islamic *jihad*. India, on the other hand, is loath to any international intervention, and this puts greater pressure on India to continue unveiling confidence-building measures that keep the Pakistanis engaged on the bilateral track and, at the same time, keep the rest of the world at bay.

From a purely tactical point of view also, bilateralism serves Pakistan's policy framework much better as it accords Pakistan an opportunity to try and change the status quo in Kashmir through the instrument of asymmetric warfare without any danger of international interference. After all, India cannot talk of bilateralism and, at the same time, want to involve the rest of the world in putting pressure on Pakistan to close down the *jihad* factory that is operating from there. Indeed, India has painted itself in a corner by taking its insistence on bilateralism to an extreme. Take, for example, the Indian aversion to any 'hyphenation' with Pakistan in its relations with the US. And yet, whenever an Indian meets an American, all that the Indian can talk about is Pakistan – US military and economic assistance to Pakistan, the insufficient pressure that the US is putting on Pakistan on the issue of "cross-border terrorism" and insisting the US declare Pakistan a terrorist state and the US plans to initiate political and social reforms inside Pakistan. Perhaps, India would be better able to achieve its objectives in Pakistan by insisting on 'hyphenation' rather than non-hyphenation!

Given the political, military and diplomatic benefits that 'bilateralism' bestows on Pakistan, it is somewhat surprising why instead of India, Pakistan has not insisted on the bilateral approach. The reason for this probably lies in the conflicting nature of relationship shared between India and Pakistan in which neither country believes that the policy of the other might actually work in its favour. Pakistan, therefore, always put its faith in third-party mediation and the UN resolutions. But towards the end of the 1990s, circumstances forced Pakistan to fall back on bilateral negotiations as the only way out of the *cul-de-sac* it found itself in on the issue of Kashmir. To its credit, Pakistan displayed great nimbleness in the conduct of its foreign policy and has always adjusted its policy to circumstances without necessarily changing its objectives.

Pakistan's strategic overreach and irresponsible adventurism in the realm of foreign policy through the use of the instrument of *jihad* had resulted in the country's diplomatic isolation. Hardly anyone – including China and the Islamic world – was willing to back Pakistan's position on Kashmir. Throughout the 1990s, Pakistan started being seen as a hotbed and exporter of Islamic terrorism, not just against India in Kashmir but also in many other parts of the world, including Bosnia, Middle East, Central Asia, Southeast Asia and, of course, Afghanistan. Within Pakistan, the *jihadi* groups were operating with impunity and were becoming more powerful by the day. The Pakistani state was fast losing its internal sovereignty to the radical Islamic groups.

The combination of diplomatic isolation and growing economic crunch forced Pakistan to reorient its policy on engaging India on a bilateral track, albeit one that was being nudged if not monitored and choreographed by a third party, namely, the US. This suited Pakistan because the use of *jihad* had served its purpose for the time being – it had brought international attention on the issue of Kashmir, which was increasingly being referred to as a "nuclear flashpoint." Pakistan could, therefore, afford to sweep the *jihad* factory under the carpet and keep it in reserve while it shifted gears and moved on the negotiating table with India. Any further continuation of unbridled *jihad* would only prove counter-productive, especially in a world that had 'changed' after 9/11.

While 9/11 was perhaps the single most important event that forced Pakistan to change its tactics and its strategy, if not its objective, there were some other significant events that both preceded and followed 9/11 that also pushed Pakistan to take the bilateral route. Among these were the nuclear tests in 1998, which for the first time brought the dissent against the national security model of the Pakistani state out in the open. The new security climate coupled with the economic sanctions that were imposed on an already struggling Pakistan economy led even mainstream commentators and analysts to advise the government to avoid getting into an unbridled arms race with India which would eventually bankrupt the country and to reappraise foreign and security policy. The Soviet syndrome started haunting many Pakistanis.

The sense of security lent by the nuclear tests enabled the then Prime Minister of Pakistan, Nawaz Sharif, to explore the bilateral option with India. This culminated in the Lahore bus diplomacy between the two countries. But the military in Pakistan was still unable to appreciate the new change. If anything, the Pakistan Army believed that the nuclear weapons provided them with the umbrella under which they could adopt an even more adventurist course inside Kashmir. The result was the incursions in the Kargil sector in the spring of 1999. The mini-war which followed ended with Pakistan having to withdraw without having anything to show for its labours. Even worse than the military defeat was the diplomatic fallout of Kargil. Pakistan's growing isolation in the international community was complete after Kargil. And if there was any residual sympathy for Pakistan in the international community, it disappeared with the military coup a few months after the Kargil conflict.

Just before 9/11, India made yet another effort to engage Pakistan on the bilateral track. This led to the disastrous summit at Agra in July 2001, a summit for which there was not a single good reason except that the government of the day felt that it too had reached a *cul-de-sac* after the failure of its Ramzan ceasefire initiative. Ironically, the invitation for the Agra Summit was issued to the very man who was responsible for the collapse of the ceasefire. The signal which this sent to the generalissimo of Pakistan was that India was suing for peace at any price. Of course, he got a bit of a shock when he realised that he had read the signal wrong. For the image conscious military ruler of Pakistan, Agra was a victory in the sense that it offered an opening out of the hole that Pakistan had dug itself into. This opening was the bilateral track. General Musharraf had realised this almost as soon as he usurped power and that's the reason he never tired of saying that he was willing to meet India anywhere, any time and at any level. And the great thing for the general was that he got all this without having to do anything in return. Agra allowed the general to live up to the image he had acquired back home and live down his image in the international community.

Then came 9/11 and the world changed. Suddenly, the *jihadi* option seemed like a millstone around the general's neck. No one in the international community was willing to turn a blind eye to the infrastructure of *jihad* that has been operating inside Pakistan with impunity for nearly two decades. While the Pakistanis understood the need for changing their policy on their Western frontier immediately after 9/11, it took many months before it finally dawned on the generals that their policy of fighting terror on their western frontier while supporting terror on the eastern frontier was no longer tenable or sustainable, at least not in the brazen manner that had been adopted until then. This meant that a political approach had to be adopted vis-à-vis India in order to wind down and bottle up the *jihad* genie. But it was equally important that India reciprocate by agreeing to talk "seriously and sincerely" with Pakistan on the vexed issue of Kashmir. This would give the Pakistan government the necessary face-saver for what would naturally be seen by right-wing elements as yet another U-turn in policy.

The need to wind down or tightly control the *jihad* against India was equally the result of the blow-back of this policy inside Pakistan – the mushrooming militias, the social regression that the growing radicalism brought about in the society, the economic fallout of *jihad* on business and investor climate, the deteriorating law and order situation and the consequent loss of internal sovereignty. Interestingly, Pakistan's domestic compulsions to wind up the *jihad* matched India's interest to see the *jihadi* infrastructure being wound up. Despite the irresistible temptation to see Pakistan stew in its own *jihadi* juices, India could hardly afford to be too bloody-minded about Pakistan's past shenanigans and refuse to give it the necessary face-saver. What is more, India also had to understand that the *jihad* genie was not something that could be bottled up overnight. It would take time and India would have to start engaging Pakistan even as Pakistan made efforts to wind up the *jihad* factory. All this, of course, was premised on Pakistan living up to its assurances of not allowing its territory or for that matter any territory under its control to be used for terrorist activities inside India.

If anything, this last factor will be extremely critical in the future trajectory of the peace process. Pakistan knows that the only real leverage it has on India is terrorism and that's one reason why the Pakistan has been chary in dismantling the infrastructure of *jihad* against India. India's willingness to enter into a dialogue with Pakistan on Kashmir to seek a stable solution to the problem reduces the utility of terrorism as an instrument to that extent. If India refuses to engage with Pakistan and encourages it to wind up the *jihad* factory by giving in on peripheral issues, the Pakistani regime will have a much more difficult time in reversing the *jihad* culture in the country. What is more, if India refuses to play ball, Pakistan will face a catch-22 situation: it will not be able to allow the *jihadis* to operate with impunity because of international factors and, at the same time, with no gains to show on the Kashmir front, it will find it difficult to crackdown on the *jihadi* infrastructure because of the fear of a domestic political backlash by right-wing elements in the political and military-bureaucratic establishment.

The Home Front as a Constraint and Compulsion

For all the diplomatic, political and economic advantages that have accrued to Pakistan by engaging in a bilateral dialogue with India, Pakistan is still not entirely convinced that this track will lead to an acceptable solution to the Kashmir issue. This is one reason why Pakistan continues to keep the *jihadi* militias in the wings. Pakistan also continues to raise the Kashmir issue in both international as well as bilateral forums with other countries so that the option of going back to international intervention in the issue is not foreclosed for the future.

There is, however, a very important domestic angle to this parallel policy. For one, it keeps the hardline, right-wing element satisfied that Pakistan has neither given up its traditional stance of internationalising the Kashmir issue nor has its given up on the UN resolutions on Kashmir. As a result, despite the reservations of the ultra-nationalist and radical Islamist lobby about the peace process with India, there has so far been no political backlash inside Pakistan. But nor has there been the creation of any significant political stake-holders in the peace process.

As of now, the peace process has not been 'marketed' to the extent that a substantial number of people 'buy' it. Part of the problem is that the contours of any possible peace deal are still not clear. Part of the problem is that the major political parties in Pakistan have not been kept in the loop on the negotiations taking place. And, part of the problem is that despite the composite dialogue framework between the two countries, the military-bureaucratic establishment is still not comfortable with the process, especially the back-channel diplomacy that seems to be moving everything. As a result, the process lacks the institutional backing required to make it 'irreversible'.

The peace process is in a sense 'personality driven' and not 'institution driven'. There is only a handful of people in both countries – perhaps not more than 5 to 10 on each side – who know what is really happening behind the scenes and the various roadmaps under consideration. Neither the bureaucracy nor the politicians have any real stake in the process as they have not been taken into confidence or consulted to any significant extent in order to evolve a consensus or at least prepare them for some kind of a deal. All that has been happening is that before and after every major meeting, some politicians and media-persons are assured that there will be no compromise on the "principles" of the Kashmir movement. Therefore, everyone except those in the loop are left speculating as to what the parameters of an eventual deal will be. And the speculation is generally within the traditional paradigm of what constitutes an acceptable solution to Kashmir. There are very few people outside the innermost circle of decision-making but with some amount of access to the inner circles, who are able to sense that there is perhaps a shift in the paradigm itself. This much becomes clear when one engages in conversations with Pakistani interlocutors. The ones who are just outside the loop of decision-making appear to be far more 'visionary' about the direction in which the process will ultimately go than those who are completely out of the loop and yet are important in their own right. The former explore the possibility of radically different and innovative solutions, while the latter stick to the old formulae. This is a major disconnect in the thinking of influential sections of the Pakistani establishment which could ultimately even sound the death-knell of the peace process.

But bridging this disconnect constitutes a great dilemma: the stage has perhaps still not been reached to publicly discuss all the various options under consideration. There is a lot to be said in favour of quiet, back-channel diplomacy that tries to establish a roadmap acceptable to both India and Pakistan before it is put before the public. On the other hand, diplomacy behind closed doors fuels speculation and misinformation about what is actually under consideration. A popular leadership can manage this gap through deft political manoeuvring, but a military regime which is deeply unpopular will find it that much more difficult to manage the politics of the peace process, especially when there is a real possibility that the political opposition may use the peace process as a handle against the military regime.

Apart from the Jamaat-i-Islami, none of the other political parties is averse to the peace process, and, in fact, are supportive of it, yet there is a danger that the peace process may become a victim of the political struggle between the military regime and the political opposition. Public anger and discontent against the regime, if channelised by the opposition into street protests, could very easily spill over against India. And as happens ever so often in subcontinental politics, any collapse of the regime due to a possible political agitation might be attributed, wrongly and with ulterior motive (by right-wing groups and lobbies) to the peace moves with India. If this happens, then the new regime will perforce slip back into the old paradigm if for no other reason than self-preservation. And the army, rather than becoming a harbinger of peace and change, will become the flag bearer of the old policy of hostility and suspicion.

How easily the peace process could dovetail with the general public discontent with the current ruling dispensation became clear after a conversation with a senior Muttahida-Majlis-e-Amal (MMA) leader who belongs to the Jamiat-e-Ulema-e-Islam (JUI), a party that is very keen on normalising relations with India.[2] For the JUI, Afghanistan is more important than Kashmir. The *jihad* in Kashmir poses a political challenge to the JUI's political leadership. Had people like Masood Azhar and Fazlur Rehman Khalil not been leading the *jihad* in Kashmir, they would have been workers in the JUI. The gain of the *jihad* has been the loss of the JUI in terms of cadre and workers and indeed political support. The JUI, however, has a political problem in that politically it simply cannot detach itself completely from the Kashmir issue, even though it might like to do this. They would be more than happy if the issue sorted itself out, and are hardly keen on adopting any sort of a hard line position on Kashmir. But this doesn't mean that the JUI will not make pro-forma statements on Kashmir, which might appear to be obstructions in the path of the peace process.

The JUI leadership has a problem in being more forthright on Kashmir because its other major partner within the MMA, the Jamaat-i-Islami (JI), is very hawkish on Kashmir. As a result, the JUI has adopted a strategy of killing two birds with one stone. They criticise the government on its Kashmir policy so that not only can they keep the JI satisfied but also use the criticism as a handle against the government. But internally, the JUI leaders say that it is better for the peace process if the MMA stays united because this way they can keep a check on the JI and temper them. The JUI also admit that their criticism of the peace process is political, and aimed not so much against India as against the current regime.[3] The JUI and indeed the MMA is approaching the issue in a way that is designed to undermine the Musharraf regime, rather than the peace process. According to the JUI, the past record of the military rulers has been terrible when it comes to protecting national interests and they give the example of Ayub Khan's signing of the Indus Waters

Treaty, Yahya Khan's blunders in East Pakistan, Zia-ul-Haq's loss of Siachen, and juxtapose these to wonder what historical blunder Musharraf will make now. As far as the JUI is concerned, they want in on the peace process in order to ensure that decisions regarding the peace process are taken after due deliberation and consultation with the elected representatives of the people, in other words, the Parliament. This is a way to sow doubts about Musharraf's competence in dealing with India as well increase the power of the Parliament and by extension, the MMA. The other line of attack is related. The MMA is asking Musharraf what he has so far to show for his 'flexibility' with India which has not yielded an inch on issues like Siachen, Sir Creek and Baglihar, let alone on Kashmir.[4]

Interestingly, while the opposition parties are not averse to a bilateral dialogue – the JUI for one would prefer that Pakistan and India solve their problems bilaterally rather than involve a third party like the US – they will use the bilateral track to accuse the government of compromising on Pakistan's traditional and 'principled' stance on securing the "right to self-determination" for the Kashmiris according to the UN resolutions. This is the line of attack that other political parties too will take as and when they start an agitation against the Musharraf regime. For parties like the Jamaat-i-Islami, going soft on India presents an ideological problem, not very different from the one that confronted the Bharatiya Janata Party (BJP) after Mr. L.K. Advani's trip to Pakistan. A senior Jamaat leader confessed that the party has taken a rabidly anti-India position for so long that despite the fact that this is no longer a politically popular slogan, the party finds it difficult to take a different line, especially since the core constituency and cadre of the party could rebel against any such move.[5] But he was candid enough to say that things are very different when a party is in opposition and gave the example of the BJP to buttress his point.

The other major political parties like the People's Party of Pakistan (PPP) and the Pakistan Muslim League-Nawaz (PML-N) too will not be averse to using the peace process to pull the regime down. This, despite the fact that they will be happy if Musharraf reaches a settlement with India on Kashmir. If anything, they would prefer it if Musharraf reaches a settlement before he is ousted because this way they can always blame the settlement on him and the army and yet continue to adhere to this settlement and not challenge it. This is again a strategy to kill two birds with one stone: a settlement with India, they believe somewhat naively, will end the influence of the army on the politics of the country because not only will it end the influence arrogated by the army as the defender of the ideological and territorial frontiers of the country but also because the politicians can use the settlement to bring down the regime. But it could easily go the other way and as mentioned earlier, the situation could force the new regime to go back on the understanding reached with India, especially since such an understanding would be more in the nature of agreements rather than a treaty delineating permanent borders. The possibility of such a reversal would increase if the military rank and file is unhappy with the peace deal reached between India and Pakistan.

The Problems in Peace Deal: Expectations vs Reality

How the domestic compulsions and constraints in either country play themselves out depends critically on whether the two countries are angling for a deal that manages the problem or one that solves it. Despite all the talk of 'conflict resolution', it appears from the qualifications which both countries have specified in public discourse that the peace process is heading towards 'conflict management'. Such an approach has an inbuilt instability which in turns creates a dilemma for the involved parties.

Any solution, whether it's in the nature of conflict resolution or conflict management, necessarily means a compromise – in the case of India, on territory, sovereignty or both, and in the case of Pakistan, on the issue of surrendering its claims over a part or even the entire portion of the state that is under India's control. This is so because the ground conditions raise questions about the ability of either country to push through its desired solution. But neither country appears ready for making such compromises.

Therefore, the question: where do the two countries want to go with the peace process? Is the peace process a journey in which the destination is not known? Is there some sort of a roadmap available directing the two sides along a known path or are the two countries exploring uncharted territory and carving their own path? Equally important is the question: what do the two sides expect to gain out of the peace process? So far, no one in either India or Pakistan has articulated what they expect to emerge out of the peace process. The only thing that is clear is that the LoC, even though it is a *de facto* border, cannot be converted into a *de jure* border.[6]

The bottom line is that Pakistan has ruled out any solution on Kashmir around the LoC. The secessionists in Jammu and Kashmir too are not willing to accept the LoC as a possible solution. Almost all the Kashmiris, at least for public consumption, speak against the partitioning of the state. In India, while the Track II types (including retired military and civil bureaucrats) have been talking of converting the LoC into an international border, no responsible government functionary has ever mentioned this as a possible solution. The fact is that India can never accept the LoC as an international border – this is constitutionally not possible as it will violate the basic feature of the Constitution. Even if all the 800 odd MPs in India vote unanimously for ceding Pakistan Occupied Kashmir to Pakistan, the Supreme Court will strike down this amendment since it violates the basic feature of the Indian Constitution, which is that the territory and integrity of the country can never be compromised.

This then means that either India gets the whole state; or Pakistan gets the entire state; or both India and Pakistan walk out of Kashmir and it becomes independent. Finally, both sides learn to live with the problem of unsettled frontiers and counter-claims, without being too bloody-minded about it. India's problem, indeed dilemma, is that while it doesn't have the political and diplomatic wherewithal to enforce a solution of its liking, any management of the conflict solution will leave the issue of permanent borders unsettled, which could erupt again in the future.

As things stand, the Indian policy appears to be to shove the difficult questions, namely Kashmir, under the carpet and concentrate on the easier things. Somewhere in the Indian thinking, the calculation is that once engagement with Pakistan is sufficiently deep and broad-based, the Kashmir problem will recede into the background and cease to be an issue, if not for the Pakistanis then at least for the Kashmiris. As far as India is concerned, if even the Kashmiris on the Indian side reconcile to their future in India, the war over Kashmir will have been won. But this is typical of an ostrich that believes that if it digs its head into the sand long enough, the storm will pass it by.

The Pakistani calculation too is somewhat similar and many Pakistanis are on record saying that India being a nation of *baniyas* and *lalas* will eventually settle the Kashmir issue on Pakistan's terms in exchange for a lucrative trading relationship and other benefits that could come India's way in the event of normalisation of relations with Pakistan. Of course, there are divisions within Pakistan as to whether the lure of benefits should precede a settlement on Kashmir or follow such a settlement.

Ultimately, Kashmir is a political question but one in which issues like ideology, religion, nationalism, terrorism all dovetail with the primary question. This is something that neither the Indian political class nor the self-important bureaucracy of India seems to have understood. The political question cannot be ducked. From India's point of view, the ideal situation will be if the political question can be addressed without involving Pakistan. But while this would probably settle the issue within India, it will mean that relations with Pakistan will remain strained, and normalisation of relations will remain a pipedream. On the other hand, any involvement of Pakistan will necessarily mean a compromise either on territory or on sovereignty, either of which India cannot countenance, or so India claims. Surprisingly enough, except for holding elections, there is hardly any worthwhile political initiative that India has taken inside the troubled state. What is worse, even the rather clumsy political initiatives that were taken by India, ignored the elected representatives in the state, who, incidentally, India never tired of flaunting to the rest of the world. All the efforts made so far have been aimed at either attracting the secessionists to join the mainstream or else dividing their ranks. But no real effort has been made to isolate the secessionists. The one great opening that was provided to India by the elected Assembly of Jammu and Kashmir – the autonomy resolution – was contemptuously rejected by the then government at the centre.

Given the sort of confusion that pervades the Indian policy establishment, it is not surprising that the Pakistanis actually believe that beyond a point India will not be able to hold on to Kashmir. The confidence-building measures (CBMs), therefore, will serve their purpose up to a point. For instance, truck traffic across the LoC will serve Pakistan more than it will serve India. Not because arms will come through trucks, but because we will restore the traditional trading route of the Valley, which was through Rawalpindi and, consequently, sever the economic linkages which mainland India has made with Kashmir over the last 60 years. Now India might be doing the Kashmiri businessman a favour but it will also be cutting its feet in Kashmir.

There are many people in both India and Pakistan who believe that Pakistan's tactics and strategy have changed in Kashmir but the objective remains wresting Kashmir from India's control. It is believed that Pakistan will now follow a two-pronged approach: one, change the political situation inside Kashmir in a way that India has no feet left to stand on. In other words, overtures will be made even to the pro-India political elements to attract them to Pakistan's position. The proposals for demilitarisation, self-governance and free movement are aimed at the hearts and minds of the Kashmiris, and no political leader in Kashmir can really oppose them in public. Already, we are seeing pro-India political leaders like Omar Abdullah and Mehbooba Mufti take a line which is increasingly moving in the direction of Pakistan.

The second prong will be a continuation of violence in Kashmir. The spike in incidents of terrorism even after the devastating earthquake is a pointer to this policy. Indeed, all available indications are that terrorism has entered a new and much more dangerous and sinister phase. In this phase, the *jihadi* militias will adopt a low profile and not strut around as they did in the past. No claims of strikes will come from the main groups which are headquartered in Pakistan.

These groups will continue to recruit and train *jihadis*, but there will be little if any infiltration from either the international border or the LoC. Any infiltration will be of such a nature that it will be difficult to implicate the Pakistani state of any involvement. In short, nothing will happen from Pakistan any more – no arms smuggling, no infiltration, no bombastic statements claiming credit for terrorist attacks. Yet, *jihad* will continue. The *jihadi* groups will use countries like Bangladesh and Nepal to infiltrate into India. They will source their arms from criminal mafias operating inside India. They will use sections of disaffected Indian citizens – Hindus, Muslims, Sikhs and Christians – to spread mayhem inside India. In all this there will be no visible Pakistani hand, so India will have no basis to blame Pakistan for any terrorism. Of course, such a strategy cannot stay hidden for long, and somewhere down the line, the hand of Pakistan will emerge clearly. But the troubling question is that if this is the Pakistani strategy, then where does it want to go with the peace process? Or is the peace process part of this strategy of unsettling the enemy with peace moves, while waging war with other means? In either case, this would mean that the peace process will collapse when the limit of India's tolerance is reached.

End-Game: Siachen as a Metaphor for the Peace Path?

Given the lack of clarity as well as divergence of views on the end-game of both India and Pakistan, the conflict over Siachen appears to be an apt metaphor for the current peace process. When the LoC was being delineated, both sides drew the map up to a particular point – NJ9842 – and left the rest of the area unmarked with the ambiguous phrase, "And thence north to the glaciers." At that time, no one really expected a fight over the icy wastes of the Siachen Glacier and so they never bothered to draw a line on this area. Something similar is happening during the current peace process. While there is a slew of CBMs and a whole lot of "thinking out of the box," the final contours of any possible settlement have still not been made clear. As a result, both sides believe that they will be able to get more than what they really expect. The question is: where do we go when we come to the point NJ9842 of the peace process?

The answer to this question depends on what sort of a relationship India wants to have with Pakistan. Does it want Pakistan to be a camp follower, a competitor, a subsidiary or a junior partner, a client state? Where does Pakistan fit into India's strategic scheme? At the same time, where does India fit into Pakistan's strategy? Unless both parts of the equation are correctly answered, any policy formulation is bound to be faulty.

The trouble is that so far India has failed to forge a coherent and consistent policy on Pakistan. In other words, India simply doesn't know what it wants on Pakistan. The standard line of the Indian establishment is: "A strong, stable and friendly Pakistan is in India's interest." Now this can be an expression of hope or desire, but it is certainly not a policy objective. Because if it is, then the next logical question is: what has India done and what is India willing to do to ensure that it achieves this policy objective? What policy instruments have been crafted to ensure this objective? Or is it the case that India would like this to happen without having to do anything about it?

Similarly, Indians never tire of saying that Kashmir is a symptom and not the reason for Indo-Pakistan problems. Well, if this is the case, then why does India concentrate so much on addressing this issue? Why doesn't India try to bring the real issue out and address that, which in turn will sort out the Kashmir problem? What is the point of trying symptomatic treatment when the real problem continues to afflict Indo-Pakistan relations?

Broadly, India can adopt two possible policy options available to it on Pakistan. The first is that India reaches the conclusion that its interests are better served by forging friendly ties with Pakistan and it works towards a Pakistan which is strong, self-assured, stable and prosperous. This option could include reaching an understanding with Pakistan on Kashmir and accommodating Pakistan in Kashmir even if this means compromising our sovereignty in the state or making concessions of territory.

The second approach is to reach the conclusion that Pakistan will continue to pose a challenge to India's security and, therefore, work on a policy of containment of Pakistan that not only minimises Pakistan's capability of harming India's interest but also doesn't distract India from its larger regional objectives.

If India decides on the first option, then settling the Kashmir issue with Pakistan is imperative. But if it is the second option that serves India's interest, then India needs to figure a way out of the peace process and to perpetuate the conflict over Kashmir.

Notes

1. *Public Opinion Trends Analyses & News Service* (New Delhi) Pakistan Section, Vol.4, No.31, pp. 202, 204, 206.
2. Author's personal conversations with JUI leaders in Islamabad, Lahore and Bahawalpur in May-June 2005.
3. Ibid.
4. Ibid.
5. Ibid., personal conversation with Jamaat-i-Islami leaders in Pakistan.
6. Indeed, all the three parties in the conflict, India Pakistan and the separatists, have taken this approach.

India-Pakistan Security Discourse

Rajesh Rajagopalan

There is a curious feature to the way in which Indians and Pakistanis, especially analysts and academicians, look at the India-Pakistan conflict. Despite decades of conflict, it is seen as the consequence of a series of disputes, which either run in combination or discretely. The constancy of the conflict appears not to have had much impact on the analysis. I suggest that it is this constancy that needs to be examined more closely in the security discourse, which has largely wallowed in the shallows of particular disputes.

The India-Pakistan conflict is one of the world's oldest. After almost six decades of conflict, there is little indication that the disagreements between the two countries are anywhere close to resolution. The neighbours have been to war at least four times, if we include the 1999 Kargil War. In the aftermath of the terrorist attack on the Indian Parliament in late 2001 and subsequent Operation Parakram mobilisation by the Indian military, India and Pakistan had come close to war yet again. The improvement in relations since then, while welcome, has only brought the relations back to a semblance of normality. There is little indication that any of the fundamental issues in the disagreements between the two countries are even close to resolution. Indeed, as of early 2006, even the progress made in the two years of unprecedented official dialogue appears to be at least slowing down.

But the security discourse in both countries does not even attempt to look at the underlying causes of the dispute. There is a tendency, common to both countries, to see the India-Pakistan conflict as the consequence of specific disputes. But such disputes come and go and the importance of even long-term disputes waxes and wanes. New disputes replace old ones, but the India-Pakistan conflict continues. On both sides, the significant elements of the security discourse are concerned with current issues and the latest headlines. These discourses cannot even lead to a common understanding of what the problem to be addressed is. And this is not just because there are obvious divergences of analysis and opinion about these individual issues of dispute. That is only part of the problem. There is a more critical issue: because much of the security discourse is concerned with the current issues of dispute, it is unlikely that these security discourses can lead to any long-lasting or fundamental solution. Below, I briefly examine some of the major concerns in the security discourse of both countries and suggest that these are only symptoms of a deeper conflict. I point to one of the possible candidates for such 'deep causes', the impressive imbalance of power in the region. I conclude with some comments on the security discourse and the challenges facing the current peace process.

Kashmir

Islamabad claims that Kashmir is the key issue.[1] Given the centrality of the dispute today, most Indians may agree that resolving Kashmir is vital to moving away from the current deadlock in the relationship, even though no solution appears immediately apparent. There is little doubt that Kashmir is a significant problem, and that Pakistan has invested substantial amounts of its national energy to its pursuit of this goal. In addition to launching the first war within months of independence, Kashmir was a major issue on the agenda of the United Nations in the 1950s, with many efforts made by the UN to find a middle ground between the two countries. In the aftermath of the 1962 War, as Indian defence forces began a long overdue modernisation, Pakistan felt that Indian military modernisation might foreclose any Pakistani options in Kashmir, leading to the 1965 War. Yet, in the quarter century between the 1965 War and the outbreak of the Kashmir rebellion in 1990, the issue was not particularly prominent in India-Pakistan interactions. New Delhi and Islamabad quarrelled over other issues – India's support for the Bangladeshi guerrillas, Pakistan's arms purchases from the US, Pakistan's support for the Khalistani terrorists in Punjab, and so on. Though Kashmir never disappeared from the menu of India-Pakistan disputes, its salience was low for about a quarter century until incompetent political meddling from New Delhi led to a rebellion in Kashmir in the late 1980s. This rebellion was supported materially and morally by Islamabad and was the direct cause of several 'crises' during the 1990s. But the increased importance of Kashmir in the bilateral dispute in the post-1990 period has tended to mask the fact that India-Pakistan tensions and disputes did not lessen during the quarter century when the Kashmir issue was dormant. Other disputes, as I have suggested above, continued to keep the relationship on the boil during much of this period. Indeed, neither the 1971 India-Pakistan War, nor the 1987 Brasstacks crisis, had anything whatsoever to do with the Kashmir dispute. What this suggests is that the resolution of the Kashmir dispute would not necessarily lead to a final settlement in South Asia. By implication, then,

Kashmir is not the central issue in the dispute between the two sides. We would need to look elsewhere for such a candidate.

It would be foolish to conclude from the above that the Kashmir issue should not be addressed, even as a central item in the dialogue between the two sides. Resolving this issue has a variety of benefits: halting the rising human costs of the conflict, both to the Kashmiris, as well as to the Indian soldiers who are deployed there and their families (who are the most invisible elements in much of this debate); reducing the levels of violence in the region; and ameliorating the dangers of escalation of this conflict from a guerrilla war to a full-fledged conventional test of arms between the two sides (with the inevitable worry about the potential for such conflicts to escalate to the nuclear level), among others. But I would suggest that the argument that Kashmir is central to the dispute is questionable, conceptually as well as empirically. Kashmir is a serious dispute, and needs to be addressed for its own merits as such, but it is more a symptom of the underlying conflict between India and Pakistan rather than the conflict itself.

The Nuclear Balance

The nuclear balance in the region is another major issue in the security discourse in India and Pakistan. Though not seen as being as central to the dispute between India and Pakistan, it is also one of the several issues that roil the security discourse in the two countries. On this issue though, despite some disagreements, there are also a number of commonalities in the discourse. Indian and Pakistani analysts disagree about a number of issues, most importantly, Pakistan's nuclear doctrine, Pakistan's (irresponsible) nuclear behaviour, Pakistan's role in nuclear proliferation, and India's acquisition of ballistic missile defences (BMD). But they broadly agree on the nuclear danger in the region and the possibility of nuclear escalation and war in South Asia. Here I focus on two of the major issues in the debate: India's pursuit of missile defences and Pakistan's nuclear doctrine. India's desire to acquire missile defences is seen as a serious escalation in Pakistan, another attempt by India to assert its superiority in the region.

Indian BMD efforts are a significant source of concern in the Pakistani nuclear discourse. Mutahir Ahmed, for example, argues that Indian missile defences will destabilise the region. It will force "China and Pakistan... to engage in nuclear build-ups and to continue established patterns of strategic cooperation."[2] For good measure, he suggests that India's pursuit of missile defences indicates its ambition to acquire absolute regional superiority in the nuclear domain. These concerns were also expressed by Pakistani officials. In early 2005, Pakistani Defence Secretary Hamid Nawaz stated that Pakistan opposed any sale of US Patriot missile defence systems to India because it would "disturb the balance of the entire region."[3] Pakistani analysts' opposition to Indian BMD appears to be based on the belief that any Indian acquisition of BMD would erode Pakistan's deterrent capabilities vis-à-vis its neighbour. On the other hand, India's BMD plans have shown little signs of progress. For example, New Delhi first considered building or acquiring missile defences a decade ago, in the mid-1990s. But these plans have yet to fructify. Part of the reason for the delay in Indian plans appears to be because the Indian government itself is uncertain about what kind of missile defences it wants. For example, after repeatedly complaining that the US was not providing it with the PAC-3 version of the Patriot BMD system, New Delhi seemed unprepared to discuss its specific needs when the US did offer the PAC-3 version. Despite the fact that Indian plans show no signs of progress, there continues to be considerable disquiet in Pakistan about the consequences of the Indian programme.

Pakistan's nuclear doctrine is yet another issue of disagreement in the security discourses in the two countries. What is most clear in this debate, on the other hand, is that there is a certain lack of clarity about what Pakistan's nuclear doctrine is. Pakistan's rather extravagant definition of its so-called "redlines,"[4] and the general acceptance in India that Pakistan may actually be willing to use its nuclear weapons if it is under pressure, have led to the assumption that Pakistan's doctrine is one where it keeps its nuclear forces on a hair-trigger, ready to use at a moment's notice. Elsewhere, I have suggested that Pakistan's doctrine is actually one which emphasises neither "first strike" nor even early use, but rather one where Pakistan reserves the right to use its nuclear weapons, possibly in a very limited or even demonstration-test manner, when the very fate of the Pakistani state and nation is at risk.[5] Needless to say, this is an extremely remote likelihood, especially as a consequence of an Indian assault. But the argument about Pakistan's readiness to use its nuclear forces is part of the general Indian security discourse about Pakistan's irresponsible behaviour that does little to advance our understanding of the sources of conflict in the region. Pakistan's nuclear doctrine is a responsible, stable, and considered response to its strategic equation with India, not an indication of "irresponsibility." To extend the argument further, it is also unclear how a more "responsible" doctrine from Pakistan might reduce India-Pakistan conflict or even tensions. Such a change may reduce the pressures on New Delhi in a crisis, but it is unclear why this should concern Pakistan.

The Conventional Balance

A major issue in at least the Pakistani security discourse is the conventional force imbalance between the two neighbours. This, of course, is a long-standing issue. The conventional force imbalance is the natural consequence of the disparity in the wealth that the two sides could devote to their conventional military forces. India, with its bigger economy, was always able to have a larger defence budget, even as it spent proportionately far less than Pakistan on its national defence. Indeed, it was this concern that propelled Zulfikar Ali Bhutto to suggest that Pakistan needed nuclear weapons. He pointed out that even an efficient, but relatively small, conventional force cannot hope to match a larger and stronger aggressor.[6] Of course, even this realisation had to wait until Pakistan suffered defeat and disaster in the 1965 War that it launched for Kashmir. Until that point, Pakistan was relatively more relaxed about the conventional imbalance in the region. Myths, such as one Pakistani soldier being equal to ten Indian ones, were partly used for comfort: President Ayub Khan's directive to General Musa, commander-in-chief of the Pakistan Army, is reported to have stated that "as a general rule, Hindu morale would not stand more than a couple of hard blows delivered at the right time and place."[7] But clearly, such myths were not the only source of comfort. Pakistan also sought advanced weapons from the West to counter Indian numerical superiority. Quality was thought sufficient to meet quantity. The purchase of the F-104 Starfighter, the M-60 Patton tank in the 1960s and the F-16 "Fighting Falcon" air superiority fighters in the 1980s, are just some of the indicators of the attempt to achieve a qualitative offset for quantitative inferiority. Developing a nuclear weapons programme was another response. It was not accidental that the "Multan decision," which led to the Pakistani nuclear weapons programme, directly followed, and was a consequence of, the disastrous 1971 War which led to the break-up of Pakistan.

Oddly, Pakistan continues to worry about the conventional balance in the region despite the nuclearisation of the region. Just a few days after the 1998 nuclear tests, Ambassador Munir Akram was telling the Special Session of the Conference on Disarmament that nuclear restraint was possible only if there was a stable conventional balance too.[8] Other Pakistani leaders have also stated that they needed a robust conventional military capability despite having nuclear weapons, because all conflicts invariably began as conventional ones.[9] As recently as in September 2005, Pakistani President Pervez Musharraf raised the issue of the conventional force imbalance during his address to the UN General Assembly, questioning in particular India's conventional military build-up. It is unclear if Pakistan will ever achieve a conventional military balance that it is comfortable with because that balance is a reflection of the disparity in the wealth of the two countries, which, with India's economic boom, is increasing rather than decreasing.

This issue has not been seriously considered by Indian analysts, who are wont to dismiss Pakistani claims either by pointing to India's two-front problem or by dismissing the notion that Indian conventional superiority is a problem. While such a response fails to give proper consideration to genuine Pakistani fears about the military imbalance in the region, the focus on the conventional military imbalance needs to go deeper to examine the roots of the imbalance rather than, yet again, treat the symptom. But this issue has at least one advantage, in that it points the direction for additional work.

Terrorism

Terrorism is a significant factor in the security discourse in both India and Pakistan but there are also important variations in the debates in the two countries about the issue. In India, long decades of struggle against varieties of secessionist and other insurgent forces have created at least some space for looking at the political roots of such issues and addressing such root cause issues. This is most evident in looking at the official army discourse on issues of internal conflicts.[10] The army's doctrine, well-established even if it is not formalised, suggests that dealing with internal rebellions is not the primary purpose or mission of the army. The primary mission remains that of dealing with external, conventional military threats, presumably from Pakistan and China, and other such sources. Internal duties are part of the "aid to civil" responsibilities of the army, and are seen as a limited mission. Though such "aid to civil" missions include many types of missions, such as disaster relief and temporary use of military forces to maintain law and order, the considerations here are primarily of the army's internal security operations and how the army approaches such tasks. For the army, these are primarily political problems, and the roots of the problem, as well as the solution to the problem, lie in political processes. The army's mission, as the army sees it, is to ensure that normalcy is restored in areas affected by insurgencies and internal rebellion so that the political process, interrupted by violence, can be restarted. Such a 'political' view of internal rebellion also suggests a number of corollary elements. Rebels are seen not as the enemy, but as misguided youths who may even have legitimate grievances. Thus, rebellion may even be the natural outcome of the failure of the political system. But, and this is critical, the solution cannot be a military one. Almost all army writings on the subject repeat this formulation faithfully: that internal rebellions, even if the result of bad or failed politics and policy, can only be solved by political processes. In essence, the solution to the failure of politics is more politics. The military's role is limited to creating the conditions for politics to resume. In addition, because internal rebellions force the army to fight its own fellow citizens, the quantum of force that is used has to be limited. Thus, internal military operations have abjured the use of heavy weapons such as artillery and tanks, or the use of combat air power in counter-insurgency operations. This is not to suggest that excesses do not happen in army counter-insurgency operations. They do. But the attitude towards internal rebellions is political rather than military, even within the army.

If internal rebellions are seen as requiring political solutions, the general security discourse in India also focusses on the role of external actors in exacerbating such conflicts. Both Pakistan and China have supported internal rebellions within India, and both are seen as part of the problem. Though the current discourse does not focus as much on China's role – reflecting the reduced Chinese activism on these issues – Pakistan continues to be seen as the source of much of the problem of terrorism in the region and the world. Indian strategic analysts, and its officialdom, are loath to accept the American claim that Pakistan is a "stalwart" ally in the war on terrorism. Part of the reason is Pakistan's strategy of "smart terrorism" which distinguishes between terror directed at India and terror directed at the US and the West. Clearly, Pakistan has discouraged the latter, and has captured terrorists wanted by the US who were hiding in Pakistan. Sometimes, this has even been done in contravention of domestic Pakistani law and due processes. This is cooperation that cannot but be seen in a positive light by Washington. On the other hand, such discriminatory strategy also allows Pakistan to not only continue its terror strategy against India but also negates the possibility that the US and India will join together to contain Pakistan's sponsorship of terror groups.

Unfortunately, in this discourse too, there is little attempt to go beyond the surface. Clearly, Pakistani support for rebellions within India has been a long-standing feature, going back to the support extended to the Naga and Mizo rebels in the 1960s and Sikh terrorists in the 1980s. One way to look at this issue is to see this as part of the normal menu of state strategic choices: India, to name only one relevant example, has also supported rebellions in East Pakistan, as well as that of the Tamils in Sri Lanka. But the frequency and consistency of the Pakistani support for such rebellions in India suggest the need for a closer examination of why Pakistan feels that such support is necessary and useful to Pakistani strategy. Unfortunately, the Indian security discourse does not examine such questions.

Above, I have suggested that many of the elements of the security discourses in the two countries are concerned with immediate policy issues rather than examining the underlying causes of conflicts between India and Pakistan. Next, I suggest one such underlying cause: the imbalance of power in the region. I must preface this by accepting that there might be other factors, such as nationalism and national identities, which are also good candidates as deep causes. I am not suggesting that the imbalance of power can provide the only good explanation. But I will let other scholars, more convinced of such explanations, make their case.[11]

The Imbalance of Power

What the above suggests is that specific disputes mask a more fundamental one. Between India and Pakistan, the more fundamental problem is Pakistan's fear of India, which is itself a consequence of the gross imbalance of power between the two countries. This imbalance is so huge that there is little need to specify it, but a couple of examples might be useful. In size (population) and wealth, two important indicators of power, Pakistan is only about a tenth that of India. Indian industry dwarfs Pakistan's, and Pakistan's defence industrial base, not inconsiderable by global and developing world standards, appears small when compared to India's. This imbalance is reflected in military terms also. Pakistan's fear of India keeps its military budget high and its attention focussed. As a proportion of its total budget, Pakistan almost always spends twice as much as India on its defence forces, but in real terms, this amounts to only about a sixth of what India spends on defence. Thus, despite putting huge strains on its economy, it has never been able to come even close to what India spends on defence.

This gross imbalance makes Pakistan's fear understandable, and repeated battlefield defeats make this imbalance intolerable. But there are no short-term solutions to this problem. In the first several decades of independence, many Pakistanis thought that India was too unwieldy to hold together. Some still may, but India's endurance — a mystery not just to the Pakistanis – cannot any longer be wished away. Pakistan has tried several strategies to overcome this gross imbalance of power in the region, in addition to building up its military capabilities. Pakistan's international alliances illustrate one way in which Pakistan attempted to even the power equation in the region. It initially aligned with the US, ostensibly to prevent the spread of global Communism, though Pakistani leaders assured both China and the Soviet Union in private that their interest in the alliance was to balance India. When Washington cosied-up to India during the Kennedy Administration, Pakistan promptly took up common cause with China against their mutual regional adversary. Though they have built up what they claim is an "all-weather" relationship, it will pass its true test only if India and China become friendlier. Indeed, as Sino-Indian relations improved, especially in the defence field, Pakistani officials have warned China that such closeness should be within strict limits. But this is ultimately a battle that Pakistan cannot win unless it can begin to match India in wealth. This is not entirely inconceivable: other relatively small nations have become wealthy as a consequence of either naturally endowed wealth (such as oil-rich states) or because they have followed successful economic policies (as in the case of the East Asian tiger economies). Short of such a change, it is unlikely that Pakistan will feel safe. Because India cannot be defeated, and it will not fall apart, it is not easy to resolve the Pakistani dilemma. India's best hope is a gradual change within Pakistan that will make Pakistan relatively less fearful of India. Having nuclear weapons and the guarantee they provide should help. Indian actions could too, which is why continuing the peace process is useful. Such actions can, in the long-term, convince Pakistan that it can live as an equal and in peace with its much larger and richer neighbour.

The above analysis suggests that there are deeper causes that prevent improvement in India-Pakistan relations that have not yet been addressed. I have suggested one possible explanation. Of course, such hypotheses need to be tested with rigour before they can be validated. But to do that, we must at least begin to look for such deeper explanations. Unfortunately, there is little indication of such examination in the security discourse in either India or Pakistan.

Conclusions

What can we conclude about the security discourse in the two countries and the prospects for the current peace process? The security discourse in India and Pakistan and the current peace process may or may not resolve the many India-Pakistan disputes. But it could slowly help Pakistan come to terms with India's size and power. Though resolution of specific disputes could help this process, what is more important is to ensure that the process continues even if there are no resolutions. There is an undue emphasis in the security discourse in both capitals on the solution of specific disputes because there is a mistaken notion that the India-Pakistan problem could be resolved if such disputes are resolved. But as long as the basic source of the conflict – Pakistan's fear of India – continues, new disputes will always rise to take the place of even those disputes than can be resolved. This fundamental problem will prevent any quick resolution to the conflict. New Delhi needs to be patient, recognising that there are no quick fixes to Pakistan's fear of India. More importantly, New Delhi has to recognise that this is a process that is internal to Pakistan, even if Indian actions can help or hinder that process.

But the peace process faces other, important challenges also. There is constant worry in New Delhi about the possibility that infiltration across the Line of Control will increase and put at risk the current peace process. The tenor of these comments suggests that if such infiltration, as well as violence within Jammu and Kashmir, increases, Indian support for the peace process will dry up. The Indian hope that the peace process will reduce the violence in Jammu and Kashmir is odd. Indeed, we should expect the violence to increase as the peace process continues, as Pakistan attempts to put pressure on the ground to increase its bargaining position at the negotiating table. From Pakistan's perspective, it makes eminent strategic sense because it forces India onto the horns of a dilemma – either abandon the peace process and be blamed for its failure, or swallow the pain. Such violence will also increase domestic pressures on the government, both from the general population and the military and other services. New Delhi, and its security analysts, need to recognise that violence could increase even if Islamabad undertakes a sincere effort – which it has not until now – to rein in the terrorist groups operating from its territory. Terrorist groups would then use terror to remain relevant to the process, if only in the spoiler role. The central point is that it we should expect the violence to go up as the dialogue continues, and particularly if the dialogue shows signs of progress.

India needs to respond to any increase in violence and infiltration, but it has few options. Over the years, New Delhi has failed to develop any military means to respond to such "low intensity violence." India's primary response to such challenges in the past has been to either complain incessantly to Washington or discontinue the dialogue or both, solutions worse than the problem. Complaining to Washington did not work even in the days before the September 11 attacks, which has made Pakistan a necessary ally for the US. New Delhi has always overestimated the power of its own logic in convincing Washington to see the light regarding Pakistan as well as the American ability to control Pakistan. It was also never very clear why Pakistani terrorism against India should be an American problem.

An appropriate response to such low-level violence will be to reply with proportionate force, using covert and special forces. But both India's military capabilities and the political commitment to use force, never very strong, have withered over the years. An additional problem for New Delhi is that it has developed no military tools to respond proportionately to such attacks. If India had such forces, it would be perfectly justified in using them to attack and destroy the bases from which these infiltrators are sent, and their communication centres and their other support infrastructure within Pakistan.

Such proportionate responses would keep the risk of escalation low, a necessary requirement in the nuclear age. Even if such retaliation is not militarily effective, it would send a political message that India would respond to attacks instead of merely complaining about them. Such responses would also reduce the incentives for the Pakistani military to convince itself that India would not respond to even more serious challenges, as it has done several times over the last half-century, and most recently in Kargil. Most importantly, if New Delhi developed such tools, it would not have to threaten to stop talking every time a group of terrorists attacked a military camp or killed Indian civilians. In the absence of such tools, the pressures on the dialogue process are likely to mount even if the peace process advances. These pressures can only be countered by recognising that there are no quick solutions to Pakistan's insecurity – and, hence, to the India-Pakistan conflict – and that India needs to develop responses other than to stop talking each time Pakistan raises the stakes with its hired guns.

Ultimately, there is a curious symmetry in the two security discourses in their insistence on focussing on immediate issues to the neglect of more fundamental causes. These individual immediate issues may come and go but the fundamental issues of disputes will remain unless such issues are deliberately addressed. That process has barely begun.

Notes

1. There is, of course, a huge quantity of material on the various aspects of the dispute. Though somewhat dated, one of the best collections of Indian and Pakistani views on the conflict can be found in Raju G.C. Thomas, ed., *Perspectives on Kashmir: The Roots of Conflict in South Asia* (Boulder: Westview Press, 1992).
2. Mutahir Ahmed, "Missile Defense and South Asia: A Pakistani Perspective," in Michael Krepon and Chris Gagne, eds., *The Impact of US Missile Defenses on Southern Asia* Report no. 46 (Washington DC.: The Henry L. Stimson Centre, 2002), p.24.
3. "Pakistan Capable to Counter India's Missile System," *People's Daily Online*. Available at <http://english.people.com.cn/20050225/eng20050225_174740.html>
4. See, for example, Paolo Cotta-Ramusino and Maurizio Martellini, *Nuclear Safety, Nuclear Stability and Nuclear Strategy in Pakistan: A Concise Report of a Visit by Landau Network – Centro Volta* (Como: Landau Network, 2002). Available at www.mi.infn.it/%7Elandnet/Doc/pakistan.pdf.
5. Rajesh Rajagopalan, *Second Strike: Arguments About Nuclear War in South Asia* (New Delhi: Penguin, 2005), especially, chapter 3.

6. Zulfikar Ali Bhutto, *The Myth of Independence* (London: Oxford University Press, 1969), pp.152-53.
7. As cited in Air Commodore Jasjit Singh (Retd.), "1965 War: The Wrong Lessons," rediff.com, October 10, 2005. Available at http://www.rediff.com/news/2005/oct/10war1.htm.
8. Statement by Ambassador Munir Akram at the Special Session of the Conference on Disarmament on June 2, 1998.
9. "Pak Must Maintain Conventional Capability," *The Hindu*, March 26, 1999; "Pakistan Still Needs Conventional Forces: COAS," *The News International*, May 16, 1999.
10. The following is based on an analysis of professional military writings found in journals produced by various Indian Army training establishments as well as regimental and other military history writings and memoirs of army officers. For a fuller treatment of the subject, see Rajesh Rajagopalan, "Restoring Normalcy: The Evolution of the Indian Army's Counterinsurgency Doctrine," *Small Wars and Insurgencies*, 11:1, Spring 2000, pp.44-68.
11. Some, indeed, have. See, for example, Ashutosh Varshney, "India, Pakistan and Kashmir: Antinomies of Nationalism," *Asian Survey*, 31:11 November 1991, pp. 1009-1010.

Crossing the Lines: A Pakistani Looks at Science and Society in India

Pervez Hoodbhoy

Pakistan-India relations underwent dramatic improvement in 2004 and 2005. But this merely reflects the fact that relations were abysmally poor earlier. Indeed, even with the so-called peace process in motion, the two countries are hardly on friendly terms. Pakistan refused Indian aid for the devastating earthquake that killed over 50,000 people in its northern region. Moreover, there remains a high degree of ignorance among the populations – university academics included – of life and people on the other side of the border. An overwhelming number of students have never met a national of their "enemy country", a notion that has yet to disappear from school textbooks.

It was, therefore, a stroke of good fortune that allowed me to visit, and also to independently assess, the state of education and science across India's hugely diverse regions. This was made possible by the award of UNESCO's Kalinga Prize for the popularisation of science. One part of the prize included a 4-week lecture tour that took me around India: Delhi, Pune, Mumbai, Bangalore, Chennai, Hyderabad, Bhubhaneswar, Cuttack, Calcutta, and then back to Delhi again before I returned home to Islamabad in mid-February. Although the prize was awarded in 2003, frosty Pakistan-India relations had made the tour impossible until 2005.

It was a relentless schedule from the first day onwards, with several lectures daily at schools, colleges, universities, research institutions, and peace groups. I chatted with children from excellent schools as well as those from rather ordinary ones; had long sessions with students and professors from colleges and universities; met with the *junta* (cooks, taxi drivers, and rickshawallas); and was invited to see ministers and chief ministers in several states, as well as the president of India.

Some Observations

- *Many Indian universities have a cosmopolitan character and are world class.* Their social culture is secular, modern, and similar to that in universities located in free societies across the world. (In Pakistan, Aga Khan University (AKU) and Lahore University of Management Sciences (LUMS) would be the closest approximations.) Male and female students freely intermingle, library and laboratory facilities are good, seminars and colloquia are frequent, and the faculty engages in research. Entrance exams are tough and competition for grades is intense. Some "deemed universities" and other institutions I visited (Tata Institute of Fundamental Research, Indian Institute of Science, Indian Institutes of Technology, Institute of Mathematical Sciences, Indian Institute of Chemical Technology, Inter-University Centre for Astronomy and Astrophysics, Jawaharlal Nehru Centre for Advanced Scientific Research, Institute of Plant Breeding, Raman Institute, Swaminathan Institute, etc.) do research work at the cutting edge of science. A strong tradition of mathematics and theoretical science forms a backbone that sustains progress in areas ranging from space exploration and super-computing to nanotechnology and biotechnology.

- *The rural-urban divide, and the class divide, are strong.* Schools and colleges in small towns have a culture steeped in religion. Here one sees hierarchy, obedience, and even servility. The national anthem is sung in schools and religious symbols are given much prominence. Some students I met were bright, but many appeared rather dull. Although most Indian colleges are co-educational (unlike in Pakistan), male and female students sit separately and are not encouraged to intermingle. It is sometimes difficult to understand the English spoken there. Where possible, I spoke in Hindi/Urdu. This enhanced my ability to communicate and also created a certain kind of bonding. There is an evident desire to improve, however, and at least some college principals go out of their way to organise events and invite guest speakers. My lecture at the Basavanagudi National College, a fairly ordinary college in Bangalore, was the 1,978th lecture by academicians over a period of 30 years! I do not know of any Pakistani college that invites speakers regularly.
- *Independent thought in India's better universities is alive and well.* Office bearers of the Jawaharlal Nehru University students union in Delhi were requested by the university's administration to present flowers to President Abdul Kalam at the annual convocation. They flatly refused, saying that he is a nuclear hawk and an appointee of a Hindu fundamentalist party. Moreover, as young women of dignity, they could not agree to act as mere flower girls presenting bouquets to a man. Eventually, the head of the physics department, also a woman, somewhat reluctantly presented flowers to Dr. Kalam but said that she

was doing so as a scientist honouring another scientist, not because she was a woman. Bravo! I have not seen comparable boldness and intellectual courage in Pakistani students. Student unions in Pakistan have been banned for two decades and so it is a moot question if any union there could have mustered similar independence of thought.

- *Taking science to the masses has become a kind of mantra all over India.* My columnist friend Praful Bidwai – a powerful critic of the Indian state and its militaristic policies – counts among India's greatest achievements the energisation of its democracy and refers to "our social movements, with their rich traditions of people's self-organisation, innovative protest and daring questioning of power." These movements have ensured that, unlike in Pakistan, land grabbers in Indian cities have found fierce resistance when they try to gobble up public spaces – parks, zoos, playgrounds, historical sites, etc. Praful should also include in his list the huge number of science popularisation movements, sometimes supported by the state but often spontaneous. These are sweeping through India's towns and villages, seeking to bring about an understanding of natural phenomena, teach simple health care, and introduce technology appropriate to a rural environment. There is not even one comparable Pakistani counterpart. I watched some science communicators, such as Arvind Gupta at IUCAA in Pune, whose infectious enthusiasm leaves children thrilled and desirous of pursuing careers in science. Individual Indian states have funded and created numerous impressive planetariums and science museums, and local organisations are putting out a huge volume of written and audio-visual science material in the local languages.
- *Attitudes of Indian scientists towards science are conservative.* Progress through science is an immensely popular notion in India, stressed by both past and present leaders. But what is science understood to be? I was a little jolted upon reading Nehru's words, written in stone at the entrance to the Jawaharlal Nehru Institute for Advanced Research in Bangalore: "I too have worshipped at the shrine of science." The notion of "worship" and "shrine of science" do not go well with the modern science and the scientific temper. Science is about challenging – not worshipping. As a secular man, Nehru was not given to worship but his metaphorical allusions to industries and factories as temples of science found full resonance. Indeed, science in India is largely seen as an instrument that enhances productive capabilities, and not as a transformational tool for producing an informed, just, and rational society. Most Indian scientists are techno-nationalists – they put their

science at the service of their state rather than the people. In this respect, Pakistan is no different.

- *India's nuclear and space programmes are nationally venerated as symbols of high achievement.* This led to India's nuclear hero, Dr. Abdul Kalam, becoming the country's president. When Dr. Kalam received me in his office, after the usual pleasantries, I expressed my regret at India having gone nuclear and causing Pakistan to follow suit. Shouldn't India now reduce dangers by initiating a process of nuclear disarmament? Dr. Kalam gave me a well-practised response: India would get rid of its nuclear weapons the very minute that America agreed to do the same. He displayed little enthusiasm for an agreement to cut off fissile material production. However, he did agree to my suggestion that exchange of academics could be an important way to build good relations between Pakistan and India.
- *Indian society remains deeply superstitious, caste divisions are important, and women still have a long way to go.* While I found myself admiring the energetic popular science movements, I was disappointed that they pay relatively little attention to the anti-scientific superstitions widely prevalent in Indian society. The *jyotishi* (astrologer) dictates the dates when a marriage is possible, and even whether a couple can marry at all. After I had given a strong pitch for fighting irrational beliefs at a meeting of science popularisation activists from villages in Northern India, a young woman asked me what to do if *"koi devi aap pay utr jayai"* (if a spirit should descend upon you). Inter-caste marriages are still frowned upon, and usually forbidden. In local newspapers, one typically reads of tragic accounts such as that of a boy and girl from different castes who jointly commit suicide after their families forbid the match. Although Indian women are freer, more visible, and more confident than their Pakistani counterparts, India is still a strongly male dominated society. However, the rapidly increasing number of bold and well-educated young women gives hope for the future.
- *Muslims in India remain at the margins of scientific research and higher education.* Hamdard University in Delhi is distinctly better than the university bearing the same name on the Pakistani side. Jamia Millia, a largely Muslim university, appears to be doing well and probably better than any Pakistani university in the field of physics. But, although Muslims form 12 percent of India's population, I met only a few Muslim scientists in leading Indian research institutes and universities. Discrimination against Muslims does not appear to be the dominant

cause. A professor at Jamia told me that an overwhelming number of Muslim students were inclined towards seeking easier (and more lucrative) professions in spite of special incentives offered to them at his university. In general, Muslims in India appear more modern and secular than in Pakistan. However, Hyderabad astonished me. Is it a total exception? In the lecture that I gave at a government women's college, there was only one young woman without a *burqa* in an audience of about a hundred. These women were surprised to learn that Pakistan – at least in most places – is more liberal than Hyderabad. The extreme conservatism in the Muslim part of the city reminds one of Peshawar.

- *There was a remarkable lack of hostility towards Pakistan.* Indeed, a desire for friendly relations was repeatedly expressed in every forum I went to. This is not to be taken lightly: many of my public lectures were either about (or on) science, but others dealt with deeply contentious issues – nuclear weapons, India-Pakistan relations, and the Kashmir conflict. Various Indian peace groups and non-governmental organisations (NGOs) organised public discussions and screenings of the two documentaries that I had made (with my friend Zia Mian): "Pakistan and India under the Nuclear Shadow", and "Crossing the Lines – Kashmir, Pakistan, India." To be sure, my views on Indian policies and actions in Kashmir occasionally provoked knee-jerk nationalistic responses and accusations of pushing "a Pakistani line". But these were infrequent and even heated exchanges always remained within the bounds of civility.
- *Ignorance about Pakistan is widespread.* In most public gatherings, and certainly in every school that I spoke at, people had never seen a Pakistani. A puzzled 12-year old girl asked me: "Sir, are you really a Pakistani?" Many Indians have a misconception of Pakistan as a medieval, theocratic state. In fact, only a few parts of Pakistan are really so. I also encountered the belief that Pakistanis have been totally muzzled and live in a police state. This is untrue – articles in the Pakistani Press are often blunter and more critical than in the Indian Press. An Indian friend hypothesised that knowledge of the other country is inversely proportional to the geographical distance between countries. Unfortunately, this will remain true unless there is a substantial exchange of visitors between the two countries.
- *Indians are deeply nationalistic and may dislike particular governments but they only rarely criticise the Indian state.* This is not difficult to understand: the democratic process has given a strong sense of participation to most citizens and has successfully forged a national identity (except in Kashmir, and parts of the northeast) that transcends the immense diversity of Indian

cultures. But this has an important downside: nationalism is easy to mobilise and highly dangerous in matters of war and conflict. I found the Indian elite (especially the former heads of nuclear, space, and technology programmes) condescending and irritatingly smug. Even if India has done well in some respects, in most others, it is still behind the rest of the world. Fortunately, Pakistani intellectuals are less attached to their nation-state and, therefore, more forthright. The reason is rather clear: three decades of military rule have dealt a serious blow to nation-building and firming up the Pakistani identity.

- *Similarities between the two countries exceed the differences.* Cities in both countries are poisoned with thick car fumes and grid-locks are frequent; megaslums and exploding populations threaten to swallow up the countryside; electricity supplies are intermittent; and water is fast disappearing from rivers and aquifers. The rural poor are fleeing to the cities, and wretched beggars with amputated limbs are casually accepted as part of the urban scenery. There is little long-term planning, and none at all for coping with the inevitable changes that global warming will soon bring.

The Way Forward

One can imagine a very large number of goodwill gestures that would help create a climate of peace between India and Pakistan. Among these is academic exchange and, in particular, the exchange of university teachers. Teaching visits could help create strong bonds. This certainly does not come at the expense of other efforts such as short school visits by students. Indeed, one hopes that the suggested exchange could be a precursor for a much wider exchange of faculty and students between Pakistani and Indian universities, and, hence, allow for increased contact between two populations that have grown apart over the decades. If sufficient people-to-people contact comes about, this could eliminate or greatly reduce the threat of confrontation between two heavily armed neighbouring states.

University teacher exchange also makes eminent economic and developmental sense: Pakistan is eagerly seeking to attract foreign faculty into its rapidly expanding university system by offering salaries 5-10 times larger than normal for scientific and technical subjects. On the other hand, India has a huge pool of accomplished teachers in its universities and research institutes.

There is evidence that some Pakistani universities would be eager to accept Indian faculty if permission is granted by the government. Indeed, although this is not generally known, there is a handful of Indian teachers employed in Pakistan. Attractive salaries, together with other reasons, would succeed in attracting many more renowned Indian teachers for short-term contracts. Some Indian universities have already indicated their interest in hiring teachers from Pakistan.

Obtaining political consent from the two national governments will require exercising quiet but effective diplomacy, perhaps from a third country. It is not possible, at the present time to get long-term (3-6 month) visas for university teachers from the other side. This is likely to be the biggest immediate hurdle. But if the ice is broken, this may lead to a situation where large numbers of academics cross borders without needing special effort or financial incentives. Extremists on both sides will oppose the idea but, if one starts small enough, there may not be excessive opposition.

India-Pakistan Relations: The Jihadi Impediment

Wilson John

Introduction

In May 2002, Pakistan President Pervez Musharraf came under compelling pressure from the international community to rein in terrorist groups following India's decision to mass troops on the border in retaliation for the December 2001 attack on the Indian Parliament. He summoned senior officials of the Inter-Services Intelligence Directorate (Pakistan's omnipotent external intelligence agency known by its infamous acronym, the ISI) and told them that *jihadi* groups operating in Kashmir will have to halt operations. Soon after, a senior ISI officer summoned *jihadi* leaders to convey this message. Incensed by the directive, one of the *jihadi* leaders said, Hassan Abbas reports, "General Musharraf has betrayed the Kashmiris after ditching the Taliban."[1]

Nothing could be more revealing than this small but insightful anecdote, coming as it does from a senior police official in Pakistan, about the depth of ties that bind *jihadi* groups and the state in Pakistan. Time and again, it has been proved, beyond any doubt, that in Pakistan, *jihadis* have for long been instruments of Pakistan's foreign policy.[2]

Pakistan has about 58 religious political parties and 24 armed *jihadi* groups,[3] most of whom were created by the Pakistan Army or the ISI, as covert instruments of the state policy to create and quell internal sectarian conflicts, intimidate opponents of the regime, ethnic separatists and moderate political parties. Some of the *jihadi* groups were later gathered under the umbrella of Harkat-ul Ansar (HuA) by the ISI[4] to support secessionist Kashmiri groups like the Jammu and Kashmir Liberation Front (JKLF) which had declared war on the Indian state in 1988. Former JKLF leader Yasin Malik is on record stating that a prominent Pakistani politician, Sheikh Rashid, federal minister of information and broadcasting in the ruling coalition government of President Musharraf, hosted his group.[5]

There is no visible change in this policy even today. For the Pakistan Army, extremist and terrorist groups (often difficult to distinguish) continue to be effective tools in managing regional interests—ensuring Pakistan's objective of maintaining a strategic depth in Afghanistan and keeping India occupied in Kashmir.[6] Thus, aided and supported by the state, these groups, over the years, more so particularly during the Musharraf rule since October 12, 1999, have successfully managed to lay the ground work for an extensive terrorist infrastructure in Pakistan[7] which includes newspapers and magazines, charitable trusts and *madrassas* (religious schools) to channelise funds and enlist and indoctrinate new recruits, new training facilities across the country and sleeper cells in the US, India, Australia, Iraq, Spain and Britain.

It is against this backdrop that this chapter would make an attempt to evaluate the growth of *jihadi* groups in Pakistan, their official patronage, and the impact Pakistan's persisting strategy of using them to promote and foster terrorism as an instrument of foreign policy will have on the peace process between India and Pakistan initiated in April 2003. This analysis, for the sake of brevity and clarity, will confine itself to two primary strands of inquiry: the status of terrorist infrastructure in Pakistan and whether there is any discernible change in Pakistan's Kashmir policy.

Genesis of Extremism

For an objective assessment, it is important to place in context how and when religious extremism acquired official patronage in Pakistan and how it became part of the global *jihad*.

Although it would not be altogether unfair to state that religious extremism was an important factor in the birth of Pakistan, the seeds of the present form of extremist ideology were sown some time in 1979[8] when President Zia ul-Haq decided to adopt Islamic laws—an Islamic penal code, a Shariat court and a system of Islamic taxes—for his country. The move infuriated the Shias[9] who took to the streets for several months before laying a siege on Islamabad. Faced with an angry mass protest across Pakistan, Zia backed down and withdrew some of the provisions of the Islamic laws. This was widely seen, especially among the Sunnis and the army, as a defiance of the Martial Law regime. The army, which has been ruling Pakistan, directly or by proxy, saw it as a threat to its hegemony and national security.[10] Two prominent Sunni religious organisations, Jamaat-e-Ulema-Pakistan (JuP) and Jamiat-e-Ulema-e-Islam (JuI), alarmed at the Shia's growing clout, supported, they believed, in large measure by a Shia-dominated Iran, decided to strike back. With the tacit support of the army, they organised two conferences with the sole objective of countering the "move by this tiny Shia minority to impose its will on Sawad-e-Azam (the great Sunni majority)."[11] The fall-out of the these two conferences was the setting up of a radical Sunni organisation called Sawad-e-Azam located in Karachi which, later, came to be known as Anjuman-e-Sipah-e-Sahaba, led by a young Sunni extremist and vice president of JuI's Punjab unit, Haq Nawaz Jhangvi. The army encouraged the growth of the group, especially in Bawahalpur and Rahimyar Khan, to be used as a "second line of defence against a possible Indian attack from Rajasthan."[12] A few years later, the Anjuman was rechristened as Sipah-e-Sahaba Pakistan (SSP), one of the most dreaded extremist groups in Pakistan today with links to various terrorist groups, besides the Taliban and Al Qaida.

These groups, spawned in *madrassas,* which flourished during the Afghan *jihad,* are supplemented by generous Saudi munificence. These *madrassas* were run by different factions of JuI which had, over a period of time, split into several groups. A large number of *madrassas,* with an average enrolment of 2,000 students, tutored (and continues to do so) young and impressionable students in a sectarian and extremist outlook.[13] One of the prominent *jihadi madrassas* is the Jamiat-ul-Ulum ul-Islamia set up by Alama Yusuf Binori[14] in Binori town, Karachi. Part of the Binori mosque, the *madrassa* has about 12 affiliate schools and an enrolment of 8,000. It was presided over by Mufti Nizamuddin Shamzai, known for his *fatwa* against the US,[15] till his assassination in June 2004. Another seminary that took part in the Afghan *jihad* was Dar-ul Uloom Haqqania at Akhora Khattak, Northwest Frontier Province (NWFP), headed by Maulana Samiul-Haq, chief of a splinter group of JuI, and friend and teacher of a large number of the Taliban leaders.[16] These seminaries, especially the one at Binori town, have been prominent recruitment and training grounds for *jihadis,* a large number of whom were drawn from the SSP cadre[17] and sent to training camps set up by the Central Intelligence Agency (CIA)-ISI combine in Afghanistan and Pakistan.[18] At one point, more than 25,000 recruits from 30 countries attended these training camps run by the Pakistan Army.[19] It was at these training camps that religious extremist groups like the SSP developed closer links with the Taliban and other terrorist groups like HuA and Hizb-ul Mujahideen (HuM), besides various other groups that were drawn to the *jihad* from Southeast Asia, Central Asia and Europe.[20]

Coalition of Terror

The ouster of the Taliban and Al Qaida from Afghanistan, following the relentless US bombing within a month of the September 11 terrorist attacks on the World Trade Centre (WTC), gave a new lease of life to various criminal, sectarian and religious groups in Pakistan that were finding it increasingly difficult to survive due to international pressure. The WTC attack had forced the Pakistan government to ban several organisations, close down their offices and freeze their bank accounts. Many of these groups would have faced a natural death had Al Qaida and Taliban elements not taken shelter in Pakistan following the US bombings in Afghanistan. These groups provided Al Qaida and other groups with logistics support to help regroup in Pakistan, developing in the process a new coalition of terrorists.[21] This was facilitated, in no less measure, by the unambiguous relationship that existed between the Pakistani military-intelligence establishment and these local extremist elements that befriended Al Qaida.

The murder of the India correspondent of *Wall Street Journal*, Daniel Pearl, in Karachi in January 2002 and the police shooting of Amjad Farooqui, one of the most wanted terrorists in Pakistan, in September 2004, revealed how Al Qaida had successfully managed to bring together various religious, sectarian and criminal groups in Pakistan into its fold. Fazl Karim, a Lashkar-e-Jhangvi (LeJ—a splinter group of SSP, more rabid and violent) activist from Rahimyar Khan (a district in Punjab) picked up for questioning three months after the killing of Pearl, was one of the first to reveal Al Qaida's merger plans in Pakistan within weeks of September 11.[22] It was Karim who held Pearl while two Yemenis slit his throat. The two Yemenis, it was later discovered, were associates of Ramzi Yousef, the main accused in the World Trade Centre attack of 1993. Subsequent investigations revealed that LeJ was only one of the several groups involved in the murder of Pearl, including many, like Amjad Farooqui, who were later accused of conspiring to kill President Musharraf.

Amjad Farooqi was shot dead by the security forces on September 26, 2004, after a five-hour gun battle. Farooqi was involved in the two assassination attempts[23] on President Musharraf along with Libyan Al Qaida operative Abu Feraj al-Libbi, Pearl murder accused Syed Omar Sheikh, activists of Jaish-e-Mohammad (JeM) and LeJ. Investigations also revealed that Farooqi, who was also involved in the hijacking of the Indian Airlines flight IC-814 in December 1999, had friends within the Pakistan Army, and had knowledge of the president's security arrangements.[24] The assassination attempts also revealed the existence of a loose confederation of terrorist and extremist groups called Brigade 313,[25] with possible links to Al Qaida. Brigade 313 was found to be an alliance of five terrorist groups—JeM, Harkat-ul Jihad al Islami, LeT, LeJ and Harkat-ul Mujahideen al Alami. Pakistan security officials believe that the assassination attempts followed a threat issued by Osama bin Laden's second-in-command, Ayman al-Zawahri, in September 2003. [26]

These two events—Pearl's murder and Farooqi's shooting—showed how Pakistan itself faced serious threats from extremist elements, a factor that might make the army deflect the trouble towards India in the near future under the guise of *jihad* in Kashmir. A Pakistani Air Force officer, Air Commodore Tariq Mahmud Ashraf summed up the situation aptly: "The fall of the Taliban introduced a new dimension in terrorism activities in Pakistan because a sizeable number of *jihadi* elements who returned to Pakistan got involved in terrorist activities here. Pakistan's worry is that this vast reservoir of trained potential terrorists has already crossed over into Pakistan and this group of individuals...have strong and established links with Pakistani religious groups and parties..."[27]

Continuing Threat

Although several terrorist and religious groups[28] have been involved in fomenting terrorism in Kashmir[29], only one—Lashkar-e-Tayyeba (LeT)—merits a closer scrutiny for the present assessment. [30] First, Lashkar is the only terrorist group which is organised on a strict hierarchical structure, has a clearly articulated agenda, generous financial resources and assets, and a large number of recruits from different parts of the world. Second, for the above reasons, it is a group which has the capability to evolve independently of the state. Third, it has escaped a greater scrutiny because of its conscious attempts to project itself independent of Al Qaida. Fourth, it has the support of the state. Fifth, it has a large network in India and is now spreading its cells in the US, Australia, Europe and Southeast Asia. Sixth, LeT is the only group that today has the wherewithal to threaten India beyond Kashmir. Seventh, the group is currently recruiting a large number of youngsters for terrorist activities, setting up new training camps and expanding its base beyond the Indian subcontinent.[31]

LeT has 2,200 offices across Pakistan and more than two dozen launching camps along the Line of Control (LoC). The group runs at least two training camps in Muzaffarabad, Pakistan Occupied Kashmir, stocked with weapons and ammunition, most of which are procured through international gun-runners.[32] The training is divided into two phases—*Daura Aam* (Basic Phase) and *Daura Khaas* (Special Phase). The first phase is of 21-day duration where students are motivated to accept *jihad* as life's mission through stories of bravery and sacrifice of martyrs. The second phase lasts for three months and involves weapons training, ambush and survival techniques.

What really drives the terrorist group's ideological indoctrination and weapons training is a concept evolved by its founder, Hafiz Saeed. His philosophy has been to merge *jihadi* education with modern curricula to train young students not only in Islamic principles but also make them adept in science and technology.[33] This, he believes, will enable them to work towards alternative models of governance and development while learning fighting skills to wage *jihad*. Saeed believes that *jihad* is essential for achieving political power.

LeT's foray into terrorist activities began with the setting up of military training camps in the eastern Afghanistan provinces of Kuntar and Pakhtia in 1987-88. But since the *jihad* in Afghan was on the wane by that time, the group, persuaded by the ISI, turned its attention towards India in 1993. Saeed directed his group to concentrate first on Kashmir before taking up the cause of liberating Junagarh (a tiny enclave in the Indian state of Gujarat) and Hyderabad (at present the capital of the Indian state of Andhra Pradesh which was a Muslim-ruled princely state before partition). Addressing one of the annual three-day congregations of his group in Muridke in February 2000, Saeed declared: "The Hindu is a mean enemy and the proper way to deal with him is the one adopted by our forefathers...who crushed them by force...We need to do the same."[34] The group carried out several spectacular suicide attacks, massacres and terrorist operations in India, including sending terrorists to occupy mountain tops in upper Drass and Batalik, the ridge overlooking the town of Kargil in Kashmir which saw the most recent battle between the troops of the two nuclear neighbours in the summer of 1999. No less daring attacks were on the Jammu and Kashmir Assembly on October 1, 2001, and on the Indian Parliament House on December 13, 2001, coming barely weeks after the terrorist attacks in the US which led the US and Pakistan to impose a ban on the group, freeze its bank accounts and severely restrict Saeed's activities. Undeterred, Saeed addressed the media on December 24, 2001, outlining his plans to reorganise and strengthen LeT. He was arrested on December 31, 2001, but not for terrorist activities. The charges against him were making inflammatory speeches and inciting public which prompted the Lahore High Court to set him free on November 19, 2002.[35]

Saeed's incarceration could have been shorter but he took the opportunity to reorganise his group, renaming the parent organisation, Markaz-e-Dawa wal Irshad to Jamaat ul-Dawa (JuD) and appointing a close confidante Maulana Abdul Wahid Kashmiri, as the new LeT chief who, soon after, declared that his group was shifting its base to the Indian Kashmir. These steps were aimed to circumvent the ban imposed by President Musharraf and avoid further international sanctions. There was another clear change in Saeed's outlook: he turned against the US.

The two most worrying aspects about LeT today are its growing strength and an ever-expanding base—it has set up sleeper cells in the US,[36] India and Australia,[37] trained terrorists from other countries and has shown a willingness to enter new operational areas like Iraq, aligning with Al Qaida's operational strategy.

Current Situation

Given the gravity of the situation, especially after the two assassination attempts on President Musharraf, it was thought that Pakistan would honour its commitments on terrorism and clear the country of terrorist and sectarian groups like LeJ and LeT, and curb cross-border terrorism. Although there had been intermittent crackdowns on these groups marked by arrests and shooting of leaders and activists, the steps remained half-hearted, betraying Pakistan's refusal to make a complete break with its past covert support for terrorist groups.[38]

Well-known Pakistani journalists and commentators[39] have documented how Saeed and his group managed to hoodwink the sanctions despite Pakistan's commitment towards the US-led war on terrorism. The group's posters were seen in urban and rural areas of Pakistan's Punjab province, urging young men to join *jihad*. The posters carried the telephone numbers of the group's scores of offices. Despite the ban, the group, in the first two years of the ban, collected Rs 710 million in anonymous donations and gifts[40]. There are also reports that the group collected $280,000 in Britain alone where over 675,000 Muslims of Pakistani origin are currently in residence.

As for facilitating terrorists to cross over to Kashmir, there is evidence that President Musharraf allowed groups like LeT small-scale infiltrations in late 2002, inviting a public reprimand from US Ambassador to Pakistan Nancy Powell, in January 2003, who demanded that Pakistan must "ensure that its pledges are implemented to prevent infiltration across the Line of Control and end the use of Pakistan as a platform for terrorism."[41] This was corroborated by LeT chief Saeed's declaration in March 2004, while addressing a Friday sermon in Lahore, that his group had recruited more than 7,000 youngsters for the Kashmir *jihad*. He also claimed that over 800 of them had so far died in Kashmir.

Saeed's claims are amply borne out by both Indian and Pakistani figures of intrusions and terrorist training camps[42] operating from Pakistan. India has prepared a list of 54 terrorist training camps currently operating in Pakistan—27 in Pakistan Occupied Kashmir, eight in Punjab, 15 in NWFP, one in Sindh and three in Northern Areas. Infiltration too has shown a discernible rise in the past few months.[43] The Pakistani media[44] had recently revealed that several training camps were activated in April 2005 and hundreds of terrorists had gathered on the LoC[45] for infiltration during the summer months.

A fact which clearly indicates the growing clout of Saeed's terrorist group, is the freedom with which he holds Friday prayers at a Lahore mosque where he exhorts his followers to take up the path of *jihad* against India and the US with renewed vigour. He appears regularly in the columns of the Urdu Press with statements condemning President Musharraf's "pro-US" and "pro-India" policies. He hosts parties for political leaders.[46] His group has been allowed to distribute *jihadi* literature freely even in government offices where they have a sizeable readership among senior officials.[47] He was even paid severance pay by the ISI to lie low when the peace process with India began taking shape.[48]

There is also disturbing evidence that various *jihadi* groups have infiltrated political parties and security forces and intelligence services. The evidence presented during the trial at Fort Attock of those accused in the December 25 attack on President Musharraf showed that *jihadi* preachers had approached soldiers at an army stadium and a special services group camp at Abottabad in 2003 asking them to take up *jihad*.[49] More alarming is the statement made by Federal Minister for Interior Aftab Ahmed Khan Sherpao that there was evidence of at least one member of the National Assembly's links with Al Qaida.[50]

There have been no curbs on the *jihadi madrasas* either despite the heat generated after the July 7 London blasts.[51] At least three of the four London bombers were supposed to have visited *madrassas* in Pakistan.[52] Although President Musharraf promised action against *madrassas* in his July 22 speech, there are serious differences within his government over the actions needed for *madrassa* reforms. Chaudhary Shujaat Hussain, president of the ruling coalition, and considered close to President Musharraf, has questioned the latter's decision to oust foreign students from *madrassas*.[53] Two members of the Cabinet, the ministers of education and religious affairs, have defended the *madrassas* by arguing that it was fallacious to link them up with extremism and terrorism. The much-touted *madrassa* reform, therefore, remains effectively stymied by these serious differences of opinion within the establishment.[54]

Target Kashmir

One of the reasons why President Musharraf has not been willing to honour his promise on cross-border terrorism is the impact it would have on Pakistan's Kashmir policy and consequently on the Pakistan Army which has sustained the cause of Kashmir over the last half-a-century for remaining the supreme arbiter of the destiny of Pakistan. Since the *jihadis*, who were operating in Kashmir, were "groomed and financed to operate in Kashmir" by the Pakistan Army, it was, and is, difficult for President Musharraf to neutralise them.[55]

President Pervez Musharraf's January 12, 2002, address to the nation reinforces what his predecessors have been emphasising on Kashmir: "Kashmir runs in our blood. No Pakistani can afford to sever links with Kashmir...We will continue to extend our moral, political and diplomatic support to Kashmiris. We will never budge from our principled stand on Kashmir."[56]

The statement represents, in a nutshell, the official policy of Pakistan on Kashmir,[57] influenced substantially by the army's perception that "Kashmir is so strategically situated that it can be used to cripple Pakistan economically and militarily."[58] The army's apprehensions were also based on the fact that the Indus, the lifeline for Pakistan, flowed from Kashmir, giving India an omnipotent weapon against the former in future. Over the years, the army exploited these fears to turn Kashmir into a question of identity, an "unfinished task of Partition."[59] When three wars and more than four decades of diplomatic offensive failed to achieve much, the Pakistan Army, supported by the political establishment, chose to exploit the presence of the band of Mujahideen,[60] returning flush with their victory in Afghanistan. The Mujahideen, within years of their involvement in Kashmir, were given the respectability of *jihad* and remained outside the purview of diplomatic scrutiny for long, till they became "terrorists" for the West. Not only did Pakistan train secessionists from Kashmir but it also recruits or volunteers from other groups and countries in carrying out acts of sabotage and killings in Kashmir, linking the cause with an emerging global *jihad*.[61] Various groups were incorporated in the new *jihad* for Kashmir[62], some already existing, others created anew, by the ISI to project Kashmir on the consciousness of the global community as a potential conflict zone in a nuclear environment by involving India in a low-cost but damaging proxy war, to aid and abet Kashmiri militants to force the secession of Kashmir; and to gainfully employ the guerilla bands returning from Afghanistan to prevent an internal law and order problem for Pakistan, already reeling under severe economic and social convulsions.

Jihad vs Peace

In one sense, President Musharraf has higher stakes in the outcome of the peace process than India. He has seemingly compromised on several contentious issues, including Kashmir, primarily to comply with the US pressure, and is seeking a *quid pro quo* from India on at least less troublesome border demarcation issues like the Sir Creek maritime boundary dispute. If the composite dialogue fails to come up with resolutions of at least some of the contentious issues between the two countries, President Musharraf might be hard put to keep the terrorist groups like LeT under check.

This could also mean a serious loss of face for the army which might revert to the proven strategies of the past, without President Musharraf. The involvement of junior officials of the Pakistan Air Force and intelligence agencies in the assassination attempts on the president, the detention of more than a dozen middle-rung officers from the army for their involvement with the Taliban in 2004 and the persistent criticism being levelled against the president by retired senior army officers for his policies towards India and the US are an indication of a growing sense of unease within the army establishment about the way Pakistan was being steered.

The vociferous religious leaders, contained for the time being by setbacks in the local by-elections and their failure to command a wider acceptance from the people, are eagerly waiting for President Musharraf to slip and falter. The composite dialogue with India, which lays emphasis on creating an atmosphere of goodwill and trust through people-to-people contact, has also generated a domestic constituency for peace in Pakistan, especially for the economic benefits it has accrued for them and the rekindling of hope that their country might just escape becoming an impoverished country ruled by religious brigands. The collapse of the peace process could unsettle these equations in a dramatically short time.

Ironically, the only way President Musharraf could ensure that such a collapse does not happen is to dismantle the terrorist infrastructure, burn the bridges, and chart a new course for himself, and his country.

By President Musharraf's own admission on July 21, 2005, terrorist groups, during his regime, have "mushroomed in cities which recruit people openly, train them, collect donations and publish and distribute *jihadi* literature."[63] What he did not say was that it could be a conscious decision on the part of Pakistan to keep the *jihadi* infrastructure alive as an insurance policy on Kashmir[64] in case the peace process, especially the dialogue on Kashmir, gets mired in bickering and protests, and fails to yield any tangible results within a visible timeframe.

The *jihadi* groups are an integral part of Pakistan's Kashmir policy and there is no discernible sign of any changes in that policy. More significantly, *jihadi* groups like LeT are critical tools for the Pakistan Army to retain control over the peace process,[65] which currently has India in the driver's seat. Giving up *jihad* could mean giving up Kashmir. The failure of the Pakistan Army's attempts to force a solution though military means in Kargil 1999 has further revived and strengthened this strategy whose origins date back to 1947-48 when the army had orchestrated an attack on Kashmir by tribal *lashkars* (army) in an attempt to redefine the ceasefire line that divided the two nations. Pakistan's insistence on omitting any references to cross-border terrorism in joint statements betrays the revival of this policy.

Another ominous indicator of such a possibility can be inferred from what Saeed said in an interview to the Urdu newspaper, *Khabrain*, on July 20,2005. He said that *fidayeen* attacks were different from suicide attacks and that the *Quran* supported the concept of *jihad*. He declared that his group "would support it and they would also extend support to the organisations, active in *jihad* anywhere in the world."[66] This statement came barely three weeks after his group launched an attack on the highly revered holy site of Ayodhya on July 5.[67] Although the attack was foiled in time before the LeT suicide attackers could damage the holy shrine, there is likelihood that the group, using local sleeper cells, might attempt another major attack on a strategic target like a holy site or a historical monument, or an important government building, disrupting the peace process,[68] which, despite claims to the contrary from the top leadership of India and Pakistan, is far from crossing the critical threshold of irreversibility.

Notes

1. Zahid Hussain, "Mission Impossible?," *Newsline* (Karachi), June 2002. Available at http://www.newsline.com.pk/NewsJune2002/cover1june.htm.
2. Stephen Philip Cohen, "The Jihadist Threat to Pakistan," *The Washington Quarterly*, Summer 2003.
3. Hassan Abbas, *Pakistan's Drift into Extremism: Allah, the Army, and America's War on Terror* (New Delhi: Pentagon Press, 2005), p.201.
4. Abbas, Ibid.
5. Zulfiqar Ali, "For the Record," *Herald* (a widely read magazine of from the Dawn group of newspapers in Pakistan), Karachi, July 2005.
6. Vali Nasr, *Testimony to the Senate Foreign Relations Committee*, July 14, 2004. Available at http://foreign.senate.gov/testimony/2004/NasrTestimony040714.pdf
7. Hussain Haqqani, "Pakistan's Terrorism Dilemma," in Satu Limaye, Robert Wirsing and Mohan Malik, eds., *Religious Radicalism and Security in South Asia* (Honolulu: Asia Pacific Centre for Security Studies, 2004), pp.351-361.
8. According to well-known American analyst on Pakistan, Stephen Cohen, the Pakistan state first "exploited radical and violent Islamic groups in 1970-1971 in East Pakistan, when the Pakistani Army called on right wing Islamic militants, notably the student wing of the JI, to terrorise, torture, and murder Bengali intellectuals, politicians and other supporters of the Bangladesh movement." See Cohen, n.2.
9. Shias follow a different interpretation of Islamic texts and are in a minority in

Pakistan. When Zia pressed ahead with his decision to impose the rule of Islam on Pakistan, Shias formed the Tehrik-e-Nifaz-e-Fiqah-e-Jafariya (Movement for the Enforcement of the Jafari Fiqh) to fight the government in Islamabad.

10. Mumtaz Ahmed, "Sectarianism and Zia," *The News* (Karachi) April 15, 1988.
11. Ahmed, Ibid.
12. Khaled Ahmed, "Islamic Extremism in Pakistan," *South Asia Journal,* Issue 2 October-December 2003. Available at http://www.southasianmedia.net/Magazine/Journal/previousissue2.htm. Ahmed said he was given the information by a retired general of the Pakistan Army during a seminar.
13. Report of the Human Rights Commission of Pakistan, 1997, Islamabad, p.222.
14. Maulana Yusuf Binori, appointed by Zia as the member of the Council of Islamic Ideology, was instrumental in the grand Deobandi alliance which became the inspiration for the *jihad.* See Ahmed, n.12 , *South Asia Journal.*, Terrorist groups like the Lashkar-e-Tayyeba and extremist groups like the SSP owe allegiance to Deobandi school of Islam which has its origins in the town of the Deoband, Moradabad disrict of the Indian state of Uttar Pradesh. A majority of the *madrassas* in Pakistan are Deobandi.
15. Khaled Ahmed, "Jehad and the Price It Extracts," *The Friday Times* (Lahore), March 8, 2001.
16. At least nine Taliban Cabinet ministers were from Haqqania. The *madrassa* has a boarding school for 1,500 students, a high school for 1,000 day scholars and 12 affiliated *madrassas.* Many of JeM's recruits also came from this seminary.
17. "Pakistan: Madrassas, Extremism and the Military," *Asia Report No. 36*, July 29, 2002, p.12, International Crisis Group.
18. Samina Ahmed, "Centralisation, Authoritarianism, and the Mismanagement of Ethnic Relations in Pakistan," in Michael E. Brown and Sumit Ganguly, eds., *Government Policies and Ethnic Relations in Asia and the Pacific* (Cambridge: MIT Press, 1997) pp.107-127. A confidential report prepared by the deputy commissioner of Sheikupura on the orders of Prime Minister Benazir Bhutto said there were at least 38 terrorist training camps within Pakistan and in Karachi itself, 43 educational institutions were being used to recruit and indoctrinate terrorist trainees. See "Secret Pak Report Admits to 38 Terrorist Training Camps," *The Hindustan Times,* May 12, 1997.
19. Ahmed Rashid, "Trouble Ahead, Trouble Behind," *Current Theory,* Vol.95, No. 600, April 1996, p.160.
20. Wilson John, "Harkat-ul Jihad al Islami," in Wilson John and Swati Parashar, eds., *Terrorism in South Asia* (New Delhi: Observer Research Foundation, 2005), pp.78-89.
21. Hasan Masnoo, "New jihadi Group Involved in US Consulate Attack?" *The Friday Times,* July 12, 2002; Afzal Nadeem, "Arab Killed Pearl after Escape Bid: Police," *The Asian Age,* July 16, 2002; Shamsul Islam Naz, "Members of Banned Outfits Join New Groups," *Dawn,* March 22, 2002; Massoud Ansari, "City of Fear", Newsline, *June* 2002; In a testimony before the US Senate Committee on Intelligence on February 11, 2003, Defence Intelligence Agency Director Vice Admiral Lowell Jacoby said, "Al Qaida appears to maintain an operational presence in Pakistan. The government of Pakistan has been a key partner in Operation Enduring Freedom and in our global war on terrorism, but despite its best efforts, Al Qaida continues to use Pakistan for transit, haven, and as a staging area for attacks." Available at http://intelligence. senate.gov/0302hrg/030211/jacoby.pdf

22. Wilson John, *Karachi: A Terror Capital in the Making* (New Delhi: Rupa-ORF, 2004); Ian Bruce, "Radical Groups Join Forces in Jihad: CIA Claims Consulate Bomb was Work of Terror Alliance," *The Herald* (Glasgow), June 17, 2002.
23. "Suspected Mastermind of Attacks on Musharraf: Top Wanted Terrorist Amjad Farooqi Killed," *Daily Times*, September 27, 2004.
24. Kamran Khan, "Farooqi's Killing Leaves Important Questions Unanswered," *The News*, (Karachi), September 28, 2004.
25. Amir Mir, "Friends Turned Foes," *The Herald Annual, (Karachi)*, January 2004.
26. Mir, Ibid.
27. Tariq Mahmud Ashraf, "Terrorism in Pakistan: The Emerging Trends," paper presented at the National Defence College, Islamabad, Pakistan, 2004.
28. See K. Santhanam, Sreedhar, Sudhir Saxena and Manish, eds., *Jihadis in Jammu and Kashmir: A Portrait Gallery* (New Delhi: Sage and Institute for Defence Studies and Analyses, 2003); Zaffar Abbas, "The Militant Brigade," *The Herald*, February 2004.
29. Two other excellent and independent works of documentation of the involvement of terrorist groups in Kashmir are: Muhammad Amir Rana, *A to Z of Jehadi Organizations in Pakistan* (Lahore: Mashal Books, 2004) and Hassan Abbas, *Pakistan's Drift into Extremism: Allah, the Army, and America's War on Terror* (New Delhi: Pentagon Press, 2005). For an Indian view, please refer to an extensive catalogue of articles written by India's most well-known counter-terrorism expert, Mr. B. Raman, which can be accessed at www.saag.com or www.orfonline.org
30. The other two that have been in the forefront of terrorism in Kashmir are Jaish-e-Mohammad and Muttahida Jihad Council. Jaish is led by Maulana Masood Azhar, one of the terrorists released by India in the IC-814 hijacking in December 1999. Although Jaish had been quite active in the Valley, its influence waned after the Maulana, a rabble rouser, fell foul with the army and the ISI after September 11. The group also suffered heavily because of infighting and struggle for the control of assets. It is my estimate that the group also lost its benefactors in West Asia around this time, forcing many of its activists to form rebel groups or merge with other groups to carry out terrorist operations. The group suffered the army's ire after it was discovered that some of the Jaish leadership was involved in the assassination attempts on President Musharraf. The Muttahida Jihad Council, led by Syed Salahuddin from his headquarters in Muzaffarabad in Pakistan Occupied Kashmir (PoK), was set up by the ISI as a coordinating centre for Kashmir operations. The council is an umbrella organisation of several small groups operating in PoK but mainly consists of members of Hizb-ul Mujahideen, one of the most prominent groups operating in Kashmir for long. Hizb, over the years, almost run to the ground by the Indian Army, has lost its supremacy to more powerful and organised terrorist groups like Lashkar-e-Taiba.
31. Wilson John, "Lashkar-e-Taiba: New Threats Posed by an Old Organization," *Terrorism Monitor*, Vol. 3, Issue 4, February 24, 2005, Jamestown Foundation, Washington DC. Available at http://www.jamestown.org/publications_details.php? volume_id=411&issue_id=3242&article_id=2369321.
32. John, Ibid.
33. Saeed Shafwat, "The Rise of Dawat ul-Irshad and Lashkar-e-Toiba," in Christopher Jaffrelot, ed., *Pakistan: Nationalism Without a Nation* (New Delhi, Manohar Publications, 2002).
34. Hafiz Mohammad Sayeed,"No More Dialogue on Kashmir" www.dawacenter.

com/magazines/voiceofislam/sep99/editorial.html (This website was taken off following the US State Department ban on the group.)

35. Pakistani analysts have argued that the judiciary had been indifferent on deciding cases of terrorism. This apathy has resulted in a large number of acquittals in the recent years. Air Commodore Tariq Mahmud Ashraf, a senior Pakistani Air Force officer, in a paper presented at the National Defence College, Pakistan, has quoted the following figures. See Ashraf, n.27.

Year	Arrested	Convicted	Acquitted
2001	131	16	115
2002	142	22	120
2003	60	00	60

36. US vs Masoud Ahmad Khan, US District Court for the Eastern District of Virginia. Accessed at http://news.findlaw.com/hdocs/docs/terrorism/uskhan70103gmot.pdf.
37. "Brigitte May Return to Give Evidence," *The Age* (Melbourne), April 25, 2004. Available at http://www.theage.com.au/articles/2004/04/25/1082831430449.html? from=storyrhs.
38. Haqqani, n. 7, pp.351-361.
39. Two excellent references are Rana's, *A to Z of Jehadi Organizations in Pakistan* and Amir Mir's *True* Face *of Jihadis.* Both these books are published by Mashal Publications, Lahore, Pakistan.
40. Mohammad Shehzad, "Banned LeT Collects Millions in Charity, Hides," *South Asia Tribune,* Issue No.35, March 23-29, 2003. Available at www.satribune.com/archives/ mar23_29_03/P1_hides.htm
41. Abbas, n.3, pp.201-216.
42. Khalid Hasan, "There are Training Camps in Mansehra," *Daily Times,* August 22, 2005.
43. Wilson John, "Forceful Intervention," *The Pioneer,* August 17, 2005. The figures for month-wise infiltration in 2005 are as follows: January - 19; February - 5; March - 7; April - 44; May - 32; June - 72; and, July - 171.
44. Amir Mir, "Musharraf's Commitment to Wipe out Jihadis Badly Exposed," *South Asia Tribune,* July 31, 2005. Available at http://www.satribune.com/archives/200507/ P1_mir2.htm.
45. For an Indian figure, refer to John, n.43.
46. "Is Pakistan Still a Launch-Pad for Terrorism?" *Daily Times,* July 18, 2005.
47. Ali Waqqar, "Banned Literature Being Distributed in Punjab Offices," *Daily Times,* August 13, 2005.
48. Husain Haqqani, *Pakistan Between Mosque and Military* (Lahore: Vanguard Publications, 2005).
49. Zaffar Abbas, "The Fifth Column," *The Herald,* June 2005.
50. Muhamad Anis, "MNA Reported to Have Links with Al Qaeda: Sherpao," *Daily Times,* September 15, 2005.
51. Ahmed Rashid, "Pakistan Wakes up to the Hatred Within," *Daily Times,* July 15, 2005.
52. "Seminaries Won't be Searched for Militants," *Daily Times,* July 17, 2005.
53. Hasan-Askari Rizvi, "Political Dynamics of Counter Terrorism," *Daily Times,* August 15, 2005.

54. "Resist MMA's Scuttling of Madrassa Reform," *Daily Times*, August 24, 2005.
55. Abbas, n.3.
56.. The English rendering of the president's complete speech can be accessed at www.pakgov.pk/President_Addresses/presidential_addresses_index.htm
57. For an Indian view of Pakistan's Kashmir policy, refer to Smruti S.Pattanaik, "Pakistan's Kashmir Policy: Objectives and Approaches," *Strategic Analysis* (a monthly journal from a well-known government-funded think-tank, the Institute of Defence Studies and Analyses based in New Delhi), Vol. XXVI, No. 2, April-June 2002.
58. Hasan-Askari Rizvi, *The Military & Politics in Pakistan* (Lahore: Progressive Publishers, 1987) pp. 39 and 46.
59. "National Security and Pakistan's Foreign Policy" *Pakistan Horizon*, April 1990, The article was based on the address by Mr Iqbal Akhund, advisor to the prime minister on foreign affairs and national secuirty, on "National Security and Pakistan's Foreign Policy in a Changing World" at the Pakistan Institute for International Affairs, April 5, 1990.
60. The following terms, *jihadis, mujahideens* and terrorists, have often been used to describe members of various religious and sectarian groups who were recruited and trained by the Pakistan Army, funded generously by Saudi Arabia, the US and its allies during the Afghan *Jihad* and after. As long the terrorists worked for the US, they remained *mujhaideens* or religious warriors. No sooner had they turned against the US, they were clubbed together first as terrorists, then increasingly as *jihadis* , primarily to associate them with Islam.
61. Haqqani, n.7.
62. Haqqani, Ibid. Haqqani quotes a confidential letter from the US secretary of state to Prime Minister Nawaz Sharif which stated that "...we are very confident of our information that your intelligence service,the Inter-Service Intelligence Directorate, and elements of the Army, are supporting Kashmiri and Sikh militants who carry out acts of terrorism...The support takes the form of providing weapons, training and assistance in infiltration...."
63. President Musharraf's address to the nation, July 22, 2006. Available at www.pakgov.pk/President_Addresses/presidential_addresses_index.htm
64. Husain Haqqani, "Extremism Still Thrives in Pakistan," *International Herald Tribune* (Paris), July 19, 2005. Available at http://www.iht.com/articles/2005/07/19/opinion/edhaqq.php.
65. Hussain Haqqani, "London Bombings and Pakistani Connection," *South Asia Tribune*, July 20, 2005. Accessed at http://www.satribune.com/archives/200507/P1_hh2.htm
66. *Khabrain*,July 21, 2005.
67. Rakesh Sinha and Alka Pande, "Ayodhya: Terror Terminated, Politics Begins," *The Indian Express*, July 6, 2005.
68. "India: Terror Attacks Could Undermine Peace Process," *The Indian Express*, July 14, 2005.

The Indus Waters and Pakistan's Water Security[1]

A.K. Pandey

Introduction

One of the unintended consequences of the Indus Waters Treaty was the close involvement of multilateral financial institutions, such as the World Bank, which have appraised and financed virtually every project of any consequence in Pakistan over the past 50 years. Reports authored and commissioned by these agencies provide a wealth of data which is freely available in the public domain.[2] In recent times, there has also been a growing literature appearing in environmental journals. The following analysis depends wholly on such published primary material.

The analysis is divided into three parts, viz. Context, Pakistan's Water Security, and Conclusions.

Context and Background

Viewed in terms of hydrology and drainage basins, Pakistan comprises three regions. In the order of importance, these are the Indus Basin, the Balochistan plateau and the Makran coast. The Indus Basin, comprising all of the Northwest Frontier Province (NWFP), Punjab, Sindh and the eastern fringe of Balochistan, accounts for about 55 per cent of Pakistan's land area but 95 per cent of its population.

The importance of the Indus is seen starkly in this statistic. If all of Pakistan had the population density of the non-Indus Basin region, the entire territory of Pakistan would support a population of less than 15 million, as against its current population of roughly 160 million.

A recent article in the *International Herald Tribune* observes that the Indus is to Pakistan what the Nile is to Egypt.[3] This is, if anything, an understatement since the Indus Basin Irrigation System (IBIS) is the largest contiguous network in the world, extending over 16 million hectares or 80 per cent of Pakistan's total cultivated land area. The total length of the canal system (including field channels) runs in the vicinity of one million kilometres.

Alternatively, to take a less statistical, more sentimental view, one may consider the fact that the two largest provinces, accounting for roughly three quarters of Pakistan's population, viz, Punjab and Sindh are named after the rivers of the Indus Basin.

Natural disasters have played an important role in the history of our subcontinent. It is worth recalling that the East Bengal cyclone of 1970 presaged and, in a manner, contributed to, the political events that followed. In India, the twenty-year Mizoram insurgency was sparked in 1959 by one season's crop failure.

More recently, the renewed troubles in Balochistan have been attributed to the severe drought that this region has suffered since 2000. This drought has severely affected the local economy, decimating the livestock population which is the principal resource and wealth of the ethnic Baloch people and causing starvation deaths without evincing any significant relief or support from the federal authorities.

Pakistan's water crisis is just one facet of a serious and growing environmental crisis afflicting the entire Indus Basin, manifested *inter alia* in the deforestation and denudation of its upper reaches, the depletion of the water retention capability of the basin as a whole, and in the lower reaches, widespread degradation and contamination of Pakistan's land and water resources. In respect of many key environmental indicators such as land under forest cover, per capita water availability and soil salinity, Pakistan figures in the globally worst affected category.

The figures in this regard are well known.[4] Per capita water availability has declined from 5,000 cubic metres per annum in 1947 to around 1,100 cubic metres per annum currently, which is the threshold for water scarcity conditions. The area under forest cover has suffered an equally precipitous decline. Pakistan today has less than 4 per cent of its land under forest cover as against the international norm of 26 per cent. Salinisation of the lower Indus Basin is all pervasive, depleting the soil and taking a mounting human toll in terms of death and chronic diseases from the intake of contaminated water.

The following section estimates that the impact of the current water/ environmental crisis varies markedly from province to province. This is briefly surveyed below.

Regional Impact

Pakistan has no institution responsible for the integrated development of the entire Indus Basin. Located as it is at the tail end of the Indus Basin Irrigation System (IBIS), Sindh must cope with its own problems, as well as the downstream impact of the localised measures of the upper riparians. It has been severely affected by the arbitrary upstream diversion of the Indus waters by Punjab, as also by poorly designed drainage projects that evacuate salinity and pollutants from upstream regions to interior Sindh. This, in turn, has seriously affected the quantity and quality of water available in the province.

Historically, the richest agricultural region in the territory now constituting Pakistan was the Indus delta. Over the centuries, the silt laden fresh waters of the Indus fertilised the delta and its farmers prospered by growing large surpluses of rice and fish for export. As a result of the upstream damming and diversion of the Indus, the delta has shrunk catastrophically; measuring 350 sq km with nine perennial streams in 1947, it has shrunk today to just 25 sq km and two perennial streams.[5]

Most arable lands in the coastal districts of Thatta and Badin and in southern Hyderabad have been rendered barren by salt-water intrusion. Drinking water supplies are contaminated and hundreds of villages in these districts have been abandoned. For those that remain, international relief agencies such as the United Nations Development Programme (UNDP) and the World Council of Churches, at the instance of the Pakistan government, provide relief by way of free food and fuel.

While the coastal districts are the worst affected, interior Sindh is not much better off. Ground water throughout the province is so saline that tubewell irrigation is impossible except in lands adjacent to the canal system. Interior Sindh was famous for its large fresh water bodies, such as the 100 sq km Manchar Lake, which hosted a large variety of flora and fauna, including 222 species of birds. The concentration of saline waste has turned most of Pakistan's lakes and wetlands into 'cesspools', which regularly causes large scale injury and death due to water poisoning, particularly in the major population centres in Sindh.[6] The residents of these wetlands who made a decent living by fishing, farming and tourism, are now chronically sick and poverty stricken.

Water deprivation is pervasive, affecting towns as well as countryside. In Karachi, for example, the municipal water supply is so erratic that this function has been taken over by a "tanker mafia", in which the federal paramilitaries, the Pakistani Rangers, play a major role. Middle class families may pay upto Rs. 5,000 per month for assured water supplies. Unusual medical disorders caused by contaminated water such as typhoid, bone deformities and renal failure have multiplied in recent years.

It is said that throughout much of Sindh, cattle are being replaced by camels. The most pressing of the province's problems, issues such as desertification, declining per capita incomes, increasing poverty ratio and frequent outbreaks of water poisoning, can be directly ascribed to the environmental degradation of the Indus Basin.

The NWFP should in theory be abundant in water resources, receiving as it does 1,000 mm of precipitation annually. Perversely, mismanagement of its natural resources has left the NWFP stricken with both water scarcity and poverty. Over 43 per cent of the NWFP's population lives below the food poverty line.

Most residents of the NWFP, Peshawar apart, are dependent on the soil, primarily animal husbandry, forestry, tobacco and maize cultivation. The roots of the present economic distress go back to the Eighties and the Afghan *jihad*. Till this time, the mountains of the NWFP were covered with thick Himalayan forests of walnut and pine which provided fuel and shelter while protecting the ecosystem, offering habitats for the area's animals, and holding the soil of the hillsides in place. Shrubs and extensive grasslands fulfilled a similar function in the lower reaches.

The influx of the Afghan refugees with their livestock and the beginnings of a road infrastructure suddenly put a high premium on the NWFP's wood and biomass resources. Inevitably, an influential "timber mafia" took over and the uncontrolled felling and trading of timber began. Today, the forest cover in the NWFP stands reduced to just 12 per cent of its original level. In many mountain areas, exposed rock is visible and the entire ecosystem degraded.[7]

The consequences of this rampant deforestation are serious soil erosion and marked scarcities of fuelwood and building timber upon which the local communities relied. Top soil losses are estimated at 150–165 tons per hectare per annum. Such arable land as remains is either extremely poor or used by drug dealers to grow opium. Lower down, the watershed, of an original 5 million hectares of grazing land, 4.3 million are now said to be devoid of vegetation.[8] Poverty and scarcity of potable water have followed.

With the loss of the NWFP's forests, Pakistan has merely 4 per cent of its land under forest cover, as against the international norm of 26 per cent. The absence of vegetation leads to a large reduction in watershed and reservoir efficiency. The Warsak Hydroelectric Dam near Peshawar, constructed in 1960, is already silted up and can generate only the run of the river power. The World Bank estimates that less than 10 per cent of Pakistan's hydroelectric potential is currently exploited, yet further development is heavily constrained by silting.[9]

Despite some efforts at reforestation by voluntary agencies such as the Agha Khan Trust, it is believed that Pakistan continues to lose timber at the rate of 5 million board-feet a year. At this rate, the country's forests may cease to exist in a decade. As it is, say researchers, 90 per cent unemployment rates are not unknown, conflict is rife, and the whole social system of the province is under stress.[10] According to the local forest conservator, the true figure for Pakistan's forest cover would be closer to 2 per cent.[11] "In the poor areas, the people are desperate. Not a blade of grass stands, not a tree, not a shrub."[12]

Balochistan is the largest province, accounting for nearly half of Pakistan's land area. The eastern quarter of the province falls within the Indus Valley, otherwise most of Balochistan forms a separate geographical basin altogether.

The arid province has long suffered Islamabad's neglect, reflected *inter alia* in the fact that it is unable to fully utilise its miniscule 3 per cent share of the Indus waters. Of 19 million hectares of cultivable land, a mere 0.33 million hectares have assured irrigation, the interior plateau and valleys having none.[13] Here, an ad hoc, private tubewell based irrigation sprang up, leading to the cultivation of water-intensive crops such as rice and sugarcane. Such practices proved unsustainable in the highly arid conditions where ground water reserves are exhausted rapidly. As a result, most of these farms and orchards are now being abandoned.

Animal husbandry, the primary occupation of the ethnic Baloch, is particularly hard hit. A prolonged drought starting in 1999 took a heavy toll, destroying well over half the livestock. Starvation deaths and large scale internal displacement of people have taken place, with international voluntary agencies called in to provide relief.

With its preferred access to scarce water resources, Punjab has not suffered the deprivation of the three smaller provinces, although the situation varies markedly between the pampered north Punjab areas and the districts of southern Punjab – the so-called Seraiki speaking areas where the situation is more akin to downstream Sindh. This situation has, in turn, fuelled the Seraiki demand for an independent province and the renegotiation of the Indus Water Treaty with a view to reclaiming the waters of the Satluj.[14]

Pakistan's Water Security

The key to Pakistan's water security paradigm lies in the seasonality of the Indus waters. The catchment of the Indus comprises a wide arc of the high Himalayas from the Panjshir Valley north of Kabul to Siachen down to eastern Ladakh. In the summer months, when the accumulated snow and glaciers melt, there is enough water in the system to meet all of Pakistan's agricultural needs plus a surplus to fill the dams and for the occasional flood. Over 80 per cent of the total mean annual flow of the Indus accrues in the five months from May – September.

The problem occurs during the winter months when, with the principal agricultural crop of Pakistan, wheat, in the fields, the Indus falls from its summer high of half a million cusecs to below 20,000 cusecs. The main tributaries of the Indus, viz. the Kabul, Chenab and Jhelum broadly follow the seasonality of the Indus although they are more rain dependent and as lower altitude rivers, rise earlier and recede later than the main Indus.

Wheat is not a particularly water-intensive crop but early watering is crucial for its planting and initial growth. The two giant hydroelectric dams at the head of the Indus Basin, viz, Tarbela and Mangla assure this early watering and, to this extent, provide a measure of wheat guarantee or what one may term a food safety net to the country. The problem is that this food safety net is getting progressively thinner and more worn out with every passing year on account of the rapid siltation of these dams.

According to the official figures, the Tarbela and Mangla Dams have already lost over 24 per cent of their total storage capacity.[15] The Indus carries the most heavy silt load of any major river in the world and this has depleted the capacity of the Tarbela, which probably retains less than two-thirds of its initial capacity of 11.5 million acre feet of water.[16] Since the Tarbela accounts for nearly two-thirds of Pakistan's total water storage capacity, this has had an impact on the water availability for the basin as a whole. Each passing year, there is a little less assured moisture for Pakistan's main agricultural crop.

This situation has given new life to an old controversy – the question of a new high dam on the Indus at Kalabagh. This controversy, which is almost as old as Pakistan itself, has always had the effect of placing Punjab in opposition to the three smaller provinces. Over the years, in a general atmosphere of distrust and perceived injustice, the position on all sides has progressively hardened and the proposed dam has acquired a political symbolism which far outweighs its technical parameters. The provincial Assemblies in all the three smaller provinces have unanimously adopted, on more than one occasion, resolutions against the Kalabagh Dam, but this has not stopped Punjabi interests, now voiced by General Musharraf himself, to revive this dam. The Kalabagh issue, like the problem of water, in general, has got steadily more intractable over the years; it belongs to a category of problems where the status quo is intolerable but any possible solution even worse.

Given the seasonality of the Indus waters, Pakistan's water crisis is in essence a ten-week window of vulnerability in the first quarter of the calendar year: with the crucial *rabbi* crop hungry for water, and seasonal flows at a minimum, even minor shortages can have a disproportionate effect. During this window of vulnerability, the waters of the Kabul and, to a lesser extent, the Chenab, acquire particular importance since these rivers are undammed and carry much of the available water precipitation.

An even more insidious problem is that of salinisation of land and water, particularly in the lower regions of the Indus Basin. The very Himalayan waters that fertilise the fields of Pakistan also bring with them harmful salts estimated at 120 metric tonnes annually which accumulate into the soil. Any properly functioning irrigation system should incorporate the means to drain the salts from the soil but this feature is lacking in the Indus Basin Irrigation System. Only 20 per cent of the annual salt deposits in the Indus Basin are being evacuated as required, the remainder being concentrated in the lower half of the Indus Basin, leading to the whole scale contamination of land and water in Sindh and Southern Punjab.[17]

The problem of salinity is not new and was noted even in the early years of the development of the Indus Basin, with President Ayub Khan seeking the assistance of President Eisenhower on this issue 40 years ago. There is some statistical evidence to suggest that the problem has taken a turn for the worse since the mid-1990s, manifesting itself in stagnant to declining agricultural productivity, a growing national poverty ratio and widening income inequalities.[18] This overall picture is, perhaps, best captured in the most recent UNDP Human Development Report which places Pakistan together with Bangladesh as the only two South Asian countries in the least developed category.[19] Another ominous indicator is the recent World Bank finding that the per capita income of Sindh has been declining steadily over the past decade.[20]

Environmental degradation has had a major impact on Pakistan's economic development and has contributed to widening inequalities in society and mounting regional disparities. Whatever economic growth Pakistan is witnessing, is concentrated in the privileged north Punjab areas apart from Karachi. In three and a half out of four provinces, viz. Sindh, Balochistan, NWFP and southern Punjab, declining per capita incomes and mounting poverty ratios are the norm and this phenomenon can be directly attributed to the crisis in availability of water, wood and other environmental resources. In southern Punjab and Sindh, contaminated water has become a serious health hazard as well.

Conclusion

The long-term viability of existing land and water management systems in Pakistan may be doubted for two principal reasons.

First of all, there is the technical problem of applying tropical flood irrigation techniques in a country, which in climatic terms, falls in the arid to semi-arid category. Unlike tropical soils where accumulated salts are leached via natural precipitation, in an arid / semi-arid environment, this natural leaching does not take place, and without extreme care, progressive salinisation is inevitable. Purely as a theoretical proposition, irrigation in arid or semi-arid climatic zones depends critically on stringent conditionalities with regard to water availability and drainage which, for the most part, are not being fulfilled in Pakistan today. For long-term viability, Pakistan must develop desert irrigation techniques which emphasise water conservation and drip and sprinkler irrigation. There is wide recognition in Pakistan that it needs such a modern irrigation system; less acknowledged is the fact that its unreformed 19th century social system, wherein powerful feudal interests claim unfettered rights to cheap and plentiful water, militates against the building of a 21st century irrigation system.

Second, and fundamentally, is the inherent inequity of the system. The present land and water management arrangements ensure that whatever sporadic economic progress Pakistan achieves is appropriated by the powerful landed interests of north Punjab. The apportionment of scarce water resources amongst the provinces does not follow any law or legal principle nor any other consensual arrangement but is governed by ad hoc arrangements which accord preferential treatment to the upstream north Punjab areas. In a general environment of water scarcity and consequent high prices for basic food and agricultural commodities, this preferential access also acts as a taxation mechanism whereby the income of the food deficit provinces is diverted to the food surplus districts of north Punjab. In effect, all the deficit provinces, viz, Sindh, Balochistan, NWFP pay a food tax to the politically influential landed gentry of north Punjab. There is a deep flaw in this system whereby a politically dominant elite flourishes on the back of its poorest and most vulnerable people.

Pakistan has, perhaps, been overanalysed as a political entity and we can gain some new and better insights by viewing it as the hydrological entity that it certainly is. The English word 'rivals' derives from the word 'river' and refers to the inherent conflict upstream and downstream interests. In Pakistan, these inherent contradictions are exacerbated in the absence of any credible means to adjudicate differences and mitigate perceived injustices. The peasant farmers who are the most acutely aware of the problems of land and water are voiceless. Religious propaganda and whipped up anti-India sentiments can obscure these internal contradictions only for a while. Ultimately, the inhabitants of the Indus Valley would realise that they have as much in common with people on the Indian side of the border as they do with their countrymen upstream or downstream to them.

Notes

1. The analysis set out below is the product of personal, academic research and has no official content or endorsement.
2. See country reports filed by the Government of Pakistan with the various United Nations / multilateral agencies dealing with global environmental issues such as the Commission on Sustainable Development, United Nations Environment Programme (UNEP), and the World Conservation Union among others. Relevant data may also be found in the Pakistani government submissions to the donor community, reports written by Pakistani technical experts on the basis of consultancies awarded by the multilateral agencies. Many such reports are available on the website of Pakistan Water Gateway, www.waterinfo.net.pk. Global media also have reports, in particular specialist journals, such as *Terra Daily, The New Agriculturist Online, Environmental News Network* (ENN). The World Conservation Union (www.iucnp.org) has done an extraordinary amount of research into the Indus Basin environmental issues, which may be accessed on their website. Some Sindhi nationalist websites also contain a wealth of references. See, for example, www.sanalist.org or www.sindh.ws. Multilateral agencies such as the World Bank, Asian Development Bank and the International Water Management Institute (IWMI) also have a wealth of data.
3. Philip R. Bowring "Kashmir's Real Story? A River Runs Through it," *International Herald Tribune / New York Times*, March 8, 2005. A similar story appeared a few days later in R. Ramesh, "Rivers Run Through It," *The Guardian*, March 16, 2005.
4. Proceedings of "Advanced Workshop on Environmental Orientation and Education" organised by the World Conservation Union (IUCN) in Islamabad April 7-9, 2005. Also "Presentation on Planning for Water Resources," submitted to the Pakistan Development Forum (PDF), held from May 12 to 14, 2003, by Dr. Shahid Amjad Chaudhry, deputy chairman, Planning Commission, Government of Pakistan.
5. This description may be seen *inter alia* in the very comprehensive reports of the World Conservation Union on "Sindh: State of Environment and Development," which looks in some detail on the impact of salt water intrusion in the Indus Delta. Available at http://www.iucn.org/places/pakistan/
6. See Zulfi Khan, "Pakistan Forgotten Genocide," *The Nation*, March, 27, 2005; Azeezuddeen Ahmad, "Sindh's Unending Suffering," *The Nation*, May 5, 2005.
7. This description is drawn from the University of Toronto case study published online under the heading Peter Gozweski & Thomas Homes–Dixen, "Environmental Scarcity and Violent Conflict: The Case of Pakistan." Available at www.library.utoronto.ca/pcs/eps/pakistan/pak1.htm
8. Ibid.
9. Ibid.
10. Ibid.
11. Michael Kamber, "Pakistan's Environmental Nightmare," *The Village Voice*, December 2001, Available at www.villagevoice.com/ews/0148, kamber,30265, 1.html
12. Kamber, Ibid.
13. See Pakistan Water Gateway website www.waterinfo.net.pk
14. Chief of Pakistan Seraiki Party (PSP) Taj Mohd. Langa quoted by the following

news reports: "Seraikis not Opposed to Kalabagh Dam: Pakistan Seraiki Party (PSP)," *Dawn*, March 29, 2005: "People Urged not to Oppose Kalabagh Dam, Thal Canal," *Jung*, March 29, 2005.

15. See, for example, "Presentation on Planning for Water Resources," presented to the Pakistan Development Forum (PDF), May, 12-14, 2003, by Dr. Shahid Amjad Chaudhry, deputy chairman, Planning Commission, Government of Pakistan.
16. Ibid.
17. Fateh Ullah Khan, "Wrong Planning Leads to Drought," May 10, 2002. Available at http://drought.iucnp.org/wrong.htm. Khan is former chairman, Indus River Systems Authority (IRSA).
18. This finding is indirectly endorsed by a World Bank Study on poverty in Pakistan which concluded: "There has been a marked deterioration in Pakistan's land, water and resource base in the past decade, which will weaken Pakistan's ability to achieve sustainable growth in productivity." See Nadeem Malik, "Economic Growth Fails to Arrest Poverty," February 7, 2005. Available at http://www.jang.com.pk/thenews/feb2005-daily/07-02-2005/main/main7.htm
19. See UN Human Development Report, 2004.
20. The World Bank has observed a decline in per capita income of Sindh, at an average negative rate of 0.5 per cent per annum over the period 1999-2004, quoted in Sabihuddin Ghousi, "Per Capita Income in Sindh Falling: WB Concept Note," *Dawn*, November 4, 2004.

Cross-Border Terrorism: A Review

Afsir Karim

Introduction

To assess the state of cross-border terrorism by the number of infiltration attempts or incidents of terrorism attacks thwarted by the security forces during a particular year or season, body counts or kill ratios can only lead to flawed conclusions about our success or failure to combat Pakistan-based cross-border terrorism. The political and military objectives of Pakistan have to be analysed objectively and the status of cross-border terrorism determined and reviewed from a long-term perspective. Cross-border terrorism has multiple aims and each of these may require a separate counter-terrorist strategy.

One of the aims of the Pakistan-based terrorist groups operating in Jammu & Kashmir (J&K) is to intimidate the government and the people by causing a large number of civilian casualties, generating shock and anger, and increasing bitterness between religious and ethnic groups. We must determine whether we have been able to counter these designs effectively. As the possibilities of lethal terrorist attacks have progressively increased with the availability of high-tech weapons to the Pakistan-based terrorist groups, new politico-military parameters for preventing, curbing or stopping terrorist attacks are required to be determined urgently by the central and state governments, if lethal terrorist attacks are to be thwarted in the future.

In the late Eighties, Pakistani-trained and Saudi-financed Afghan War veterans were unleashed in J&K. Pakistan-sponsored terrorism, thereafter, became an instrument of covert war against India. This form of warfare employing terrorism as an adjunct of war has been aptly described as "simply the contemporary name given to, and the modern permutation of, warfare deliberately waged against civilians with the purpose of destroying their will to support either leaders or policies that the agents of such violence find objectionable."[1]

To effectively counter sponsored and insurgent-terrorism launched from bases in Pakistan, the overall pattern of their operations and *modus operandi* have to be studied carefully because, besides carrying on the campaigns of terror, the movement aims to discredit the government and raise doubts about its legitimacy by subversion and other means. Their front organisations assert that they are the true representatives of the people (the Hurriyat in Kashmir, is a typical example of this kind) and the incumbent elected government has been imposed on the people. It is necessary to demolish such arguments by putting forward persuasive claims of legitimacy while actively combating terrorism; elections that were held in J&K in 2002 successfully established the legitimacy of the government and this proved a setback for the terrorists, separatists and their supporters. However,. propaganda campaigns carried out by terrorist organisations and their supporters have yet to be rebutted effectively through political initiatives and administrative measures of a positive kind. All legitimate means of bringing out the truth in front of the people must be employed; the information war has to be won by the government at any cost to diminish the local support available to the terrorists. The government's claims can only be convincing if the facts correspond with the evidence on the ground. It is necessary to expose the negative effects of the terrorist activities and the damage they are causing to the people and the economy of J&K. However, false claims of success or popular support that can be seen as an obvious form of propaganda will prove counter-productive and negate the purpose and thrust of political and administrative initiatives. It should be realised that people are seldom deceived by false propaganda.

Another aim of sponsored terrorism is to radically change or influence the behaviour pattern of the people by generating abnormal fear. Acts of terror are also motivated by revenge and religious hatred planted in the minds of foreign terrorists by the distorted *jihadi* ideology. Assassination of various political opponents and massacre of minority groups in J&K are examples of this kind of mindset. Terrorism has caused wanton destruction in J&K but has not led to the achievement of the political or military objectives of Pakistan or the separatist groups. Caleb Carr rightly argues, "Terrorism stiffens enemy resolve, it is self-defeating and has never achieved – nor will ever achieve – long-term success."[2]

Pakistan-sponsored terrorism against India has gradually assumed the shape of an 'uncomfortable' shadow war that is being waged for attaining long-term political and strategic objectives. India needs a coherent policy to deal effectively with this situation. In the absence of a multi-disciplined expert body for formulating long-term strategies and coordinating counter-terrorist policies, it is difficult to deal effectively with Pakistan-sponsored terrorism in J&K.

Pakistan/Pakistan Occupied Kashmir(PoK) based fundamentalist groups launched in J&K foment socio-economic unrest and create fear in the minds of the common people about the dangers posed to their religious identity or freedom. In this environment, extremists engineer incidents calculated to generate communal tensions under the pretext of safeguarding the religious identities of both Muslims and Hindus. Taking advantage of the ensuing chaos, various internal and external elements take a hand in spreading violence and terrorism.

Pakistan is sponsoring terrorism and instigating violence to achieve its long-term strategic and political agenda by using terrorism as a foreign policy tool that translates into unconventional warfare. Sponsored terrorism has gradually attained dangerous dimensions in J&K because the government and the intelligence agencies have failed to read the pattern of this new kind of offensive by Pakistan. The offensive launched in 1989 constituted a serious threat to regional stability besides posing a threat to India's composite culture and national integrity. Pakistan has remained undeterred because of our own flawed policies and the reluctance of the US and the international community to either indict or persuade Pakistan to stop sponsoring terrorism. Pakistan, as a strategic ally of the US in its war on terrorism, has little fear of facing sanctions or any other punitive measures. The international community has yet to respond to India's requests to compel Pakistan to demolish the *jihadi* terrorist network that is targeting several countries across international borders besides India.

Defensive measures seldom deter or prevent transnational terrorist attacks; a vigorous offensive campaign against the terrorists and their sponsors is required to deal with the menace. Accurate and timely intelligence is a prerequisite for any offensive action against terrorists; we seem to lack such intelligence capability. President Bush has sanctioned creation of a new "Terrorist Threat Integration Centre" for the working of intelligence agencies under one roof to detect and prevent terrorist attacks. There is little doubt that we need similar organisations for countering transnational terrorism; for safeguarding our assets, critical economic infrastructure; and for preventing mass casualty terrorist attacks. The aim should be to combine all elements of national power to combat terrorism in its various manifestations that endanger national security

Terrorists have been most brutal and unsparing in J&K against non-Muslims and political opponents. The Pakistani propaganda machine has, however, been able to convince several countries of the world that these terrorists are freedom fighters. Since no definition of terrorism is ever likely to be universally acceptable, such a ploy still works. According to J. Bowyer Bell

"The very word [terrorism] becomes a litmus test for dearly held beliefs, so that a brief conversation on terrorist matters with almost any one reveals a special world view, an interpretation of the nature of man and a glimpse of the desired future."[3]

The situation in J&K is delicately balanced, infiltration from Pakistan continues and peace has yet to return to the state, regardless of our periodic claims to the contrary. The internal situation in J&K continues to cause concern and has yet to reach a turning point while the India–Pakistan dialogue and confidence-building measures are well underway without many problems. Although the government of J&K has achieved a measure of success in bringing people back to the mainstream and restoring normalcy in the state, much more is still required to be done to restore peaceful conditions. The sponsored and domestic terrorist groups supported by international fundamentalist organisations outside of, and within, J&K, and their leaders, continue to foment violence, and the blood of innocents is still being shed. There is little cooperation between political parties within J&K. And this makes the situation politically volatile, creating an environment in which terrorist groups are able to operate with impunity. The Congress, the Bharatiya Janata Party (BJP) and other national parties continue to be at loggerheads, ignoring national interests in J&K and a national consensus or a joint strategy for J&K is still not in sight.

Pakistan is following a dual policy of continuing the dialogue and supporting and launching groups which carry out terrorist activities in J&K. Pakistani policy-makers still seem to believe that pressure must be maintained on India through terrorist attacks otherwise India will not be in the required frame of mind to continue talks on J&K. Pakistan also seems to believe that the logical end of the process should be that India accepts the demands of the separatist groups and agrees to the solution of the J&K problem as proposed by Pakistan. A change in Pakistani policy on supporting fundamentalist groups may be on the cards, as some recent statements of General Musharraf indicate, but the actual position will be known only if there is a change in the ground situation; one has to wait and watch.

Aims and Objectives of Pak-Sponsored Terrorism

Pakistan's aims in the past have been rather over-ambitious but clear-cut and well focussed; these can be summarised as under:

- To wrest away Muslim majority areas of J&K through a combination of political subversion and armed movements.

- Use terrorism to overawe the people and the state authorities and make them submit to Pakistani designs.
- Awaken Islamic fundamentalism to obviate any chance of compromise between the people of J&K and the Indian government.
- To thwart the independence movement in J&K and convert it into a pro-Pakistan movement.
- Bring the Kashmir problem back to the centre-stage at the international level and to present India as a highly repressive state, which is using military power to suppress a popular uprising in J&K.

The Campaign, 1989- 2005

By the end of 1987, a visible pro-Pakistan bias had emerged in the Valley and the anti-Indian activities and propaganda of the Jamaat-i-Islami (Kashmir) (JI-K) and its militant wings had increased greatly. Pakistan had by now trained a large number of Kashmiri youths from both sides of the Line of Control (LoC) for subversion and terrorism. Arms, explosives, financial support and bases were also provided to them in PoK and Pakistan. After the end of the war in Afghanistan, war veterans were sent to lead the terrorists in J&K.

The following important developments took place in J&K during this period:

- The administrative machinery, including the police forces, was subverted by infiltration of well-trained agents.
- JI(K) became a force to reckon with and it declared its intention of establishing an Islamic state of Kashmir, in collusion with Pakistan.
- By December 1989, an organised phase of terrorism was launched in J&K by Pakistan: the Jammu and Kashmir Liberation Front (JKLF) was gradually sidelined and Islamic radical terrorist groups like the Hizb-ul-Mujahideen, and others took over.

The movement passed through the following main stages in the initial phases:

- Random bomb attacks, assassination of selected political figures who would not support the armed struggle against India.
- Mass protests by the people, violence on the streets resembling the *intifada* of the Palestinians.
- Subversion of the civil administration and the police forces of J&K.
- Discrediting the Indian security forces in the eyes of the people.
- Random massacres of innocent Hindus and Sikhs to drive out minorities from selected areas and overawe the people.

By 1991, Pakistan had gained great expertise in planning covert operations and terrorist groups trained in the terrorist camps in Afghanistan and Pakistan were ready for operations in J&K. A proxy war through highly trained *jihadi* groups was eventually launched. A psychological war phase preceded the armed action, to mentally prepare the people of J&K for a prolonged anti-Indian armed struggle. A virulent anti-India campaign was launched, and an indoctrination process and training of Kashmiri youth to create pro-Pakistan cadres formed an essential part of this campaign. The armed struggle was meant to create a no–win situation for the Indian security forces and to demonstrate the inability of the government of J&K to stop the terrorist onslaught. The overall objective in 1990-2005 was a graduated escalation of violence and subversion of the administrative apparatus. The following plans were put into motion:

- The J&K government and its administrative machinery were put on the defensive and became totally ineffective.
- Brutal attacks on political opponents and members of minority communities demoralised the people.
- Religious places were used as bases by the terrorists to inhibit attacks by the armed forces.
- Communalisation of the situation by well-calculated political moves and massacre of minorities to drive them away, particularly the Kashmiri Pandits: this was used to invigorate the fundamentalist movement.
- Engineering of events to invite tough government measures which directly affected the common people, calculated to increase the alienation of the people.
- Doubts were cast about the legitimacy of the J&K government through a well-organised media campaign.
- Increased use of high–tech weapons, command, control and communication system, use of remotely controlled devices to blast army and police vehicles became a common occurrence.
- Intensification of propaganda about the supposed atrocities of the armed forces, sophisticated methods of use of doctored video films to present a distorted picture of actual events; highlighting these through the electronic media.
- Extensive use of cyber–terrorism and hacking of civil and military websites.
- Advent of *fidayeens* who acted in small groups with the main aim of causing maximum casualties on the security forces and attacking high security areas.
- Massive propaganda drive against Sufi Islam and the composite Kashmiri culture, dubbing both as anti–Islamic.

- Efforts of changing demographic balances in areas north of the Chenab River were intensified.

From 1995 onwards, a new campaign to terrorise the urban population of big towns, bomb blasts in railway tracks/ stations and bazaars was started in Jammu, and the establishment of well-concealed special recruiting centres for Muslim youths in Jammu region for reinforcing terrorist groups, already operating in various areas, came to light. The frequency of improvised explosive device (IED) blasts on various segments of the National Highway in Jammu increased manifold and caused large numbers of casualties.

There has been no let up in terrorism since then. Pakistan-based terrorists crossed all bounds when they attacked the J&K Assembly in October 2001 and followed it up by an attack on December 13, 2001, on the Indian Parliament, the main symbol of India's sovereignty. This brought the two countries to the brink of war; as cross-border terrorism continues, the danger of war between the two countries persists.

In the years 2003-05, there was some reduction in the scale of infiltration but not in the scale of terrorist attacks or subversive activities. The current situation is fluid and dangerous and we cannot let our guard down in these circumstances. In 2005, there was a spurt in terrorist attacks against soft targets, including school children and other bystanders. A large number of terrorists were gunned down in repeated clashes between the security forces and members of radical terrorist groups but their attacks continued unabated; a number of army and paramilitary personnel were killed in various attacks across the state.

In April 2005, violence erupted once the arrangements of starting the Srinagar-Muzaffarabad bus service were finalised: terrorists set off a country-made bomb near Pattan town on the route of the cross-border bus service, wounding seven road workers who were digging the highway. The bomb went off less than an hour after soldiers had defused two powerful landmines a few miles away on the same road. Just before the start of the Srinagar-Muzaffarabad bus service, two suicide bombers attacked the Tourist Reception Centre at Srinagar where 24 passengers were lodged, awaiting the launching ceremony. Even though the security officials expected militants to mount attacks to intimidate people and derail the bus service, they were unable to stop them. The security forces further intensified vigilance as militants issued fresh threats, but several lethal attacks were mounted against civil and military targets These examples are being quoted here to reassert the fact that the claims of the security forces that they have more or less stopped the infiltration or that the terrorist violence has been controlled do not fully match the situation on the ground.

Some Measures to Counter Pak-Sponsored Terrorism

The present efforts of curbing cross-border terrorism by Pakistan are not particularly encouraging because of its internal compulsions, and India has yet to find convincing methods of drawing international attention to the inadequate efforts of Pakistan. The international community is still not quite certain whether the terrorist activities in J&K are indigenous or transnational; different countries view things differently. The awareness of the long-term adverse implications of terrorism for the region is still rather limited in various countries.

The first requirement is, of course, the peaceful resolution of the conflict between Pakistan and India; however, regional and international efforts would also be necessary for establishing a cooperative framework for peace. Post-modern terrorism has set entirely new norms and it seems no country can be entirely safe from surprise attacks. It is virtually impossible to defend all the vulnerable areas all the time; however, proper handling of a situation can either make most attacks ineffective or greatly reduce the damage. In our environment, the adverse political impact of terrorist attacks has to be defused, the possible ethnic or religious fallout has to be anticipated and controlled. As most terrorist groups operating against India are based in Pakistan or PoK, their base areas and support organisations must be brought under unbearable pressure through diplomatic channels.

No quarter should be given to groups or individuals who are colluding with the terrorists in attacking educational institutions, killing ordinary citizens or holding the country to ransom. No deal should be made with those who demand release of prisoners or withdrawal of troops without any intention of curbing or discouraging terrorist activities. Safe passage or other concessions should be denied to the terrorists who indulge in killing innocent citizens—they should either be killed or captured. Terrorists who are captured after an attack or a siege must be tried by special courts and given appropriate punishment with speed.

To prevent or thwart attempts to kill innocent citizens in temples, theatres or cinema halls, innovative tactics, dedicated intelligence and well-planned counter- operations will be required. To deal with hit and run terrorist attacks in bazaars and public places, few options are available other than efficient police work aided by good intelligence. It is, however, necessary to ensure that the terrorists do not get away unscathed after an attack under any circumstances.

Indiscriminate use of force by the security forces and the police can be a critical factor in conflict escalation and increasing the alienation of the people. Comparative studies regarding the relationship between harsh measures and escalation of conflicts show that there is need of evolving methods of using force in a manner that causes minimum collateral damage.

Cross-border terrorist attacks can be substantially reduced if:

- Consensus is reached between India and Pakistan to jointly meet the threats of cross-border and domestic terrorism.
- Awareness of the threats of terrorism is increased at the regional level and coordinated efforts are made to track down terrorists operating in the region.
- Permanent organisations are created and regional plans are developed for countering terrorism.

Political, economic, social and military measures have to be enmeshed for countering terrorism effectively; compartmentalisation of counter-terrorist efforts militate against well thought out and coordinated planning and actions. Special organisations can play a significant role in establishing a counter-terrorist framework. Terrorist-specific regional intelligence cells provided with dedicated funds and equipment to detect sleeper cells, watch terrorist movements and anticipate their plans would be necessary.

Crisis management schemes, indicating focal points for national and state level resources for combating terrorism are required to be coordinated. Assets and financial resources for countering terrorism must be pooled. Overall coordination between civil and military/paramilitary organisations to counter cross-border terrorism has still not been achieved in J&K.

Conclusions

Terrorists deliberately target non-combatants to instil fear in those who directly witness the act or to affect a lager targeted group. Terrorists violate all normative values; they believe that the more horrible the act, the better to affect the targeted entity. No rules of human conduct are respected as long as the act of terror serves the purpose of the perpetrators. The abnormal intensity of force used by the terrorists against civilians and soft targets sets terrorism apart from all other categories of violence. Acts of wanton killing of innocent citizens during wars are well known but killing of civilians as symbolic acts to spread terror in peace-time is peculiar to terrorism.

Terrorism, if allowed to linger on, can take the shape of a prolonged shadow war, as the case is in J&K. Religious extremism and terrorism provoke internal conflicts to damage the secular and democratic ethos of a country with the aim of eventually destabilising it by prolonged covert warfare. Generally, no solid evidence can be mustered against a state that is sponsoring terrorism as it uses proxies and mercenaries instead of employing its own armed forces. Deterring the threats posed by international terrorism, whether state-sponsored or otherwise, is a difficult and complex task that cannot be accomplished by any one country without international cooperation. A multi-dimensional approach including international support is necessary besides innovative political and diplomatic initiatives to combat terrorism.

Countering sponsored-terrorism is much more complex than an ordinary military enterprise: equal importance has to be given to a wide range of non-conventional or paramilitary options unlike conventional military operations. Military operations do not prove very effective in an environment where the terrorists operate in small groups from safe bases that are made available to them within the region. New technologies, air mobility, sophisticated communication systems combined with innovative and daring tactics can, however, greatly help the counter-terrorist forces in catching the terrorists off guard and destroying their bases.

India has been facing the challenge of terrorism for many decades but terrorism acquired a more dangerous dimension in the 1990s when Pakistan adopted insurgent-terrorism as a means of achieving its political and strategic objectives in the subcontinent through *jihadi* groups. The fundamentalist organisations in Pakistan, with the active support of the armed forces, gradually mobilised vast resources of manpower, arms and finances, to carry out armed trans-border operations across the LoC and some other parts of India. India was, thus, confronted with multiple long-term threats to its territorial integrity and national unity by a new kind of aggression by Pakistan in the form of unconventional warfare: sponsored terrorism and subversive activities for achieving long-term political and territorial objectives under a nuclear shield.

International terrorism has in the recent past led to wars in West Asia, Afghanistan and Sri Lanka, and lately it brought India-Pakistan to the brink of a major war. One of the main dangers of continued cross-border terrorism is that it can lead to a full-fledged war between India and Pakistan. As both countries have nuclear weapons, even a nuclear war cannot be ruled out. Although the US and its allies have been calling J&K the most dangerous place on earth, they have done little to either persuade or coerce Pakistan to demolish the terrorist network that operates from its soil.

Pakistani Islamists, a conglomerate of several radical groups, want to bring the entire subcontinent under their sway; fundamentalism and terror serve their purpose of gaining political objectives and, therefore, their focus remains on achieving political power by using terrorism and religious fundamentalism. Hate is being openly propagated by radical organisations against religious minorities in various parts of J&K, leading to communal tensions.

The rise of terrorism in J&K coincided with the defeat of the Soviet forces in Afghanistan and the consequent American withdrawal from the region that left the field open for radical Islamic groups and led to the spread of terrorism and aggravation of politico-religious conflicts in Central Asia, Afghanistan, Pakistan and Kashmir. Transnational terrorism became the favoured form of warfare since it is comparatively risk free in the nuclear era. It is extremely difficult for the targeted country to counter this kind of aggression politically without waging a full-fledged conventional war.

India has faced ethno-religious conflicts and terrorism for more than two decades; Pakistan took advantage of this situation to lend support to separatist movements; the motivation was to destabilise and weaken India, and wrest away Kashmir. Terrorist attacks were used to intimidate the government by causing large numbers of casualties among civilians; the attacks were also meant to increase bitterness and mistrust between various ethnic and religious factions in India. The advent of *jihadi* terrorism in J&K started a far more devastating and violent phase against India. The menace of *jihadi* terrorism remained unchecked because its destructive potential was neither understood nor countered effectively for a long time, either by the state or central leadership. Terrorist attacks may gradually become more destructive and lethal with the availability of more sophisticated weapons to the terrorist groups; India has yet to take concrete steps to counter this threat.

Terrorist operations are based on military principles from an offensive perspective and the terrorists have an advantage of choosing targets which are virtually impossible to protect at all times. Although terrorism *per se* has never succeeded in bringing about a political change, terrorism combined with political movements can cause serious political disruption in a country.

It has been amply demonstrated that terrorism cannot be dealt with effectively by armed action only. The political leadership must address the root causes of the growing fundamentalist mindset and socio-economic factors responsible for alienation in J&K. Indoctrination has to be curbed at the grass-roots, in various religious-based political institutions which preach hatred and presently function unchecked.

Both Pakistan and India are under considerable pressure from the international community to reach an amicable solution to the J&K imbroglio. After 9/11, the issue has received greater international attention because of the growing clout of the fundamentalist groups in Pakistan and their potential to start a war between India and Pakistan which may turn into a nuclear confrontation.

It is necessary to survey the entire landscape surrounding international and transnational terrorism for formulating appropriate strategies. The planning has to commence after a comprehensive study of counter-terrorist policies: a policy statement must issue from the highest authority encompassing all forms of terrorism, clearly defining the goals that have to be achieved and decisions on the counter-terrorist infrastructure that will be established

The assistance of the media is essential to change public perceptions of various incidents of terrorist related violence in J&K and their effects on the well-being of the people and their democratic rights. The security forces should be trained to be sensitive to the predispositions of the domestic population in keeping with their religious and cultural beliefs and customs.

Notes

1. Caleb Carr, *The Lessons of Terror* (New York: Random House, Inc, 2002), p.6.
2. Carr, Ibid., pp.11-15.
3. Donald J. Hanle, *Terrorism the Newest Face of War* (Pergamon-Brassey's International Defense Publishers, Inc. 1989), p.104.

Peace Building in Jammu Kashmir

The Peace Process: A View From Jammu

Rekha Chowdhary

To locate the peace process in the specificity of Jammu is to reflect on the complexity that underlies this process. Such a complexity is defined by the plurality and political divergence within the state, which resonates in the context of conflict as well. The conflict that the present peace process aims to address, though having implications for the whole of the state, is region-specific and is located mainly in the ethno-cultural politics of Kashmir. This imparts an intricacy to the whole process. The peace process cannot attain a momentum until it addresses the specificity of the conflict and yet it cannot be isolated from the larger reality of the state.

Viewing the peace process from Jammu, therefore, helps not only to situate it in the larger perspective of the state but also to emphasise the internal dynamics of the process, laying bare a variety of issues and concerns. These issues and concerns are vital and need to be addressed for the peace process to have a lasting effect.

Specificity of the Context of Conflict and Implications for Jammu

As stated above, there is a specificity to the context of conflict which can be historically located in the identity politics of Kashmir. Ever since the 1920s, when the Kashmiri political consciousness came to be organised, this politics has been acquiring various forms.[1] The extraordinary circumstances in which this state was placed in the post-1947 period led to the sharpening of the politics of Kashmiri identity. These circumstances were defined both by the external situation (the hostility between India and Pakistan; the division of the state between the Indian and Pakistani administered parts; and the internationalisation of the Kashmir issue in the context of the Cold War), as well as by the internal circumstances (the undemocratic and intrusive politics of the centre and systematic erosion of the constitutionally guaranteed autonomy). Steering towards the issue of Kashmir's relationship with the Indian state, the identity politics of Kashmir, since 1947, has been taking various turns and twists and having a range of manifestations – ranging from the demand for plebiscite to restoration of autonomy of the state. In its present phase, starting from 1989, this politics has manifested itself in the form of separatist and militant politics. Such politics, rooted in the indigenous context of political alienation, has been fermented by the systematic support that it has received from Pakistan.

This context of militancy and separatism defines the core of the conflict that the present peace process (both between India and Pakistan as well as between the Indian government and the separatist leadership of Kashmir) is aiming to address. The specificity of this context becomes clear from the fact that the politics of separatism that gained sufficient depth in Kashmir failed to have similar impact in other parts of the state. Though militancy has had implications for the whole of the state, separatist politics has remained, more or less, confined to the Valley of Kashmir.

Separatism, therefore, does not form the predominant political sentiment of Jammu region. Its manifestation in Kashmir in the early Nineties did not have much effect on the political responses even of the Muslim dominated population in this region. Neither the mass upsurge of the early period nor the later political responses, especially the continued identification with the separatist sentiment, have been replicated in this region. This is despite the fact that there has been a very strong presence of militant outfits in many parts of this region. So much so, that there has been no significant presence of either the All Parties Hurriyat Conference (APHC), the main separatist organisation of Kashmir, or any other leading separatist organisation. If one finds a milieu of separatism in this region, it is in the Kashmiri-speaking part of the Doda district. This district, that lies on the southern border of Kashmir, has a large number of people of Kashmir-origin who still identify with the Kashmiri culture and to some extent also follow the Kashmiri politics. However, even here, separatism could not acquire the same form as it did in the Valley of Kashmir. It is a fact that militancy had spread here quite early; but what attracted militants to this area was the difficult hilly terrain of the district, making it convenient for them to have their hideouts, rather than the popular separatist sentiments.

The case of Doda having been influenced by the politics of separatism, even to the limited extent, makes it very clear that the separatist movement has an ethno-cultural rather than a merely religious basis. Other than this Kashmiri speaking part of the region, the separatist movement has not found much support in other Muslim-dominated areas of Jammu. It is important to note that the districts of Poonch and Rajouri, the two predominantly Muslim districts of the region bordering with Pakistan administered Kashmir, remained untouched even by militancy for quite some time.[2] It was only in the late Nineties that these areas became active in militancy-related activities, mostly externally supported.[3] The complicity of the local population in the militancy, especially among the Gujjars inhabiting the upper reaches of these areas, however, has been less based upon emotional reasons and more on material and situational ones – they are either forced to provide food and shelter to the militants or are lured by money.

An analysis of the political responses within Jammu leads to the conclusion that religion does not form the basis of the conflict at hand. The fact that there is no homogenised Muslim response in the state becomes clear not only in the context of the separatist politics but also in the context of other political responses. In all the three Muslim-dominated districts of Jammu, viz., Doda, Poonch and Rajouri, the people share a sense of antagonism against the "Kashmir-dominated" structure of power. For the backwardness and marginalisation that the people of these areas suffer, both the political elite of Jammu as well as of Kashmir are held responsible. Despite their identification with the Kashmiri culture, the people even of the Kashmiri belt of Doda, emphasise their marginalisation by claiming their position within the words "and" in the nomenclature of the state "Jammu and Kashmir" – arguing that they fit neither in Jammu nor in Kashmir as they are ignored by the elite of both the regions.[4] Among the common grievances that the people of this district have against the Kashmiri leadership is the deliberate neglect of the area, especially its tourist potential.

The dominant political concerns of people of these Muslim dominated areas, therefore, rather than being linked to the separatist politics, emanate from the position of their backwardness and marginalisation. As these areas are far-flung, mostly in the treacherous mountainous belt, and are peripheral in the process of development and distribution of resources, the political demands here mostly have their developmental basis. Hence, rather than the demand for *Azadi*, these areas echo with the demands like the organisation of Hill Councils, jobs in the government sector, political reservations and other concessions. The identity politics that resounds in these areas is linked with the local competition for resources between the Gujjars who have attained the Scheduled Tribe status and the Paharis who are demanding such a status.

What comes to be highlighted in the above analysis is the context of plurality and political divergence within the state. Jammu and Kashmir represents a very interesting context of plurality that persists from the social to the political realities of the state. There is a blend of different religions, languages, cultures and tribes. Of all the regions, Jammu is the most heterogeneous. Though Hindus form the majority here, Muslims also have a strong presence.[5] However, the religious division does not define the social or political existence of the people of the region as other affinities based on caste, clan, community and tribe cut across the religious divide.[6]

Social diversity is matched by a multiplicity of political voices and a variety of identity politics. Kashmiri identity politics that underscores the "Kashmir problem" (as the conflict is generally known), though relatively more widespread, is neither inclusive of all the political responses within the state nor internally homogenous. Like all other kinds of identity politics that claim exclusivity and distinctiveness, it leaves outside its margins a vast political space where a number of other identities get constructed and politicised.

Regional Divide: A Challenge to the Peace Process

The political divergence has often become the basis of politicisation by the political groups and organisations situated in the Jammu region. Right from the time of the state's accession in 1947, politics has been generated around the issue of Jammu's regional interest vis-à-vis Kashmir.[7] The political discourse of regional discrimination and political deprivation has been popularised at the commonsensical level in the urban areas of the region by political parties across the ideological divide. During the last one and half decades of militancy, the Kashmir-specific nature of the movement has helped boost such a political discourse and has generated a regional politics that has taken various forms. While for many political parties and organisations, this has led to the emphasis on the demand for "regional autonomy," for many others, it has led to a counter politics of "separatism." Under different banners, a number of organisations, mostly holding their links with the Rashtriya Swayamsevak Sangh (RSS), have raised the demand for reorganisation of the state and separation of Jammu from Kashmir (on the logic of incompatibility of the political aspirations of the people of Jammu with those of Kashmir).[8] Though these demands have failed to have much impact on the overall politics of the region, they have sharpened the politics of the regional divide.

It is this context of political divergence at the inter-regional level that makes the process of peace most challenging, especially at the internal level – between the Government of India and the separatist leadership of Kashmir. The local sensitivities in this context assume importance because the issue of political divergence between Kashmir and Jammu itself is highly politicised. To illustrate such sensitivities one can refer to the 'autonomy' debate that was initiated by the National Conference (NC) government in early 2000. Seeking to present "restoration of autonomy guaranteed to the state in its pristine form" as the basis for solution to the "Kashmir problem," the state government had initiated a debate with the centre around the question of restoration of the pre-1953 status of the state. However, the debate put the NC government on the back foot as the Government of India completely rejected the demand.[9] One of the reasons for such a response of the central government was that the debate had raised emotions against the demand for autonomy in Jammu. Though the regional divide that was projected on the issue of autonomy was more apparent than real, the fact that the debate had been initiated by the Kashmiri leadership and had remained thoroughly Kashmir-centric without responding to the political sensitivities of Jammu region resulted in strong reactions against it.[10]

Balraj Puri, a well-known analyst of the politics of Jammu and Kashmir, recognising the political divergence between the two regions, has been forcefully arguing about the close linkage between the "Kashmir tangle" and the political responses of the Jammu region.[11] According to him, there is no possibility of the resolution of the Kashmir problem in isolation, without addressing the political discontent of Jammu region. Such political discontent, in his view, has been located in the nature of the power politics of the state which is Kashmir-centric and ignores the regional aspirations of Jammu. While recognising the need to address the Kashmiri discontent, preferably through restoring the state autonomy, he has been making a strong case for "regional autonomy" of Jammu. Jammu, he argues, provides a strong clue to the Kashmir tangle. In his opinion, there are two dimensions of the problem: one related to Kashmir that lies at the realm of the centre-state relations and the other related to Jammu that lies at the intra-state and inter-regional level. The two dimensions are so entangled that without resolving the one, the other cannot be resolved. All efforts made by the centre to deal with the Kashmir issue, without addressing Jammu's discontent vis-à-vis Kashmir, have faced some opposition from Jammu, mainly because these did not address Jammu's discontent.

While there is much in Puri's argument that can be contested[12], one cannot completely ignore it. Progress in the process cannot be achieved if it remains exclusively Kashmir-oriented and does not extend to the other regions. The regional chauvinistic forces may use it to sharpen the inter-regional differences and generate divisive politics. For peace to attain momentum in the state, therefore, it is important that the process becomes inclusive enough to incorporate divergent political demands and involve the political elite of all the three regions of the state.

This brings into focus the issue of "representation."

Issue of Representation

Since the peace process initiated by the Government of India takes cognisance of the need to involve the political leadership that claims to represent the people, the questions as to who initiates the dialogue and on what grounds does it take place remain crucial for peace to be sustained in the whole state. Aggressive political articulation of the regional politics during the last one and half decades has resulted in the demand that the process of conflict resolution should be both inclusive and participatory – inclusive enough to incorporate the political voices of the Jammu region and participatory enough to provide an opportunity to the regional leadership to negotiate the regional interest. Therefore, much before the Government of India took the decision to hold a dialogue with the separatist leadership, the issue of representation had already assumed importance. The political demands made by the separatist organisations, especially those relating to self-determination for the whole of Jammu and Kashmir, were contested by a variety of organisations located in Jammu and Ladakh. As against the separatist claim of the all-pervasive and all-inclusive nature of the movement, counter-claims about the limited nature of separatist politics were made by various organisations like the Ladakh Buddhist Association (LBA), Bharatiya Janta Party (BJP), Jammu Mukti Morcha (JMM), Jammu State Morcha (JSM), Panun Kashmir, etc. All these organisations, claiming to represent the Ladakhis, the Jammu people or the Kashmiri pundits, sought to affirm faith in Indian nationalism, on the one hand, and asserted the distinct political aspirations of each of these groups, on the other. The claims of these organisations obviously were highly exaggerated and did not reflect the internal plurality of each region or group they sought to represent. However, despite such exaggerations, the political assertions made by these organisations resulted in fracturing the claims of singular, unified and homogenised politics in Jammu and Kashmir. It also helped develop sensitivity among all the politically active groups within the state about the incapacity of any one organisation or movement to represent all sections of society or to speak about the interest of the whole state from one platform. [13]

With the Government of India initiating the peace process with the separatist leaders of Kashmir, the groups and organisations contesting the separatist political stance have been demanding that the process be broadened to include other political viewpoints. Though there is a general acceptance to the idea of dialogue with the separatists, it is expected that as progress in this direction is made, other political groups will also be involved.

However, the complexity to the issue of peace and dialogue is provided not as much by the multiplicity of political voices as by their divergence. It is in this context of political divergence that the idea of an intra-state dialogue has acquired prominence.

Intra-State Dialogue

The demand for an intra-state dialogue has been raised not only by the Jammu-based political leaders who fear marginalisation of their voices in the process of peace but also by the Kashmiri separatists who concede the possibility of failure of the process in the absence of an internal synchronisation of political views. Abdul Gani Lone, the leader of the People's Conference, was among the first separatist leaders who recognised the need to engage the voices outside the separatist politics to evolve a broad-based consensus towards the resolution of the Kashmir problem. He had organised the first such meetings in Jammu where leaders across the political spectrum were invited to voice their opinion on the issue.

The idea of engaging the alternative political voices has come to be accepted generally by the separatist political leadership and, as the peace process started gaining ground in the last two years, it has been voiced more forcefully by a number of leaders. Mirwaiz Omar Farooq, the leader of the APHC(A) (the faction of the separatist organisation that has entered into dialogue with the Government of India) has been prominent among those separatist leaders who feel the necessity of intra-state dialogue. For him and many others, intra-state dialogue forms the third essential layer of the peace process, along with the other two layers – the dialogue between India-Pakistan and the dialogue between India and the Kashmiris.

Intra-state dialogue assumes importance in the context of the multiple identity politics within the state that has been sharpened during the period of militancy. Much of such identity politics, operating in terms of "we" and "they," has been constructed around polarity between different regions and sub-regions. Thus, it is not only the politics of "Jammu versus Kashmir" or "Kashmir versus Ladakh" that has been sharpened in the last few years, but also the politics of "Leh versus Kargil," "Jammu versus Doda" and "Jammu versus Poonch-Rajouri," etc. The internal polarisation that is taking place, consequently, has dangerous potential as it can give substance to divisive agendas. To nip such divisive tendencies in the bud, it becomes important to build bridges between the regions and sub-regions through the process of dialogue.

In the absence of such a dialogue, the peace process aiming to address the core of conflict, especially the feeling of alienation in Kashmir, may generate tensions within the state. The heightened sensitivities, promoted by multiple levels of identity politics, may generate an environment which might be unsettling. It may, therefore, be important to confront the differences and evolve a consensus through an internal dialogue. Evolving a consensus in the face of the existing political differences is not that difficult a task. In many ways, the differences are superficial and acquire a larger than life image due to the way these are politicised. The political ethos of the state that is defined by diversities, plurality, toleration and secular values ultimately prevails.

Peace Process and Maintaining Political Ethos of the State

Diversities, as the experience of the state in general and of Jammu region in particular shows, rather than polarising people, make way for a plural society. The multiple and overlapping identities have a very healthy influence on the political and social life. The divisive tendencies, though operating on the surface, fail to transcend beyond a point. That is the reason why the state has not been witness to any major communal tension, specifically in the post-independence period.[14] The non-sectarian approach of the people has continued in the most difficult period of militancy even when there have been enough provocations in that direction. Numerous targeted killings of minorities, both in the Valley of Kashmir as well as in Jammu region have also failed to upset the secular ethos of the state.[15]

Maintaining the plural character of the state becomes the essential element of the process of peace. This is more so when peace is viewed from Jammu – the reason being that Jammu is more heterogeneous as compared to the rest of the two regions of the state, and plurality is the way of life here. The secular ethos has been reinforced here through the historical experiences of people. Despite the deliberate provocations by the militants to communalise the region, inter-community relations have remained, more or less, intact. (This has been so despite the fact that every situation of targeted killing has been matched by the communal mobilisation by the Hindu rightist forces.) With the exception of one or two outbursts in the towns of Doda or Rajouri, the traditional communal amity has not been disturbed.

The reflection of the secular ethos can be seen in the political responses of the region. Despite the vociferous Hindu-oriented politics in the towns of Jammu and Kathua districts, the region has maintained the tradition of centrist politics and parties. Such politics has been sustained, more or less, during the period of militancy as well.[16]

The secular and plural ethos of the region, therefore, clearly negates any kind of simplistic religion-based process of conflict resolution. Hence, there is no popular support to the divisive formulas that have been offered, from time to time, by the international think-tanks or even by certain political groups or leaders nearer at home or in Pakistan. These formulas are based upon the logic that the Muslims of the region form one political unit along with the Muslims of Kashmir and, therefore, need to be clubbed with them for the purposes of any future political design. Those following this logic erroneously tend to see the religious divide as the major political divide in the state and tend to deal with the complexity of the state through simplified communally divisive formulas. A number of such formulas have been floated from time to time – like the Chenab formula, the series of formulas offered by the US-based Kashmir Study Group, or the more recent Musharraf's multi-regional formula (as well as the internal demands of organisations like the JSM and LBA to reorganise the state by separating Jammu and Ladakh from Kashmir). These formulas, as this paper has attempted to show, are not matched with the ground reality and clearly negate the traditional tenor of the region. That is why these formulas are not taken very seriously at the local level.

It is the plurality of the state in which people have a common stake and, therefore, maintaining its sanctity remains one of the most important concerns of the region. It is this stake which makes Jammu a very important constituency of peace. This constituency of peace is as substantial as, if not bigger than, the conflict-ridden Kashmir. Stakes in peace here are located in the context of conflict as well as in the context of its plurality.

Jammu: The Peace Constituency

To say that Jammu is not implicated in the separatist politics is not to argue that the conflict does not have its implications for Jammu. In fact, in certain ways, this region has experienced the conflict in much more intense and incisive ways as compared to the Kashmir region. The region has had to face the impact not only of partition but also of the hostility between India and Pakistan, not only during the major wars but also during other periods of 'peace-time.' Therefore, the region has a greater stake in peace, [17] especially in the cessation of hostilities between the two countries.[18]

Jammu region has been implicated in the conflict right from the time of partition. The division of the state, while leaving the Valley almost compact, divided the area and people of Jammu region between two different political dispensations – one under Indian administration and the other under Pakistani administration. Like all other places which were adversely affected by partition, the Jammu belt also witnessed the horrors of violence, bloodshed and migration. So huge was the impact of division that it resulted in effecting a substantial change in the demographic pattern on both sides of the divide. While on the Pakistani administered side, the region was bereft of any Hindu population, on the Indian side, the number of Muslims was drastically reduced. From a Muslim-dominated region, it now acquired the status of a Hindu-majority region. Migration of the people from both sides resulted in a large population of the region acquiring the status of refugees. In fact, for the people inhabiting either side of the Line of Control (LoC), the line dividing the two parts has been very fluid as they have been moving from one side to the other all through the last five decades. (The migration, on a very big scale involving thousands of families, it is understood, took place during the 1965 and 1971 Wars. In the 1971 War, in fact, lots of people were divided as Chamb area falling on the Indian side of Jammu division went to the other side.)

The division of the region and the continued movement of people through the porous borders has generated the phenomenon of "Divided Families." Notwithstanding the fact that this phenomenon underlies one of the major demands of the Kashmiri separatists – that the borders be opened and people be allowed free movement across the two sides of Kashmir – it is here that the impact of division is actually felt. The whole belt of the LoC around the districts of Poonch and Rajouri is inhabited by a number of such divided families who have the greatest stake in the opening of the borders. For these people, opening of the Uri-Muzaffarabad Road has been a real movement forward.

The urge for open borders and normalcy of relations across the border has not been limited to the people with the divided families but is shared by many others in the Jammu region. Despite the division for more than five decades, people on both the sides of the border have not been able to reconcile to the partition and remain nostalgic about the 'other' side. The memory of partition, though painful, evokes a strong emotional response for those who had to migrate from their native places. The desire to revisit these places, therefore, remains very intense. A glimpse of such emotional response can be seen from the many of the memoirs recorded by a group of "Jammuites" in Pakistan who were forced to leave Jammu in 1947 in the wake of the violence. Nostalgia for Jammu remains strong for all of them, despite the bitter memory of bloodshed and migration. The following excerpts from Rehmatullah Rad's and Khalid Hasan's book are self-expressive:[19]

> ...Even today, I would gladly return to Jammu, if I could, though cities by themselves are just so much mortar, stone and earth. Cities in the end are the people who live in them. And, of course, the people of my childhood, are lost in the mists of time. The world has moved on. But the world that we once knew

> was a calmer, a more magical, a more caring place. Partition and 1947 brought that world to an end. Those Muslims of Jammu who survived were forced to flee to Pakistan where they remained strangers and are so to this day. The generation that was born in Pakistan and grew up there, of course, knows nothing of Jammu and the way of life which was special to Jammu. .. Our parents, who are all dead and gone now, were never able to reconcile themselves to the loss of that way of life. As long as they lived, they kept missing Jammu, hoping, at least in their early years of Pakistan, that very soon things would settle down and they would return to Jammu. After some years, they gave up the hope. But they never overcame their nostalgia and their love of Jammu. (Khalid Hasan)[20]
>
> There was something about that city which was different, otherwise why would one feel haunted so many years later by its eternal magic.(Sorraya Khurshid) [21]
>
> We people were forced out of Jammu and overnight turned into refugees. Helpless and without friends, we got scattered in various parts of Pakistan…what was it about that city that still draws us back? What was its magic? What was it about its ambience that still sends us in a trance though so many years have passed since we left it behind? Maybe it was the great fellow-feeling that existed among its people. It did not matter what caste, family, tribe or clan one belonged to: we treated one another as if we were members of the same family… It is over half a century since we left Jammu but we still remember it…(Aziz Kash).[22]

An illustration of the emotional bond that the migrated population has with the native places can be seen from the response of many of the migrated people on the Indian side of Jammu region as well. Those who migrated to Jammu from the side of Pakistani administered Kashmir made conscious efforts to sustain, the memory of their places of origin, as well as their language and culture. Thus, the "Muzaffarabadis," the "Mirpuris," "Kotliwale," "Poonchis" are the ethno-cultural groups which have kept their pre-partition identity alive and have remained emotionally attached to it. Despite the fact that this identity is horizontally divided between the Hindus on the Indian side and the Muslims on the Pakistani side, the emotional bond remains very strong. Thus, the immersion of the old Mirpur town after the construction of Mangla Dam evokes sufficient emotional response from the Mirpuris on this side. On a number of occasions, the Mirpuris have expressed their solidarity with the Mirpuris on the other side. The same has been true of the Muzaffarabadis or the Poonchis.

It is because of this emotional chord that the demand to open borders has found strong supporters in this part of the state. During the last two years of the peace process, there has been sufficient lobbying by individuals, social and political groups for the opening of borders. This is significant because in the international parlance, it is in the ethnic-Kashmiri (Valley-based) identity that a continuity is seen. That there is a continuity of the ethnic Jammu identity, is a point that needs to be highlighted. It is here that the idea of borders being irrelevant assumes automatic acceptance.[23]

The human bond that exists between the people across the two sides of the LoC has not diminished despite the impact that these people have had to bear of the hostility between India and Pakistan. In fact, as the recent experience of the earthquake has shown, the bond has become stronger. The massive human and material loss on the side of Pakistani administered Kashmir after the earthquake that took place on October 8, 2005, has evoked strong emotional responses on the Indian side and people here have offered support to people on the other side. Much before help could come from the rest of the world, a number of small but significant initiatives were taken by the people on both sides of the border to help each other. The border had dissolved, in fact, for many who chose to go across the other side to be of immediate assistance to those facing misery brought about by the disaster. Responding to the urge of the people to meet each other on the two sides of the LoC, the Governments of India and Pakistan decided to open a number of points from where people could go across and meet their relatives and send the relief material. So huge was the response to this initiative that during the first day of the opening of the Poonch-Rawalkot point, hundreds of local people had gathered in the Pakistani administered Kashmir. The Pakistani police, in fact, had to use force to disperse a mob of people who had gathered in the expectation of meeting their relatives on the other side of the border.

It is in the light of the above that one can argue that Jammu, as it expands on the two sides of the border, offers all the opportunities for a fresh outlook on the relationship, not only between the people on the two sides of the erstwhile State of Jammu and Kashmir, but also between India and Pakistan. It is here that one can experience the idea of "irrelevance of borders" in its actuality and see the obliteration of the territorial approach to the relations between India and Pakistan.[24] As a cultural bridge between the two sides of divided "Kashmir," Jammu provides a positive space not only for the ongoing peace process but also for the future linkage between India and Pakistan.

Notes

1. For an in-depth analysis of socio-economic forces influencing the process of construction and assertion of Kashmiri identity till the 1947 period, see Chitralekha Zutshi, *The Languages of Belongings: Islam, Regional Identity and the*

Making of Kashmir (Delhi: Permanent Black, 2003) and Mridu Roy, *Hindu Rulers, Muslim Subjects: Islam, Rights and the History of Kashmir* (Princeton: Princeton University Press, 2004).

2. Eighty-five per cent of the people of Poonch district and 65 per cent of the people of Rajouri district are Muslims.
3. A distinction may be drawn between militancy and the separatist movement. In Kashmir, militancy operates in the environment of separatist politics. Separatist sentiment is a popular sentiment and, therefore, even as there is general opposition to violence perpetrated through militancy, there is a great sense of identification with separatism. In Poonch-Rajouri area, there has been no such relationship between the two. Since there was no similar separatist sentiment in these areas, the nature of militancy is different. That does not mean that there is no local recruitment, but the reasons for joining militancy are not ideological.
4. This understanding is based on the author's personal interviews held in July 2005 during visits to Doda, Baderwah and Kishtwar, the three major towns of Doda district. The manifestation of this feeling was there in almost every interview.
5. However, the division between the two communities is not very neat and clean and the presence of the two communities makes an interesting context of mixed living within the region. Apart from the districts of Jammu and Kathua which are predominantly Hindu (but which also have a significant presence of Gujjars, all Muslims), and Poonch district which is predominantly Muslim (but is having a significant number of Hindus and a concentration of Hindu population in its towns), the rest of the three districts of Udhampur, Kathua and Rajouri have a spread of mixed population. Doda, one of the largest districts of the region, exemplifies the complexity in the religious terms – the majority Muslim population is matched by an almost even number of Hindus who form all patterns of even division as in the towns of Baderwah and Kishtwar, of one community dominating as in the case of the town of Doda, of villages having a majority of Muslim population and a minority of Hindu population and vice-versa and even all-Muslim or all-Hindu villages.
6. The Muslims of the region, for instance, are not one homogeneous category as their identification with their tribe, caste or clan is greater and gets reflected in the variety of identity politics that operates in this region. Thus, the Rajput Muslims tend to distance themselves from Gujjars and Paharis, both Muslim tribal communities. The later two also are mutually engaged in a competitive relationship over the issue of tribal status and reservation.
7. The tone of this politics was set in 1952 in a major agitation launched by the Praja Parishad, a Jammu-based party having close linkage with the RSS and Bharatiya Jana Sangh. The agitation echoing the slogans of *"Ek Vidhan, Ek Pradhan, Ek Nishan"* (one Constitution, one president and one symbol) contested the basis of the special constitutional status guaranteed by Article 370 of the Indian Constitution. Projecting the full constitutional integration of the state with India as the political aspiration of Jammu, the Praja Parishad sought to emphasise the divergence between the politics of Jammu and Kashmir. The regional divide was further sharpened due to the Kashmir-centric nature of power politics in which the political elite of Jammu region was perpetually deprived of a share in political power. This has had the effect of generating a politics in this region around the issues of "regional imbalances" and "regional discrimination."

8. Though the RSS has been pursuing the idea of division of the state since the mid-Nineties, it came out openly in its favour just before the 2002 Assembly elections when it helped organise the Jammu State Morcha (JSM) with the demand for a separate state for Jammu. However, the JSM failed to get support for its idea of division of the state of J&K. It could register its victory only in one Assembly constituency in Jammu region.
9. The National Conference had contested the 1996 Assembly election by invoking the demand of state autonomy. However, while seeking a mandate from Jammu region, it had also supported the idea of regional autonomy. Soon after taking over the power, the NC government had constituted the State Autonomy Committee (SAC) and the Regional Autonomy Committee (RAC). While the State Autonomy Committee had recommended the restoration of autonomy enjoyed by the state in the pre-1953 period, the Regional Autonomy Committee, contesting the existing definition of regions, had recommended fresh reorganisation of regions. Instead of the known three regions of Jammu, Kashmir and Ladakh, it had recommended eight regions, dividing Jammu and Kashmir into three regions each and dividing Ladakh into two regions.
10. Apart from the State Autonomy Committee Report, the recommendations of the Regional Autonomy Committee Report were also highly politicised. The idea of division of the existing regions, especially of Jammu region into three regions was seen as a ploy by the NC government to push the very question of regional autonomy to the background.
11. For a detailed overview of Balraj Puri's arguments, refer to his *Simmering Volcano: Study of Jammu's Relations with Kashmir* (Delhi: Sterling, 1983); *Jammu and Kashmir: Triumph and Tragedy of Indian Federalism* (Delhi: Sterling, 1981); *Jammu: A Clue to Kashmir Tangle* (Delhi: 1966).
12. For instance, the argument that power has remained concentrated in Kashmir, can be contested on the ground that instead of regional dispersion of power, there is a class-based concentration of power and the mass of Kashmiris have been as much distanced from power as the people from Jammu.
13. With the passage of time, there have been clear indications that even the Kashmiri political response is not unified and cannot be represented either by one political organisation or under the banner of one kind of politics.
14. The partition of 1947, however, did have its impact on Jammu region as it resulted in the killing and migration of Muslims and Hindus in the region of Jammu. The Kashmir Valley, however, remained totally peaceful.
15. On a number of occasions, the minorities have been targeted by the militants with a specific purpose to provoke a communal response. Some of the most gruesome killings of minorities include the killings of 14 bus passangers in Sarthal, Doda district in 1994; 7 Kashmiri pundits in Sangrampora in 1997; 23 Kashmiri pundits in Wandhama in 1998; 25 members of a wedding party in Chapnari, Doda, in 1998; 26 Kashmiri pundits in Prankot in 1998; 15 labourers in Anantnag in 1999; 34 Sikhs in Chattisinghpora in 2000; 21 villagers killed in Kunda Pogal, Banihal, in 2000; 24 Kashmiri pundits in Nadimarg in 2003.
16. The BJP could find a foothold in the militancy-infested areas of the region and could even increase its electoral base in the region during the peak of the militancy. In 1996, the party could attain as many as eight seats in the State Assembly. This was an exceptional response of the region. The maximum number of seats that the party could win earlier was three. But in the 2002 Assembly

elections, it could not repeat its performance of the earlier election and it could win only one seat in the urban belt of Jammu district.

17. Among those people in the region who form a very strong constituency of peace, the most significant are those who live near the LoC and international boundary (IB) as these are the people who have suffered directly from the hostilities between India and Pakistan. As the borders have generally remained volatile, with shelling on a regular basis, these people have been witness to multiple displacements. To give a more recent example, Akhnoor sector that was the most hard hit in the deployment of forces saw migration of people in large numbers; 45,000 people from border villages of this sector had to flee to safer places. Many of these people are still located in the camps near Jammu city.
18. With the present ceasefire in force, the borders have become quiet for the first time. There is a sense of relief and also hope that the peace will become permanent so that people do not have to be bothered by the mining of their fields, frequent migrations and uncertainties not only in relation to their livelihood (especially for those dependent on agriculture) but also in terms of quality of their life.
19. Rehmatullah Rad and Khalid Hasan, *Memory Lane to Jammu* (Lahore: Sang-E-Meel Publication, 2004).
20. Khalid Hassan, "The Jammu That Was," in Rad and Hasan, Ibid., p.144.
21. Sorraya Khurshid, "My Jammu Memories," in Rad and Hasan, Ibid., pp.67-68.
22. Aziz Kash, "A Jammu Rememberance," in Rad and Hasan, Ibid., p.149.
23. Apart from all these groups which have been affected by the situation of conflict in one way or the other, many others urge for the free movement between the two sides of the state. The trading class (mostly Hindus) that resides mostly in the urban centres of the region, has been demanding the opening of multiple routes in Jammu region. This class is looking for business opportunities that the traditional natural trading routes can provide.
24. Jammu has a rich cultural heritage which not only provides examples of communal harmony but also of shared spiritual spaces. Shrines that are found all over the region are visited by people belonging to all the religions. So strong is the emotional bond of people with these shrines that even the borders and hostilities between India and Pakistan have not been able to dampen it. The shrine of Baba Chamliyal in Samba Sector is one such example. The annual festival in this 300-year-old shrine brings thousands of Pakistani devotees of this saint (incidentally, a Hindu) to the border. It is different matter, however, that they cannot visit the actual site and that they offer their *chadar* and receive their share of *shakkar* and *sharbat* through the help of Indian and Pakistani rangers.

The Peace Process: View From Leh

P. Stobdan

Historical Backdrop

For most people in Ladakh, the phrase "peace process" is a misnomer as to what it means to their present life and future destiny. Ladakh is peaceful, devoid of any conflict within and outside. One of the biggest tragedies for Ladakh in recent history has been its geo-political orientation from a Central Asian to South Asian outlook. This rather imposed subcontinental association has gravely distorted the very identity of Ladakh as a political unit in the trans-Himalayan region. Fortunately, the geographical barriers militated against Ladakh's exposure to the subcontinental influence. For instance, the ideological struggle of Buddhism versus Hinduism did not extend beyond Kashmir. However, a wave of Islamic preachers successfully reached Ladakh around the 13th century, transforming to an extent its cultural complexity. In fact, the rulers of Ladakh even sought military aid from the Mughal emperors to repel successive Tibetan onslaughts.

The early political dynamics of Ladakh was primarily associated with the Tibetan civilisational movement. A mélange of feudalism and Lamaism formed the traditional socio-political culture of the western Himalayan kingdom – although not exactly an ethno-geographical parameter but sectarian differences compelled Ladakh's rulers to maintain considerable distance from Tibet itself. Ladakh as an independent western Himalayan kingdom existed since 1930 AD. The kingdom was born out of several small sovereign principalities, unified by King Lhachen-Palgigon. The kingdom reached its political height during the Namgyal Dynasty (15th -16th centuries) and lasted until 1842 when it was conquered by the Dogras.

The Dogra rule decisively shaped the future course of Ladakh's politics. The Dogras and later the Kashmiris systematically subjugated and undermined Ladakh's identity, its culture and political rights. The Dogras, although they failed in their religious mission of Hinduising the Buddhist Ladakh, effectively cut off its old links, except the trade and commercial ties with Tibet. For the British, Ladakh was only of strategic importance against the Chinese and Russian threats. It did not fit into the British mercantile design, even though the idea of opening a Pashmina processing unit in Leh by William Moorcroft who was a veterinarian and in charge of the East India Company's stud farm at Calcutta was the only exception. The Moravian Christians too failed to hasten the spread of Christianity among the Buddhists of Ladakh in the early 19th century.

Ladakh and J&K

Ladakh's perception about its place in Jammu and Kashmir (J&K) has its genesis in an age-old political contradiction. The state, formed in March 1846 under the Treaty of Amritsar between the British and Jammu ruler Gulab Singh, was devoid of any geo-political character. Many people in Ladakh, including the Shias of Kargil and Baltistan, showed dismay over the irretrievable merger of their identity with J&K. Frederic Drew who served as governor in Ladakh in the 19th century remarked, "[T]he territories of Jammu and Kashmir have no other bond of cohesion than the fact of Maharaja's rule, no simple name for it exists."[1] In fact, the Kashmiris themselves launched movements such as the Quit Kashmir Movement (1946) and Scrap Amritsar Treaty crusade (1924) for the abrogation of the 1846 Treaty.

In fact, Ladakh had no case, at the time of the independence movement, to put forward its view except that its people felt emotionally and spiritually closer to Tibet. Nonetheless, the sole organisation in the region, the Ladakh Buddhist Association (LBA), was actively guided by a few Kashmiri pundits to put forward a case for separating Ladakh from J&K in favour of an administrative solution within the Indian system. In fact, the pundits also conspired to form a Youngman Buddhist Association (YBA) with the aim to Indianise Buddhism in Ladakh. The move to create the YBA was in consonance with similar movements launched elsewhere in India, Sri Lanka and Burma.

A memorandum to Maharaja Hari Singh and to the prime minister of India on May 4, 1949, by Cheewang Rigzin, president, LBA, opposed the proposed plebiscite and demanded that Ladakh be governed either by the maharaja without tagging it on to Kashmir, amalgamated with Jammu to form a separate province or be permitted to join East Punjab. While doing so, the people of Ladakh gave historical reasons of their bond with the people of Jammu (military conquest) and not with Kashmir as it was the Dogra king who conquered Ladakh in 1834, whereas Kashmir came into Dogra possession 12 years later, in 1846. It was argued that Sheikh Abdullah's case for a unitary set-up, was to be seen only in the context of the Amritsar Treaty – which bears upon the Valley only. Failing all options, they would be forced to consider the option of reuniting with Tibet. The memorandum underlined the strategic and commercial importance of neighbouring Tibet and China, with Leh as the nerve centre of the Central Asian trade. Neither Maharaja Hari Singh nor Jawaharlal Nehru responded to the appeal. Pundit advisors suggested that Ladakh should have been allowed to go its own way with the collapse of the maharaja's hereditary rule. Even otherwise, the constitutional link between Ladakh and the Dogras ceased to be operative with the fall of the monarchy in 1948. However, the choice of the majority in Ladakh found expression in the self-proclaimed leader of the Ladakhis, Kushok Bakula's statements that Ladakh be allowed to join Tibet.

It seemed that Sheikh Abdullah astutely manipulated Ladakh's case. In order to convince the Buddhist clergy, Sheikh, *inter alia,* drew their attention to the horrifying state of the Tibetans under the Chinese influence. This was to foster a sense of anxiety among the lamas for the security of their land and religion. Sheikh Abdullah also orchestrated events such as arresting mock Russian agents in Leh Bazar, indicating that there was a perceived threat to Buddhism from the Soviets across Chinese Turkistan. These factors strongly impelled the lamas to choose Sheikh Abdullah as a lesser evil than the Chinese or Russian Communists. Sheikh Abdullah also shrewdly won the hearts of the lamas by exempting the monasteries, which owned major lands, from the state land reforms Act brought about by him in the early 1950s. Given the clergy's greater concern for monastic rather than the people's affairs, it was not difficult for the Kashmiri leadership to placate them. Consequently, Sheikh Abdullah brought Kushok Bakula to represent Ladakh in the first Constituent Assembly in 1952. Bakula's signing the draft Constitution that envisaged a unitary state with a clear concentration of powers in the Valley was a gross political blunder and a historical tragedy that decisively shaped the status of Ladakh in J&K.

Ladakh's maladjustment with J&K started from the very beginning. Clearly, the Kashmiri leadership had no interest in Ladakh. They enjoyed a free hand in exercising sabre-rattling and jingoism towards the region's Buddhist heritage. They disdainfully referred to the people as Boto (non-Muslim). The Kashmiri elite sought greater autonomy and funds for the state but denied Ladakh its share. The people of Ladakh have all along accused the Kashmiri leadership of allowing systematic discrimination against them. In fact, every enquiry commission, including the Gajendragadkar Commission (1967-68), the Sikri Commission (1979-80), the Wazir Commission (1982-83) and the Singhal Committee (1998) have invariably acknowledged in unambiguous language that the ruling class has all along treated Ladakh shabbily. The commissions cited innumerable instances of discrimination and the Valley's apathy *vis-à-vis* Ladakh.

Repeated agitations by the Buddhists of Ladakh for separation from Kashmir were quelled by using force. The protests ranged from the demand for "greater autonomy" in the 1950s, "NEFA-type" administration in the 1960s, "central administration" in the 1970s, "free Ladakh from Kashmir" in the 1980s to the demand for "Union Territory"(UT) status in the 1990s. While it is also true that even though the people of Ladakh accepted the *fait accompli*, New Delhi tended to open its own direct line of communication with Ladakh. Although the China factor always compelled the central government to stay in touch with Ladakh, there had been tendencies to pitch the local leaders against Srinagar whenever New Delhi felt it necessary to do so.

Divide and Rule

The leadership of the Valley assiduously coopted ambitious leaders from Ladakh for inclusion in the nomenclature of *Darbar* in the Valley. Whenever they failed in this strategy, the Kashmiri leadership tended to communalise Ladakh's politics by pitting the Muslims in Ladakh against the Buddhists or at times encouraging factionalism within the Buddhist population. Sheikh Abdullah not only divided the region into two districts along communal lines, but also initiated measures to create a "Greater Kashmir" to include Ladakh in it. The splintering of Ladakh on communal lines helped the Valley leaders curb the centrifugal trend of thought in Ladakh. Sheikh Abdullah's "Greater Kashmir" concept heightened suspicion among the Buddhists that he was attempting to Islamise Ladakh and relegate the Buddhists into a minority within Ladakh. The LBA, in the early 1970s, even carried out a movement demanding allocation of land to the Tibetan refugees in Ladakh. This resulted in sharp polarisation of Ladakh along communal lines, with Shia majority Kargil joining hands with the Kashmiris. The "Greater Kashmir" idea influenced the polity in Ladakh throughout the 1980s and 1990s that effectively divided the sentiments of the people – Muslim Kargil supporting the Kashmiri cause and Buddhist Leh demanding regional identity. The separation has not only hurt the sentiments of the people of Kargil but also created confusion and a gulf between Kargil and Ladakh. This artificial division along communal lines is still being used as a convenient argument to quell any strong voice from Ladakh in the current discourse on the Kashmir issue.

Kashmiri Struggle and Ladakh

Interestingly, Ladakh's agitation against Kashmiri rule in Ladakh coincided with the beginning of the present phase of the crisis in Kashmir. A violent struggle launched by the LBA, in 1989, giving the call to free Ladakh from

Kashmir could be brought under control only after a tripartite agreement among the representatives of the LBA, the state government and the central government was signed in October 1993. The LBA then rescinded the demand for UT status in favour of an Autonomous Hill Council (AHC). Throughout the 1990s, Ladakh remained bogged down with its own affairs, such as the non-implementation of provisions stated in the tripartite agreement. The Farooq Abdullah government was the main hurdle in the non-implementation of the provisions. The power for the Ladakh Autonomous Hill Development Council (LAHDC) was curtailed by the National Conference (NC). LAHDC leaders such as Thufstan Chewang and Rigzin Jora remained vocal about Abdullah's efforts at undermining the LAHDC's autonomy, and as such, Ladakh's attention was not at all to focus on the peace process or the Indo-Pak conflict on the Kashmir issue. In political terms, Ladakh remained unfazed by the Kashmiri secessionist movement. In other words, Leh remained indifferent to the ongoing crisis. Most of Ladakh's political organisations, barring the Congress Party, neither supported nor condemned the Kashmiri struggle for independence. The lack of support from the Kargil Muslims for UT status dampened Ladakh's struggles. By this time, it was clear that the "Greater Kashmir" drive had sufficiently engulfed part of Ladakh. Kargil strongly resented any move to club it with the Ladakhi identity and felt it necessary to affiliate with the Valley, despite the fact that Kargil is ethnically, linguistically and socially closer to the wider Ladakh region.

Pakistan and Ladakh

In 1948, the Pakistani Ibex and Eskimo Forces captured Kargil and Drass and advanced further up to Leh. They were pushed back around the onset of winter in November that year. The Pakistan Army has seen Kargil as a strategic point for a long time. Historically, its location at the crossroads between Skardu and Leh and Kashgar and Srinagar prompted it to play an important military and commercial role. Kargil has a unique strategic position, as it opens up four valleys (Drass-Suru-Wakha-Indus). The Pakistani military always considered Kargil a chokepoint for operations in Ladakh. During the Kargil conflict, the Pakistan Army used a three-pronged strategy to cut off Drass and Kargil from Leh and Srinagar before Zojila was cleared. The aim was to enter the Indus Valley through Batalik and Chorbatla to capture areas up to Khaltse, and enter Shayok Valley to recapture 254 sq miles of Turtuk, comprising five villages, Chalungka, Thang, Tyakshi, Pharol and Turtuk. But for the early opening of the Zojila in April that year, the Pakistan Army would have certainly accomplished its objectives.

Pakistan has been eyeing Ladakh for years, primarily to regain areas it lost to India since 1971. However, it has faced difficulties on two accounts. First, unlike in the Valley, Ladakh was not ripe for an Islamic revolution, though attempts were made to communalise the region through subversive means. Secondly, the topography (naked mountains) was not favourable for guerrilla operations. To overcome these, since the summer of 1997, Pakistan had resorted to large-scale occasional artillery shelling in Kargil. The aim was to terrorise the sequestered people in order to push and scare them away from the high ridges. This tactic has helped the Pakistan Army significantly in undermining Indian intelligence-gathering abilities. The aim was also to disperse the Kargil Shias to move towards the areas under Buddhist control. A significant number of Shias from Drass and Kargil were shifted during the conflict to Leh. A strategy was also devised to swell the Muslim population through both conversion and migration.[2]

Pakistan also used the battle-hardened Afghan militia, the Mujahideen, who had fought the Soviets in the Hind Kush and Pamir heights. It raised a militia locally to suit the terrain and climate. The objective was to disrupt communications, destroy supply dumps and gain the support of the local populace as it was hoped that there would be a general popular uprising. Essentially, the Kargil War revealed a well thought-out Pakistani plan for an Islamic uprising in Ladakh too—a plot hatched nine years prior to the conflict. What made it worse was that Sheikh Abdullah decided to separate Kargil from Ladakh as a separate administrative zone. This was done on July 1, 1979, a year after the Iranian Revolution. The step has helped the Pakistani cause considerably.

In the early 1990s, the Shias of Kargil not only refused to support UT status for Ladakh but also rejected the offer of an Autonomous Hill Council (AHC) status, essentially to mark their solidarity with the Kashmiri cause. It was widely perceived then that acceptance of the AHC by Kargil would not have been appreciated by the Kashmiri secessionist groups, despite the fact that the vast majority of people in Kargil supported the idea of an AHC. However, it is true that the Muslims of Kargil did not join the Kashmiri secessionist forces. Impressions, however, prevailed that elements from Kargil had colluded with the Pakistan Army, especially the role they played in passing on accurate information about key installations in Kargil. It was precisely for this reason that the Indian Army had to carry out, though without success, the "Sadbhavana" campaign in the aftermath of Kargil to win the hearts of the Shia population along the Line of Control (LoC) in the Kargil-Ladakh sector.

The Kargil crisis, from Ladakh's perspective, was not a case of intelligence failure. The Pakistani thrust into the Ladakh sector was clear since 1997. By intruding into Kargil, Pakistan wished to open a qualitatively new front *vis-à-vis* India. While gaining control over the mountain heights, it wanted to politically widen the scope of the Kashmir conflict on the ground. The Pakistanis also concluded, as evident from the broadcasts from Radio Azad Kashmir and Radio Skardu, that the Buddhist Ladakh too was getting averse to India's rule. The Pakistanis carried on subversive activities in Ladakh through infiltration and dumping arms across the Turtuk sector. There were also reports of large caches of arms found in and around Leh. Post-Kargil, attempts were made by the Kashmiri militants to infiltrate into Ladakh through Doda and Kishtowar areas. Terrorists killed monks in Zanskar Valley, evoking a sharp reaction from the Buddhists in Ladakh.

The LBA in one of its meeting observed that the bulk seizures of Pakistani arms and ammunition from Turtuk villages had shocked the peace-loving population of Ladakh. They accused the state government of being unsatisfactory and lackadaisical in the handling of this case. It demanded that the state government should get the Central Bureau of Investigation (CBI)to investigate the mass stocking of arms in the region. The former Chairman of the Ladakh Autonomous Hill Development Council (LAHDC) Thupstan Chewang said Pakistan-based terrorist groups had attempted to create a network in Ladakh, but the geographical nature and the climatic conditions of Ladakh prevented them from spreading their tentacles.[3] However, the Kashmiri militants came to Ladakh in the garb of traders and antique dealers from Srinagar. Nevertheless, in the absence of any local support, their actions remained dormant. The destruction of the Bamiyan Buddha by the Taliban regime in Afghanistan triggered tensions in Ladakh although the situation remained under control.

The Peace Process and Ladakh

The Siachen conflict, the Kargil intrusion and the communal divide were, in a sense, designed to bring the Ladakh region into the fold of the Indo-Pak conflict, which otherwise remained confined to the Valley. However, they did not provoke the people of Ladakh. Ladakh's response to the Kashmir crisis and the Indo-Pak conflict could be described as indifferent and cold. It is widely understood that Ladakh has no intentions to dispute or reject the aspirations of the people of Kashmir Valley. However, it needs to be underlined that the people of Ladakh have never opposed the Kashmiri struggle except for condemning certain acts of terrorism that hurt the people of Ladakh. It is also necessary to underline the fact that the separatists also never targeted or intimidated the people of Ladakh. Nonetheless, the Indo-Pak conflict in Ladakh, the Siachen issue and the Kargil conflict have inevitably highlighted the need for involving Ladakh in the peace process. From the Pakistani perspective, this was important to widen the scope of the conflict, but India too, invariably, pushed the Ladakh factor, albeit without any seriousness, to counter the secessionists' arguments. The Ladakh factor was particularly added to the Kashmir conflict in the aftermath of the Kargil conflict by the National Democratic Alliance (NDA) government to provide a contrasting view on the issue to weaken the Kashmiri case. The special interlocutors appointed by the NDA government and continued by the United Progressive Front (UPA) government consulted sections of the Buddhist and Shia communities of Ladakh. However, those interactions and efforts to involve Ladakh have not been worthwhile to form a perspective in a meaningful way. The view from Leh was that the people of Ladakh have nothing to do with the ongoing crisis, and that their main political goal is to separate from Kashmir in favour of a self-rule mechanism in the form of a UT status to run their affairs.[4] At the same time, the people of Ladakh are aware that such a result is not going to come about easily and that their fate is linked inextricably to the final resolution of the Kashmir issue. The most favoured perception in Ladakh is to allow Kashmir to find its own way in whatever manner and then deal with the situation accordingly. Privately, people in Ladakh would prefer Kashmir finding a solution outside the Indian framework so that they could take up their own case separately. It needs to be firmly understood that Ladakh's engagement with the state is necessitated by technical reasons, in terms of the government's allocations of developmental funds. Both politically and psychologically, Ladakh does not relate to the J&K dynamics. For example, Ladakh vociferously opposed any move by the centre to restore the pre-1953 status. Former Union Minister and Congress leader P. Namgyal is reported to have said that the pre-1953 status to Kashmir should be restored only once Ladakh and Jammu are separated from the Valley. The concept of *Kashmiriyat* too is a misnomer for Ladakh. The Valley leadership has applied double standards on the issue of division while justifying separation from India on communal lines but has resisted J&K's division to safeguard the secular ethos of the state.

The issue of "greater autonomy" and "regional autonomy" as recommended by the state's Regional Autonomy Committee (RAC) also never excited Ladakh and was rejected as a ploy to reaffirm Kashmiri monopoly over the state. Barring a handful of Abdullah's NC supporters, an overwhelming majority of the people of Ladakh, both Muslims and Buddhists, vehemently opposed the idea of autonomy as resolved in the J&K Legislative Assembly on June 26, 2000. Autonomy was never seen as a panacea and would only prolong the agonies – further aggravating the existing inter-regional tensions in the state.

Trifurcation was seen as a viable solution to the problems confronting the people of Jammu, Kashmir and Ladakh. A reorganisation of the state was sought on the lines of other states such as UP, Bihar, Punjab and MP. The people of Jammu and even the Kashmiri pundits in their campaign for trifurcation of J&K invariably tagged their cause with that of Ladakh. They too referred to Ladakh's suffering at the hands of the Valley leaders whenever it was necessary for them to do so. Since 2000, the idea of trifurcation has gained currency. Indian leaders, including L.K. Advani, did not rule out trifurcation of J&K into Jammu, Kashmir and Ladakh but only within the four corners of the Indian Constitution. The Rashtriya Swayamsevak Sangh (RSS) in its June 30, 2000, Kurukshetra resolution, called for the trifurcation of J&K. This was also the view advocated by the people of Jammu but opposed by the National Conference and Congress Party. *Inter alia*, trifurcation was perceived to be advantageous in that it would restrict the area of contention to Kashmir and facilitate the task of the government to curb militancy effectively. Similarly, the Vishva Hindu Parishad (VHP) too supported separate statehood for Jammu and union territory status for Ladakh. It believed that concentrating power only in Kashmir Valley is highly unjustified and discriminatory. It is quite possible that the Ladakh Buddhist Association's call for rejection of the pre-1953 type RAC report and the suggested trifurcation of J&K into two states and one union territory was inspired by the right-wing BJP, VHP and RSS.

The people of Ladakh also did not respond to various initiatives for intra-Kashmir dialogues even though they noted the political alienation of the people of Ladakh and Gilgit-Baltistan. Such initiatives often advocated a solution to J&K by restoring the state in its entirety while preserving its plurality, democratic and federal nature. Since the Ladakh region is larger in size than Kashmir and Jammu combined, the idea of rechristening the state as Jammu, Kashmir & Ladakh State was suggested by some to eliminate a sense of isolation and provide a sense of belonging.

It is, however, true that the views of the Kargil Shias differ from those of Leh. Firstly, Kargil seeks a direct ethnic affinity with the people of Baltistan and never reconciled to the separation of people sharing a common sectarian identity. For decades, the Shias accepted the division as a *fait accompli* due to the frozen nature of Indo-Pak relations. Also, what kept the Kargil Shias away from the

Indo-Pak conflict were the sectarian differences with Pakistan. Islamabad's repeated persecution of Shias in the Northern Areas has had a negative impact on the Shias of Kargil. In the changed circumstances, the peace process has particularly opened up opportunities for the Shias to raise a voice in favour of greater cross-border interaction with the Northern Areas, including the opening of the bus service between Kargil and Skardu. As the process of confidence-building measures (CBMs) evolved, the demand for starting the bus service gained greater currency. This point has singularly dominated the Shias' meetings with the central government's interlocutors on Kashmir.

The need for Ladakh factoring in the peace process or CBMs, from New Delhi's perspective, is also being argued on the ground that the process has to be J&K-centric rather Valley-centric. Hence, the idea of opening the Sailkote-Jammu and Kargil-Skardu bus services was added to strengthen the argument. Nonetheless, it is necessary to emphasise here that opening of the Kargil-Skardu road would be fraught with dangerous security and political consequences in the long term. The opening of the road would push Kargil closer to Skardu, Pakistan Occupied Kashmir (PoK) and Islamabad, which in turn would have ideological implications, including spillover of Islamisation into Ladakh. Unlike India's axis to Kargil through Pir Punjal and Zojila (which remains closed for 8 months in a year) Pakistan will have an all-weather road to Kargil.

The Shias of Kargil in their appeal to the interlocutor, made a substantive point that the centre has never involved the people of Ladakh region in the Indo-Pak peace process, despite the fact that over 70 per cent territory illegally occupied by Pakistan belonged to Ladakh and not Jammu or Kashmir. They argued that the All Parties Hurriyat Conference (APHC) represents only the Valley's voice and not the sentiments of the entire state.[5] This, in fact, poses a logical question of whether the parties are contesting for population or the territory.

It has become rather appropriate to mention Ladakh as one of the key areas in international relations, particularly in the Indo-Pak context. During his visit to Ladakh in June 2005, the Indian prime minister made a number of very bold proclamations about the importance of peace in the region. He also said, "[N]ow the time has come and we should try to convert this battlefield (Siachen Glacier) into a peace mountain."[6] In the context of Ladakh, the phrase, "peace process" is being used indiscriminately and merely to seek a divergent view. To the people of Ladakh, the Indo-Pak peace process is diplomatic jargon with no meaning and devoid of true commitment to peace and justice. Someone has correctly stated, "Hopefully, India and Pakistan will not start using that dreadful phrase, especially with reference to Ladakh because it would be seen as one of the few generalisations that can be made about the peaceful societies. The people of Ladakh not only strongly believe in peacefulness, they also create real processes—social systems and cultural values—to make sure those beliefs translate into reality." Therefore, it is highly unlikely that Ladakh's perception with regard to being associated with the state would undergo any change in the medium or longer term.

New Dynamics

Something is silently brewing in the trans-Himalayan zone of Gilgit, Baltistan and Ladakh. Leh observed martyr's day on August 27 to mark the police killing of peaceful demonstrators in 1989. On August 25, Gyalo Tundup, the pro-Chinese brother of the Dalai Lama, reached Leh clandestinely to brief the Tibetan leader, who was in retreat in Ladakh. On August 31, when the Dalai Lama visited Turktuk, (a Shia pocket salvaged from Pakistan in 1971) for the first time, the people turned hysterical. The event marked Dalai's complete supremacy in the western Himalayas. Dalai Lama's leadership is incontestable in the region.

Across in Baltistan, November 1 marks the day of its subjugation by Pakistan. "Northern Areas" has been restive since 1988 when Pakistani police burnt Shia protestors alive. If Baltistan dissented against atrocities under Pakistan's federally administered rule since 1948, Ladakh is increasingly seeking to sever its ties with Kashmir. The growing resentment in Ladakh and Baltistan could eventually expose the much-hyped Kashmir issue. Interestingly, Kashmir comprises less than 10 per cent of J&K territory. With Jammu covering 11.8 per cent, the remaining 78.5 per cent is neither Jammu nor Kashmir.

Kashmir was only an estate of the Dogras, bought under the British law. Ladakh-Gilgit-Baltistan (LBG) measuring 174,376 sq km was conquered by the Dogras (1833-1846) and, hence, has a brighter case for political freedom than Kashmir. The maharaja's fall (1948) led to Pakistan capturing Gilgit and Baltistan (77,675 sq km), while Ladakh (96,701 sq km) remained as part of J&K. Since then, only China has contested the Indo-Pak rivalry in the trans-Himalayas. By the early 1960s, Beijing firmly sliced 37,000 sq km (Aksai Chin) from Ladakh, and 5,180 sq km (Shaksgam and Muztagh Valley) from Baltistan. China today controls over 24.5 per cent of LGB territory.

Over four decades of military contests by Pakistan, China and India have turned the region into a protracted battlefield that led to colossal damage, including radioactive induced effects on the region. For long, people have complained about the psychological impact of perpetual war and conflict.

They suffered horrifying cultural onslaughts. Baltistan and Gilgit witnessed Punjabi forays and if the Urduisation process wiped out the archaic Balti and Purig languages, fundamentalists obliterated the unique Nur-Bakhshia tradition of the *Kubrawiya* Sufi order. The situation has been no better in Ladakh either. The Kashmiris exercised a jingoistic policy towards the Buddhist heritage.

Strangely, it took over five decades for the Hindu masters to discover that the holy Indus originated from Ladakh. The BJP's reign led the zealous L.K. Advani to spearhead saffronisation of Ladakh. The state sponsored annual "Sindhu Darshan" drew lakhs of people to rinse out their feet in Leh's pristine water – adding Indus to the list of the country's polluted rivers. Many Indians took pride in it – accomplishing the unfinished task of Adi Shankaracharya!! Pakistani editorials viewed this as another Sikkim in the making. In reality, Advani sowed the seeds for future conflict in the Himalayas. In the aftermath of the Kargil conflict, the NDA government tried to be more benevolent in giving economic incentives to Ladakh. There was a newfound recognition of Ladakh in the Indian mind because of the Kargil War. Apart from initiating the Sindhu Darshan festivities, the NDA government pushed the agenda of opening the Ladakh route to Kailash Mansarovar for pilgrimage. They promised to take up the issue strongly with the Chinese even if it meant compromising with Beijing on the border issue. For the BJP, saffronisation of Ladakh was more important, particularly in the light of Ladakh becoming vulnerable to Islamic invasion.

In Baltistan, resentment has been growing against the settlement of Pathans, Punjabis and Afghan refugees. In Ladakh, Tibetan refugees introduced the politics of reincarnation, sectarianism and crime, which are threatening the Ladakhis' basic values and culture, a la *wahhabi* sectarian rhetoric that has been destabilising Balti society since 1996.

The "self-rule" demand of Baltistan is as old as the independence of Pakistan. But since the 1990s, Baltistan's demand has shifted from civil rights to complete independence from Pakistan along the 1948 UN resolution. A movement launched by the Karakoram Students Organisation (KSO) and Baltistan Students Federation (BSF) against Punjabis grabbing jobs gave birth to the formation of the Balwaristan National Front (BNF). The founder, Nawaz Khan Naji, envisaged Balwaristan (land of heights) reflecting a common history, geography and culture of people from Chitral to Ladakh. The BNF's flag shows icy mountain peaks and an ibex as its national symbol. Moreover, people are rallying around Gohar Aman of Yasin who is being resurrected as the region's legendary hero. Today, the Karakoram National

Movement (KNM), Boloristan Democratic Front (BDF), Gilgit-Baltistan National Conference (GBNC) and Northern Areas United Front (NAUF) among others sustain the anti-Pakistan rhetoric; they even seek the return of territory from China.

In Ladakh, the protests have traditionally been against Kashmiri exploitation. But in 1989, the LBA raised anti-India slogans. It then threatened to take up arms. The protests also had a pro-China colour. The LBA's demand for a UT status was, however, rescinded in favour of a Ladakh Autonomous Hill Development Council (LAHDC) in 1993. But the issue resurfaced in 2002, with the Ladakh Union Territory Front (LUTF) staking fresh demands, which is nothing but a smokescreen for larger things to come. The LUTF's demand is becoming more vociferous, with extremist and irredentist overtones. This was reflected in its past agitation. In the recent case, during the election for the LAHDC, the LUTF leadership expressed similar sentiments. However, the Government of India remained silent on the issue of UT status for Ladakh. Union Home Minister Shivraj Patil was non-committal about the Government of India's stand on the demand for the grant of UT status to Ladakh when he visited the region in November 2004. Patil said that the issue (demand for UT status) "can join or break the unity." He added, "Whether it can be done or not or how it can be done, we are not in a position to say." This indicated India's over-cautiousness on the issue.

There appears to be complete harmony and commonality of views between the people of Gilgit-Baltistan and Ladakh region, despite the fact that there have been no opportunities for a dialogue between the divided erstwhile Ladakh Wazarat. There is an emerging trend of Ladakh and Baltistan (L&B) increasingly seeking a solution out of the South Asian quandary. This is happening when both Baltistan and Ladakh are becoming the hottest destinations for international tourists. Baltistan is more popular than Pakistan. Ladakh has already become a playground for political and cultural actors.

Interestingly, prominent figures in Ladakh, in a security related seminar in 2004, questioned New Delhi's wisdom of buying peace with China by bartering away territories of Ladakh.[7] *Inter alia*, they censured India's utter failure in stopping China and Pakistan from transgressing Ladakh territory. They considered the Indian Army to be a demoralised force and India's lack of commitment for the region disillusioned them. New Delhi has almost forgotten that Ladakh owned an enclave of six villages at the foothills of Mount Kailash until the 1960s. A chilling comment in the foreign media was that "Indian exploitation, Indian inability to defend Ladakh and the weakness of the historical association between India and Ladakh carries the message that Ladakh, like Kashmir, should separate from India and go its own way."[8] New Delhi needs to be cautious about any miscalculation in Ladakh: as an expert has said, the prevailing relative peace was solely due to the people's faith in non-violence, which couldn't be guaranteed in the long run.[9] No wonder, the adroit Chinese are not in a hurry to strike a deal.

Conclusion

From Ladakh's point of view, the current *status quo* in J&K is unendurable and is against the democratic and political aspiration of various nationalities. Ladakh is likely to pursue a persuasive policy to safeguard its interests. Ladakh's opposition to engagement with any process so far has been due to its belief that even an autonomous J&K state would seal its political fate with the Valley. Leh's strategy so far has been to put its political lot with New Delhi, hoping that the latter will protect its interests even in the worst situation. New Delhi's assessment that Ladakh, along with Jammu, will opt to remain with India could turn out to be a wrong one. The situation may be changing fast in the region. There is an increasing awareness that putting all the eggs in Delhi's basket would be wrong. Moreover, Delhi's attitude has throughout been to ignore the Ladakh factor to appease the Kashmiris.

Certainly, the problem cannot be resolved without restructuring the state. The political logic in maintaining the state as a single political unit needs to be explained sooner or later and Ladakh too realises that relying only on Delhi may not sufficiently address its interests. The power brokers of the National Conference and the Congress Party have so far vehemently thwarted Ladakh's support for the division of J&K. With the emerging new political reality that has come to the fore during the recent LAHDC election, there is every possibility that Ladakh too will appreciate separation of regions, to form political entities of their own. There is near convergence of views between the APHC, Pakistan government, RSS and Ladakh – all of them driving at a reconstruction of the state, something along the Owen Dixon Plan of 1950.

It is interesting that unlike the NC and the Congress, the separatist groups are more inclined to recognise Ladakh's case. Former Chairman of the Hurriyat Conference, Sayeed Ali Shah Geelani did admit that the current struggle is only of the Kashmiris and not of the people of J&K. He said that even the division of J&K, as a consensus decision arrived at in tripartite talks among India, Pakistan and the people of Kashmir, would be acceptable. To that extent, even the proposal moved by General Musharraf to divide the state into seven regions, demilitarise them and change their status was welcomed by the people of Ladakh. There was absolutely no contradiction between what he said and Ladakh's demand, except in the fact that Pakistan wanted to separate Kargil from Ladakh. However, this issue is a separate point of debate. Nonetheless, Pakistan has recognised that Ladakh too has the right to exist as a separate political entity outside Kashmir. Islamabad's latest proposal for "self-governance" and the APHC's proposal to create a United States of Jammu and Kashmir emphasise the same point, which would be a welcome sign for Ladakh. There is growing scope for the Kashmiri leadership, including the APHC, to seek a dialogue process with the people of Ladakh, Baltistan and Gilgit before they talk about tripartite talks among India, Pakistan and the people of Kashmir.

Notes

1. Frederic Drew, *The Northern Barrier of India: A Popular Account of the Jammoo and Kashmir Territories with Illustrations* (London: Edward Stanford, 1877) 1st edition. Reprinted by Light & Life Publishers, Jammu. 1971. Cited in "Why Union Territory Status for Ladakh?" A Memorandum to members of the Indian Parliament by Tsering Samphel, *Kashmir Sentinel*, August 2002 Issue. Samphel was the president of the Ladakh Buddhist Association (LBA).
2. See P. Stobdan, "Lapses in Ladakh," *Indian Express*, July 7, 1999. The observations are based on the field study done by the author at the time of the Kargil War.
3. "Ladakh Foils Terrorist Attempts for Base," *Daily Excelsior*, June 4, 2005.
4. This view was expressed to the central government's interlocutor on Kashmir Shri N.N. Vohra, who was trying to seek Ladakhi opinion on the Kashmir issue. The central government in New Delhi, during the BJP rule, had tried consulting all the regions of J&K. The Ladakhis refused to spell out their position on the Kashmir crisis excepting putting forward their own case for UT status.
5. Views expressed to this author by Shri. N.N. Vohra, the centre's interlocutor for Jammu and Kashmir.
6. "Peacefulness in Ladakh, Part 1: Designate a Peace Mountain," June 16, 2005. Available at http://www.peacefulsocieties.org/NAR/050616lada1.html.
7. Views expressed during the deliberations of the seminar on "India-China Relations: Peace & Tranquillity Across Frontier," August 11, 2004, Leh. The seminar was organised by the University of Jammu, Indian Pugwash Society, New Delhi and 14 Corps of the Indian Army, based in Leh. Experts from Delhi, Jammu, Indian Army and prominent members of Ladakhi civil society participated in the seminar.
8. P. Stobdan, "Mishandling Ladakh May Prove Costly," *Ladags Melong*, Vol. 1, Issue 1, Spring/May 7-8, 1995; reproduced from *The Times of India*.
9. The view was expressed by Cheewang Smanla, a prominent Ladakhi intellectual. Deliberations of the seminar on "India-China Relations: Peace & Tranquillity Across Frontier," August 11, 2004, Leh.

Peace Process and Imperatives of Resolving the Kashmir Problem

Noor Ahmad Baba

The Problem and its Dimensions

The first step in addressing a problem with a view to resolving it is to admit its existence and understand it in its different dimensions. Fortunately, today, people across the subcontinent and the world admit the existence of the Kashmir problem and the need for its resolution. But differences surface as soon as we come to the contours of what constitutes this problem and the elements that could constitute, or contribute to, its solution. Most people concerned with this issue admit its complexity not only in terms of its origin but also its dimensions and manifestations. But for most people in Kashmir, the problem is rooted in certain identifiable objective causes and factors rooted in history, in its internal dimensions and also in relation to India and Pakistan. Maharaja Hari Singh's signing of the Instrument of Accession with the Indian Union did not carry legitimacy vis-à-vis the people of Kashmir as his own legitimacy to rule the state had been questioned by the predominant majority of his subjects. It was for this non-representative character of the maharaja that the government of India offered to refer the final decision about the issue of accession to the people of the state. Even Sheikh Abdullah who, as a leader of the dominant party in the national movement in Kashmir, was supposed to endorse the accession, tried his utmost to delegitimise the whole process by campaigning for Kashmir's right to self-determination continuously for twenty-two years between 1953 and 1975. The Government of India also made a bold commitment, both locally and internationally, that the state's future would "be settled by a reference to its people." The UN resolutions also endorsed the position that the final dispensation of Kashmir would be made according to the will of the people, ascertained through a plebiscite. The popular mistrust was accentuated by the fact that the special position that was secured by the state within the Indian Constitution under Article 370, was eroded through regimes which had no base in the people. State sponsored electoral rigging, non-functional democracy and continued repressive order within the state only helped to reinforce the discontent and alienation of the people and helped buttress their desire for the right to self-determination. The continued division of the state and its people between the Indian and the Pakistani controlled parts, the persistent contestation on Kashmir between India and Pakistan and the international recognition to the disputed nature of Kashmir only served to reinforce the legitimacy of this claim in the minds of the people.

These factors together make it a two-dimensional problem with different layers of manifestations. In its internal dimensions, it is primarily a problem for its people, with many tangible political, psychological, economic and moral bases rooted in history. Simultaneously, it is an international dispute between India and Pakistan, with a degree of recognition from the international community. Internally, the people of Kashmir have been bearing the brunt of the issue in the worst possible manner, and externally, this problem has also afflicted the subcontinent for more than half a century. For most part of their history, the two countries used their resources – diplomatic, political, military and economic – only to undermine each other in whatever way they could. They remained so obsessed towards each other that each one ignored more dangerous security challenges from within and without. Therefore, we cannot close our eyes to wish it away. It needs to be taken head-on to see that it is addressed and resolved once for all.

Imperatives of Indo-Pak Detente

Indo-Pak nuclearisation in 1998 turned out to be a turning point in Indo-Pak relations, as the open war in their case became a practical impossibility. However, it took six years for the two countries to gain this realisation, at a substantial human and material cost. Not that nobody on both sides had the vision to understand it then. There were people like A.B. Vajpayee and Nawaz Sharif who had an inkling of the new situation. Nevertheless, to make many people with lesser vision realise this, the two sides had to go through the traumatic experiences of Kargil and the post-Parliament attack troops mobilisation on the borders. The relationship between the two countries during this short period of about six years since 1998 reflects all the predicaments, paradoxes and complexities that have characterised the Indo-Pak hot/cold war continuum ever since their birth in 1947. This brief period has seen the two countries carrying out tit-for-tat nuclear explosions that made this region potentially one of the most dangerous places in the world. It was followed by the emotional euphoria of peace building at Lahore, again to be scuttled through the Kargil incursions. Then there was the failure of the Agra Summit, followed by the contention on the issue of "cross border terrorism" and the attack on the Indian Parliament that led the two countries almost to the brink of war.

The year 2003 was beset with confusing signals of hopes for peace and apprehensions of a continued conflict and bitterness in the relationship, to be followed by a new hope in January 2004. The current thaw between India and Pakistan indicates a growing understanding on both sides that peace has no alternative and that it is indispensable for economic and social development in a region long held hostage by a protracted conflict. Each country seems to be showing flexibility and has expressed a willingness to go beyond its rigid positions on the problems that face them. Enhanced people-to-people contacts are beginning, which could play an important role in creating the much needed domestic support for peace and dispelling mutual public suspicion and mistrust. The process needs to be strengthened further. This, in the context of the changing global scenario, and combined with some other developments in relation to Kashmir, indicates that there has never ever been an atmosphere so conducive for addressing the Kashmir dispute as there is today.

Violence: Origins and Implications

Any serious attempt at resolving the dispute in the interest of promoting peace in the region should begin with developing a realistic appreciation of all the important dimensions of this dispute. We must begin with an admission that all major conflicts are generally rooted in certain objective historical situations. Every conflict passes through different phases and may have divergent manifestations, but its underlying causes continue to be broadly the same. With the passage of time, such a conflict becomes an integral part of the collective subconscious of the society in which it emerges. This is true of the Kashmir conflict also. Therefore, in spite of the occasional-changing manifestation of the conflict in Kashmir, its underlying causes and the core concerns have not only remained unchanged but will continue to be the same till they are meaningfully addressed and resolved. We must note that the present problem in Kashmir is not basically the problem of militancy. In fact, militancy has been the outcome of the Kashmir problem. The source of all protests is some sort of serious dissatisfaction with the existing political arrangement. It takes a violent form only when the normal and peaceful channels of the expression of dissent get blocked and constrain the disgruntled to revolt in a violent form.

However, whatever its causes may be, its consequences are mostly undesirable and harmful to society. This is what has happened in Kashmir also. The eruption of militancy in Kashmir in the late 1980s was spontaneous and confined to a committed group of young men dedicated to the cause of independence of the state. But probably under its own logic, the violence went out of control, leading to the emergence of a very large number of militant groups, with little coordination, working for divergent ends. Many lumpen and criminal elements also joined the militancy as they found it a profitable venture to attain personal aggrandisement. In this situation, the activation and large-scale mobilisation of security agencies (military and paramilitary forces) with enormous and arbitrary powers (Public Safety Act, Armed Forces Special Powers Act, Disturbed Areas Act, TADA, and POTA), and their lack of sensitivity and sympathy for the local population made the situation much more complex and terribly dangerous. The common person was badly caught in this terrible crossfire. The situation became worse as with the greater pressure from security forces, politico-ideologically less committed cadres and criminal elements within the militants changed their side to become what came to be known as pro-government/renegade militants. These so-called reformed militants, operating in liaison with, or on behalf of, the army and paramilitary forces, also "emerged as a major menace in many areas of the Valley." Their activities included "murder, rape, kidnapping, extortion and smuggling." They also became a convenient conduit of corruption, extortion and repression for the security agencies. The latter manifestation of them has been the SOG (Special Operation Group). The late 1990s brought a new brand of militants from within and without, with an ideology and programme that had little or no linkage with the common people's aspirations in Kashmir. Some of them eschew a sort of pan-Islamic agenda, with little concern for the common Kashmiris' aspirations. Therefore, today's militancy is, to a great extent, devoid of any social links within Kashmiri society. However, this common man's distancing from the militancy should not be construed as a change of heart on the basic issues of the movement. In fact, greater repression by state agencies and indiscriminate violation of human rights, further alienated the people from the existing political set-up. In this situation, the present elected government in the state, working under a number of constraints, has not been able to deliver anything worthwhile that could help to change the ground situation in Kashmir in any meaningful way.

In a way, the use of violence has only helped to further distance the common Kashmiri simultaneously from both India and Pakistan for the first time in its history since 1947.

In short, the cycle of violence has brought a lot of misery to the common person in Kashmir. The estimate of the number of people who lost their lives in the turmoil ranges between 40,000(official estimate) to over 100,000 (unofficial estimate). This is in addition to the tremendous economic, social, psychological and material loss that the people had to suffer in the process. There is probably no family left in Kashmir which has not been adversely affected by the situation. Naturally, in this situation of anarchy, insecurity, universal fear and uncertainty, there is no section of society in Kashmir that has remained unaffected. This is even true about the security forces operating there. There have been credible reports of their suffering from depression and other psychological disorders, resulting in a growing number of suicides and killings of colleagues.

Therefore, the common Kashmiri looks to the peace process with hope that this might be the end to the problem that has, socially, psychologically, emotionally and politically, besieged him for more than half a century. The important development which has to have a bearing on the situation in Kashmir and South Asia is the undermining of violence as a mechanism of securing solutions to problems, particularly in the post 9/11 scenario. Any violence, even if rooted in objective factors, has generally very negative implications for the common man in whose name it is generally used. Today's state has a tremendous repressive capacity, with a tremendous coercive machinery at its disposal to handle all private violence with much more comprehensive and superior violence. Therefore, in this process, the defenceless and vulnerable civilian population suffers the worst in a variety of ways. This, as we noted earlier, has happened also in Kashmir. Even the Indian leadership should realise that the employment of repressive means to address political grievances does not resolve issues but only furthers alienation and hostility.

Imperatives of Addressing Kashmir

Because of the changing imperatives, now both India and Pakistan are committed to ending violence (terrorism) in its all manifestations. Since Kashmir has seen a high degree of state coercion and repression, suggestions like demilitarisation make a lot of sense in Kashmir. Kashmir, as very often suggested, has seen the largest concentration of military and paramilitary forces, in a relatively small area, which has made its ecology – both social and physical – highly vulnerable. The parties concerned need to ensure the end of the cycle of violence to facilitate the process of the demilitarisation of Jammu and Kashmir (J&K), and transform it into a zone of peace that, instead of dividing, binds India and Pakistan into a relationship of friendship and cooperation and a joint commitment for human development in the region.

We need to negotiate, and arrive at, some common ground for addressing the Kashmir issue. However, till reaching that level of understanding of going beyond beaten tracks, we need to promote some objective conditions in Kashmir that ease the common man's life across different regions. This, at a minimum should include scrapping of all repressive laws, immediate and unconditional release of all political prisoners and allowing conditions in which open and free political discourse is promoted among the divergent sections of the society.

Some attributes of the New World Order have opened up a variety of new possibilities and prospects for the two countries and the people of South Asia that could not be thought of until a few years back. There is growing realisation that instead of narrowly defined national security, economic and human development should get priority in the governmental agenda. One of the attributes of this is the global process of transition from the nation-state to a larger cooperative order at the level of identifiable regions. In this context, the European Union is an example to emulate for countries of other regions. South Asia is also aiming to move in this direction by developing the South Asian Association for Regional Cooperation (SAARC) as an effective mechanism of regional cooperation. It is because of this factor that in recent years the progress of SAARC in this direction, in both formulating ideals and practice, has been relatively significant. This process, in a way, is gradually undermining highly sanctified borders globally, with implications for South Asia. The European lead in this direction is significant because the notion of nation-state was born, and borrowed from, there. Europe has considerably transcended this divisive loyalty among peoples of different countries and this is being gradually followed in other regions of the world. This development has to have a positive bearing on the course of relationships in South Asia in finding an answer to some of the dimensions of the Kashmir issue. The principled acceptance of, and steps towards, softening of borders across the Line of Control (LoC) could not have been possible without this development. But we need to admit that we have to cover a lot of ground to actualise the potential and possibilities in this process.

The post-colonial leadership in the Third World was unable to use federalism as an imaginative and dynamic mechanism for addressing the plural character of their societies. Many of the problems that these societies faced in their nation -building process were a result of their lack of creative imagination to use the potential of federal dynamics for the purpose. Similarly, in its initial years, the leadership within India did not have a positive attitude to a viable federal arrangement, particularly vis-à-vis situations (like Kashmir and the northeast) that required a greater degree of accommodation. One factor that added to the complication of the Kashmir problem was that the Indian leadership was reluctant to grant and respect Kashmir's autonomous status which it had to grant to it because of certain strategic/tactical considerations. It is because of this reason that they tried their best to undo this at the first opportunity they got. Today, the objective situation in relation to federal arrangements has considerably changed. This may have some practical relevance in dealing with some of the dimensions of the Kashmir issue which include evolving a more viable relationship among the various regions of the state, in tune with their plural character. Today, in the words of former Prime Minister A.B. Vajpayee, "In our search for a lasting solution to the Kashmir problem, both in its internal and external dimensions, we shall not traverse solely on the beaten track of the past. Mindsets will have to be altered and historical baggage jettisoned."[1]

Kashmir: To Be Rescued From the Secluded Periphery

The broad lessons that we need to draw from history in relation to Kashmir are several. One of the dimensions of the Kashmir issue has been the division between the two Kashmirs. Even though it is not generally realised, this fact has socially and economically strangulated the people of the Kashmir Valley. It needs to be noted that historically, Kashmir has been at the crossroads of civilisational, social and economic currents through different directions and passages. That is why it has had very close trade and cultural relations with places in China, Tibet, a number of cities in Central Asia, Afghanistan, Iran, not to speak of close connections with the north and more particularly northwestern Indian subcontinent. Of various passages, the Jhelum Valley road via Muzaffarabad has been the most important link that connected the Valley of Kashmir with the rest of the world for trade, people-to-people contact and exchange of cultural and social influences. The 1947 political development, resulting in the division of the Indian subcontinent and the *de facto* division of J&K, the placement of its two parts under the actual control of two different and hostile states, and the resultant hardening of borders, pushed the Valley to a number of social, psychological, political and economic disadvantages. Kashmir was relegated to a status of a secluded periphery, and in addition, the emotional and psychological implications of the division of the people cannot be ignored. From a position of being connected through a number of passages, it became practically dependent on a fair weather road that is less dependable and lengthier to connect people to the centres of trade and for other types of interaction. The disadvantages of political uncertainty and impact of the on-going conflict created their own disadvantages and problems of a serious nature for the people of Kashmir.

The starting of the bus service on April 7 and opening of five border points in itself is a small thing as it involves only a small number of passenger exchanges in a month under its present schedule. But this is important because only some time back, even this small development would have been impossible to imagine happening. One also hopes that in the context of the changing character of Indo-Pak relations, the process is taken further and the J.V. Road becomes functional for frequent travel of people, removing the psychological barriers between the two divided parts. It also needs to be combined with free flow of goods across the road. It is this development that is going to have a tremendous positive impact on the economy of the people, as this route is going to have great economic advantage for the transportation of goods and services to the outside world, because of the relative advantages of security, distance and smoothness. Unlike the existing highly unreliable and fair weather road joining Kashmir with India via Banihal, many consider the Srinagar-Muzaffarabad road to be one of the world's better mountainous routes. This will help restore to the Valley its lost centrality from its present status of relative seclusion. As per estimates by local vendors, if the road is opened for trade, fruit growers can save around Rs.30 per 20 kg apple box on account of freight alone. Compared to Bombay port, where the Kashmiri traders presently take their goods, Karachi port is about 1,200 km nearer to Kashmir. As against the distance of 3,000 km between Bombay and Srinagar, Karachi is only 1,800 km away from the Valley. By taking the products to Karachi port, the apple industry alone is expected to save "around Rs.1,400 crore on freight alone." Hence, allowing trade through the Srinagar-Muzaffarabad route will make Kashmiri goods more competitive in the international market. Significantly, Prime Minister Manmohan Singh, in his speech at the inaugural ceremony of the bus service, hinted at the opening of more roads and extending them from the travel of people to vibrant trade activity even to Central Asia. However, the greater barrier for Kashmiris to the outside world, particularly Pakistan and Pakistan Administered Kashmir, has been securing travel documents. That position remains almost the same. That is the reason why the opening of Srinagar-Muzaffarabad road has not inspired many people in Kashmir. Progress on this front is vitally important to make the peace process meaningful for the common Kashmiri.

Conclusion: To Begin With

To conclude, we need to accept the fact that the problem is more of its people than the problem of territory between the two states. It is acknowledged that the problem is complex and may not be easy to resolve in one go. But at the outset, we need to appreciate its existence, and the centrality of its resolution to the viability and durability of the peace process. There is a need for stating in clear terms the commitment to resolve it in its different dimensions. We need to exhibit courage and employ a high degree of creative imagination to address the issue in a manner that all parties have a feeling of gaining, not losing. It provides for structural foundations for promoting peace, prosperity and happiness across the Indo-Pak subcontinent. This is the challenge to our resolve and imagination. The process of peace should not be seen as aimed at buying time, particularly in Kashmir. That may jeopardise the whole process, which we cannot afford. In order to add to the credibilty of the process, we must immediately initiate measures that make a positive difference to the people in Kashmir. What has been achieved so far has been directed at improving the Indo-Pak relations. In the context of Kashmir, whatever has been done is only of symbolic nature. We need to immediately initiate confidence-building measures (CBMs) which would make a difference to the plight of the people in Kashmir and ameliorate their sufferings. The minimum steps that are required in this direction are the following:

1. Common understanding/undertaking between and among all the concerned parties that violence is immediately stopped from all sides.
2. There is need for substantial decrease of military/paramilitary forces from all residential areas as part of a broader understanding to resolve the issue.
3. All political prisoners should be immediately and unconditionally released.
4. All human rights groups, including Amnesty International, should have free access to the people on both sides of the LoC.
5. All repressive laws that restrict freedom of movement, discussion, debate and mobilisation such as the Armed Forces Special Powers Act and Public Safety Act, should be immediately withdrawn so that the people/parties of all shades of political opinion have full freedom for political debate and mobilisation and discussion across regions, communities and ethnic formations.
6. The opening of free movement and interaction across the LoC should be encouraged.
7. Dialogue across regions and communities should be encouraged with a view to finding common grounds for an acceptable and workable relationship.

This has to be done not as an end in itself but as a means to create the right atmosphere for a final resolution of the issue. What is needed is to address the issue with all seriousness and with a spirit of fraternity across the region in a manner that instead of reinforcing the divisions across communities, regions and borders, becomes the basis for a greater union in South Asia. The solution has to undo the division of the state about which people on both sides of the LoC feel strongly. In view of its heterogeneous character, the political framework has to be drawn to accommodate the plurality within and across regions. The political entity, thus, evolved should be a completely demilitarised zone and needs to be so formulated as to promote unity rather than discord across South Asia. There are many imaginative ways of doing it, provided there is the will to do so. In this process, we may benefit from many such examples of conflict resolution in similar situations across the globe and the suggestions and solutions developed by various agencies with the specific objective of addressing the Kashmir issue.

Notes

1. Prime Minister Atal Bihari Vajpayee, "Time to Resolve Problems of the Past; Time to Move on Towards a Better Future," January 1, 2001. Available at http://www.indianembassy.org/special/cabinet/Primeminister/pm_january_01_2001.htm

Kashmir: How to Grasp the Nettle

Prem Shankar Jha

When President Musharraf met Prime Minister Manmohan Singh for dinner in New York, in September 2005, he dropped a bombshell at the very beginning of the meeting. The time had come, he said, to move from confidence-building measures designed to normalise India-Pakistan relations and restore links between the two parts of Kashmir, to finding a solution to the core issue itself. While the details of what the two heads of government said to each other remain undisclosed, enough has been revealed over the following months to confirm that Musharraf raised two issues: some form of limited self-rule for the Kashmiris, perhaps within a federal model, and "joint control" over the state by India and Pakistan.

Musharraf took the prime minister and his advisers by surprise, but the surprise was in large part of India's own making, for Musharraf had not merely been sending feelers in this direction for some time; he had also taken decisive action within Pakistan to pave the way towards a settlement that would conform to the parameters he had first set forth at the Agra Summit, and then sharply defined in his April 2005 meeting with Manmohan Singh in New Delhi. At Agra, he had suggested a four-step resolution process whose first and most important step was to have been the rejection of any solution that either country found unacceptable. In Delhi, the two leaders had decided that since the Line of Control as an international border was not acceptable to Pakistan and any redrawing of current borders was not acceptable to India, the only way forward was, in effect, to eliminate the border between the two parts of Kashmir by making it "irrelevant". This agreement had itself come days after the most important breakthrough in India-Pakistan relations, the opening of the road between Muzaffarabad and Srinagar, on April 7, 2005.

In the months that followed, President Musharraf had moved swiftly to create conditions in Pakistan for the implementation of the Delhi Agreement. Apart from giving a succession of Press conferences to explain the agreement to fellow Pakistanis, he completed his government's dissociation from the hard line Kashmiri leader, Ali Shah Geelani, and announced his decision to work with the moderate wing of the Hurriyat led by Mirwaiz Umar Farooq, in the most public manner possible by inviting him and other "pro-independence" leaders to Islamabad and giving them the full red carpet treatment while they were there. This was a process that had been started by Prime Minister Shaukat Aziz when he visited Delhi in January 2005, and was taken a long step forward by Musharraf himself during a three—and—half hour meeting with the leaders of all factions of the Kashmiri nationalist movement in Delhi in April 2005.

What the Indian prime minister's advisers had failed to discern was that these measures were not aimed at 'softening' New Delhi for some as yet unspecified purpose, or 'capturing' the Mirwaiz faction of the Hurriyat so much as for preparing Pakistan to accept a final solution that was immeasurably far removed from its original claim to the whole of the state and its demand for a plebiscite that would make its inhabitants choose between only two options – India or Pakistan. However obvious this may have seemed to Indians, and however much Pakistanis may have privately feared that this was unattainable, a public acceptance of the position that Pakistan could not have the whole of Kashmir, that the UN resolutions could not be implemented, and that there was a third option for Kashmiris – self-rule – came as a seismic shock to the Pakistani people. Musharraf had begun preparing the ground more than a year previously when he said that Pakistan was prepared to move away from the UN resolutions if India too was prepared to move from its established position on Kashmir. He took this process a long way further when he calculatedly sent up a trial balloon suggesting a federal solution for the whole of Kashmir "within constraints" at an *Iftar* party in October 2004. Both these sallies had met vociferous criticism in the Pakistani Press and think-tanks. The April agreement appeared to even moderate and constructive opinion-makers like Ayaz Amir of *Dawn* as having gone a step too far and given away essential Pakistani positions, with nothing to show in return. In the weeks that followed, a groundswell mounted in Pakistan that Musharraf had been taken for a ride by the wily Indians.

New Delhi was taken by surprise because it had not understood the significance of this groundswell. For three years, Musharraf had relied upon the public's, and especially the intelligentsia's, growing disillusionment with the policy of perpetual confrontation to oppose the hawks in his establishment. Now the very ground on which he stood had begun to shake. To regain control, he had to show results, and that meant that he had to move quickly towards the resolution of the core issue.

The Official Positions no Longer Yield a Viable Solution

Given the fog of mutual suspicion that surrounds the issue, perhaps the best starting point in the search for a solution to the Kashmir dispute is, as President Musharraf said before and after the Agra Summit, to rule out the solutions that one or other country cannot live with. The first two solutions that will have to be rejected are the original demands of the two countries, which still remain their official positions. Since the early Fifties, Pakistan has been calling upon India to honour its commitment to hold a plebiscite in the state of Jammu and Kashmir to decide whether it should belong to Pakistan or India. But a moment's reflection should show not only that this is no longer feasible, but that were it so, it would almost certainly result in Pakistan losing Azad Kashmir.

The main problem with a plebiscite today remains what it was in 1948, namely, determining precisely who would be qualified to vote in it. In 1948, as correspondence to be found in the British Library shows, Pakistan was worried that it might lose the plebiscite if a large number of Kashmiri Muslims (especially from Jammu, Poonch and Rajouri) who had crossed , or been driven over, the border into Pakistan, were not allowed to vote. By the same token, it wanted all the Hindus and Sikhs who, it claimed, had settled in Jammu after partition, to be excluded from the vote. These demands constituted a tall order, but Nehru accepted them, at least initially. However, Karachi's fear was revealing. If in a state with 77 per cent Muslims, it was afraid that the absence of a relatively small proportion would make all the difference, then it already knew that a large proportion of the Muslims, i.e. the followers of Sheikh Abdullah, who made up a majority in the Valley, would not vote to join Pakistan.

The problem of deciding who could vote has become all but insurmountable today. Three-quarters to four-fifths of the inhabitants of Jammu and Kashmir in1947 are dead. Their progeny have the right to vote but who precisely are they, and how will they prove their right to vote if they do not reside in one or other part of the old princely state? How will they do so if they reside abroad? Several lakhs, mainly from Pakistan Occupied Kashmir (PoK) have taken citizenship there. Should they even be considered for inclusion in the voters' list? One would have thought not.

The truth, as the British conceded in private memoranda between the Commonwealth Relations Office in London and the UK delegation to the UN in 1948, is that ascertaining who should be allowed to vote on the basis of origin was difficult even then. It would be almost impossible today. In practice, one would have to confine the plebiscite to the present population of the

Jammu and Kashmir princely state. That would go even more heavily against Pakistan today than in 1947, because while Jammu has filled up with Hindus and Sikhs, Azad Kashmir has lost much of its original Muslim population.

Some idea of what could happen in Indian Kashmir if there was a plebiscite today was obtained by a MORI poll commissioned by the UK-based "Friends of Kashmir" which is headed by the veteran champion of Kashmiri accession to Pakistan, Lord Avebury. Held in April 2002, it showed that given two choices, India or Pakistan, 61 per cent favoured staying in India and only 6 percent favoured joining Pakistan.

The Indian government is, needless to say, aware of the implications of the changing population composition, as indeed of the MORI poll. But the reason why it will not even consider a plebiscite today is that in a plebiscite Pakistan would have absolutely no option but to appeal to the Kashmiris on the basis of religion. That would inflame communal passions and just probably set off a Hindu backlash in India. No one who has the good of the subcontinent at heart could possibly want to do that.

If a plebiscite is out, then so is the Indian claim that the whole of Jammu and Kashmir should belong to India. It is true that Maharaja Hari Singh acceded to India under the Indian Independence Act. It is also true, as I have indicated elsewhere, that he did not sign the Instrument of Accession under duress, but had been trying to accede to India without much success since the middle of September 1947, i.e five weeks before the raiders from the Northwest Frontier Province (NWFP) arrived in Kashmir.[1] But Nehru's government knew, although it never conceded it in public, that there had been a fairly spontaneous revolt in the Jhelum Valley and other parts of what is now Azad Kashmir, against the maharajah's decision to accede to India. This was because the Muslims of Jhelum Poonch and Rajouri were ethnically entirely different from those of the Vale of Kashmir. They were for the most part Mirpuris, who spoke Punjabi and had little in common with the Kashmiri speaking people of the Vale. That is one of the reasons why he accepted a ceasefire without trying to recover the Jhelum Valley or all of Poonch. That is also one of the reasons why Mrs. Indira Gandhi signed the Shimla Agreement which conceded Azad Kashmir to Pakistan so long as Pakistan did the same for Jammu and Kashmir, till a final agreement could be hammered out.

Legal and ethnic issues apart, there is another powerful reason why despite all its advocacy of a plebiscite, Pakistan cannot even contemplate a mode of settlement that could bring the whole of Maharaja Hari Singh's Kashmir into India. For that would make India contiguous with the NWFP. In 1947, this was unthinkable, for Pakistan had won a plebiscite in the NWFP under a property qualification that allowed only 7 per cent of the population to vote, by a single percentage point. It had still to subjugate the Khudai Khidmatgars who had been adamantly opposed to partition and had won an election with a nearly two-thirds majority, only a year earlier. A common border with India would have made the infant state of Pakistan indefensible from the start. That was the reason Lieutenant General Akbar Khan gave in his book, *Raiders in Kashmir*, for sending the Pathan tribesmen to Kashmir. Until very recently, Pakistanis could have claimed that the Pathans have been more or less fully assimilated into the Pakistani state, but after Pakistan became an ally of the US in its invasion of Afghanistan, can anyone lay bets that this will never come undone? In particular, can anyone be sure of what would happen to Pakhtoon sentiment if the US were to ask the Pakistan Army to punish the Pakhtoon tribes that are sheltering the Taliban in the Tribal Areas, and General Musharraf or a future leader were to comply? (Since this was written, that has already happened.)

Defence is planned not on the basis of intentions but capabilities. Thus, so long as it is theoretically possible for the Pathans to demand secession from Pakistan on one ground or another, Pakistan needs a buffer between India and the NWFP. That is what Azad Kashmir provides.

Now that we have eliminated both the official positions, are there any intermediate, more acceptable solutions available? Over the years, both India and Pakistan have mooted one alternative each. India has let it be known in private that it will accept the Line of Control (LoC) as the international border, with or without some rectifications. Pakistan has often mentioned, although never formally, the possibility of implementing what is known as the Dixon Plan, after Sir Owen Dixon, although it was in fact first mooted during the first days of the tribal invasion by V.P. Menon. This is, to leave Jammu and Ladakh with India and transfer the Valley to Pakistan. A variant of this plan would make the Valley a UN trust territory for a specified number of years, to be followed by a plebiscite in the Valley alone. The plebiscite would give Kashmiris only two choices — India or Pakistan.

The LoC as International Border

The Indian proposal has a good deal of international support. Not only has the LoC endured for 55 years, but there are ceasefire lines all over the world, that have, through the passage of time, become accepted as international boundaries. Other countries have become tired of the Kashmir dispute and grown increasingly apprehensive of its potential to trigger a war on the subcontinent that could turn nuclear. The Shimla Agreement of 1972, moreover, strongly pointed towards the LoC becoming the basis for a final settlement of the Kashmir "situation", after the resumption of normal relations between the two countries. If all else failed, India could insist on this particular meaning of the agreement and would probably get abundant support abroad for its interpretation.

In any case, India is so much larger than Pakistan, and has so much more staying power, and, therefore, is capable of forcing this 'solution' to the Kashmir dispute on Pakistan. Its army is in control of the state; it seems capable of accepting the level of attrition that the *jihadis* from Pakistan are capable of inflicting almost indefinitely; the genuine Kashmiri insurgency has been over since 1994 and violence in the state is nourished almost entirely by 'guest militants' and by an as yet small band of Kashmiri Wahhabi elements. Thermal imaging and other new equipment has sharply raised the kill rate of *jihadis* crossing from the other side of the LoC. Kashmiris are tired of the insurgency and pine for peace. They may, therefore, in the end, settle for fair elections and their own government in Kashmir.

This will become the solution if India and Pakistan are never able to find common ground, but for India to opt for this 'solution' without making every effort to take Pakistan on board would be shortsighted. For it would do nothing to resolve the tension between it and Pakistan. So long as that continues, all Pakistan governments will be tempted to keep nourishing *jihadis* for Kashmir on one border, while kowtowing to the US and relentlessly pursuing another kind of *jihad* on the other border. It does not need much intuition to see that this policy is not sustainable in the long run. Sooner or later, therefore, Pakistan will get dragged into the vortex of violence that is being created in Afghanistan and the Middle East.

The Dixon Plan

If the LoC is not an optimal solution even from India's point of view, the Dixon Plan is even more impracticable. Whatever may have been possible in 1947, when V. P. Menon first mooted the idea to the British acting high commissioner in Delhi, such a solution would be totally unacceptable to India for the same reasons as the original UN proposal. If no plebiscite can be held without Pakistan appealing to communal sentiment in Kashmir, then no part of India can be ceded simply because it is a Muslim majority area. The risk that communal passions will not remain confined to Kashmir alone, and could trigger a powerful backlash against Muslims in India is one that no responsible Indian government can take. The fact that India is a democracy and that the Bharatiya Janata Party (BJP) would pounce on any such arrangement as a betrayal of the nation, hardly needs to be underlined.

There are, however, weightier reasons for not conceding such a demand. The original Dixon Plan has been bypassed by time. In 1947, the Kashmiris, along with the subjects of other princely states, were treated as chattel that could be handed over from one ruler to another at will. Today, after eleven elections, (including three that all concede were fair elections, in 1977, 1983 and 2002), and a huge spread of literacy and higher education in the Valley, this is no longer possible. Kashmir has a militantly nationalistic intelligentsia, extremely conscious of "Kashmiriyat" — its Kashmiri identity — which will not allow anyone else to decide its fate.

A Plebiscite with Three Options

What is theoretically possible is a plebiscite with three options — Pakistan, India and independence. We have no clear indication of how people in the Valley would vote if they were given three choices, because the only scientific opinion poll, the MORI poll, was so obviously designed to give Pakistan ammunition for use against India in international fora that its questionnaire did not even contain the third option of independence. But if the 29 per cent who claimed they were "undecided" between Pakistan and India can be assumed to have been in favour of independence, and if all of them can be assumed to have been from Kashmir Valley — both tall but not totally unwarranted assumptions — then it would seem that somewhere around 60 to 65 per cent of Kashmir Valley dwellers would opt for independence.

A three-option plebiscite would greatly reduce the risk of a communal backlash in India against Muslims. But the question would immediately arise: why should Kashmir Valley be singled out for such a plebiscite? Why should the three options not be extended to the whole of the original state of Kashmir? At the very least, why should it not include Azad Kashmir? There is, after all, a substantial movement for independence in Azad Kashmir too.

A long moment's reflection shows that neither Pakistan nor India would be receptive to the idea of a three option plebiscite. In India, no ruling coalition, acting on its own, would be able to endorse such a proposal, because it would be immediately accused by the opposition of betraying the nation. Any major constitutional change in Kashmir, or any step that could require such a change would have to be endorsed by all the major parties in the country. Such an endorsement would be exceedingly hard to obtain. Not only would the opposition accuse the government of giving away a part of the country, but it would endanger the federal structure of the country. Kashmir would become a precedent for every aspiring state leader trying to whip up public support to win a state election. That is a risk that no central government in Delhi will ever take.

Pakistan has demonstrated its aversion to the idea by never once endorsing it during five decades of incessant campaigning to secure Kashmir. Even when it was inciting the leaders of the Jammu and Kashmir Liberation Front (JKLF) to take up arms against India, during talks held in Muzaffarabad, in the late 1980s, it never offered the "third option." In February 1992, when the Pakistani security forces fired upon JKLF cadres trying to cross the LoC into Indian Kashmir at Chinari, Prime Minister Nawaz Sharif was sufficiently rattled by the reaction to endorse the third option of independence for Kashmir. The storm that broke out in Pakistan forced him to issue retractions every few hours for the next two days. The plain truth is that for all the strategic and military reasons cited above, Pakistan cannot endorse any solution that makes it run the risk of losing Azad Kashmir.

Is a Condominium Feasible?

But what if India and Pakistan agreed to join the Valley to all or the larger part of Azad Kashmir and turn it into a kind of condominium? This would involve giving the new state of Kashmir sovereignty in all internal affairs and jointly guaranteeing its defence against external threats. Proposals for limited or constrained sovereignty somewhat along these lines have been put forward by the New York based Kashmir Study Group headed by Farouq Kathwari. This proposal has the merit of meeting the aspirations of the majority of the Kashmiris while largely avoiding the risk of a communal backlash in India. However, at the present state of India-Pakistan relations, it suffers from one fatal flaw. Any joint guarantee of security or for that matter the implementation of any agreement between the two countries to respect Kashmir's sovereignty presupposes a high degree of trust between the two countries. That trust is precisely what does not exist today. In its absence, Pakistan will constantly wonder whether every agreement Srinagar signs with New Delhi does not signal a closer integration with India. It will view every seat offered in an Indian medical or engineering college to a Kashmiri, every new road or rail link between India and Kashmir, and every addition to the Indian armed forces in Ladakh or Jammu as part of a larger design to reabsorb Kashmir into India.

India will entertain similar fears about Pakistan. In addition, after fifty years and three attempts by Pakistan to annex Kashmir, a condominium arrangement of the above kind will not really end the suspicion in New Delhi that Pakistan's main purpose is to get the Indian Army out of Kashmir so that it can make a fourth attempt on terms far more favourable than those that exist today. Nor will a condominium arrangement necessarily bind organisations like the Lashkar-e-Tayyeba or the Jaish-e-Muhammad. New Delhi will, moreover, view the arrival in Kashmir of every Maulvi preaching orthodox Deobandi, Wahhabi or Ahl-e-Hadis variants of Islam, as preparation for fomenting a rebellion on religious grounds by discrediting Rishi Islam and, thereby, undermining one of the main pillars of Kashmiriyat. Indeed, many of the key leaders of Kashmiri nationalism today regard the 1972 decision by a Congress government in Kashmir to lift the ban on the Jamaat-i-Islami as the first and most grievous blow against Kashmiriyat, and it was dealt not by Pakistan but by India[2].

Such suspicions will make it difficult for India not to keep troops in a constant state of readiness for reentering Kashmir. There will, in short, be no peace and no let-up of tension. In many ways, therefore, we will all find ourselves back where we were in 1947.

Towards a Lasting Solution

The above discussion brings us at last to what in this writer's opinion is the key requirement of a lasting solution to the Kashmir problem. This is the building up of trust between the two countries. Without trust, no solution is likely to endure. But trust too cannot be built up in a day. We, therefore, need to establish a process — a phased succession of actions by both countries — whose successful implementation will build up trust step by step, even as it leads towards a final solution. What is more, this final solution cannot be one that is acceptable only to India and Pakistan. It must be acceptable to the people of Kashmir too. It must, in short, be one in which all parties give up some of their aspirations in exchange for the benefits of lasting peace, but from which none emerges as a loser.

Both Delhi and Islamabad, in their saner moments acknowledge that what is needed is to start the process and go step by step, without jumping to its end point. But even this movement gets bogged down before it starts because each fears that the other will try to push the process itself in a direction the other does not want to go — India towards acceptance of the LoC, and Pakistan towards some version of the Dixon Plan. That is why, watching the numerous abortive attempts to start the dialogue since the mid- Nineties, this author has come to the conclusion that the process cannot be divorced completely from the end. Both countries need to have an idea of the kind of solution that they could accept and sell to their own people, even before the process of détente begins. This need not be a precise idea. Indeed, there would be virtue in imprecision because it would enlarge the room for negotiation. But if there is not some narrowing of the gap that exists at present between even the 'informal' positions held by Delhi and Islamabad, it will be difficult even for discussions in process not to get bogged down.

Let me, therefore, take the bull by the horns and suggest the broad outlines of what a final settlement of the Kashmir dispute could look like, and the process by which India and Pakistan could arrive at it. To do so, we do not have to invent something new. History has enough examples of how similar problems have been resolved elsewhere.

Learning From the Tyrol

The model this author has in mind is that of the Tyrol, a German speaking trans-Alpine region, which falls partly in Austria and partly in Italy. Southern Tyrol came into Italy after the fall of the Austro-Hungarian Empire in 1918, and enjoyed a troubled relationship with it for the major part of the 20th century. All that is a part of the past. The reason is that, well before the formation of the European Union, Italy and Austria had learned how to turn the existence of Tyrol between them from a big minus into a big plus. Today, Southern Tyrol enjoys a considerable measure of autonomy within Italy, with its own elections and its own laws over a wide range of subjects. It enjoys immense tax advantages in comparison to the rest of Italy, which make it a magnet for industry. It has complete freedom of communications with Northern Tyrol, with Austria and with the rest of Europe. People from the rest of Europe are free to visit, to trade with, invest and live in the Tyrol. Tyroleans, needless to say, enjoy unhindered access to both Italy and Austria and now, of course, the whole of Europe. What Italy and Austria have done is to reduce the significance of the international border between the two parts to the point where it no longer impinges upon the lives of the people of Tyrol, Austria and Italy.

Yet Southern Tyrol remains a part of Italy and Northern Tyrol of Austria. The foreign relations of the two parts remain securely in the hands of the two countries. They vote separately for the European Parliament. Presumably, their defence, insofar as it is not subsumed in the defence arrangements of the European Union and North Atlantic Treaty Organisation (NATO), would also be the separate responsibility of the two countries. The Tyrol is, therefore, a sort of condominium, in which the areas of responsibility for defence and foreign affairs of the region have been demarcated by history instead of by explicit agreement.

The key element in the success of the arrangement between Austria and Italy is trust. Admittedly, it has taken the better part of half a century to build. But India and Pakistan can do it in a much shorter period of time.

- Today, the defining event that created the two Kashmirs is already half a century behind us.
- In the intervening years, we have both learned, and the Kashmiris have learned, that there is no military solution to the problem.
- On paper at least, both the Kashmirs enjoy immense autonomy. Indian Kashmir has a separate Constitution and the power to redefine its relations with India. It has used this power to increase integration in the past but can use it to reduce it too if it wants to. Pakistan has throughout maintained the fiction that Azad Kashmir is an independent nation, although this has been even more of a fiction than Kashmir's autonomy. An essential stage in the step by step resolution of the Kashmir problem would be to clothe this skeletal autonomy with real flesh.
- India and Pakistan can then allow the elected representatives of the two Kashmirs to decide whether or not they want to set up a common consultative council and the subjects on which they will coordinate their policies. High on their list, of course, will come the opening of the LoC between the two parts at various crossing points for travel and trade between the two Kashmirs. It will then be up to India and Pakistan to work out how this will be confined only to Kashmiris.
- But why should it remain confined to the Kashmiris? Why should Pakistanis not be enabled to visit Indian Kashmir and Indians not be allowed to visit Azad Kashmir and the Northern Areas? The people of these regions can only gain from the increase in the tourism that will result. Greater contact will also break down stereotypes and build friendships.
- The next obvious step would be to extend freedom of trade and transit between the two Kashmirs to freedom of trade and transit for Kashmiris from each part of Kashmir with the whole of the other country. In practice, this would be difficult to keep separate from a more general move towards full trading and consular relations between India and Pakistan. But that is something that civil society in Pakistan is already asking for with increasing assertiveness, for the simple reason that its benefits for Pakistan far outweigh its benefits for India.

The process outlined above will take several years to work out because it is immensely complex. But it is worth remembering that the European Union also came into being a full thirty years after the creation of the European Common Market. What we need to remember is that in the building up of trust, the first steps are the most difficult. If India and Pakistan agree, however tacitly, that the above road is broadly the only one that they can follow, then each step that they go down it will make the next step easier and the process itself faster. In the end the benefits of a simultaneous resolution of the Kashmir dispute and the coming into being of a South Asian Association for Regional Cooperation (SAARC) free market, will so far outweigh the costs that people will be left wondering why it all took so long.

Notes

1. See Prem Shankar Jha, *India 1947: The Origins of a Dispute* (New Delhi: Oxford University Press, 2003).
2. Yaseen Malik wrote a book while in jail in which he said this explicitly. Yaseen Malik, *Our Real Crime* (Jammu: Jammu and Kashmir Liberation Front, 1994). See pp.103-115.

Resolving the Kashmir Issue: A Dream Worth Dreaming

Pran Chopra

Some formulations clarify a proposition by compressing it in a few phrases. Some only obfuscate it. The formulation before us does both. Up to a point, it shows the way forward. But then it brings us face to face with an obstacle, and we can go further only if we put the phrases aside and confront realities.

The formulation, which began to circulate about 20 years ago in its earlier versions, basically is that if we solve the problem "in" Kashmir, the problem "of" Kashmir will be solved automatically. The logic encapsulated here is that once the people of Kashmir are given a domestic dispensation which satisfies them, they will have no grievances left against India, the problem "in" Kashmir will be solved, and that will also solve the problem "of" Kashmir because Pakistan will no longer be able to push militants into Kashmir. They will find no local discontents behind which they may hide.

This view of the problem "of" Kashmir credits Pakistan with having no interest in Kashmir other than to ensure, through intrusive militancy, that India yields to the wishes of the Kashmiris, and having ensured that, Pakistan like the good Samaritan it is , will leave Kashmir and India free to work out in peace such mutual arrangements as may satisfy both. Anyone who thinks that this is possible should study something else.

A converse formulation of this proposition is that once India settles all its other disputes with Pakistan, which constitute the problem "of" Kashmir, Pakistan will leave New Delhi alone to sort out the problem "in" Kashmir in any way it may wish to do so. That formulation sees Pakistan as interested in Kashmir only for using it as a lever for extracting more concessions out of India for Pakistan, and having got them, it will forget Kashmir. Anyone who believes that need not study anything.

Each formulation implies that when either "problem" is "solved", the other will automatically vanish because neither of them has a life independently of the other. But that is not so. Each has a life in a third variable, which is that every regime in Pakistan has had a long-term interest in using the problems "of" and "in" Kashmir in the service of its ambitions regarding both Kashmir and the rest of India. They are in this yoke together. They will be relieved of the yoke only when the conviction is carried home to Pakistan that it is only hurting itself in trying to hit India by hitting Kashmir.

Hitherto, the history of the yoke has been somewhat as follows: whenever resentment against "India" rises among the people of "Kashmir", Pakistan gets a chance to step up its intrusions, and it never fails to do so. Conversely, whenever such intrusions increase, even if they do so for reasons unconnected with the temper within Kashmir, they aggravate the problem "in" Kashmir.

This has been happening a great deal in recent weeks, in a measure which cannot be explained as another seasonal spurt in the externally aided militancy in Kashmir. The reasons for the more recent stepping up of violence in Kashmir are a part of the problem "in" Kashmir, of course, as well as a part of the problem "of" Kashmir. But let us not forget causes which lie farther afield.

Whenever America presses Pakistan a little harder, as it has been doing in recent years, to curb the anti-American activities of Pakistan-based militants in Afghanistan, Pakistan has found it convenient to push the more hardened ones among them into Kashmir. Thereby, it kills many birds with one stone. It aggravates both the problems "of" and "in" Kashmir for India. It tells the discontented in Kashmir that it is continuing to help them against India. And it earns credit with America by reducing the anti-American pressure in Afghanistan.

This has been happening more in very recent years than earlier. That is probably why the new lot of militants injected into Kashmir are tougher, and are armed with more deadly weapons. Their actions, tactics, and firepower, are more like what they have developed in Afghanistan and other West Asian trouble spots than they are like the actions of the raw militancy that was practised in Kashmir until a few years ago.

This change has also benefited those indigenous elements in Kashmir who have been bitten harder by the anti-Indian bug. That has brought the problems "of" and "in" Kashmir closer together. Correspondingly, this has also made it more necessary to bring about closer coordination between security steps against militancy for dealing with the problem "of" Kashmir , and political initiatives for resolving the problem "in" Kashmir, while, at the same time, keeping one's guard up regarding Pakistan's more distant ambitions.

Because of this background, it has also become more difficult now to sustain the optimism with which these problems began to be thought about a couple of years ago. In that state of mind, it was assumed by some that the "in" problem was now so much closer to resolution that the "of" problem could be left to bus drivers. That optimism now needs a harder look.

But there is no need for anyone to press the panic button. Sagacity has paid handsome dividends in recent times. It must be given more room to pay more as we take some critical decisions which are due in the near future. All that is being suggested here is that too much optimism invites disappointments and recrimination, and we should avoid this risk. India should take all the necessary security measures, and take them even more firmly than before, for dealing with the problem "of" Kashmir.

But, for solving the problem "in" Kashmir, India must now enlist the strength of the whole of Jammu and Kashmir, and that strength should not be underestimated. As the most important single unit of what constituted the former state of Jammu and Kashmir, and as the most important city in the state, the Valley of Kashmir and the city of Srinagar must resume their former role as the magnetic centre of the state.

This road may turn out to be long. But there are rewards to reap at the end of it. Opportunity calls, as the shadow of the Taliban recedes.

Until the early 1970s, there was a widespread apprehension in India that there was bloodier mindedness in Pakistan against India than could be disarmed only by political adroitness and gestures of peace, and harder measures against Pakistan by India would always be blocked by Pakistan's anti-Soviet friends. This negative assessment led to negative measures.

But much of this changed with the Bangladesh War. The whole world and even sections of American opinion, and Chinese too quite unexpectedly, began to see the South Asian scene very differently. That is why I titled my book on that war, published in 1972, as *India's Second Liberation*.[1]

Many changes for the better in India's relations with Pakistan could have followed from that. But this possibility was frustrated for close upon twenty years by a chain of events which were to prove to be most unfortunate for the whole of the South Asian region and even further afield.

The chain began with Zulfikar Ali Bhutto's betrayal of the promises he made to Indira Gandhi at the Shimla Conference in 1972. Then followed more than a decade of Zia's dictatorship in Pakistan which included the "assassination" of Bhutto (to quote a part of the title of another book of mine on this period), then the Soviet intervention in Afghanistan, then the equally thoughtless joint intervention there by Pakistan and the United States. The rise of the Taliban followed as a global phenomenon, and India's apprehensions acquired new dimensions. No one seemed to have an answer to the appeal of fundamentalism.

But despite all that, something changed basically in the India-Pakistan context of the problems "of" and "in" Kashmir, as was shown by a different and more benign chain of events.

This chain was given an auspicious and most significant start by the succession of confidential dialogues between the Indian Prime Minister at that time, Mr I.K. Gujral, and his Pakistani counterpart, Nawaz Sharif. The basis of this chain must be understood if we are to continue to maintain the right balance in handling the twin problems "of" and "in" Kashmir.

Writing about these dialogues in 2004, Mr Gujral wrote, "Nawaz Sharif and I met four times , at Male, New York, Edingburgh and Dhaka within ten months." Thus, both lived up to their publicly stated resolve that "the dialogue must never stop."[2] He wrote further: "Every meeting generated a better understanding and narrowed the areas of dissent."[3]

This was an important reason why public opinion in India (and in Pakistan too, though perhaps to a smaller extent) not only accepted but rejoiced over Prime Minister Vajpayee's bus journey to Pakistan. It was also during this phase that the principle of simultaneous discussion on all issues took shape, which has assisted both countries in ensuring continuity of discussion between them till now. The principle of continuity in a composite frame has again been at work in the Indo-Pakistan talks underway.

As the talks proceeded, a promising change took place "in" Kashmir. For the first time ever, militancy lost a substantial part of its Kashmiri constituency. This part revolted against the controllers of the militancy, who were based in Pakistan, and it turned its face towards other ways of bringing Kashmiri ambitions to fruit.

That bred other changes too. For the first time in about 20 years, such elections were held in Kashmir which international and Indian opinion generally, and broad sections of Kashmiri opinion also, accepted as fair. Significant numbers of Kashmiris took part in them in defiance of dire threats held out against them by the militants, and the assassination of one of the most popular "Kashmiri nationalists," Abdul Ghani Lone. I have discussed these elections in greater detail in parts of my book, *Scene Changes in Kashmir, Pakistan and India* (2003).[4] But their significance has been further enhanced by certain events which followed.

The issue of the state's accession to India did not figure in the elections directly. But the majority of the votes were polled by those who did not oppose the accession, and those who did were not able to prevent a heavy overall turnout despite their deadly attacks on polling stations. Then, and for the first time ever, a coalition government was formed in Jammu and Kashmir which, in fair elections, had proved that it had the support of all the main regions of the state on the Indian side of the Line of Control (LoC), and was also in power in New Delhi, and in which India's largest political party also had a substantial share of responsibility. The electoral momentum has continued since then as well. Early in 2005, even civic elections, which normally lack the glamour of legislative elections, attracted a record 70 per cent voter turnout despite exceptionally heavy snowfalls.

The wisdom shown by the Congress, and particularly by the party President, Mrs. Sonia Gandhi, made it possible for a senior and trusted Kashmiri leader to form the government though his party had fewer members in the house than the Congress had. Because of its electoral and political credentials, the new government became a better carrier of two messages in the succeeding months than any government in the state had been able to be since the late 1980s.

First, the Valley-based partner in the government, the People's Democratic Party (PDP), was better able to convey to the people of the country a sharper awareness of what security lapses and excesses were doing to the political climate in the state; and second, the Congress partner was better able to convince the people of the state that security needs would be met better if they were backed by equitable development. In both respects, the state government had a better status in the eyes of the state and the country, and a better record of performance, than any government in the state since the mid-1980s.

Events outside the electoral arena also were momentous. Musharraf was forced to put his Kargil dagger back into its sheath, while the Indian Army and Air Force won new laurels and experience in very unexpected and exceptional battles. Both events made India's ultimate success more likely in the war against terrorism, and they also had a beneficial fall-out on the politics of both the "in" and "of" problems. They reinvigorated the peace process which Prime Minister Vajpayee had initiated with his bus ride to Pakistan and which Musharraf had tried to bury on the Kargil heights. Prime Minister Manmohan Singh carried the process forward in a more intimately intra-Kashmir form which had the potential for greater good.

Pakistan nearly scuttled that process also with its customary itch to be too clever by half, as will be narrated later. But in spite of that, both the "in Kashmir" and "of Kashmir" aspects of the problem stand today at the edge of greater possibilities than have been created by any Indo-Pakistan initiative since the talks between Gujral and Nawaz Sharif, or Vajpayee's visit to the National Monument of Pakistan.

The people of the state of Jammu and Kashmir were not a direct or active party to these initiatives between New Delhi and Islamabad. But the people of the Indian side of the state were more intimately associated with them than the people of the Pakistan side. This was because of the richer and more democratic association between New Delhi and Srinagar than between Islamabad and Muzaffarabad. This had always been the case. But it became much more so after the latest elections to the legislature of the state on the Indian side. As explained above, these elections and the state government which resulted from them brought the national government in New Delhi and the state government in Srinagar into a closer political partnership.

On the other hand, when the President of Pakistan, General Musharraf, extinguished even such democracy as had existed in Pakistan under Prime Minister Nawaz Sharif and some of his predecessors, the people of the Pakistan side of Kashmir lost even such indirect association with Indo-Pakistan initiatives as they could have claimed till then. This difference between the two sides of the state had often come in the way of certain civil society efforts which had been made from time to time to build bridges within the state, to by-pass the much deeper gulf between the two countries at the national level.

But the growing dissatisfaction of the people in "Azad Kashmir" with their political deprivation in Pakistan had something to do with some very welcome developments which followed earlier this year, as an effort to build bridges between the two sides of Kashmir was added to the on-going effort to build them between India and Pakistan.

During the first six months of 2005, this intra-Kashmir effort came closer to a more palpable success than at any time before. This period saw the most extensively popular and participatory effort ever made by the governments of the two countries, and more so by the governments and people of the two sides of the state, to open the gates for the people of both sides of the state to resume all manner of connections between themselves. They managed to make a more promising start than they had ever made before.

Precisely to protect this effort from the baleful effects of the deeper differences between the two countries at the national level, and also to simplify the travel documents so that more people could access them in both parts of Kashmir, it was decided that people on each side of the LoC could cross over to the other side without formal passport procedures, and only on the basis of local identity papers. But such travels would be limited to the boundaries of the original and undivided state of Jammu and Kashmir. If anyone wanted to cross either into "India" or "Pakistan", he must carry the regular passport of his country.

Never was an India-Pakistan initiative so warmly welcomed by the people of both sides of the state, nor were visitors from either side so cheered by such throngs of people on their arrival from the other side. All manner of trade and travel exchanges between the two sides began to be discussed. Some of that might have been ignited by the acute sense which the people of Kashmir have for trading and other business opportunities. But more important than that was the feeling of good cheer which the occasion aroused on both sides of the state.

There were some very precious straws in that wind as the visitors were greeted by their hosts in Srinagar. Like the revival of old friendships, re-telling of childhood memories of days lived in ancestral homes, reaching for the underpinnings of the old sense of having been together in the formerly single state of Jammu and Kashmir. Like anticipations of multiplying the linkages while yet remaining true to respective rituals and values. Like the taste of the politics of free elections which, while being denied to most parts of Pakistan from time to time, have been most denied to the people of what is, ironically, called Azad Kashmir.

Encouraging too is the fact that people from each side began to see more virtues in the people and institutions on the other side than they had seen before. Visitors from the Indian to the Pakistani side did not see the latter only as a lost slice of the former state but as a shared bridge to lands and peoples and markets beyond Pakistan which are better reached by land than through distant Indian ports. Much noticed by visitors from the Pakistani side was the smooth change of governments which elections had brought about in both New Delhi and Srinagar, and particularly how the Indian people had chosen, in freely contested elections, a Sikh to be the prime minister and a Muslim to be their president, to mention the two "minority" communities of India which the people of Pakistan have most often been shown by their leaders as oppressed by the Hindu majority. Nor would the visitors have failed to notice that the present prime minister and the present president, though neither is a "Hindu" , are among the most highly respected and admired incumbents who have ever graced these offices since India became independent.

There are reasons to think that there was more here than just the holiday spirit of a weekend trip. All this was a part of the "Scene Changes in Kashmir, India, and Pakistan" which this author has discussed in a book bearing the same name[5], that is well before the "happening" which engulfed the LoC some time ago. They were the background which gave more substance to the latest "scenes". Such background as the unprecedented elections held on the Indian side nearly three years earlier, and the unique character of the state government which resulted from that. Or the bold bid by Kashmiri dissidents to break away from the shackles of Pakistan, a bid because of which Abdul Ghani Lone was shot by Pakistan-based terrorists. Or things like the resentment felt on the Pakistan side of the state over attempts by all governments in Pakistan, from the Bhuttos to Musharraf, to kill the "*azadi*" of Azad Kashmir as completely in constitutional law as it had been killed already in political fact. And now, on top of it all, the contrast between the status of the two sides of the LoC which the visitors from the Pakistan side were now experiencing directly, and most of them for the first time, the contrast between the insignificance of "Azad Kashmir" in the national affairs of Pakistan and the important role being played by Kashmiri politicians on the Indian side of the state and, more importantly, in India's national affairs, the current chief minister of the state being a former home minister in the national government in New Delhi. Another Kashmiri of great promise who narrowly lost the chance to be the chief minister of the state was at one time India's junior minister of external affairs.

It is difficult to say what further steps would have been taken by India and Pakistan in the course of time if this first effort at building cordial relations between the two sides of the state had not been scuttled. But little room was left for this speculation when Pakistan decided to sprinkle sand on the pudding. India had agreed that any dissident Kashmiri would be just as free as any other resident of either side of Jammu and Kashmir to cross the LoC without a passport, but like everyone else, he too must travel only up to the Pakistan border. He would cross over into Pakistan only if he had obtained an Indian passport for the purpose, as any Indian must for going out of the country.

This condition applied to all who crossed the LoC but was particularly relevant in the case of some prominent Kashmiri dissidents who had been asking for India's permission to travel to Pakistan as the chosen representatives of Kashmir. India had no problem with their going to Pakistan, though only in their personal capacity and not as "chosen representatives", but it was required that they, like everyone else, must apply for Indian passports. This some of them had refused to do because it involved describing themselves Indian citizens. At this point, Pakistan succumbed once again to its weakness for playing clever tricks instead of choosing the wiser course. It led selected dissidents into Pakistan by giving them visas on its own papers.

India's public reaction was mild. India only said that Pakistan had violated an agreement and must "bear the onus for doing so." What "bearing the onus" would mean was not spelt out. It should have been, even if the onus was not as significant as it was made to look by the manner in which the threat of it was held out by the Indian foreign secretary. It is good for everyone to be reminded that agreements are meant to be observed. It smoothens the way for bigger agreements in future. But this was not done.

It would be surprising if there was or would be no consequence. The least that is likely to follow is a damper on a repeat of what had turned out to be a festival of visitors. Pakistan will be less free in letting people travel to the Indian side, and those who are allowed will be directed to keep their enthusiasm in check. In general, there will be discouragement of the state level *bhai chara* which was seen to be building up between the two sides.

How discouraging it will be, or how it will help either India or Pakistan or the people of either side of Kashmir, is hard to tell. But there is no doubt about what the Indian response should be. Pakistan watchers in Srinagar must, of course, observe how the people of "Azad Kashmir" react to the cold shower to which they might be subjected by Pakistan. But there are India matters too on which they must keep a wary eye.

For example, the question which was very important at one time, that is whether Mufti Mohammad Sayeed of the PDP, who was the chief minister of Jammu and Kashmir at that time, should step down after completing the three-year term for which he was chosen under a rotational agreement with the larger party, the Congress. Under the agreement, the next chief minister was to be from the Congress, and the party faithful strongly urged that this must be ensured "in the interests of the party."

But what is interesting to recall now is that the maximum acclaim the Congress won after the last election was not for its electoral performance, good though it was, but for its decision, which, to her credit, was entirely Sonia Gandhi's, to step back and to let the first term in that post go to the Mufti, who is Kashmiri to the core and unquestionably was the best candidate. The interests of the country and the state were better served that way.

Mufti Mohammed Sayeed also further enhanced his stature by his performance, and all the more so because the Congress had no match for him in its own ranks within the state. It could have brought in some prominent figure from outside the state. But that would have exposed it to certain risks. One, an outsider with limited experience of the fluid politics of the state might have slipped on "an outsider" peel , and the National Conference would have been tempted then to make the most use of that event. That could also have persuaded some fleet footed MLAs of other parties to cross over to the National Conference.

The second risk is more important, and more relevant to the present discussion. Conditions on the Indian side of the LoC need to be at their most attractive best if there is to be an effective follow-up to the impressions of Srinagar which have been carried back by the recent visitors from across the border. That requires a very sensitive finger on the pulse of things, and very updated assessment of the scope for cooperation between the two sides of the state. An invitation to political uncertainties in Srinagar would hardly be helpful. This needs to be kept in the scales for weighing what is good for the Congress against what is good for the state and the country.

Equally important it is, and for similar reasons, that the government in New Delhi must remember, and fulfill, certain promises that it made to Srinagar in the 1975 agreement. It is probably the best agreement that was ever reached between Srinagar and New Delhi since the accession of the state to India. It underlines the sanctity of the accession on the subjects on which the accession was signed by Sheikh Abdullah when he was the unquestionable embodiment of the will of the people of the state. At the same time, it provides for a mutual review of such extensions of the accession as were added in subsequent years by governments of the state whose democratic credentials were less than perfect. Most of these additions are either inconsequential or have been welcomed in the state, such as bringing the state judiciary within the purview of the Indian Supreme Court. But the manner in which the agreement was emasculated is as reprehensible as its contents are praiseworthy.

The review was promised to Sheikh Abdullah in reasonably plain language, by Mrs. Indira Gandhi herself, and probably with honest intentions. Then the merchants of words got into the act. The text is as ambiguous as skilful draftsmen can make it, phrases were used which could be interpreted whichever way subsequent calculations might warrant, and according to the participants and others who were close to the scene at that time and were interviewed by the author later on, closer scrutiny by Abdullah's colleagues was inhibited by his belief that he had established a high level of confidence with Mrs. Gandhi.

Worse befell him later. By the time the first state Assembly was elected and the first state government was formed after the signing of the agreement, which would be the main state agents for starting action on its implementation, Sheikh Abdullah was already a man much in physical and mental decline.

He was also caught in the cross-fire of contradictory advice from two close colleagues, each suspicious of the agreement but for opposite reasons. One was a traditional opponent of the accession in the first place, and wanted none of the hard reaffirmation of the accession as couched in the drafts. The other was a clever lawyer from Jammu, who did not like the greater and more discretionary powers Srinagar would get in the affairs of the state if detailed control over the state by the centre were to be whittled down, as it would be under the agreement.

The upshot of it all was what can only be called a mockery of the stated intention behind the agreement. While that intention was to invite the state to make any recommendation it wanted for a review of the terms of the extended accession, all that the Assembly asked for was some changes in the ceremonial aspects of the accession. When asked how this happened, one of the main actors of the day gave a blow by blow account of how Sheikh Abdullah was by-passed, and then he added, “Sheikh Saheb was a very tired man, and we had all the power.”

It is time to revive, respect, and implement that agreement. India must deliver on the promise to review the clauses which were added to the act of accession at a time when the state was under an undemocratic dispensation. That will strengthen, not weaken, the accession itself. That would be the best answer to the problem “in” Kashmir. It would also help in the fulfillment of India’s assurance, which was subsequently snatched away in a totally unjustified manner, that such “autonomy” as might be negotiated between New Delhi and Srinagar would be conferred on the latter by stages.

The result would so enhance the profile of Srinagar and the Valley in the whole of the undivided state, and, in fact, further afield, that fulfillment of the dream of their *de-facto* leadership of the region would follow, whatever local or regional politics, laws, and Constitutions might say. Expectations of such a status are realistic enough to goad Srinagar into doing all it can in the meantime to earn goodwill and trust in all parts of the former state, and enhance the talents of all its parts.

There are some features of the present geo-polity of the state which are probably beyond all that we mean by the problem “of” and the problem “in” the state. These features include what Pakistan calls the “Northern Areas” and which it has virtually incorporated in Pakistan, taking them quite out of the ambit of what it calls “Azad Kashmir”; and what both Pakistan and India treat as territories ceded to China by Pakistan in 1963. Both are entangled in world politics at the highest level. Moreover, it is unlikely that the area “ceded” to China will return to Jammu and Kashmir any time soon. But that time will come sooner if a more coherent Jammu and Kashmir can in the meantime more firmly register its presence in the whole region.

That, of course, means addressing the problem “in” Kashmir in a larger sense, which would include addressing such parts of the problem “of” Kashmir which impinge directly on the state, and addressing in other ways such parts of the problem “of” Kashmir which impinge directly on Pakistan. That is why this road may be long. But the “dream”, nevertheless, remains “worth dreaming”.

Notes

1. Pran Chopra, *India's Second Liberation* (Delhi: Vikas Publishing House,1972).
2. Inder Kumar Gujral, *Viewpoint: Civilization, Democracy and Foreign Policy* (New Delhi: Allied Publishers 2004), p. 109.
3. Gujral, Ibid., p. 139.
4. Pran Chopra, *Scene Changes in Kashmir, India and Pakistan* (New Delhi: Gyan Publishing House, 2003).
5. Ibid.

Jammu and Kashmir: The Internal Dimension

Radhavinod Raju

Two Indian prime ministers, at two different times, have broadly laid down the limits that the Indian state would go to in the search for an acceptable solution to the Kashmir problem. Narasimha Rao was essentially addressing the people of Jammu and Kashmir (J&K), from far away Burkina Faso, when he said that "sky was the limit" in regard to autonomy that could be worked out for J&K. And the present Prime Minister, Manmohan Singh was addressing Pakistan, when he said from Kashmir, that there cannot be any redrawing of boundaries, or a further division of India on communal lines, in an attempt to solve the Kashmir problem. This then appears to be the maximum position that India is willing to go to, to secure peace in J&K.

It is accepted, by both Pakistan and India, that there cannot be a military solution to this problem. India under Vajpayee turned nuclear in the summer of 1998 and Pakistan, under Nawaz Sharif, followed suit quickly. While many pundits around the globe felt that this has put a stop to military adventures against each other by either country, the Pakistanis had different ideas. Using militant groups under their control, adventurous incursions were made into Kargil during the following winter, believing that the world would intervene if India took steps to reclaim the territory forcibly. Strategic locations and areas in the upper reaches of Kargil were occupied by Pakistani regulars under the guise of *jihadis* and freedom fighters, with a commanding view of the National Highway linking Ladakh with the rest of the country. This resulted in the defence of Ladakh and Siachen becoming vulnerable. Security pundits had already declared that South Asia was a nuclear flashpoint. But there was no hesitation in the Indian political leadership deciding to mount a limited operation, using even air power, to launch a counter-attack to reclaim the territory – heavy casualties notwithstanding. This was a clear indication that India would not hesitate to defend its territorial integrity, whatever be the cost. And the entire comity of nations hailed the Indian stand. The net result of this Pakistani misadventure was that the Line of Control (LoC) in J&K became virtually sacrosanct.

It has now become clear to Pakistan that whatever nomenclature it might design for its overt and covert actions to use force and cunning to snatch the state of J&K from the Indian union, it has no chance of success. 9/11, and now 7/7, and further the clandestine fillip that the Pakistani A.Q. Khan gave to nuclear proliferation, have all combined and placed severe constraints and limitations on that country's options for annexing J&K. Where does it take us from here? A peace process was set rolling by Vajpayee in 2003, and both countries have affirmed, again and again, that it is "irreversible." Leaders of both countries have met in both capitals as well as on the sidelines of international gatherings, and appear confident, notwithstanding minor hiccups and irritants, that they shall go ahead with the process. It is in this background that this paper attempts to look at various factors infringing on the internal situation in the state.

Let us see how the Pakistanis have been looking at the unfolding situation. Taking advantage of internal problems in the state, and the huge border with innumerable passes, all of which could not have been manned by the Indian forces, Pakistan encouraged, trained, armed and financed various groups of Kashmiri youth to militate against the state and central governments in J&K. It was naïve on their part to think that the Indian state would pack up and go at the first signs of militancy, after the Soviet experience in Afghanistan. They did not realise that we were fighting to preserve the unity and integrity of our country.

With the vast experience that the Indians have of managing internal law and order problems, and the genuine political space that the Indian democracy was capable of giving to divergent voices, it was only a matter of time before the Kashmir disturbances would be controlled by the Indian state. To counter this the Pakistani agency, Inter-Services Intelligence (ISI), which had master-minded the internal revolt, broke the Kashmiri groups into a number of militant organisations, playing favourites, starved the pro-independence, secular group Jammu and Kashmir Liberation Front (JKLF) which had spearheaded the movement of funds and weapons, and finally when the local boys began to tire out, injected the *jihadi* poison into the movement. The large number of foreign terrorists who have perished in J&K, and the numbers that still fight the Indian security forces in the name of *jihad*[1], has clearly exposed the ISI's role in the continuing covert war that Pakistan has unleashed against this country.

Let us see the result of the ongoing Pakistani adventure in J&K. This low intensity war has been on since 1990. In these years, till the end of August 2005, over 15,700 civilians were reported killed in terrorist action, including over 3,330 in cross-firing between terrorists and members of the security forces and related law and order problems. Over 4,750 members of the security forces, including nearly 800 officers and men of the J&K Police, were killed in fighting militancy and terrorism during this period. The ratio of men killed, to that of the total strength of the organisation, is the highest in the case of J&K Police. As against this, nearly 20,000 terrorists were killed by the security forces in this period.[2] Thus, loss of human lives in over fourteen years of Pakistan inspired cross-border terrorism is a staggering 40,000, and this tragedy needs to be seen in the light of the fact that Pakistan is not an inch closer to realising its dream of annexing Kashmir. If anything, this adventure has economically weakened Pakistan, it has been identified as the hub of international terrorist activity by the outside world, its *madrassa*-based education system, which has spawned terrorists worldwide, has come under international scrutiny, and its government has had to take action – under outside pressure – to check the growth of this system. On the other hand, India, along with China, is fast emerging as an economic superpower, and with its strong institutions, professional military, and its abiding faith in democracy has gone far ahead of Pakistan.

Following initiatives taken by the National Democratic Alliance (NDA) government headed by Vajpayee, and the Pakistani response, a ceasefire has come to stay along the border, giving tremendous relief to residents along the borders. In a joint statement issued after the meeting of Prime Minister Vajpayee and President Musharraf in Islamabad, in early 2004, Pakistan had given an undertaking that its territory would not be allowed to be used for any anti-India activity. We may now see the situation on the ground following this understanding.

In this period, according to the security forces, infiltration of terrorists has seen ups and downs, but overall, there has been some reduction. Terrorist incidents have also shown downward trends, including human losses among civilians and members of the security forces.[3] But there are clear indications that the terrorist infrastructure in Pakistan is intact, and their network in J&K is quite active. This network has retained a capacity to strike in any part of the state. During this year, terrorists have focussed their attention on Srinagar, the summer capital of the state, resulting in several *fidayeen* attacks and attacks using grenades and other improvised explosive devices, including the *fidayeen* attack on the Tourist Reception Centre on the eve of the inaugural Srinagar-Muzaffarabad bus service.

Pakistan is trying to tell the world that it has done all that is possible to check infiltration of *jihadis* into J&K, and that what happens here can be checked by India only by taking steps to solve the "core" issue of Kashmir. There are pro-Pak groups in J&K, particularly the Hurriyat (G) led by Geelani, who criticises the Pakistani policy of seeking a peaceful solution of the Kashmir problem with

India. The four *jihadi* groups currently operating in J&K, who call themselves the G4, consisting of the Save Kashmir Movement, Farzandan-e-Millat, Al-Mansoorian and Al-Arifeen also oppose the Pakistan government's policy. They issued threats to the passengers of the first Srinagar-Muzaffarabad bus, and were critical of the talks of the moderate Hurriyat group led by Omar Farooq, with the Government of India. These four groups are front organisations for the Lashkar-e-Tayyeba, with very close links to the Hizb-ul Mujahideen and the Jaish-e- Mohammad.

It is difficult to accept that these hardline groups, both separatists and terrorists, are operating outside the control of Pakistan's ISI. There are substantial intelligence inputs that would show that these *jihadi* groups are in touch with their handlers in Pakistan, and can summon *fidayeens* for targeted attacks in the Valley whenever they want. This happened at the time of the *fidayeen* attack on the Tourist Reception Centre complex on the eve of the inaugural Srinagar- Muzaffarabad Bus Service.

From this, it is clear that the Pakistan government is actively pursuing a dual policy – swearing by the peace process and continuing with official level meetings in either capitals, and allowing a number of confidence-building measures, but also continuing to provide clandestine support to *jihadi* groups to "safeguard" their interest in Kashmir. In this connection, it is useful to quote from an article written by a leading Pakistani strategic analyst which appeared around the time of the Agra Summit in mid-2001.[4] Commenting on the support of the United States, the European Union and Russia for each other on issues like Palestine and Chechnya, this analyst wrote, "If these are the realities, can any small power go counter to the trend? Or specifically, can Pakistan counter the Russian-Western support for India? On the Kashmir issue, it can, if the situation on the ground is sustained. In other words, the freedom struggle in IHK (Indian held Kashmir) cannot fade out because that is the only real pressure on the international community and India – especially the Indian military. Dialogue must not be accompanied by a cessation of the military struggle on the ground until substantive progress has been made." To Pakistan, substantive progress on Kashmir means only one thing – handing over Kashmir to Pakistan. This then is the policy of the Pakistan government – continuing dialogue accompanied by continuing covert military struggle to soften and bring India around to its point of view. If 40,000 more innocent lives perish in this futile exercise, so be it! If each year, the Indian security forces eliminate about 1,000 terrorists, there will be infiltration bids to keep the level of active terrorists in the state the same as the earlier years, all the promises notwithstanding. A clever reference to the

Indian forces along the boundary, and the fence that has come up on the Indian side would be made by claiming that even such obstacles could not prevent the "freedom fighters" from getting into J&K because of their sheer determination. This then is the reality on the ground.

This does not mean that this policy of Pakistan has not been criticised within Pakistan. A clear perception has emerged in Pakistan that the current policy is meant solely to keep the military in power. According to an analyst there, Pakistan fought two and a half wars against India to wrest Kashmir from Indian control, or at least to change the status-quo on Kashmir. The first war was fought in 1947-48, the second in 1965 and the third in Kargil in 1999, calling the last one a predictable disaster and "General Musharraf's personal contribution to the annals of Kashmir warfare."[5] Far from focussing attention on the need for a Kashmir solution, Kargil put the spotlight on Pakistan's sponsorship of "cross-border terrorism." Following September 11 and American and Indian pressure, General Musharraf was compelled to give assurances about rolling up *jihad* in Kashmir. The Kargil misadventure resulted in making the Line of Control more or less a permanent one: it "marks the farthermost limits of Pakistani military prowess.....there can be nothing more concrete than this." A clear statement from a perceptive analyst was that it was impossible for Pakistan, with or without nuclear weapons, to snatch Kashmir from India militarily.[6] This opinion in Pakistan has realised that even though the Pakistani establishment would like division of the state on communal lines, and that a section of Kashmiri opinion favours accession to Pakistan, the majority opinion in the Valley would rather have independence. While commenting on General Musharraf's call for "sincerity" in solving the Kashmir dispute, the analyst asks whether Pakistan expects India to do voluntarily on the basis of "sincerity" what it failed to make India do militarily. And on Pakistan's harping on the "core" issue, the analyst adds that having got used to the loss of East Pakistan, which was half of Pakistan, how can Kashmir become a "core" issue when it was never a part of Pakistan. According to this analyst, the talk of core issue has served to make the military "the holiest cow" in Pakistan and that, as a result, the Pakistani "military today is far bigger than when there was both West and East Pakistan to defend."

An opinion is gradually emerging in Pakistan on the outlines of an acceptable solution based on " realism."[7] Pakistan simply cannot hope to get, on the negotiating table what it has failed to win on the battlefield, and that those favouring independence in Kashmir cannot get it because both India and Pakistan "cannot countenance this idea." The opinion also accepts that the Security Council resolutions calling for plebiscite, "for all their relevance or life left in them" are virtually dead, and that it is better to begin from ground realities. On this aspect of "ground realities," this emerging opinion laments that there cannot be "going round the Line of Control," and that this line will remain the effective frontier dividing Kashmir. Pakistan's efforts, both overt and covert, right from 1947 till the Kargil adventure of 1999 and beyond have only succeeded in making this line more permanent and that if "ever a case can be made out for a farewell to arms, it is here."

The picture that emerges is very unclear. A peace process is on and both governments are supporting the process. The covert war using *jihadis* continues to ensure pressure on the international community and the Indian security forces, looking for a Kashmir solution favourable to Pakistan. To this end, the *jihadi* infrastructure in Pakistan is intact, and the main protagonists of the anti-India *jihadis*, Azhar Masood of the Jaish-e-Mohammad and Hafiz Saeed of the Lashker-e-Tayyeba, are strutting about breathing fire. But the emergence of an opinion in Pakistan that this war will fetch no results and that it is much better to focus on economic and social upliftment of the masses in that country is the one silver lining in these dense clouds.

On our side, terrorist incidents continue in different parts of the state, targeting members of the security forces, alleged informers, political activists and civilians. The security forces, of which J&K Police is a vital and integral part, are handling the situation with a lot of self-confidence, conscious of the rights of civilians all the time. Due to deliberate and conscious efforts, a large number of civilian oriented activities and programmes are undertaken by the police, army and paramilitary forces to bring them closer to the people they serve.

In a recent attack on an army vehicle using an improvised explosive device, in which nine jawans (soldiers) were killed and several injured, there was no reaction from the security forces – but in a few weeks, the J&K Police succeeded in busting a Hizb-ul Mujahideen ring which was involved in this and other such attacks. This is because of better training, based on experience gained over all these years. This is not to say that incidents of human rights violations have been totally controlled. Such incidents do take place now and then, and get highlighted by an aggressive anti-establishment media. But immediate measures are taken to check them and punish the guilty. With pinpointed anti-terrorist operations based on accurate intelligence, better border management and sustained investigations to expose illegal activities of upper-ground supporters, including those who provide safe-havens, infrastructural support and *hawala* funding, it is expected that sooner rather than later, greater relief will be provided to the peace-starved citizens of this state.

But that would address only one side of the problem. The opening of the Srinagar-Muzaffarabad road has suddenly focussed attention on related developmental and emotional issues. With the two governments agreeing to open more such routes to connect the people of Jammu with Sialkot and Mirpur, and those of Leh and Kargil with Gilgit and Skardu, the possibilities of trade and commerce loom large in the skyline along with reuniting of divided families. People-to-people contact is already on the increase, and this is bound to ease tensions. The rise in tourists visiting different parts of the Valley is unprecedented this year when we look at the last 15 years. People move around freely, and interact with members of the security forces easily and with growing confidence. There was a tremendous response from the people during the local elections, and there is a clear feeling of empowerment – that they can make and break governments and demand accountability and transparency in government functioning. The Right to Information Act and the corresponding rules that were passed recently have gone a long way to give the feeling of empowerment to the people.

The two Punjabs have already started coming closer. Maximum bloodshed during partition was in this zone. Punjabi domination in Pakistan is well known. And the main cause for the lack of trust between the two countries is ascribed to this Punjabi domination of Pakistan and the bloodletting during partition. If the two Punjabs, with all the distrust and the 1965 and 1971 Wars behind them, can get closer on the platform of Punjabiyat, with the two Chief Ministers, Parvez Elahi of Pakistani Punjab and Capt. Amarinder Singh of Indian Punjab publicly hugging each other, with inter-Punjab games and trade, commerce and tourism as the agenda, there is no reason why similar inter-Kashmir activities cannot be visualised. A more relaxed and trusting environment in the India-Pakistan context will not only bring emotional happiness to hundreds of thousands of people of this state, across boundaries, but also give a tremendous boost to economic development, with huge markets for Kashmiri produce, both agricultural and handicrafts, with a number of routes opening on every side.

A number of Pakistanis now visit different parts of India for expert medical help. We should open our universities and other institutions to Pakistanis to enable them to enjoy the fruits of higher education, and get exposed to the strengths of Indian democracy. A Pakistani commentator wrote, "Indian democracy triumphs and we feel humiliated." Atal Behari Vajpayee's conceding defeat when it became clear that the party he led was trailing the Congress was a normal exercise in any parliamentary democracy, and it has happened in India again and again, but this single political exercise in a democracy was "thoroughly amazing" for Pakistanis. Indian democracy, with all its imperfections, is a functioning democracy where every shade of opinion, and all religious minorities, get space for political expression. Some of the highest learning centres of Islam function in India. Muslims have distinguished themselves in every field, be it politics, art, sports, music, computers and information technology, medicine – you name it, and we have icons with millions of Indian fans rooting for them.

Kashmiri Muslims can be found in every part of the country today, settled in the farthest corners of South India and doing well. Kashmiris go to every learning centre in India for higher education – thanks to militancy and disturbances in Kashmir, one of the unexpected but fruitful fallouts of Pakistan's undeclared war in Kashmir. Many highly qualified Kashmiris are gainfully employed in their own state, working for multinationals. These boys and girls are focussed on their education and development, rather than fall prey to the machinations of the *jihadi* terrorists. When finally the few thousand Kashmiri boys still in Pakistan, who have wasted the best parts of their lives listening to fanciful stories of Indian atrocities on their people and *jihadi* literature, return to Kashmir, there will be hardly any place for them in a forward looking economic environment, unless they are willing to start from the beginning, cutting their losses. In fact, the J&K government should prepare plans for their anticipated return, and the J&K Police, currently spearheading the fight against *jihadi* terrorists, should prepare contingency plans to cope with a sharp rise in conventional crime.

The current peace initiative between India and Pakistan has been widely acclaimed by a cross-section of Kashmiri opinion, even though the few *jihadi* groups, and their political cousins of the Hurriyat(G), have condemned the talks. Amidst this unfolding drama, one hears alternate voices, hitherto dwelling only on the theme of independence, commenting that "meddled polity has scuttled the evolution of a responsible political process, throwing up natural leaders representative of the public sentiment. Instead, an array of superficially imposed substitutes failing to deliver has eroded the very institution giving rise to deep-seated suspicion."[8] Such voices have called for ascertaining the representative character of the leaders using some form of ballot – to establish the legitimacy and credibility of any leader. Looking at the drastically changed dynamics of the environment at the inception of the movement in 1989, "from ideological geo-strategy" to the present "information driven geo-economics," one writer calls for a rethink and a trans-positioning from the ideal to realism, contending that an economically strengthened, and a diplomatically and militarily stronger India would be too powerful for them to take on.[9]

Similarly, there are some voices in Pakistan emphasising that geography can be a huge advantage for Pakistan, instead of a millstone around its neck. Predicting that a new Great Game is going to begin in the area, one analyst says that there will be more than two contenders this time, with Russia, the United States, China, India and possibly the European Union, all vying with each other to reach the enormous energy potential in the region for their growing industrial and economic needs.[10] He further suggested that instead of continuing rivalry with India, Pakistan must take advantage of its position to "become the hinge that connects these two economic giants, providing transit facilities to the rapidly growing trade between India and China and become the energy hub for the flow of natural gas to these energy deficit countries." The scene in these parts is thus rapidly changing – with enormous potential for economic growth. Once barriers of trust are crossed, water management, which is a continuing source of tensions between the two countries, can easily become a tremendous source of strength, mutual trust and rapid development. But the problem is the continuing *jihad*. President Musharraf recently said that the time is ripe for a solution of Kashmir. If after all these realities and destructions, Pakistan thinks that there can be a solution in which Kashmir goes to that country, despite pragmatic voices calling for a u-turn of the *jihadi* policy *a la* the Taliban in Afghanistan, and in pursuance of this hard headed policy, *jihadi* terrorists, in their effort to put pressure on India and its security forces, continue to inflict pain and hurt on Kashmiris in their hope of a 1,000 cuts to bleed India, one can only pity the common people who are affected by their blind actions. This year itself, till August end, 657 terrorists were eliminated by the Indian security forces, including dozens of top leaders; 173 members of the security forces and 383 civilians also got killed in these operations.[11] India has learned to take these losses. Prime Minister Manmohan Singh has made it clear that continuing *jihadi* activities can jeopardise the peace process. The limits to which India is prepared to go have also been clearly laid down. There are excellent prospects for peace, and peace can bring happiness and prosperity to all and give dignity and self-respect back to the Kashmiris. India has agreed to reduce military strength in the Valley if terrorist activities come down, infiltration of terrorists stops and the terrorist infrastructure in Pakistan is dismantled. However, it would be a serious mistake if these confidence-building measures are construed as dilution or weakening of the national will of the people of India to protect and preserve the unity and territorial integrity of this country. The J&K Police is today a fine fighting machine – caring for the people, but spearheading the fight against terrorists. The police, along with their colleagues in the paramilitary and army, will continue to remain alert and keep their powder dry to face any challenge against the unity and integrity of the state and the country.

Notes

1. According to the data available with the J&K Police.
2. Ibid.
3. Ibid.
4. Shirin Mazari, "Emerging Rules of the Game," *Kashmir Times*, June 13, 2001.
5. Ayaz Amir, "A Sincere Approach to Kashmir," *The Dawn*, June 11, 2004.
6. Amir, Ibid.
7. For example, see Ayaz Amir, "Can We Pull it off This Time?" *The Dawn*, May 9, 2003.
8. Asma Khan Lone, "The Journey Beyond," *Greater Kashmir*, September 5, 2005.
9. Lone, Ibid.
10. Shahid Javed Burki, "Geography is Destiny," *The Dawn*, August 30, 2005.
11. Data available with the J&K Police.

India-Pakistan Relations: The Way Forward

India-Pakistan Neemrana Initiative: An Experiment in Track Two Diplomacy

Satish Kumar

Introduction

The 1990s comprised a rather turbulent phase in India-Pakistan relations. After the Afghan *jihad* against the Soviet invasion of 1979 came to an end and the Soviet troops withdrew in 1989, the Pakistani military establishment took advantage of the fresh political discontent and organised an insurgency in Jammu and Kashmir. Amidst high tension in 1990 and the scare of a nuclear show-down between India and Pakistan, the US Information Centre in New Delhi, took the 'initiative' to organise a Track Two group of eminent Indians and Pakistanis.

It took a few months to identify and put together ten Indians and ten Pakistanis with experience and stature in the fields of academia, diplomacy, military affairs, and journalism. In October 1991, these twenty persons accompanied by some senior officials from the US Embassy in India were taken to the Neemrana Fort resort in Rajasthan, about 70 km from Delhi, to provide the right environment for candid and concentrated discussions away from the distractions of Delhi. To acclimatise the participants to the vicissitudes of complex negotiations and to impress upon them the need to produce results in a fixed timeframe, the US Embassy personnel staged a play called "A Walk in the Woods" based on the highly important Reagan-Gorbachev Summit in Reykjavik, Iceland, in 1987. The play depicted a Russian and an American diplomat thrown at each other in a closed environment for days together until they produced an agreement.

"Track Two" is an important part of multi-track diplomacy, the efficacy of which was exemplified by the long history of its success between the US and the USSR during the Cold War. The most classic case was that of the Dartmouth Conference which was instituted in 1959 when President Dwight D. Eisenhower of the United States asked Norman Cousins, the editor of the *Saturday Review*, to get together some prominent US and Soviet citizens on a single platform to discuss US-Soviet relations. These meetings, initially held in Dartmouth College, were continued on a regular basis for more than 29 years. The two issues that were entrusted to the two separate task forces and were regularly discussed every six months were arms control and regional issues. Besides, the plenary meetings took place every twelve or eighteen months. The Dartmouth Process was believed to have led to improved US-Soviet communication and understanding on a wide range of issues.

But what exactly is Track Two diplomacy? John W. McDonald, in his essay on "Further Exploration of Track Two Diplomacy"[1] gives five categories of Multi-Track Diplomacy.[2] These are:

Track I: Official, government to government diplomatic interaction.

Track II: Unofficial, analytical, policy-oriented, problem solving efforts by skilled, educated, experienced and professionally informed private citizens of a particular country interacting with similar citizens of another country.

Track III: Businessmen-to-Businessmen contacts in the private sector to promote free enterprise between countries and their multinational corporations.

Track IV: Citizen-to-Citizen exchange programmes of various kinds, such as scientific, cultural, academic, students, and youth exchange programmes, and exchanges in the entertainment industry involving films, music, arts, sports, etc.

Track V: Media-to-Media based efforts designed to expose and educate large segments of the population to the philosophy, ideas, culture, and aspirations of the other nation, society, or ethnic group with whom they are in conflict.

Among all these forms of diplomatic exchanges, Track Two Diplomacy has assumed significance next only to Track One, and finds a respectable place in serious literature on conflict resolution. Given their expertise in handling specific issues with regard to the conflict, the well-informed citizens chosen to carry forth the Track Two dialogue have often succeeded in creating a conducive environment for conflict resolution. They do so by providing appropriate inputs to their governments and through their writings and speeches.

The term Track Two diplomacy was coined by a former American diplomat Joseph Montville in 1981 to describe the "unofficial, informal interaction between members of adversary groups or nations which aims to develop strategies, influence public opinion, and organise human and material resources in ways that might help resolve their conflict."[3] Louis Diamond and

John McDonald, co-founders of the Institute for Multi-Track Diplomacy in Washington D.C. have defined Track Two diplomacy in essence as the "realm of professional, non-governmental action attempting to analyse, prevent, resolve and manage (intrastate and interstate) conflicts."[4] The Neemrana Dialogue can be said to be a classic example of Track Two diplomacy.

The Neemrana Dialogue

The India-Pakistan Neemrana Initiative (IPNI), the official name by which this dialogue is called, has some distinctive features which make it different from various other multi-track processes in the context of Indo-Pak relations. These features may be enumerated as follows:

(i) The regularity and frequency of these meetings. The Neemrana Dialogue participants have met regularly twice a year, alternately in India and Pakistan. So far, the dialogue has had 25 meetings, the last one having taken place in New Delhi in December 2005.

(ii) High level of expertise and eminence on both sides. The delegations on both sides have had former foreign secretaries, former vice-chiefs of the army, navy or air force, former senior professors of international relations, former financial administrators, former editors, senior economists, journalists, senior educationists and strategic affairs experts.

(iii) The dialogue from the very beginning has had a precise and agreed agenda. The issues regularly discussed were:
   (a) Internal situation in both countries;
   (b) Respective views on the international security environment affecting Indo-Pak relations;
   (c) Kashmir question and Indo-Pak peace process;
   (d) Nuclear issues;
   (e) Trade and economic issues;
   (f) Cultural cooperation, people-to-people contacts, visa problems, etc.;
   (g) Ad-hoc issues like cooperation in the fields of science and technology, agriculture, education, etc.

(iv) Feedback to the government, but no cue from the government. The delegations tried to maintain their independent and non-official character by taking no cue from the government before every meeting. The delegations, however, kept their respective governments informed of the outcome of their deliberations and submitted to the governments agreed recommendations on specific issues. At times, these recommendations were accepted and implemented.

(v) Influencing public opinion through speeches and writings. Since the dialogue meetings were held behind closed doors, members on both sides tried to influence public opinion in favour of reconciliation through research and newspaper writings, and participation in seminars and conferences.

(vi) Avoiding media publicity. In view of the hostility of certain sections of society to any Indo-Pak dialogue in the initial stages, it was decided that the dialogue would be kept completely closed to the media. The occasional leaks and speculations, however, could not do any damage to the continuation of the dialogue. This feature in particular distinguishes the Neemrana Dialogue from other multiple tracks of diplomacy between India and Pakistan which were prone to give immediate extensive publicity to their endeavours.

(vii) Attributing names in any report or write-up on the proceedings of Neemrana Dialogue was completely prohibited. This enabled the members to express their views in the dialogue freely and forcefully.

There were two ground rules which were agreed upon at the first meeting of the dialogue in October 1991 at Neemrana and which enabled the dialogue to move forward. They were, one, that no member would repeat the history of any issue in Indo-Pak relations, which should be taken as known, and two, that no member would reiterate the official or governmental position on any issue, so that it becomes possible to break new ground in resolving the conflict.

Some Achievements

Questions are often raised about the usefulness of the Neemrana Dialogue and whether it has made any real contribution to India-Pakistan reconciliation. There is no doubt that any Track Two process can at best lend a helping hand in creating the right environment between two conflicting nations. Real progress can take place only at the Track One level which is authorised to take decisions and implement them. But in a highly complex strategic environment, every fresh idea counts, and such ideas do get generated if the level of expertise in Track Two is sufficiently high and the attitude on both sides is positive. In-depth analysis of certain issues at the Track Two meetings, imbued with mature insights and independent thinking, sometimes produces solutions which would not be thinkable at the Track One level.

At the second Neemrana Dialogue in Lahore in January 1992, a thorough discussion was held on the Pakistani proposal of a nuclear weapons free zone in South Asia. Both the delegations had recognised expertise in the nuclear field. When it was realised in the course of the discussion that it would not be possible for the two countries to roll back their nuclear programmes, the two delegations agreed that the two countries should work towards making South Asia a nuclear weapons "safe zone". In other words, instead of working at cross purposes, the two countries should work towards a common goal which was achievable. Although there was already an agreement in place (since 1988) by which the two countries were committed to exchange lists of their nuclear facilities every year, the suggestion for a nuclear weapons safe zone that emerged from the Neemrana Second Round helped in giving a positive direction to the nuclear debate in India and Pakistan.

In 1995, members of the Neemrana Dialogue decided to meet Kashmiri leaders, including dissidents on both sides of the dividing line. The meetings with dissident Kashmiri leaders on the Indian side were facilitated by India's Neemrana members, and vice versa on the Pakistani side. After the meetings, the Indian side recommended to Prime Minister P.V. Narasimha Rao that steps should be taken to grant greater autonomy to the state of Jammu and Kashmir. Prime Minister Rao arranged a visit of five members of the Indian delegation to Kashmir for a closer on the spot assessment and had another discussion with them on their return. It was soon after this discussion that he made an offer in the Parliament that the people of Kashmir could be granted "Autonomy short of *Azadi,*" and that the "sky is the limit."

In 1995 and 1996, joint papers were produced by the Indian and Pakistani participants in the Neemrana Dialogue on two important issues, that is, "Options for a Kashmir Solution" and "Military CBMs Between India and Pakistan." The papers were drafted by task forces representing both the delegations and were approved by the plenary meetings. The papers were then submitted to the two governments, the Kashmir paper to the Foreign Office of each country and the CBMs paper to the respective army chiefs.

In 1997, when I.K. Gujral was the Indian prime minister, the Neemrana delegation of India prevailed upon him to liberalise the visa policy with regard to Pakistan. Mr. Gujral had kept track of the deliberations in the Neemrana Dialogue through frequent meetings with the Indian and Pakistani members. His attitude had always been that of facilitating travel and communication for the people of both countries.

In October 2004, the Neemrana Dialogue which was held in New Delhi took up the question of the Srinagar-Muzaffarabad bus service and the difficulties that bedevilled this proposal. Further progress on this proposal was stuck on the nature of documents which must be examined at the border before the passengers could be allowed to board the bus. While India insisted that the passports to be shown at the check post, Pakistan was opposed to it. The Neemrana Dialogue members worked out a substitute arrangement which was submitted to the two foreign ministers. The foreign ministers reacted favourably and submitted the document to their Foreign Offices. The document was fine tuned further and eventually became the basis of the system implemented by the two governments.

Some Limitations of Track Two Diplomacy

Even though Track Two diplomacy is conducted by men of stature and credibility, it suffers from some inherent limitations. One such limitation is excessive consciousness of national interest on the part of the participants and their tendency to be sympathetic to the respective official positions. Such tendencies become more pronounced in moments of crisis. For instance, at the time of "Operation Parakram" in 2002, when India deployed more than 7,00,000 troops on the Pakistan border in the wake of the terrorist attack on India's Parliament House on December 13, 2001, the role of Track Two diplomacy would normally have been considered as extremely relevant. But the Neemrana Dialogue was completely suspended during the period. It was resumed only after the crisis was over.

There is another limitation which perhaps is not peculiar to Track Two diplomacy and can be discerned in Track One diplomacy as well. This pertains to the tendency of the stronger partner to lecture down to the weaker partner and to sermonise it on how it should behave or what positions it should take in the course of negotiations. There were occasions when this happened during the Neemrana discussions as well. This can lead to further rigidifying the behaviour of the weaker partner.

Yet another limitation is the apathy and cynicism on the part of the bureaucratic establishment in the Foreign Offices of the countries concerned. The bureaucratic establishment normally provides the personnel for Track One dialogue. There are occasions when it is found to be reluctant to give due importance to the considered views of Track Two people, even though the political leadership is more receptive to the inputs emanating from Track Two. The success of Track Two dialogue, therefore, very much depends on the composition of Track Two delegations and the stature of their leadership. The more influential and eminent the chairman and members are, the greater are the chances of their success. The success has to be measured not only in terms of what the deliberations of Track Two produce but also whether the outcome makes an impact on the deliberations of Track One.

Finally, the self-imposed limitation of the Neemrana Dialogue to work anonymously. It has been pointed out by some observers that the decision of the Neemrana Initiative not to engage with the mass media has reduced its ability to affect public opinion and thereby exert indirect influence on policy-making.[5] It must, however, be pointed out that the sensitivity of some recommendations made from time to time by the Neemrana Initiative to the two governments would still require the principle of anonymity to be maintained. The general tenor of discussions, with emphasis on positive elements, can perhaps be shared with the media with good effect.

Relevance of Track Two Diplomacy

At the end, it is necessary to deal with the question of how relevant is Track Two diplomacy in any peace process. In the structure of a peace process delineated by Harold Saunders in his book *The Other Walls*,[6] he lays down five stages through which it proceeds. These stages are:

(i) Defining the problem (pertaining to any conflict situation);
(ii) Developing a commitment (on the part of the parties to the conflict) to negotiate;
(iii) Arranging a negotiation (between the parties to the conflict);
(iv) The negotiation process (towards reaching an agreement);
(v) Implementing the agreement.

This author's experience in Track Two would suggest that it can be of great help in the first two stages of the peace process. The members of Track Two, on the basis of their expertise, can contribute to public discourse in such a manner that the problem sounds more amenable to a solution than otherwise. They can help define the problem in terms that reduce the gap in the positions of the two sides. Similarly, Track Two personnel, through their writings and speeches, can help strengthen the resolve of the parties to come to the negotiating table. Once they are on the table, the negotiating process can acquire a momentum which leads to some agreement, even if incrementally.

Notes

1. Louis Kriesberg and Stuart Thorson, eds., *Timing the De-Escalation of International Conflicts* (Syracuse: Syracuse University Press, 1991).
2. He later expanded them into nine in Louis Diamond and John McDonald, *Multi-track Diplomacy: A Systems Approach to Peace* (Connecticut: Kumarian Press, 1996).
3. Joseph V. Montville, "The Arrow and the Olive Branch: A Case for Track Two Diplomacy," in John W. Mc Donald and Diane B. Bendahmane, eds., *Conflict*

Resolution: Track Two Diplomacy (Washington D.C.: Institute for Multi-Track Diplomacy, 1995), p.9.

4. Diamond and McDonald, Ibid.
5. See Manjrika Sewak, *Multi-Track Diplomacy Between India and Pakistan: A Conceptual Framework for Sustainable Security*, RCSS Policy Studies 30 (New Delhi: Manohar, 2005), p.67.
6. Harold Saunders, *The Other Walls: The Arab-Israeli Peace Process in a Global Perspective* (New Delhi: Affiliated East-West Press, 1992), pp.22-38.

India-Pakistan Relations: Is the Peace Process "Irreversible"?

Frédéric Grare

Six years after the Kargil War, and a period of particularly strained relations which saw the two countries deploying more than a million troops along the border during the winter of 2001-2002, India and Pakistan are experiencing one of those periods of calm and hope which have often marked their turbulent history. The composite dialogue initiated by the then Indian Prime Minister Atal Behari Vajpayee and the Pakistani President Pervez Musharraf during the 12th Southeast Asian Association for Regional Cooperation (SAARC) summit of January 2004, held in Islamabad, marked the beginning of a new – although rather uncertain – phase, by the official acceptance that all disputes ought to be resolved only through dialogue.

The two countries had experienced similar developments in the past but the nuclear capabilities demonstrated by the tests of 1998 and the two subsequent crises between the two countries gave this new phase of dialogue an unprecedented urgency. Two years after its beginning, however, the peace process has not yet experienced a setback but achieved no major breakthrough either. The outcome so far has been limited to secondary issues, such as the ceasefire along the Line of Control (LoC) or the release of civilian prisoners, although the agreements related to ballistic missiles tests notifications, operationalisation of the 'hotline' between the foreign secretaries are likely to diminish the nuclear risk and, therefore, reassure the international community.

Talks have so far failed to resolve traditional disputes. One may argue that given the situation which prevailed between the two countries two years ago, the process is itself an achievement. The decrease in violence and the quasi "freeze" of the conflict have benefited the local populations and have allowed the talks to go on. However, as rightly observed by Teresita Schaffer, "[c]ommitment to talking may keep violence down for a time, but will not, by itself, solve the problems between India and Pakistan."[1] In this perspective, the situation in the Kashmir Valley remains the key issue. Violence from both sides has decreased but has not disappeared and the management of the political process may well create additional difficulties. Pakistan's President Pervez Musharraf and Indian

Prime Minister Manmohan Singh have declared the peace process irreversible but this process is still flawed with a number of risks which could jeopardise and ultimately destroy it.

This chapter intends to examine the evolution of the peace process between India and Pakistan and the trends which characterise it. It attempts to identify the risks associated with it as well as the constraints that the two countries are facing and examine various scenarios regarding the future of the process. It does so by taking into account the bilateral, Pakistani and Indian dimensions of the problem, in particular when considering the Kashmir issue. The potential consequences of the recent earthquake are also analysed in this context.

India-Pakistan Bilateral Dialogue: Some Real But Limited Progress

Assessing the ongoing peace process between India and Pakistan is a difficult and frustrating exercise. The outcomes have been so far below expectations for both the parties and the most significant progress has, perhaps, not been the most visible one. As stated above, the peace process has so far experienced no setback but, reviewing the achievement made within the framework of the composite dialogue, on the sidelines of the plenary meeting of the 60th UN General Assembly session, Prime Minister Manmohan Singh and President Musharraf could only reiterate their commitment to ensure a peaceful settlement of all pending issues and did not announce any breakthrough.[2] A little over two years into the peace process, the progress made is important but limited.

Agreements related to ballistic missile test pre-notification and the operationalisation of the 'hotline' between the two foreign secretaries or the upgrading of the existing hotline between the two Directors-General of Military Operations (DGMOs)[3], are important developments to limit nuclear risks and are likely to reassure, not only the two protagonists but also the international community. Progress on conventional confidence-building measures (CBMs) related to the implementation of the 1991 agreement between Pakistan and India on air space violations, the commitment not to develop any new post and defence work along the LoC, the monthly flag meetings between local commanders, or the speedy return of inadvertent LoC crossers are also steps in the right direction. Similarly, the ceasefire on the LoC and the release of the fishermen and civilian prisoners who have completed their term, do benefit local populations but such measures do not constitute major steps although they are undoubtedly a sign of abatement of tension.

The state of their economic relations is a good example of the actual achievements of the Indo-Pakistan dialogue. The trade between the two countries has more than doubled over the last 12 months. It should, however, be observed that bilateral trade started from an incredibly low level (less than 1 per cent of the global trade of the two countries) and remains too low to constrain either of the two countries politically. Moreover, the increase is totally asymmetrical and benefits, for obvious reasons, India much more than Pakistan. This reinforces the fears of the latter that India wishes to advance the peace process only in the fields in which it is likely to gain, without having to make any substantial concessions in areas that Pakistan considers more important.

However, the traditional issues of contention between the two countries remain. Not only Kashmir, which is unlikely to be agreed upon any time soon, but neither Siachen, nor Sir Creek and even less the water problem created by the dispute over the Wullar Barrage and Baglihar Dam, have yet been settled. Interestingly, all these issues are technical in nature and legal mechanisms already exist or could be identified to solve them. India and Pakistan had even reached agreements on Siachen and the Wullar Dam respectively in 1992 and 1991, although neither of the two agreements was signed. Sir Creek is a classical case of boundary delimitation for which the 1982 Law of the Sea Convention (of which the two countries are a party) provides a formal dispute settlement mechanism that neither of the two countries has ever invoked. The continuation of these disputes, the worst being Siachen, from which the two countries would like to withdraw but are supposedly prevented to do so by technical obstacles which would be easy to bypass, is an indicator of the actual level of distrust between the two countries.

The most spectacular measure, the opening of the Srinagar-Muzaffarabad bus line, on April 7, 2005, was essentially a symbolic gesture. Although it is officially aimed at reuniting the divided families, so far it has benefited only a few carefully chosen ones by the security agencies.[4] As such, it does illustrate the limits of the "people-to-people diplomacy." Civil societies are part of the process only within the narrow limits defined by the two governments.

The Peace Process and the Situation in Kashmir

Far more important, however, for the future of the peace process is the situation in Kashmir. Security remains the key issue, and implies examining two sets of problems: the relationship between the local population and the Indian security forces, on the one hand, and the evolution of the militancy, on the other. Both the militancy and the Indian security forces take their legitimacy from the presence and the behaviour of the other in the Valley and have developed over the years a complex relationship not only with each other but also with the population against whose interests their own interests converge sometimes.

Evolution of Militancy in Kashmir

Violence has declined in the Kashmir Valley but militancy has not disappeared although the number of active organisations has diminished. Hizb-ul Mujahideen, Lashkar-e-Tayyeba, Jaish-e-Mohammad, Jamiat-ul-Mujahideen and, to a lesser extent, Al Umar, continue to operate in the Valley under various names.[5] However, strategies of both infiltration and combat have changed. Larger groups of Mujahideen (consisting of 20 to 30 people) now attempt infiltration. As the fences, unattended ground sensors and other security measures make the infiltration more difficult, these groups almost always engage the Indian security forces in fire. A number of Mujahideen get killed but some escape. Once in the Valley, they no longer operate in large groups but remain distributed in many areas and operate as cellular units.

Combat strategies have also changed. Car bomb blasts were, until recently, unknown in the Valley but have proved to be very cost-effective as they minimise the exposure of the militants, kill the maximum number of people and ensure maximum publicity as the psychological impact is far greater than in the traditional bullet battles. However, even for the Mujahideen, they also have a negative aspect as they kill civilians indiscriminately (the ratio being three civilians for one member of the security forces) and, thus, alienate segments of the population, creating at the same time a rift between the predominantly Kashmiri organisations and the Pakistani ones.

Pakistan's responsibility in this process is beyond doubt.The Mujahideen are said to receive training and equipment for high altitude infiltration. Moreover, the link between the Mujahideen and the Pakistan Army units stationed along the LoC is recognised by the militants themselves. This raises the issue of both Pakistan's expectation and strategy vis-à-vis the peace process. President Musharraf's statement of November 30, 2004, proposing a three-point formula, including the identification of seven regions according to ethnic and geographical criteria, the demilitarisation of the entire region and a change of status for the seven regions which could have included options "like a condominium, UN control or any other agreed formula" and his call for a national debate on Kashmir, had generated the hope that Islamabad was gradually coming to terms with the reality that India would never accept any substantial change of Kashmir's status and that the Pakistani leadership was now looking for ways to politically sell its new position.

The new flexibility demonstrated by the Pakistani leadership did not imply any renouncement of Pakistan's demand for sovereignty over Kashmir but the proposal of a condominium of the region could be considered an implicit acceptance of India's. It was more or less consistent with Manmohan Singh's subsequent declaration in April 2005, according to which borders could not be changed but could be made irrelevant. This amounted to saying that, provided borders remained officially unchanged, Pakistan's role in Kashmir could be negotiated which constituted *de facto* a major concession from India. The resumption of militancy, however, seems to indicate that hardline views still prevail within decision-making circles.

The significance of the resumption of militancy is still an open question. It may simply be a negotiating tactic and the perceived need to pressurise New Delhi. It may also lead to the question of whether the Pakistani leadership, aware that it was in a bad cycle, has simply been trying to buy time from the very beginning of the peace process.[6] Although it certainly reflects the thinking from the part of the military, the intelligence community, and the Islamic organisations committed to "freeing" Kashmir from Hindu dominance, this may be too cynical a view. The debate over the future of the former princely state and Pakistan's policy has been real in Islamabad, with many concluding that, much to their regret, "India's position [had] been accepted by Pakistan," without any significant concession from New Delhi. In this case, the reasons for what could be considered a u-turn in Islamabad's position are still unclear and may in turn lead to the question of whether Pakistan has a clearly defined strategy regarding Kashmir.

Sustainability of the Peace Process

This situation raises the issue of the sustainability of the ongoing peace process, although it does not seem threatened in the short run, due to the international constraints on India, and even more on Pakistan, following the 1999, 9/11 and 2002 crises but also because of India's own aspirations to great power status which forces it to project the image of a responsible power.

Following the 1998 nuclear tests by India and Pakistan, Kashmir, which was until then considered a regional conflict without any major international consequence, became a concern for the international community. The stake was no less than the possibility of a nuclear conflagration in South Asia. For Pakistan, the possession of nuclear weapons was supposed to prevent India from engaging in a full conventional war, and the subsequent possibility to conduct a conflict, at a sub-conventional level, in Kashmir. Hence, Islamabad's support to the Mujahideen operating in the Kashmir Valley. For India, conventional war remains a possibility, up to a certain level of violence.

In such a context, the main difficulty was the assessment of the nuclear threshold of the enemy. Conventional escalation remained a theoretical option but the conflict spectrum, from terrorism to nuclear war through guerrilla warfare and conventional war, was reduced, in practice, to its extremes.

Such a dilemma was put to test twice, in 1999 and 2002. In 1999, US intervention and Chinese neutrality convinced Pakistan to withdraw its troops from the mountains over the city of Kargil, where regular and irregular elements had been infiltrated and were controlling the road between Leh and Srinagar. For the first time, nuclear weapons had played a major (although silent) role in a conflict in the Indian subcontinent. It also incidentally convinced India that, contrary to Pakistan's belief, the internationalisation of the Kashmir dispute would not necessarily be to its detriment.

The 2001-02 incident was preceded by another one of similar nature. When, after a series of terrorist attacks – one of them, on December 13, 2001, against the Indian Parliament in New Delhi – India mobilised its troops along the LoC and the international border with Pakistan, it could not ignore that none of the envisaged scenarios of limited conflict provided any guarantees against an escalation with possible nuclear implications. As India only has a limited strategic superiority in Kashmir, it could expect significant gains only by bypassing Kashmir and launching a conventional large scale operation. However, Pakistan's weakness inevitably raised the possibility that it may be tempted to use its nuclear weapons. The risk of paralysis of the conventionally dominant actor, India, led it to call indirectly on the international community (essentially the United States) to pressurise Pakistan and have the infiltration of militants in Kashmir stopped.

The two crises dramatically changed the international perception of the Kashmir issue. It could no longer be ignored or dismissed as merely a regional conflict without any potential global consequences. 9/11 only reinforced the international perception of the unacceptability of terrorism as a means of solving international disputes. Pakistan was marginalised and understood that international intervention in the Kashmir dispute would not necessarily work in its favour.

Although for different reasons and to an extent varying in degree, normalising relations became an imperative for both countries. Pakistan needs to rebuild its international image, shattered not only by the two above mentioned crises but also its support to the Taliban regime in Afghanistan, and focus on its domestic social, political and economic problems, whereas India, with global status aspirations, needs, although with much less urgency, to sustain the image of the responsible regional power it had demonstrated during the two crises. Getting out of the peace process is, therefore, not an option for either of the two countries.

However, the requirements from both of them are very different. India can attain its objectives by simply participating in the peace process without any real obligation of result. Whatever additional benefits it gets from it will be a gain but, even the continuation of terrorism, although unwelcome, will not affect its goals. Pakistan, on the contrary, needs to demonstrate a clear readiness to compromise on its previous claims in order to restore its international standing. Whatever the actual intentions of the Indian leadership, dialogue for India means, first and foremost, conflict management, whereas it means conflict resolution for Pakistan, although, as already described, the debate about the nature of this resolution is still going on. As this asymmetry of expectations determines, at each stage, an asymmetry of perception regarding the outcome, the risk is that one of the parties to the conflict could develop the impression that the other is reaping all the benefits. For the reasons mentioned above, this would not be sufficient to end the peace process but could potentially render it meaningless.

The Relationship Between the Local Population and the Indian Armed Forces

Pakistan's support to militancy does not exonerate India from all responsibilities. Relations between the Kashmiri civilian population and the Indian security forces have always been problematic. Ordinary people still feel caught between two guns and claim more and more openly that they have been deceived by both the militants and the Indian security forces. Few issues are as consensual across the entire local political spectrum as the condemnation of the heavy presence, and lack of respect for human rights, of the latter. The Indian security forces are for many the symbol of the "colonial" character of the Indian presence in Kashmir and, for Islamabad, give legitimacy to Pakistan's support to the Kashmiri cause and the militant struggle.

There have been endless debates on the number of Indian troops (both military and paramilitary) posted in the Valley and although their withdrawal would certainly be considered by most locals as the real first sign of New Delhi's willingness to solve the Kashmir issue, the point here is not to engage in a useless debate about numbers[7] but to discuss the adequacy of their response to the militancy with the objective of alienating it further from the population in the light of the decline of violence observed over the past two years.

This decline required that an attempt be made to satisfy some of the basic demands of the population and win them over. The Indian government tried to address partially the situation by disbanding some of the renegade units,[8] by trying to improve the training of the troops operating on the ground and bringing awareness of human rights issues among the military and paramilitary troops. As a result, the human rights situation has improved in the cities and the district capitals but remains disastrous in the rural areas.[9] Although violence from the militancy has declined, human rights violations by the Indian security forces have not been reduced to the same extent. The most immediate consequence is the central government's failure to capitalise on the fact that the population is tired of violence and sometimes willing to cooperate against militancy.

Too many interests are involved for violence to disappear overnight. Too many people have experienced the power of the guns to simply renounce it. Militancy justifies the presence of the Indian security forces. Both extort money from the population while politicians from all sides benefit from the uncertainty created by the situation. As a result, the security of ordinary citizens has improved only marginally in large parts of the region.

A Sceptical Kashmiri Population

The peace process remains, therefore, an abstraction for large segments of the Kashmiri population although the economic activity is improving. Tourism, (mostly of Hindu pilgrims) has resumed and benefits the people directly involved in the industry (craftmen, taxi drivers, hotel owners, etc.). The global economic situation of the state of Jammu and Kashmir has improved,[10] but scepticism still prevails. Besides the limited impact of the Muzaffarabad-Srinagar bus, decisions to open other inter-Kashmiri routes of communication are still awaited. A bus between Poonch and Rawalakot is planned and the modalities of the Amritsar-Lahore and Nankana Sahib-Amritsar bus services are currently being studied but these measures are perceived as mere promises. Some even doubt the economic rationale of trade between the two parts of Kashmir.[11]

The US$ 5 billion investment promised by Prime Minister Manmohan Singh on November 17, 2004, to improve the situation in Kashmir is too recent to be truly effective. Although work has started on some important infrastructure projects, measures affecting the day-to-day life of the local population such as the electrification of all villages will materialise only in 2007 at best. Moreover, despite improvement on the security front, industrial investment remains very unequal between the various parts of the state.[12]

Even when they benefit from it, many understand that that these economic measures have been taken to facilitate the integration of the state of Jammu and Kashmir within the Indian Union, but consider that, as welcome as it may be, the improvement of the economic situation can in no way be a substitute for a political solution of the conflict which, for many, if not the vast majority of the Kashmiris, can be only independence or a large amount of autonomy. The fact that out of the 24,000 jobs to be created, as announced by the prime minister in November 2004, 10,000 are in the security forces, added to the growing economic dependence vis-à-vis New Delhi,[13] makes many fear that Delhi may just be trying to expand its control over the state.

New Delhi and the Political Representation of the Kashmiris

Such scepticism is understandable given the last 18 years of mistrust and deception by the Kashmiris and the various central governments. It demonstrates that, no matter how successful Delhi's economic policies could be in the future, the Kashmir problem is and will remain primarily a political one. It also underlines the need to associate more closely the Kashmiri population to the peace process and, therefore, to identify its representatives.

The recent visits of the leaders of the moderate faction of the All Parties Hurriyat Conference (APHC) to Pakistan and their meetings with the Indian prime minister have raised a number of issues, the first of them being their representative character and the significance of the move. For a long period of time, New Delhi was reluctant to give the impression of recognising the APHC and did not want any interference by Pakistan in a dialogue which was essentially meant to be a track of negotiation independent of Pakistan. Pakistan itself had always been suspicious of an organisation it did believe to be ready to deal with the Indian central government, should circumstances allow, and was relying almost exclusively on the former leader of the Kashmiri Jamaat-i-Islami, Syed Ali Shah Geelani.

Following the surprisingly positive April meeting between Pervez Musharraf and Manmohan Singh, the authorisation given to APHC to travel to Pakistan could be interpreted as the sign of a real rapprochement between the two countries. Pakistan was not marginalised and in exchange let the dialogue be conducted between Pakistan and the APHC without interfering through *jihadi* groups. Such a position was almost a u-turn compared to the attitude which prevailed during the 2002 election campaign when one of the most prominent APHC leaders, Abdul Ghani Lone, had been assassinated, most probably on Islamabad's orders.

This development is no doubt a positive one. But it is not without risks for the internal situation in Kashmir. The agenda of the talks between Prime Minister Manmohan Singh and the moderate leaders of the APHC tends to dilute their specificity as compared to mainstream parties that have also always officially opposed the violations of human rights, demanded the release of political prisoners and asked for the withdrawal of the Indian security forces. Should the segment of the population, for whom independence is the only solution for Kashmir, feel betrayed[14] or simply no longer represented, they may be tempted by more radical groups, operating outside known political organisations. Such groups already exist. Observers in Srinagar describe the emergence of a strong undercurrent, particularly active among the Kashmiri youth.

Much of the challenge for the Indian authorities in the months and years to come will be to prevent the creation of a political vacuum which could potentially be filled by these emerging forces. It will also have to devise a mechanism by which the population will be associated with the peace process and be in a position to appropriate it rather than being a mere spectator.

Potential Consequences of the Earthquake on the Peace Process

Surprisingly, the massive earthquake which affected both the Pakistani and Indian sides of Kashmir and the Northwest Frontier Province on October 8, 2005, may give the peace process a new impetus. Within hours of the earthquake, Indian Prime Minister Manmohan Singh called Pakistani President Pervez Musharraf to offer humanitarian help, a gesture that the Pakistani president reciprocated with a similar offer for the victims in the Indian part of Kashmir, but Pakistan turned down the Indian offer of helicopters for rescue operations and ruled out rescue operations with India. Later on, however, Islamabad accepted Delhi's offer of tents, food, blankets and medicines[15] and a few days later, proposed to open the LoC.

Besides the welcome relief for the local populations, the move certainly carries a political dimension whose scope is still difficult to assess. The initial reluctance of the Pakistani authority to accept the Indian offer certainly shows that relations are not yet easy between the two countries but their later acceptance of the aid could have a tremendous impact on Pakistani public opinion. Joint relief effort should boost confidence and help bring people together. It will also show India as a benevolent power and make it undoubtedly more difficult in the future, for any Pakistani government, to demonise India for political purposes, should the temptation arise.

In the short-term, the earthquake should halt the ongoing infiltrations and weaken militant groups. Although it warned that it would not allow Indian troops to carry out relief work in the Pakistani part of Kashmir, the United Jihad Council announced a temporary truce in the devastated areas and set up several medical camps in Muzaffarabad.[16]

Like the overall population, militant movements have seen their ranks depleted by the earthquake. The Lashkar-e-Tayebba, for example, has admitted extensive damage to its infrastructure and the death of at least 70 of its cadres.[17] Other movements have also been affected. The destruction of the training camps in the Pakistani part of Kashmir and the Northwest Frontier Province, combined with the coming winter, may hinder their operations for some time. This does not constitute a guarantee that militant violence may not resume after a few months and may even reinforce the popularity of some militant organisations as they are participating in the rescue effort, but may create a new situation in which relief and reconstruction will prevail over political consideration and raise the cost of any renewed activism.

Conclusion

Over the past 10 years, India and Pakistan have, perhaps, never seemed so close to peace, but the peace process between the two countries remains undoubtedly extremely fragile. It has, so far, experienced no setbacks but there is still little incentive for the two countries to move forward. Issues such as Siachen, Sir Creek or even Baglihar and Wullar may be resolved but the core problem, Kashmir, is unlikely to be resolved any time soon. Despite the diplomatic and political space opened by the Indian prime minister, Kashmir still remains a zero sum game.

One could argue that the small steps of diplomacy which have so far characterised the peace process may ultimately lead to spectacular results. Yet, without any perspective for a quick resolution of the Kashmir issue, the most likely outcome for the months to come is a "cold peace". Short of a comprehensive peace, this would certainly be the most acceptable scenario but would only be the beginning of a new phase of unstable equilibrium.

At the same time, getting out of the peace process would prove too costly for either of the two actors to deliberately sabotage it. In that sense, the statement of Prime Minister Manmohan Singh and President Pervez Musharraf in Delhi, according to which the peace process is "irreversible", should still be understood as a commitment to the process and not to any particular outcome.

"It is normal for periods of energy and progress to alternate with episodes of slower activity,"[18] and frustrating as it may look, the present scenario would already be a success, should violence be stopped. This absence of violence alone would, by itself, be a positive development and would create a dynamic of its own, as the cost of resuming violence for the instigator of the hostilities increases each time. But despite the earthquake, and Pakistani reinsurance, there is no guarantee that violence will not resume at the end of the winter.

This necessitates renewed international vigilance. Despite the fact that Kashmir became an object of international concern due to the nuclear issue, the international community should not lose interest in it because of the CBMs adopted on the nuclear and missile issues. The agreement reached on (dealing with the pre-notification of flight testing of ballistic missiles) was not the first of its kind. The two countries had already in the past, put in place communication measures designed to prevent misunderstanding.

Finally, as stated by Teresita Schaffer, the main achievement of the past 18 months is perhaps the personal relationship the two leaders have developed over the last months.[19] This could be their most important asset if they want to achieve substantial results in the peace process but it will last only as long as they last in power. Political majorities are volatile, especially for the Indian prime minister who seems already isolated on the Indo-Pakistan issue within his own government. As for the Pakistani president, who is accountable to one and only one constituency, the army, the question is whether he has yet made up his mind as to where he ultimately wants to lead Pakistan.

Notes

1. Although one may observe that, as time passes, it will be increasingly costly for any of the two protagonists to resume violence.
2. See *Joint Statement India-Pakistan in New York,* September 14, 2005, http/::meaindia.nic.in/speech/2005/09/14js01.htm
3. *Joint Statement, Second Round of Expert Level Talks Between India and Pakistan on Conventional Confidence Building Measures*, New Delhi, August 8, 2005, http://meaindia.nic.in/speech/2005/08/08da01htm
4. Moreover, the vast majority of the divided families are not from the Valley but from Jammu.
5. Save our Kashmir, Al Nasreen, Al Afreen, Farazan-e-Islam, Al Mansoorah claim responsibility for most of the attacks perpetuated in the Valley but are only cover names for the organisations mentioned in the text.
6. *See India and Pakistan : Is Peace Real this Time, a Conversation Between Husain Haqqani and Ashley Tellis,* (Washington D.C. Carnegie Endowment for International Peace, 2004), p. 7.
7. Estimates about the number of troops in the Valley vary from 70,000 to more than a million, according to some separatist organisations.
8. Although many of their former members are now part of the police or other bodies of the Indian security fores.

9. A fact admitted even by some separatist leaders.
10. A fact recognised even by hardliners such as Syed Ali Shah Gilani.
11. Interview with Omar Abdullah, Srinagar, September 9, 2005.
12. Rs. 4 billion in Jammu but only Rs. 400 million in the Valley. Source: Jammu and Kashmir Chamber of Commerce and Industry.
13. From 47 per cent in 1973-74, this dependence rose to 86 per cent in 2001-02.
14. Such slogans were shouted at the Mirvaiz, Omar Farooq, when he came back from Delhi after the talks with the Indian prime minister.
15. http ://abcnews.go.com/International/wireStory/id=1199913
16. *Wall Street Journal*, October 12, 2005.
17. B. Raman, "Quake Impact on Jihadi Terrorism", South Asia Analysis Group, Paper No. 1573, October 12, 2005, http://www.saag.org/papers16/paper1573.html
18. Teresita Schaffer, "India and Pakistan : Still Moving Forward," *South Asia Monitor*, No.87, October 1, 2005.
19. Schaffer, Ibid.

India-Pakistan Bilateral Dynamics

Kapil Kak

More than seven years after Kargil, and a period of immensely strained and tense India-Pakistan bilateral environment that saw deployment of nearly a million and a half troops on their border during 2001-02, India-Pakistan relations have acquired a measure of stability. The India-initiated, US-facilitated and mutually evolved peace process appears largely on track. For not only has the November 2003 ceasefire along the Line of Control (LoC) – said to have been brokered by the United States – the first time in fourteen years remained inviolate, but the raft of positive gains flowing from the January 2004 Islamabad joint declaration and the composite bilateral dialogue have been palpable, notably at the people-to-people level.

India's rising profile as a responsible international player with enhanced 'hard' and 'soft' power, even as it remains the world's foremost victim of trans-national terrorism, has coincided with the transformed post-Cold War and post-9/11 global environment. Five years ago, the terrorist attacks on the Jammu and Kashmir (J&K) Assembly and India's Parliament (October 1, and December 13, 2001 respectively) – widely believed to have been planned and executed from across the border – began to make for a greater understanding by the world community on India's compulsion to defend its territorial integrity and the ideology of its polity.[1] And nuclearisation of the subcontinent and its attendant implications on the conflict spectrum have lent a new edge to the importance of strategic stability between India and Pakistan. The international community has, thus, become a key stakeholder in the ongoing peace process.

Worryingly, Pakistan continues to be mired in a malevolent and poisonous cultural mix of religious extremism, *jihadi* terrorism, sectarianism and ethnic separatism (in Balochistan) that has the potential to destabilise the country from within. These internal fault lines – and the morbid fear of India leveraging the same to pose a grave security threat – constitute a major factor in Pakistan's India policies. Cross-border terrorism remains one such arrow – perhaps the only leverage against India – in the quiver of the army-dominated establishment in that country, notwithstanding the recent improvements in bilateral relations.

Completion of three phases of the composite dialogue on a positive note, beginning of a fourth round and the many humanitarian confidence-building measures (CBMs) initiated – including cross-LoC connectivities and five meeting points – have brought relief to many divided families on both sides. Internally as well, Jammu and Kashmir has witnessed an improved environment. First, the people's faith in the democratic process and the perception of their empowerment to make or break governments and local bodies through free, fair and impartial elections has been greatly heightened. Second, a steep reduction in overall levels of violence in the state, witnessed since 2002, has brought about socio-economic revival and near normality. Third, New Delhi has demonstrated a persistent willingness to pursue the ongoing dialogue with moderate separatist groups and representatives of various regions, sub-regions and ethnic groups to evolve a mutually acceptable approach to resolve the issue of J&K – three round table conferences having been concluded with the unsurprising non-participation in the last two rounds by even the moderate Pakistan-supported Umar Farooq-led All Parties Hurriyat Conference.

The bilateral India-Pakistan track witnessed a near crisis on account of what has been widely perceived as Pakistan-sponsored and locally activated Mumbai train blasts of July 2006 that killed nearly 200 innocent commuters. Foreign secretary level talks were postponed, but thanks to the United Progressive Alliance (UPA) government's steadfastness and a shade of 'positive unilateralism', the dialogue process has since resumed. It would be too soon, however, to celebrate the transition of the situation from 'stability' to 'normality' as this is arguably "predicated not only on Pakistan's demonstrable renunciation of proxy war as a strategic tool and dismantling the terrorist infrastructure but in generating (greater) stability as precursor to bilateral normalization."[2]

This concluding chapter would attempt to explore and analyse the trends and pointers of global perspectives and regional imperatives on India-Pakistan dynamics. It would be necessary to evaluate Pakistan's domestic compulsions for the policy options its 'establishment' has had to generate in relation to India. Trend lines in the internalities of the J&K issue and how these affect both the India-Pakistan bilateral track and internal peace merit exploration and analysis. Lastly and importantly, an attempt would be made to analyse the problems and prospects of the ongoing bilateral peace process and how new pathways could be explored to make it not only irreversible but also self-sustaining and enduring for the future.

Global and Regional Impulses

Global and regional impulses that have served as drivers for the forward movement on the India-Pakistan bilateral track have been as numerous as these have been complex. In early 1999, Prime Minister Atal Bihari Vajpayee's decision to travel across the border, symbolically by bus, to sign the Lahore Peace Accord with Prime Minister Nawaz Sharif was internationally hailed as a statesmanlike and bold initiative. But as the former was to rue later: "The Lahore bus was diverted to Kargil." With over a decade-long export of terrorism to India by that time, Pakistan attempted to drive a bus through the concept of non-intervention in the internal affairs of a nation – the central pillar of the Westphalian nation-state – that was also reiterated in the 1972 Shimla Agreement. Islamabad sought to dangerously destabilise conventional and nuclear deterrence between the nuclear-armed neighbours, a development that would not remain unaddressed by a greatly concerned globalised and networked world, notably the great powers.

Indeed, the Kargil conflict triggered the somewhat grim descending bilateral spiral that was to last five long years. Far from the intended objective of helping focus on the so-called "freedom struggle" in J&K, Kargil served to unite the international community against Pakistan's military misadventure, thereby rendering the LoC sacrosanct. The stillborn Agra Summit, the Pakistan-sponsored attack on the J&K Assembly and then the potentially grave suicide attack on India's Parliament, said to have been masterminded by the Pakistan-based terrorist organisations, Jaish-e-Mohammed (JeM) and Lashkar-e-Tayyeba (LeT), exacerbated the situation. Global and regional concerns soared to a new high, as India's threshold of tolerance was perceived to have been breached yet again.

Mobilisation of India's army, navy and air force for a possible war in response to what Prime Minister Vajpayee then described as the attack "on our sovereignty, on our self-respect and a challenge to our democratic system" not only aimed to serve a notice directly to Pakistan to rein in support to cross-border terrorism or face the consequences of a war but also powerfully sought to nudge the international community to lean even more heavily on President Musharraf to change tack or be witness to the prospect of a regional conventional conflict under a nuclear overhang. As Frederic Grare argues in his chapter in this volume, "The crises of Kargil... attack on India's Parliament... and military mobilisation on the borders dramatically changed the international perspective of the severity of India-Pakistan problems as being no longer considered as part of a regional conflict but with immense global consequences." The main objective in the diplomatic forays of the key international players like the US, the European Union (EU) (notably Britain) and China – and to a lesser extent Japan and Russia – in the India-Pakistan dynamics has been to push the two countries towards stability in bilateral relations and, thus, obviate conflict that has politically worrisome nuclear dimensions.

Clearly, it was in response to this credible military challenge from India and the intense diplomatic pressure from the West that Musharraf made the historic address to his people on January 12, 2002, in which he promised to transform Pakistan into a moderate Muslim state: "There was to be no internal extremism and no safe haven for terrorists operating across Pakistan's borders." A joke making the rounds in Pakistan after the speech was that if the pious, Islamic Zia died in 1988, he was *finally buried* on January 12, 2002.[3] During another important speech on May 27, 2002, when faced again with imminent military actions by India, he repeated five times that Pakistan will never allow the export of terrorism from within Pakistan. At that time, Albert Camus' words applied to the Pakistani military leadership's dilemma so aptly: "In the best ordered life, a moment always comes when the scenery collapses." The year 2002 can, thus, be clearly identified as a turning point in Pakistan's security policy in relation to India in that it had to compulsorily lower the threshold of transnational violence in Jammu and Kashmir. This trend has sustained over nearly five years and is clearly reflected in the vastly improved situation on the ground in the troubled J&K state.

Evidently, Pakistan's strategic overreach and irresponsible adventurism in the realm of foreign policy through the use of the instrument of *jihad* has resulted in the country's diplomatic isolation. Hardly anyone, including China and the Islamic world, was willing to back Pakistan's position on Kashmir.[4] In a blow to Islamabad's counter-terrorism credentials, China for the first time publicly acknowledged the existence of terrorist camps within the territory of Pakistan. This was mentioned in official court documents relating to the trial of an Uighur prosecuted in Urumchi (Xinjiang) for terrorist activities and plotting to split the country.[5] Referring to his single-handed efforts to cool international temperatures against Pakistan, President Musharraf in February 2005 candidly admitted to Pakistan being faced with four accusations: "(a) All the terrorist activity in Afghanistan had its base in Pakistan; (b) all the freedom struggle in Indian held Kashmir was cross-border terrorism from Pakistan; (c) all the nuclear proliferation in the world has its source in Pakistan; and (d) Pakistan is an intolerant militant extremist society." Musharraf admitted to having "succeeded considerably but not sufficiently to project the reality of Pakistan as a progressive, moderate Islamic State."[6]

We need to remind ourselves that the US ambition and resolve to sustain a world order dominated by it and pursue *Pax Americana* through what it has termed "the war on global terrorism" with Pakistan's willing cooperation, saved the latter from being targeted initially. Today, the confidence deficit between the US and the international community, on the one hand, and Pakistan, on the other, continues to persist. "The US Quadrennial Review Report (2006) speaks of US prepartions to act in cases where a state that possesses WMD loses control of its weapons, especially nuclear devices. It is no secret that this a reference to Pakistan."[7]

Unambiguously reflecting anxieties on account of American pressures, years earlier, it was President Musharraf who had cited strategic assets and Kashmir policy as the primary drivers for his volte-face in turning against the Taliban in Afghanistan. Moreover, as Maleeha Lodhi, Pakistan's high commissioner to the UK, averred, "Globalisation is unleashing new dynamics and creating imperatives for cooperation, reshaping Pakistani and Indian perceptions."[8] Thus, normalisation of relations with India, an emerging global power that is also the strategic partner of the world's sole superpower, is far more important for Pakistan today than it was in the early years of its life as an independent state. The US perceives a palpably democratic, multi-cultural and economically and militarily strong India in the context of the spectacular rise of China and worldwide upsurge in Islamic extremism. Not to contain China, but as a soft balancer that can "exert a moderating influence on the polices of both China and Pakistan."[9]

For the first times since independence, India's bilateral relations with each of the great powers and important countries have never been as close as these are today. For Pakistan, besides international isolation, an economic situation that has the potential to run aground and a near domestic turmoil have compelled it to make a temporary peace with India. The deployment of nearly 80,000 troops on its western border has added to its discomfiture and is indicative of the regional compulsions Pakistan faces. Even the army is aware of India's growing strategic and economic power and Pakistan's relative decline, which appear to have prompted the decision to soften Pakistan's position on Kashmir. Unsurprisingly, evolving a convergent vision for a future of peace and cooperation for the entire region becomes an imperative for both sides, and constitutes a great challenge for both countries.

Afghanistan could prove a testing ground, as it is currently witness to the resurgence and regrouping of the Taliban in the southern and eastern regions, marginalisation of anti-Pakistan forces, and vastly increased clout of warlords at the cost of the India-backed Karzai regime in Kabul. The fluid and uncertain security situation in Islamabad is indeed an unsettling prospect for all the global and regional stakeholders, except possibly the army establishment, for which an unstable Afghanistan is the next best option after one dominated by Pakistan, the worst option being an Afghanistan under India's influence. Traditional notions of Afghanistan providing strategic depth to Pakistan and any increase in India's influence in the former being an inverse function of the latter's security appear somewhat archaic today. A stable Afghanistan at peace with its neighbours is in the security interests of both India and Pakistan, and both need to evolve a *modus vivendi*.

There appears little doubt that India persuaded itself to show greater flexibility in its approach to Pakistan as evidenced by Vajpayee's highly symbolic speech from the soil of J&K state at the Sher-e-Kashmir Cricket Stadium at Srinagar on April 18, 2003, when he offered India's hand of friendship to Pakistan yet again. The earlier insistence on there being no prospects of talks without Pakistan putting an end to cross-border terrorism stood obviously dropped. The changed posture resulted not only from the gentle nudges of the US and the EU but was the result of a confidence flowing from: (a) a successful coercive military mobilisation; (b) universally acclaimed free elections for the J&K Legislative Assembly; (c) sharp decline in levels of militancy; and (d) commencement of talks on the issue of J&K with elected representatives and moderate separatist elements.

Pakistan's Internal Fault Lines: Impact on Peace Process

In the evolution of a framework for cooperative bilateralism with India, Pakistan's domestic compulsion – flowing from its internal fault lines – would invariably influence the outcome. This has been a notable feature of the post-Zia-ul-Haq era of "Islamisation" and the well known military-Mujahideen nexus that has for long been substantial, endemic and deep-rooted and has only recently come under strain. Notwithstanding the change in mindset of large sections of the public in both countries towards each other and a slew of CBMs that have been introduced, many raise the questions of whether the ongoing peace process constitutes a tactical pause of convenience or is it a genuine transformation in Pakistan's India policy? This is because Pakistan is perceived by many as embarked on a dual policy: continuance with talks, CBMs and other measures, with simultaneous assistance to *jihadi* terrorists in J&K and elsewhere, at least at a threshold that compels India to make concessions. A similar dualism is evident in Afghanistan: provide clandestine support to the Taliban and undertake operations against it as an important constituent of the North Atlantic Treaty Organisation (NATO) coalition! For it is believed that if "Musharraf acts too forcefully against the Pashtun tribal groups, he risks a political backlash and perhaps even an Islamic coup."[10] It is the fear of this worst-case scenario – implausible as it actually appears on the ground – that drives the support of the US State Department and the bulk of the Western world for the military leadership in Pakistan.

It would be useful to recall that it was during the East Pakistan crisis (1971) that a nexus between the Pakistan Army and the fundamentalists was created and this has continued ever since. The Jamaat-i-Islami organised the infamous terrorist groups Al Badr and Al Shams to kill Bengali nationalists during the liberation movement in East Pakistan.[11] The army's role was redefined as the defender of Pakistan's ideological frontiers. To the surprise of many, Ahmediyas were declared a non-Muslim minority through a 1974 legislation during the premiership of a liberal, not so religious-minded Zulfiquar Ali Bhutto. But it was during the tenure of Zia-ut-Haq as president that Jamaat-i-Islami cadres were mobilised in strength; extremist groups, which subscribed to the belief that *jihad* against non-Muslims was mandatory, were encouraged; and, sectarian Sunni-Shia conflict received a major boost. "Pakistan's fundamentalist parties exported Deobandi *Wahabi* ideology to Afghanistan and India's J&K, both of which were earlier largely free from such ideological currents... The nexus between the military and Mujahideen that had taken shape during Zia-ul-Haq's regime has been carried forward and strengthened during the Musharraf regime. The Pakistani state has been completely identified with religion as interpreted by one school of Islam."[12]

Terrorist organisations banned under US/Western pressure quickly re-surface under different names, without any action by the authorities. Narcotics trafficking, large scale money laundering and diffusion of weapons and small arms into society – the oxygen of terrorism – have not been curbed in any meaningful way. Transnational terrorism as an extension of politics (and war) by other means is perceived across the political spectrum as the only real leverage against India. This perhaps explains the establishment's wariness in dismantling the infrastructure of *jihadi* terrorism against India. The strategy for sub-conventional war, evolved initially in Afghanistan and replicated later in J&K, is founded primarily on religious extremism. The underlying characteristic is the belief that the political system of Makkah and Medina of 1,400 years ago should be emulated today in every detail. A serious side effect of Pakistan's transformation into the epicentre of global Islamic extremism and militancy has been the cancerous growth of inter-sectarian violence. There are concerns that the Pakistani state is fast losing its internal sovereignty to the radical Islamic groups.

The rise of Islamic fundamentalism in Pakistan has had serious implications for social and political stability in the region and a highly volatile impact on relations among communities adhering to different faiths.[13] Its impact has been experienced even on the Indian side of the LoC through heightened inter-regional tensions between the provinces of Kashmir, Jammu and Ladakh that run counter to the historical, pluralistic, accommodative and secular tradition in J&K. But there is seemingly a positive underside to the situation in Pakistan. As Stephen Cohen has observed, "Despite the rise of sectarian violence and the better performance of the Islamic and religious parties, there is no 'green wave' washing over Pakistan; most for its citizens remain devout Muslims but are not attracted to Islamic extremism."[14] Perhaps, in the long-term timeline of 15-20 years or so, this silver lining could augur well for vastly improved India-Pakistan bilateral relations and prevalence of peace, stability and tranquillity in the subcontinent.

In the medium term, concerns persist on the deep-rooted linkages between the military and the Mujahideen on common convictions and strategic interests, notably with regard to Kashmir and Afghanistan. First, as evidenced by the success of the coalition Muttahida-Majlis-e-Amal (MMA) in the last (2002) elections, the army exploits the Mujahideen for its competition with the mainstream political parties like the Pakistan Muslim League (Nawaz) and People's Party of Pakistan (PPP). The Mujahideen are perceived as an effective answer to the recent Nawaz Sharif-Benazir Bhutto joint promulgation of the charter of democracy. Still, serious efforts are reportedly being made to seal a deal with Benazir Bhutto for her return to politics on the condition she supports Musharraf's presidency "in uniform" and an institutionalised role for the army in Pakistan's policy. There are also pointers in the recent past of a growing unease among Pakistan's religious parties and organisations over President Musharraf's efforts to marginalise them under growing international pressure to contain violent extremist-religious forces that threaten not only regional peace and security, notably that of India, Pakistan and Afghanistan, but beyond the Indian subcontinent as well.

Second, the army's need for the so-called freedom fighters in Kashmir is met by the Mujahideen – a compulsion that helps sustain a working relationship. The Jamaat-i-Islami has a pronounced hawkish stand on Kashmir while the Jamiat-e-Ulema-e-Islam is said to be far more focussed on Afghanistan. On the other hand, the Jamaat-ul-Dawa provides the terrorist cadres through its militant arm, the LeT. Third, the *madrassas* serve as a catchment area for helping raise the pitch of "Islam in danger," sustaining cross-border terrorism – albeit at relatively lower levels – and in neutralising the fragile democratic forces. In a chilling development, the post-October 2005 earthquake in Pakistan occupied Kashmir (PoK) witnessed how the army permitted and encouraged cadres of the LeT to undertake relief work, a decision that served to provide legitimacy and socialisation to a banned terrorist organisation. Fourth, the army has in the past "not only used the threat of India as the pretext to browbeat the people of Pakistan into submission but also manipulated domestic politics to perpetuate itself in power... It is a ruling class in the Marxian sense of the term with definite interests to safeguard."[15] Today, virtually all the national assets such as authorities, corporations and government departments are under the thumb of some 500 military officers masquerading as civilians.[16] These perquisites of power can only increase in the future as the military's domination in setting domestic and external agendas is unlikely to diminish in the years ahead, regardless of the recent agitations following the sacking of Pakistan's Chief Justice. "The absence of a serious challenge strengthens the military's power, which, in turn, further weakens civilian institutions."[17]

An important question that merits an answer is: what are the prospects for continuance of the army's direct role in politics, the military-Mujahideen nexus, and the internal reform process – all of which will have a bearing on the irreversibility of the India-Pakistan peace process? Pakistan's psycho-pathological quest for parity with India persists and the frustration would only increase – with the gap widening still more – as the latter's far larger economy sustains a Gross Domestic Product (GDP) growth of 8 per cent or more in the years ahead. Despite having lost its influence in Afghanistan and the commercial-strategic pitch in Central Asia, continued US support – a carrot and stick mix – would be predicated to Pakistan's effective assistance in the war against Al Qaida-Taliban. As for China, for its own strategy vis-à-vis both the US and India, its support to Pakistan is unlikely to waver and may well enhance as China assumes the status of a global giant. The other important world players, Russia, the EU and Japan have also, through diplomatic moves, sought to nudge Pakistan away from the extremist-religious and terrorism-oriented path it has tended to follow.

Distrust of India and intolerance for diversity at home make reforms of institutions a questionable option. Given the fragility of mainstream democratic forces and civil society – a free Press in this information age notwithstanding – the army has shown no signs of abandoning its parasitic role. To quote *The Economist*:

> ..in his seven long years in office, he (Musharraf) has insinuated the army into every nook and cranny of Pakistani public life, weakening institutions that were feeble already.... A nuclear-armed Pakistan, intertwined with a chaotic and Taliban-dominated Afghanistan is not a settling prospect. It has all happened

> before, of course. The result was September 11th , swiftly followed by a terrorist attack in Delhi that came close to starting a full-scale war between Pakistan and India.[18]

From the foregoing arguments, it would be realistic to infer that the grammar of uncertainty in India-Pakistan relations, thus, lies deeply anchored in Pakistan's internalities. With the economy no longer under a severe strain as it was when the army coup took place, and international aid flowing generously, only very high levels of external and domestic-societal pressure could compel an internal rethink.

To be sure, only a politically stable Pakistan that has high stakes in its socio-economic growth and development in a genuinely peaceful and tranquil environment can distance itself from providing refuge to terrorists and sponsoring their activities across its borders. As to the peace process, the limitations imposed by Pakistan's internal problems are obvious. "There can be no lasting solution to the Kashmir problem till such time there is full and effective civilian control over the Pakistan Army."[19] In this context, Stephen Cohen offers an insightful perspective:

> Pakistan's military leaders must come to a better understanding of the new international environment and a more objective assessment of India, as well as Pakistan's own deep structural and social problems. Pakistan is a case in which an excellent army depends upon a failing economy, a divided society, and unreliable politicians. The army lacks the the political system, the opportunity to learn and grow; its tolerance for the mistakes of others is very low, yet its performance, when in power, has usually dug the hole deeper.[20]

In the recent past, Pakistan's internalities have shown two widely devergent trends. At one level, there are signs of a glimmer of promise. Landlords are more able to keep rural *mullahs* in check, selective changes in extremist-oriented government-cleared educational textbooks on the refrain of India-as-the-enemy are in the offing, *madrassas* are sought to be brought under closer supervision, and the media are being increasingly accessed. These developments augur well for improved India-Pakistan bilateral ties. To quote *The Economist* again, "Pakistan's beleaguered liberals are hoping for a cultural return from the Middle East, where General Zia dragged them." According to Khalid Ahmed, a thoughtful Pakistani journalist: "If we lost our culture through Talibanism in the west (of the country), we can get it back from India, where our culture is still alive." The flip side, however, is worrisome. With the war in Afghanistan having spilled over – militarily and ideologically – into Pakistan, the country is getting increasingly Talibanised. The Pakistan Army appears unable to control the *jihadi* forces on its side of the Durand Line, compelling the NATO-led forces to initiate hot pursuit, including aerial attacks which further inflame anti-American and anti-Musharraf sentiment within Pakistan. The army's unwillingness to take measures against *jihadi* elements who have illegally occupied buildings in the heart of Islamabad to police society as a moral brigade upholding the Islamic way of life is a reflection of this worrisome domestic trend in Pakistan.

Peace Process: The Internal J&K Track

Ironically enough, India's military mobilisation on the LoC and border with Pakistan in the winter of 2001-02 served to create an appropriate ground environment for successful conduct of the universally-acclaimed free and fair elections to the State Assembly in 2002. Braving the Pakistan-sponsored terrorists' bullets that killed over 700 political workers, the people's participation and faith in the democratic process and the perception of their empowerment to make or break governments and local bodies (in subsequent municipal elections) has been greatly heightened. Implicit in the perspective is "the expression of faith in the policy of the democratic idiom to unleash sufficient political energy and imagination to help find a solution to the Kashmir problem."[21] It needs to be underscored that separatist sections that have kept themselves away from elections since 1989 are yet to become part of the electoral process. The representative strength of separatists of all hues – moderate as also hardline – merits careful evaluation. Rough assessments by political pundits suggest that in free, fair and impartial elections, their number in the 87-member J&K Assembly is unlikely to exceed 15. Could that be the reason for even the moderate separatists shying away from elections? Or are they testing the waters to seek a tentative political outcome that enables them to join the fray in October 2008 when elections are due next?

A distinct trend of reduction in salient parameters of terrorist violence is also evident. Specifically, the daily total rate of killings, including civilians, security forces and militants, came down from 10 in 2003 to 7 in 2004 to 5 in 2005 to a little over 3 in 2006.[22] This trend has sustained over the first quarter of 2007 as well. It would be useful to recall that terrorist violence had been likewise brought firmly under control in 1993-94 and 1997-98 but regrettably these successes were not leveraged by way of a political breakthrough – mistakes that should advisedly not be repeated.

The reopening of the Srinagar-Muzaffarabad and Poonch-Rawalakot bus services has been widely welcomed not only in J&K but internationally as well. A bilateral agreement is now in place to also utilise the Srinagar-Muzaffarabad route for cross-LoC trade. Pakistan's long delayed acquiescence for opening the Kargil-Skardu route for reestablishing the age-old links between Ladakh and Kargil, on the one hand, and Gilgit and Skardu, on the other, is indeed a welcome development. "New ideas are emerging to enhance cooperation in areas like education, health and disaster management on both sides of the LoC."[23]

All these measures and ongoing initiatives, together with the near four-year-long ceasefire on the LoC and return of quasi-normalcy, have whetted the people's yearning for lasting and enduring peace. Yet contradictions stare one in the face: even as "mainstream political parties hold large and impressive rallies, big processions of mourners still accompany dead bodies of militants." Alienation of a sizeable percentage of the population in the Valley, emanating from resentment against the centre, anger over violation of human rights, dilemmas on religious trends and lack of employment opportunities, constitutes a major challenge to the centre and the state government.

Kashmir's social landscape has also witnessed "a sweeping crisis in the criss-crossing of different political ideologies and a shift towards a new Islamic orthodoxy." Seminaries and *madrassas* influenced by the Deobandi school of thought ("preaching pure, intrinsic Islam") have came up in hundreds, thanks to the influence of trends across the border and LoC, and look down upon the Sufi-dominated orientation of Kashmiris being "antithetical to the spirit of monotheistic Islam." Dominant religious and political movements from the Tablighi Jamaat (an offshoot of the Deobandi school) to the politico-religious secessionist group Jamaat-i-Islami, the chief propagator of Deobandi thought in Kashmir, continue their sweep.[24] The Jamaat Ahl-e-Hadith, from which the LeT is said to draw its ideological beliefs, claims over a million followers in the state. There have been terrorist attacks on renowned mystic Sufis, and leaders of the syncretic Barelvi sects.

The unchecked growth of the Valley's religious right that forcibly seeks to impose reactionary moral codes on society has ominous implications for the India-Pakistan peace process and the way Jammu and Kashmir moves forward. Similar trend lines of a different hue are visible in Jammu and Ladakh as well. As a counter-movement, there has also been a renewed upsurge for a return to the uniquely syncretic and moderate Kashmiriyat so deeply ingrained in the Valley's psyche by its renowned sages-philosophers Sheikh-ul-Alam Sheikh Noorddin Noorani (Nunda Rishi) and Lal Ded

(Lalleshwari). The trend of reassertion and rejuvenation of moderate, secular and inclusive forces is a welcome development not only for the state but for India-Pakistan relations as well. Such moderate and inclusive forces must prevail, for religious orthodoxy and extremism carry with them the seeds of perpetual conflict, turbulence and violence. The duly elected political representatives of the people, civil society activists and academics need to actively support the positive forces that have a huge potential to thwart the efforts of hardliner elements across the border/LoC that have caused bloodshed and mayhem in J&K for 18 years.

Contrary to received wisdom, J&K is not a socio-economic problem. First, the unemployment/underemployment figures as also literacy levels match the national level. Second, only 6.25 per cent of the population is below the poverty line against the national average of 26 per cent. Although socio-economic inequities are sharp, it is said to have the second highest per capita income among all the states in India. J&K also has the second highest government employees to population ratio in the country. Third, the power situation, like in the rest of India is far from satisfactory – the position being particularly acute for people in the Valley during the freezing cold of the winter months. Lastly, perhaps, enhanced levels of electrification and broadband information technology (IT) services for expanded job opportunities could be the thrust areas for development along with a mission-mode approach for time-bound completion of railway projects into the Valley, construction of the old Shopian-Bilfalaz-Rajauri Mughal road, as an alternative to the national highway across the Banihal Pass, as also a third alternative road to Ladakh. While these socio-economic thrusts are doubtless important, approaches to meet the people's genuine political aspirations are equally, if not more, important. The crux of the problem is the need for the removal of inequities through a politically-driven strategy. For it has rightly been said that a substantial part of the Indian security establishment remains wedded to the idea that the separatists can be sidelined through economic development, job creation and greater accountability in the bureaucracy. Few are willing to see that a political reconciliation needs to come first.[25]

The series of Prime Minister Manmohan Singh-initiated round table conferences were aimed to identify sources of the people's alienation, overcome the trust deficit and psychologically reintegrate the state with India. These conferences, the third of which concluded in April 2007, have breathed life in the dialogue process of the internal dimension of the peace process. Four of the five working groups set up to recommend (a) CBMs across segments of society; (b) strengthening relations across the LoC; (c) economic development of J&K; and (d) ensuring good governance in the state have made comprehensive, grassroots oriented and creative sets of recommendations. Provision of an oversight body to ensure coordination and fast track implementation of the recommendations should prove useful. However, the report of the fifth working group on the more complex question of recommending a new mode of centre-J&K state relations is still awaited.

Zero tolerance for human rights violations recommended by two of the working groups, strengthening the State Human Rights Commission, review and revocation of the Armed Forces Special Powers Act, effective implementation of the Right to Information Act, opening up of half-a-dozen more travel routes across the LoC and recognition of the rights of Kashmiri Pundit migrants to return to their places of original residence, among many other proposals, have the potential to reverse alienation, provide a measure of reconciliation for people devastated by the near two-decade-long terrorist violence and indirectly provide a positive momentum to the India-Pakistan bilateral peace process track.

Bilateral Peace Process: Prospects and Problems

At this early stage of the peace process, the substance and pace of the bilateral CBMs under consideration and in the offing – especially those specific to Jammu and Kashmir – along with the Government of India's dialogue with the Kashmiri political leadership for relegitimising the political process and exploring creative solutions, constitute the key to a forward movement. It is the inter-relational dynamics of the two tracks that would shape future bilateral relations, with the composite dialogue, joint commission and the joint terror mechanism (unsurprisingly much maligned by some in both countries) serving as effective frameworks to discuss and resolve intractable issues and bring about the much-needed transformation.

For the first time since independence, there is room for guided optimism on account of the marginal but perceptible reduction in the overhang of distrust. A certain degree of calm characterises the larger relationship. And the prospects of achieving the Holy Grail of stability prior to normalisation of relations on a good neighbourly foundation have indeed brightened. The spoiler in the process remains Pakistan's employment of transnational terrorism, the only leverage against India, which the former has shown no signs of jettisoning. As India's Foreign Secretary Shiv Shankar Menon averred: "We have stressed to Pakistan that the success of the dialogue precess is predicated to Pakistan fulfilling its commitment not to permit any territory under its control to be used to support terrorism in any manner."[26]

Thoughful, liberal-minded and forward-looking elements in the establishments and societies of both countries recognise the need for evolving policy choices and creative initiatives for a constructive engagement to secure an enabling environment to meet the national security objectives of continued and rapid social and economic growth and development of their people. India and Pakistan have to fight together the common enemies of poverty, religious extremism, international terrorism, energy insecurity and ecological and environmental challenges. Both sides need to underscore the salience of deeper and sustained engagement and continuance of the across-the-board, multi-level and multi-point dialogue even in the expected absence of big-ticket breakthroughs and in the face of risk of emergence of wild cards. The Mumbai train blasts of August 2006 serve as one example. As the Samjhauta Express incident later so vividly demonstrated, in this terrorist attack, India and Pakistan were both targets of forces determined to derail the peace process. Similar spoilers could emerge in the future as well; such contingencies need to be factored into the dialogue calculus.

There is need for the two countries to demonstrate greater flexibilities and willingness to offer mutual concessions – not necessarily in equal measure by both – to settle less intractable bilateral issues. Delineation of the maritime boundary at Sir Creek and resolution of the Tulbul Navigation/Wullar Barrage and Siachen issues fall in this category. As for Sir Creek, under United Nations Commission for Law of Seas (UNCLOS) stipulations, the two countries would forfeit claims over extended exclusive economic zones in the event the maritime boundary issue in the Arabian Sea remains unresolved by 2009.

Siachen could also lend itself to expeditious resolution if the Indian defence establishment sacrificed its somewhat overcautious and inflexible operational-level perspectives at the altar of more valuable strategic gains. An icy wasteland, this glacier has no strategic value by way of military, political or economic significance. Insistence on Pakistan authenticating Indian Army deployments in this disputed sector prior to redeployment on the plea that the Pakistan Army may surreptitiously occupy the vacated Saltoro ridge along the actual ground position line is tantamount to self-deterrence. Maps/satellite images of Indian deployments could be published worldwide, including Pakistan, to project to the international community the factual deployment. In any event, given Pakistan's past track record, including Kargil, what prevents its army from occupying positions vacated by India even after it authenticates these in a Siachen agreement?

The aforementioned flexibilities and mutual concessions, duly calibrated, would serve to generate confidence and strengthen the peace-with-India constituencies in Pakistan against the radical Islamists who reject the peace process as "Musharraf's U-turn," "surrender" or "national humiliation." A jointly conceived and planned peace park-cum-glaciological studies centre alluded to by Prime Minister Manmohan Singh during his visit to Leh in June 2005, could be a good way forward until the finalisation of the border/LoC in this sector is mutully resolved. It is to be hoped that the proposed park would include both the Saltoro and Baltoro ridges. India's show of flexibility would strengthen the Pakistani establishment in this delicate phase of the peace process for the leadership there to signal to the *jihadi* groups that Islamabad has achieved something. This, of course, raises the larger question of whether Musharraf can bring all the stakeholders amongst the domestic constituencies on board the peace process, notably on Kashmir.

For India, adoption of a multi-layered approach towards encouraging the fledgling civil society in Pakistan by extensive people-to-people, socio-cultural academic, educational, tourism and economic linkages would create the appropriate critical mass. This is particularly so for the Pakistani heartland of Punjab and Sindh because 40 per cent of the terrorists in India belong to these provinces, and over the years 90 per cent of the visa seekers are said to be from Sindh. As India takes the lead in these initiatives, it must simultaneously sustain diplomatic moves in directions that ensure there is a calibrated international strategy to put the onus of making and bolstering peace squarely on Pakistan, ending violence being the prerequisite.

On the vexed issue of Jammu and Kashmir, President Musharraf's proposal envisages division of Jammu and Kashmir into "distinct" regions followed by demilitarisation and self-governance (presumably in PoK and Northern Areas as well) and joint India-Pakistan management of the state. Prime Minister Manmohan Singh, in turn, at the inauguration of the Amritsar-Nankana Sahib bus service on March 24, 2006, proposed making borders irrelevant towards making them "just lines" on a map, people on both sides of the LoC being able to move freely and trade with one another, and people of the two parts of J&K, with active encouragement of the Governments of India and Pakistan working out cooperative and consultative mechanisms so as to maximise the gains of cooperation in solving problems of socio-economic development of the region.[27] Clearly, such a declaratory congruence that seeks end of violence, making borders irrelevant and focusses on issues of political devolution/autonomy/self-governance marks a policy shift in the right direction and has tremendous potential to be mutually acceptable to a vast majority of stakeholders in both India, Pakistan and the two parts of J&K across the LoC.

In working out the broad concepts and elements on the ground, the devil, however, could be in the details. Demilitarisation cannot imply forsaking the sovereign right to deploy forces in one's territory, even as the Government of India is committed to a phased reduction and movement out of security forces from the state commensurate with elimination of Pakistan-supported terrorist violence. Also, given the thin line that separates 'religion' and 'region' in J&K, within the all-encompassing heterogeneity, pluralism and mutual accommodation, creation of new regions would create enthno-religious fault lines that are presently absent. Moreover, while joint cooperative and consultative mechanisms would be a highly desirable and feasible proposition, stretching this to joint political management that erodes sovereignty but may not undermine it, is unlikely to find acceptance in India. For the forty-odd seemingly well-reasoned solutions to J&K all envisage India having to make concessions and reduce the magnitude of its political control.

The challenge for political leaders engaged with the peace process is to segregate the political and territorial dimensions of the demand for self-determination and work toward safeguarding the political rights of the people of J&K. Most important, territorial independence of J&K will not "resolve the Kashmir problem because it it not supported by *all the people of the state*" (emphasis in original).[28] Having two autonomous entities of Jammu and Kashmir and PoK, including the Northern Areas, straddling the LoC with mutually guaranteed inter and intra-regional politico-economic decentralisation could be one way forward. Devolution of power to district level, with *halqa majlis (gram sabhas)* at the grassroots, integrated with trade and economic dividends, would serve to challenge the insurgent and the malcontent in J&K. A detailed and workable devolutionary model on these lines has been developed and proposed by India's Information Commissioner Wajahat Habibullah, a former J&K cadre Indian Administrative Service officer. In addition, hassle-free movement of people – not necessarily divided family members – unhindered trade and commerce, and mutual cooperative mechanisms on issues of ecology, forestry, water resources, energy, tourism, disaster management, etc under a jointly-conceived Regional Council of elected representatives from the respective sides, functioning under a central apex-level India-Pakistan Council, could be yet another gainful pathway ahead. Given the political will and determination to resolve highly complex problems, many creative and meaningful options could be pursued along this broad line of approach.

On the issue of increased bilateral trade and economic linkages, India and Pakistan have a long and challenging journey ahead, more specifically in the South Asian Association of Regional Cooperation (SAARC). It has remained mired in bureaucracy, unjustified mistrust and under-exploitation of intra-SAARC trade which today is less than 2 per cent of GDP in contrast to East Asia's healthy 20 per cent. Given their market size, India, Pakistan and Bangladesh have a key economic role in moving SAARC forward, with India's recent economic successes perceived as providing huge opportunities in the region. Mutual economic cooperation by India and Pakistan would help reach the goal of an eventual South Asian Economic Union by 2020, starting with a South Asian Free Trade Area by 2010, and a Customs Union by 2015, all of which already stand delayed. These were the recommendations of a report, *SAARC Vision Beyond the Year 2020*, prepared by a Group of Eminent Persons set up in 1998.

India-Pakistan trade through official channels has doubled in recent years to $1 billion, with the informal trade (read cross-border smuggling and through third countries) touching $3 billion. India's extension of most favoured nation status to Pakistan has yet to be reciprocated. Clearly, the opportunity of rapid economic growth in India and Pakistan needs to be leveraged for open borders, increased trade, investment and economic relations, and promotion of economic integration. Such a framework would doubtless create mutual inter-dependencies, enlarge constituencies of peace on both sides of the border and develop vested interests in each other's security and prosperity.

Conclusion

Since the mutally agreed ceasefire on the LoC of November 2003, India-Pakistan relations have acquired a measure of sustained stability, four phases of the composite dialogue having been completed on a positive note. Diplomatic forays of key international players like the US, the EU (notably Britain) and China – and to a lesser extent Japan and Russia – have helped bring about this outcome. For the first time since independence, India's bilateral relations with each of the great powers, including China and to an extent Pakistan, have never been as close as these are today. In contrast, there is a distinct confidence deficit between the international community and Pakistan. Its domestic turmoil, crises in Balochistan and Waziristan, and deployment of nearly 80,000 troops on the Afghan border seem to have compelled it to make peace with India even as people on both sides of the border are increasingly demystifying the myth of the 'other' and forging closer people-to-people linkages. The rise of Islamic extremism in Pakistan, the army's unwillingness to abandon its parasitic and predatory political role and that of transnational terrorism as an instant of

India-related security policy continue to have the potential to serve as a powerful spoiler in the peace process.

Concurrently, a distinct downward trend in salient parameters of terrorist violence in J&K, combined with cross-LoC CBMs and vastly increased people-to-people linkages, have imparted a fresh dynamism to improved India-Pakistan relations. The leadership on both sides has recognised the need to evolve policy choices and creative initiatives for finding a common ground on long-unresolved bilateral issues, including J&K. Significantly, President Musharraf's proposals and Prime Minister Manmohan Singh's specific ideas, that seek to end violence, make borders irrelevant and focus on issues of political devolution/autonomy/self-governance mark a policy shift that would be acceptable to a vast majority of stakeholders in both India, Pakistan and the two parts of J&K across the LoC. Successes here would doubtless enhance the potential of the peace process to become irreversible. In addition, leveraging the opportunity of rapid economic growth in India and Pakistan for open borders, increased trade and investment and promotion of regional economic integration would pay rich bilateral dividends. Creation of such inter-dependencies would enlarge constituencies of peace, security, stability and prosperity – the real Holy Grail of the ongoing peace process.

Notes

1. Kapil Kak, "Changing Parameters of Cross-Border Terrorism," in Ajay Darshan Behera and Mathew Joseph, eds., *Pakistan in a Changing Strategic Context* (New Delhi: Knowledge World, 2004), p.240.
2. Kak, Ibid.
3. Stephen Philip Cohen, *The Idea of Pakistan* (New Delhi:Oxford University Press, 2005), p.92.
4. In his chapter in this volume, Sushant Sareen has convincingly argued how the whole world tended to shun Pakistan and was not inclined to back it on the Kashmir issue. This indeed is a seminal change that is likely to stay immutable for decades ahead unless New Delhi yet again fritters away the opportunities that beckon on both the India-Pakistan and New Delhi-Srinagar tracks.
5. Press Trust of India news report in *The Indian Express*, April 20,2007, p.10.
6. Malini Parthasarathy refers to these accusations quoting President Pervez Musharraf's website "From the President's Desk" in her chapter in this volume, "Engaging Pakistan: From the NDA to the UPA."
7. K. Subrahmanyam, "A Case of Sour Grapes," *The Times of India*, May 3, 2006, p.28.
8. Maleeha Lodhi, "Nuclear Cloud Over South Asia," *The Times of India*, May 3, 2006, p.28.
9. Hussain Haqqani, "Dialogue Needs a Common Language," *The Indian Express*, April 6, 2006, p.9.

10. "Pakistan, America's Limited Partner," Editorial in *The Boston Globe*, March 1, 2007, reproduced in *The Indian Express*, March 2,2007, p.10.
11. Kalim Bahadur, "Regional Implications of the Rise of Islamic Fundamentalism in Pakistan," *Strategic Analysis*, January-March 2006, p.13.
12. Bahadur, Ibid., pp.16-17.
13. Bahadur, Ibid., p.9.
14. Cohen, n.3, p.12.
15. Satish Kumar, "Reassessing Pakistan as a Long-Term Security Threat," Public Lecture No.7, CPR Lecture Series 2002-03, Centre for Policy Reserch, New Delhi, pp.8-9.
16. M. Iliyas Khan, "Manufacturing a Mandate," *Herald*, May 2002, p.31.
17. For a thoughtful, perceptive and analytical exposition on the role of the army in the future of Pakistan and its international relations, see Ayesha Siddiqa, *Military Inc* (London: Pluto Press, 2007), pp.243-253.
18. "The Trouble With Pakistan: The Country Everyone Should Worry About," *The Economist*, July 8, 2006, p.12.
19. K. Subrahmanyam, "Pak Hand in Kashmir," *The Times of India*, August 26, 2002.
20. Cohen n.3, p.130.
21. Harish Khare, "Who is Afraid of Peace with Pakistan?" *The Hindu*, April 26, 2006, p.10.
22. For an official perspective on a three-pronged strategy in Jammu and Kashmir, of coordinated operations, economic development and psychological initiatives, see S.K. Sinha, "Jammu and Kashmir: Past, Present and Future," *USI Journal*, April-June 2005, pp. 189-196.
23. G. Parthasarathy, "The India-Pakistan Composite Dialogue," *Security and Society*, Summer 2006.
24. For an analytical and thoughtful analysis of the schools of religious orthodoxy, currently prevalent in the Kashmir Valley, see Riyaz Wani, "Clash of Canons," *The Sunday Express*, December 10, 2006, p.16, and Praveen Swami, "Behind the Silver Lining the Storm Clouds," *The Hindu*, March 22, 2007, p.10.
25. Prem Shankar Jha, "Directions Unknown,"*The Hindustan Times*, April 8, 2005, p.10.
26. Shivshankar Menon, Foreign Secretary of India, Text of the speech on "The Challenges Ahead for India's Foreign Policy," delivered at Observer Research Foundation, New Delhi, on April 10, 2007.
27. For a comprehensive and informative survey and analysis of the approaches to resolving the issue of Jammu and Kashmir, see G. Parthasarathy and Radha Kumar *Frameworks for a Kashmir Settlement* (New Delh: Policy Group Publication, 2006), pp.2-10.
28. An insightful and deeply analytical evaluation of the policy choices of India and Pakistan with regard to the peace process has been made by Navnita Chadha Behera in *Demystifying Kashmir*(New Delhi: Pearson Education, 2007), pp.236-277.

Index